The God Hypothesis

The God Hypothesis

Discovering Design in Our
"Just Right" Goldilocks Universe

Michael A. Corey

ROWMAN & LITTLEFIELD PUBLISHERS, INC.
Lanham • Boulder • New York • Oxford

ROWMAN & LITTLEFIELD PUBLISHERS, INC.

Published in the United States of America
by Rowman & Littlefield Publishers, Inc.
4720 Boston Way, Lanham, Maryland 20706
www.rowmanlittlefield.com

12 Hid's Copse Road
Cumnor Hill, Oxford OX2 9JJ, England

British Library Cataloguing in Publication Information Available

Library of Congress Cataloging-in-Publication Data

Corey, Michael Anthony, 1957–
    The God hypothesis : discovering design in our "just right" Goldilocks universe /
Michael A. Corey.
        p. cm.
    Includes bibliographical references and index.
    ISBN 0-7425-2054-4 (alk. paper)
        1. God—Proof, Cosmological. 2. God—Proof, Teleological. 3. Anthropic principle.
4. Natural theology. 5. Evolution—Religious aspects. 6. Religion and science. 7. Theism.
I. Title.

BT102 .C6724 2002
212—dc21   2001049209

Printed in the United States of America

∞™ The paper used in this publication meets the minimum requirements of
American National Standard for Information Sciences—Permanence of Paper for
Printed Library Materials, ANSI/NISO Z39.48-1992.

~

Contents

~

Preface

Goldilocks tasted Papa Bear's porridge, but it was too hot. She tasted Mama Bear's porridge, but it was too cold. She tasted Baby Bear's porridge, and it was just right! So, she ate it all up.

—"Goldilocks and the Three Bears"

For thousands of years, careful thinkers have recognized that we live in a world that is very well suited for the existence of life. This realization has been confirmed in recent years by the plethora of scientific discoveries pertaining to the "just right" status of the entire cosmos with respect to the existence of living organisms.

That is to say, in a universe that could have been utterly hostile to the needs of life, we have found that precisely the opposite state of affairs is actually the case, namely, that the universe literally *caters* to the needs of living organisms in thousands of different ways. The ancients intuitively realized this, but modern science has now confirmed their suspicion to a very high degree of accuracy. For we now know that the universe comprises a number of essential structural features called "the fundamental constants of nature." They are called "constants" because their respective numerical values are thought to have remained unchanged from the very beginning of the universe to the present day.[1] Indeed, it is their fixed status that has imparted a degree of fidelity and stability to the universe that would have been impossible to achieve otherwise.

The strength of the gravitational force, which is one of nature's most fundamental building blocks, provides a good case in point. The numerical value that is associated with the gravitational constant, g, is 6.67×10^{-11}, and this value appears to have remained rock steady from the birth of the universe to the present day. However, the most remarkable thing about the gravitational constant isn't its fixed nature as such, but rather its perfect fit for the needs of life. For had the strength of the gravitational force been even slightly different, the universe would have been "stillborn," and we wouldn't be here to discuss the fact. This is all the more remarkable because the gravitational constant could conceivably have occupied an infinite number of possible values. Yet, out of this endless sea of possible strengths, nature ended up choosing the *only one* that happens to be "just right" for the needs of life. This phenomenon can be likened to the mythical figure of Goldilocks, who ended up choosing the one bowl of porridge that was "just right" for her own taste buds.

This "just right" status is now known to apply to *all* of nature's fundamental constants, and not just to the strength of gravity. Indeed, this could very well turn out to be the single most perplexing conundrum in all of modern science. For whereas scientists and philosophers have long been aware of the fact that we live in a "just right" world and universe, they have nevertheless been at a near total loss to explain why this might be so.

In the remainder of this book we will be exploring this fascinating issue in greater detail. Our goal will be to maneuver our way through the existing scientific evidence, so that we can hopefully identify the single most likely explanation for our "just right" cosmological status.

The Reemergence of Natural Theology

Natural theology is the time-honored discipline that seeks to elucidate religious knowledge entirely through a rational study of the natural world. At one time natural theology was the dominant mode of reasoning in the scientific realm, with many of the founding fathers of the modern scientific movement being counted as active devotees. However, with the advent of the Darwinian revolution in 1859, the discipline of natural theology all but disappeared from the intellectual scene, due to the growing belief that natural selection could produce complex designs without the aid of a larger Designer.[2] In recent years, though, natural theology has quietly staged an aggressive comeback, thanks largely to a growing amount of empirical information regarding our fine-tuned, "anthropic" universe. It is because of this massive scientific expansion that the Hand of God is now becoming increasingly evident throughout the various natural sciences.

Like a phoenix arising out of the desert, natural theology has boldly returned to the intellectual scene, stronger than ever. In this sense it has come full circle, because the modern scientific movement actually began with the brilliant work of such natural theologians as Newton, Kepler, and Boyle. These scientific pioneers were compelled to look for cosmic order in the first place because they were utterly convinced that a Divine Law-Giver had originally laid down these laws in a comprehensible fashion. Without the pursuit of natural theology, then, the modern scientific movement probably would have never gotten off the ground.[3]

We will be embracing the reborn discipline of natural theology throughout the remainder of this book. Our efforts will be focused on two of natural theology's historical holy grails—proving the existence of God through a detailed analysis of the physical universe and inferring the various attributes of God using *only* the empirical data of modern science as an interpretive guide. In the process, we will be seeking to establish guidelines for a continuing dialogue between science and religion. These guidelines will revolve around a fundamental reconceptualization of science itself, so that God is actually *included* in the scientist's underlying set of axiomatic assumptions. For insofar as it can be shown that the role of God is actually *presupposed* in these foundational premises, then the long-standing dispute between science and religion—and hence between evolution and creation—will essentially be resolved once and for all, since there will no longer be any fundamental differences separating them. Best of all, this reconceptualization of science will provide a "conceptual conduit" through which we will be able to return the idea of supernatural agency to its proper role within the modern scientific method.

Notes

1. The fixed status of nature's fundamental constants, both throughout the present universe and also extending into the distant past, has been empirically verified many times over. Although a significant part of this verification process has been accomplished in the laboratory using direct empirical measurements, this method is insufficient in and of itself to establish the historical invariance of these parameters. In order for this latter goal to be accomplished, scientists typically have to resort to an *indirect* process of mathematical verification, in which these fundamental numerical values are plugged into cosmological equations that date all the way back to within 10^{-43} seconds of the Big Bang. If these equations can subsequently be seen to yield accurate solutions that are corroborated by other independent measurements, then it can safely be concluded that the constants themselves have probably been invariant from the very beginning. This supposed invariance is further supported by the almost complete lack of any conceivable mechanism by which these fundamental parameters could have varied over the course of cosmic evolution.

2. Actually, we should have recognized all along that the Darwinian revolution was incapable of obviating the need for an Intelligent Designer, because the process of natural selection is inherently incapable of explaining its own origin, as we shall see in more detail in chapter 9.

3. Kenneth R. Miller, *Finding Darwin's God* (New York: HarperCollins, 1999), 196.

~

Introduction

I do not feel like an alien in this universe.

—Freeman Dyson

The rise of science in our modern culture has inevitably brought with it a variety of religious questions in both the professional and lay communities. Given the tremendous success that scientists have had in describing the natural world as a self-contained, self-sufficient unit, it is only natural to wonder whether a supernatural Designer exists at all. For if scientists are capable of working their magic without making a single reference to an Intelligent Designer, then why should we continue to hold on to this seemingly outmoded concept?

The underlying philosophical foundation of the modern scientific enterprise, known as *metaphysical naturalism*, greatly buttresses this apparent inference, because it asserts that the realm of material particles is the only type of existence in the entire universe. When this philosophical worldview is coupled with the biochemical power of self-organization and the apparent self-sufficiency of the present universal order, there seems to be no need for a Creator at all. This was precisely Carl Sagan's point in his introduction to Stephen Hawking's best-selling book *A Brief History of Time*. Upon noting the causal independence of the present cosmic scheme, Sagan openly questioned what type of function—if any—that a Creator could possibly have in a seemingly self-reliant universe such as our own.

No wonder there is so much lingering doubt and skepticism about God in our society today. Millions of people have bought into the idea that modern

1

science has somehow supplanted the role of God in the present cosmic order, and the many technological breakthroughs that have transpired in recent years have only served to reinforce this perception. The basic idea here is that the scientific consensus regarding God's putative nonexistence *must* be correct, since scientists have been so remarkably successful in describing the various inner workings of the universe itself. It isn't surprising, then, that millions of people around the world now believe that modern science has somehow done away with our need for a Creator altogether.

The Principle of Deceptive Appearances

But science has also taught us that mere appearances can be deceiving. This is one of the great unifying principles in all of the natural sciences, for as researchers have repeatedly learned over the years, *things are rarely, if ever, the way they outwardly seem to the naked eye.* For instance, the earth has the superficial appearance of being flat, and for thousands of years people actually believed this to be the case. Today, however, we know that the earth is a sphere that only *appears* to be flat when it is viewed from an earthbound perspective. Similarly, the universe itself has the superficial appearance of being stationary, but we now know that it is expanding at a very high rate of speed.[1]

The stars are inherently deceptive as well, insofar as they superficially appear to be tiny points of light in the night sky. We now know, however, that they are huge suns just like our own sun. The only reason they appear to be so small is because they are so far away. This same principle—which we can call the Principle of Deceptive Appearances—can also be applied to the local realm of material objects, because the physical items we see all around us clearly *seem* to be totally solid in nature. The chair I am presently sitting on, for instance, *seems* to be a solid object, but it really isn't. Like all material objects, it is comprised mostly of empty space.

It isn't too much of a stretch here to suggest that this Principle of Deceptive Appearances probably applies throughout the natural realm, particularly given the prior validity of the Principle of Universality, which states that the same general laws and principles are likely to be applicable throughout the cosmos. Insofar as this is the case, it means that mere appearances will indeed tend to be deceiving throughout the cosmos, especially in the most complex areas of universal reality.

But if this is so, then why shouldn't the Principle of Deceptive Appearances[2] also be applicable to the prospect of Intelligent Design? There is little doubt that the universe itself superficially appears to be undesigned, at least in the sense of not having a blatantly obvious Creator. Three reasons for this can be cited. First, a concrete Designer isn't directly visible or otherwise immediately apparent to us. Second, the universe appears to be a completely self-sufficient mechanism because of its remarkable self-organizing power, and this detail alone seems to totally obviate the need for a larger Designer. The third reason why the universe appears to be undesigned is because no cosmic Power has intervened to prevent the many instances of catastrophic suffering that have transpired throughout our history. One would think that if a transcendent Creator really existed, He would have intervened to stop such unspeakable human evils as the Holocaust or Hiroshima long before they ever got out of hand, just as a good human father would naturally do if his children suddenly started butchering one another. Yet this doesn't seem to have happened a single time in our history, at least not in a way that is outwardly apparent.

It is primarily for these reasons that the universe superficially appears to be without a Creator. Even so, Michael Shermer reports that 28.6 percent of American believers have been able to see beyond these superficial appearances, insofar as they cited "good design of the universe" as the primary reason for why they believe in God.[3]

The modern scientific community, by contrast, has continued to take the universe's ostensible lack of a Designer at face value. For while approximately 40 percent of working scientists claim[4] to believe in God, the official scientific consensus is that the Darwinian revolution has conveniently dispensed with the need for a Designer altogether, since modern evolutionary theory is now capable of elucidating a mechanism by which "apparent design" can be mimicked by natural processes alone. In this case, the scientific skeptic is using the Principle of Deceptive Appearances to argue that design, and not a lack of it, is the deceptive appearance of the natural world that must itself be dispelled. There are two reasons why the scientific skeptic tends to believe this: (1) because most of our scientific forefathers believed in design and (2) because the majority of people around the world believe that the entire universe was created by a Higher Power.

However, these two criteria don't really describe the superficial appearance of the universe *itself*. They merely describe the various *beliefs* about design that other people have held over the years. But this isn't the type of "deceptive appearance" that the Principle of Deceptive Appearances is referring to. This Principle is instead referring to the "naked" appearance of the universe itself, entirely apart from the contaminating influences of other people's beliefs. Now, when we look at the universe from this particular vantage point, we see that it does indeed appear to be undesigned after all, for the three reasons cited above. On this level of analysis, the beliefs and rationalizations regarding design that other people have concocted over the years are irrelevant as far as the Principle of Deceptive Appearances is concerned, because this Principle is merely concerned with the superficial appearance of things, and not with our subsequent ideas about them.

Insofar as this is so, we can see that a process of scientific self-deception seems to have taken hold of the scientific community. For one thing, it simply doesn't follow that a Designer is unnecessary simply because there are natural self-organizing processes at work in the universe that can build complex designs "on their own." This is a question-begging pseudo-explanation that doesn't even attempt to address the true question that is at issue here, which is where these underlying self-organizing powers *themselves* ultimately came from. It also doesn't follow that a Designer cannot exist simply because He hasn't intervened to prevent various instances of moral evil throughout the past. This conclusion conveniently ignores the possibility that these moral evils may have a higher, morally justifiable purpose in the world, which would explain why a good God continues to allow them to exist.[5]

Moreover, it makes no sense to reject design altogether simply because the modern neo-Darwinian synthesis claims that it is no longer necessary. We mustn't forget that there is tremendous pressure for the modern scientist to publicly affirm the validity and importance of the neo-Darwinian perspective, simply because everyone else in the scientific community is banking their lives on it. This is an instance where a Principle of the Emperor's New Clothes can be applied to modern science, since no one wants to appear ignorant in front of their colleagues, particularly when it comes to the heated debate between evolution and creation.

At the same time, though, no one wants to continue to affirm a mistaken belief for the wrong reasons, either. Yet, this is precisely what appears to be happening in modern science today, because of the immense political pressure to conform to the dictates of nontheistic evolutionism.[6] Every so often, though, a scientist comes along who has the courage to publicly declare that "the Emperor has no clothes," because he or she can suddenly see beyond this scientific cloak of self-deception. The world-renowned paleoichthyologist Colin Patterson, senior paleontologist of the British Museum of Natural History and author of the book *Evolution*, provides a good case in point. In 1981, Patterson voiced his concerns about the validity of Darwinian evolution in front of an entire audience of his evolutionary colleagues. In so doing, he essentially declared that "the Emperor has no clothes":

> Last year I had a sudden realization. For over twenty years I had thought I was working on evolution in some way. One morning I woke up and something had

happened in the night; and it struck me that I had been working on this stuff for twenty years and there was not one thing I knew about it. That's quite a shock, to learn that one can be so misled so long. . . . So for the last few weeks I've tried putting a simple question to various people. . . . Can you tell me anything you know about evolution, any one thing . . . that is true? All I got was silence. . . . The absence of answers seems to suggest that . . . evolution does not convey knowledge, or, if so, I haven't yet heard of it. . . . I think many people in this room would acknowledge that during the last few years, if you had thought about it at all, you have experienced a shift from evolution as knowledge to evolution as faith. I know that it's true of me and I think it is true of a good many of you here. . . . Evolution not only conveys no knowledge but seems somehow to convey anti-knowledge.[7]

In quoting Patterson's enigmatic words, I'm not suggesting that the neo-Darwinian synthesis is mistaken in every way. Not at all. This would be throwing the proverbial baby out with the bathwater, and it would also fly in the face of numerous empirical observations regarding the common descent of all life forms. I am simply asserting here that the nontheistic version of modern evolutionary theory is mistaken, because the very process of evolution *itself* appears to be incoherent in the absence of a larger Creator. From this integrated theoretical perspective, the pitting of evolution against creation is ill conceived, because *both* positions appear to be metaphysically intertwined with one another.[8] The Providential Evolutionists of the nineteenth century, such as Mivart, Chambers, and Gray, instinctively recognized this, but modern evolutionists today have lost sight of this essential connection between God and evolution.

Now, if we take the widespread validity of the Principle of Deceptive Appearances as a cosmic precedent, it follows that the superficial lack of a Designer in the universe will probably turn out to be deceiving as well. After all, if this Principle of Deceptive Appearances is known to apply to so many other things in the natural realm, then why shouldn't it also be equally applicable to the question of universal origins? This being the case, what possible justification can there be for continuing to take the universe's ostensible lack of a Designer at face value?

The "epistemic distance stipulation" in theology lends further support to this contention, for as John Hick has pointed out, the world must superficially appear as if there is no God if human freedom is to remain intact.[9] That is to say, if the Divine Reality were blatantly obvious to everyone, our behavioral freedom would necessarily be short-circuited by our direct perception of God's great Glory, and this is something that is generally deemed to be incompatible with our existence as free-willed beings. This is why the world ostensibly must be created *etsi deus non daretur*, "as if there were no God."[10]

It is this epistemic distance stipulation that seems to account for the widespread validity of the Principle of Deceptive Appearances throughout the natural sciences. For insofar as God must be temporarily[11] veiled by His creation, it follows that He would probably *want* to design a world in which mere appearances are deceiving—because the whole idea here is to infuse some much-needed ambiguity into the creation, so that human freedom can be preserved as a result.

This conclusion is supported by the paradoxical—and hence unexpected—nature of the physical universe itself. But this is just another way of saying that the universe is far more surprising than any of us could have ever guessed, and it is this realization that ultimately leaves room for an Intelligent Designer. For even though God may no longer be *directly* needed to explain natural events, it doesn't follow from this that He isn't needed *at all*. To the contrary, the idea of God appears to be an implicit feature of most cosmological and biological theories, and it is this realization that threatens to turn our entire scientific understanding of the universe on its head, because the missing ingredient in virtually every aspect of modern science appears to be none other than God Himself.

We can, therefore, begin moving in the right direction by attempting to view the evidence from cosmology entirely on its own terms. When we do so, a startling possibility begins to present itself; namely, that the role of a Creator may actually be *presupposed* in virtually all of our scientific theories. To the extent that this turns out to be so, it means that the concept of God may ultimately be required to make sense out of modern science. We will begin to see how in the next chapter.

Notes

1. This static appearance of the heavens is so compelling that even Einstein himself was once fooled by it.

2. If God is the Author of the physical universe, then He is also the Author of the Principle of Deceptive Appearances, and this may partly explain His presumed inclusion under its overall rubric.

3. Michael Shermer, *How We Believe* (New York: Freeman, 2000), 78–87.

4. Shermer, *How We Believe*, 72.

5. M. A. Corey, *Evolution and the Problem of Natural Evil* (Lanham, Md.: University Press of America, 2000), 191–258.

6. I am distinguishing here between the nontheistic and theistic forms of modern evolutionary theory. For although I accept the empirical evidence of evolution itself, I believe that this evidence is ultimately theistic in nature, despite its superficial appearance to the

contrary. According to this unified perspective, what passes for nontheistic evolution in modern science today is actually theistic evolution in disguise.

7. Quoted in Jeremy Rifkin, *Algeny* (New York: Viking, 1983), 113.

8. There is yet another aspect of modern neo-Darwinism that appears to be in error, namely, its application to the problem of universal origins. For while natural selection may indeed be capable of explaining how the fittest variants in any given population are capable of surviving, so they can spread their genes to future generations, it is inherently incapable of explaining the origin of its own selective power (see chapter 9). It is also inherently incapable of explaining the origin of our fine-tuned universe as well, even though several theorists have proposed using natural selection to accomplish this very thing (see chapter 11).

9. John Hick, *Evil and the God of Love* (New York: Harper and Row, 1977), 281.

10. This separation between God and humanity clearly can't be physical in nature. It must instead be epistemically based, because it is at the level of our own conscious awareness that we are most vulnerable to a perception of the Divine.

11. The epistemic distance stipulation will ostensibly remain in force until the human developmental process is essentially completed, because this is when our inner volitional center will be mature enough to be able to tolerate a direct experience of the Divine without compromising our inner capacity for free choice.

CHAPTER ONE

~

Self-Organization and Our "Just Right" Universe

God has put a secret art into the forces of Nature so as to enable it to fashion itself out of chaos into a perfect world system.

—Immanuel Kant

Napoleon, in one of the most notable conversations in the entire history of science, is reported to have once asked the French scientist Pierre Simone de Laplace about the role of God in his scientific worldview. Laplace is said to have replied with the enigmatic words, "Sir, I have no need of that hypothesis."

And so it goes. The apparent self-sufficiency of our physical universe has caused many great thinkers to do away with the idea of a supernatural Creator altogether. The rationale is simply that on the face of it, there doesn't seem to be any *scientific* need for God in the present cosmic system, since the universe as we now know it superficially seems to be capable of generating all of its own causes and effects, without any need for an external Designer. The molecular phenomenon of self-organization greatly buttresses this apparent inference, because if atoms and molecules have the power to organize themselves into progressively greater instances of complexity (which they do), then there seems to be even less of a reason to invoke a supernatural Being to explain the nature of the cosmos.

The basic idea here is that if we can use natural cause and effect processes to explain the various events that transpire in our universe, there is subsequently no real need—at least from a scientific point of view—to invoke the creative activity of an Intelligent Designer. Such an invocation, on this naturalistic view, is not only redundant (again because the universe seems to be capable of generating all of its own immediate effects), it also seems to be unnecessarily complex, since a much simpler hypothesis (namely, one without God in it) appears to be just as effective in explaining why the universe is the way it is.

This Principle of Theoretical Economy, known as "Ockham's Razor" (after the great philosopher William of Ockham), is one of the main guiding principles of modern science. According to this principle, one should not "multiply causes beyond necessity" when one attempts to devise a valid scientific hypothesis. Indeed, the history of science has repeatedly confirmed Ockham's insight, insofar as the simplest hypothesis in any given discipline has more often than not turned out to be the correct one.

However, when we attempt to apply Ockham's Razor to the question of God's possible relationship to the universe, it seems to suggest that God is an unnecessary ingredient in the present cosmic scheme, since the universe, on the face of it, seems to be capable of producing all of its own causes and effects without any outside help.

The astronomer Carl Sagan reiterates this basic message in his introduction to Stephen Hawking's book *A Brief History of Time*. Upon noting the causal self-sufficiency of the present cosmic scheme, Sagan wonders what type of function a creator would have, if any, in such a universe. Sagan's point, if I understand him correctly, is that there is no real need for God in a universe in which all observable effects are regularly produced by natural cause and effect processes.

Such a view, however, turns out to be both philosophically naïve and scientifically untenable. For insofar as God exists at all, then it is clear that He *must* be the author of the present universal scheme (which includes the material process of self-organization). It is also clear that He *must* function as the underlying structural foundation for generic physical existence as well.

Moreover, there is no good reason for presuming that the metaphysical "buck" of the universe actually stops with the apparent self-sufficiency of material particles as such. For while atoms and molecules do indeed possess an amazing capacity for self-organization, we still do not know where this capacity ultimately came from. And since there isn't a shred of evidence indicating that this property has always existed, we can't simply assume the prior existence of this self-organizing power in an axiomatic manner.

Nevertheless, many informed individuals continue to insist that the property of self-organization was somehow responsible for generating its own origin long ago. Such a *non sequitur* conclusion, however, is tantamount to assuming that the self-organizing power of a modern automobile factory was somehow responsible for its own origin at some point in the past. We know, however, that this cannot possibly be true, because such a profound level of automation *cannot* be responsible for generating its own self-organizing character. It is far too complex and technologically sophisticated for that.

We also know that the finite property of self-organization couldn't possibly have been responsible for its own origin, because there was a definite point in the past before it ever existed. This follows from the very finitude of the larger universe itself. According to the Principle of Sufficient Reason, though, all finite objects and events *must* have a sufficient reason or explanation for their existence, causal or otherwise.[1] Therefore, the self-organizing power of the universe *must* have had a larger reason for its own existence outside itself. The only way out of this bind is if it could somehow be demonstrated that this self-organizing property is eternal in nature, because in this case there would never have been a point in time where an explanation would actually be needed. But the phenomenon of self-organization is clearly *not* eternal in nature (because not even the universe itself is eternal), so the Principle of Sufficient Reason demands that it must have a larger explanation outside itself.

This conclusion becomes all the more compelling when we realize that the fundamental laws and constants of nature did *not* gradually evolve into their present life-supporting character through a process of natural selection, as is widely believed. Instead, they spontaneously came into existence with the origin of the universe itself, perfectly calibrated and ready for action.[2]

This being the case, it is profoundly counterintuitive to use the universe's ostensible self-sufficiency and self-organizing power as evidence against an Intelligent Designer, because it begs the much deeper question that is ultimately at issue here, which is this: Precisely *where* did the universe get this seemingly self-sufficient character to begin with? It is useless to assert that the universe has always had this particular quality, as we have seen, because we know for an empirical fact that it did not. Indeed, according to a growing mountain of empirical data, the universe has most definitely not been around forever. Instead, it roared into being out of apparent nothingness some 15–20 billion years ago in an epic event known as the "Big Bang." Prior to this point, there was no such thing as space, matter, or even time.[3]

So we know that there was a definite point in the past before which the phenomenon of self-organization ever existed. The upshot of this realization is that we really do need to find a suitable explanation for this particular property. Interestingly enough, modern science has nothing to say about this critical issue. Scientists simply assume the prior, unexplained existence of this self-organizing power in an axiomatic manner, and for good reason—because this sort of axiomatic assumption is a necessary prerequisite for doing good science. Why? Because one has to start somewhere before one can make appreciable progress in any type of goal-oriented endeavor. It is one thing, however, to assume the prior existence of a self-organizing universe for the sake of doing good science, and quite another to use this axiomatic assumption as a tool for obviating the need for an Intelligent Designer. Nevertheless, many scientists continue to do this very thing. "Why," they ask, "should we invoke the creative activity of a Supreme Being if the universe itself is entirely capable of bringing about its own causes and effects with no outside help?"

The problem with this widespread belief is that it puts the proverbial cart before the horse since it doesn't explain where the universe's putative self-sufficiency *itself* ultimately came from. It is important to keep in mind, though, that modern science has absolutely no explanation for this particular phenomenon, apart from the deliberate workings of an Intelligent Designer.

Indeed, as we will be seeing in more detail in the coming pages, there is a very compelling reason to include God in our scientific theorizing: His contribution to the natural sciences is desperately needed in order to make sense out of the present universal scheme. Insofar as this is so, we now have a way to bypass God's exclusion from the universe on the basis of Ockham's Razor: this principle of theoretical economy only applies to those elements of a scientific hypothesis that are superfluous, and therefore unnecessary. But if the role of God turns out to be essential for the production of the present universal format, then this very necessity ultimately prevents Him from being excluded by Ockham's Razor. This is good news for religious believers everywhere, because it means that the role of God in the universe cannot be obviated by the drive for theoretical economy in the natural sciences.

The Emerging Dialogue between Science and Religion

Of all the intellectual issues that have surfaced in recent years, none has captured the popular imagination like the relationship between science and religion. Once believed to be conceptually incompatible, these former intellectual opponents are now engaged in an exciting new dialogue with one another, with very positive repercussions taking place for both sides.

Researchers working at the interface between science and religion have proposed a wide variety of possible strategies for relating modern science to religion, ranging from a complete separation of the two fields to a near-total conceptual integration. Although several different criteria have been used to determine the best way to relate these two areas to one another, the most important one, by far, has to do with the inherent compatibility between the data of science and the data of religion. The basic question that is at issue here is straightforward. Are these two fields of study conceptually compatible at all? If so, in what way?

I will be contending in the remainder of this book that the respective fields of science and religion are conceptually compatible with one another after all. Indeed, I will be arguing that they are so inherently compatible that the facts of science can actually be used to construct a compelling probabilistic proof for the existence of an Intelligent Designer.

In order to accomplish this goal, however, we must first endeavor to examine the existing scientific evidence entirely on its own terms. We need to do this in order to better discern the general direction in which nature's finger is pointing. For this to be possible, though, we must first abandon as many preconceived notions as possible regarding science and the existence of God so that we can then examine the scientific evidence in a fresh, relatively unbiased manner. Our strategy will be to take the empirical findings of modern science at face value so that we can then see in which direction they naturally seem to be pointing. If they appear to point away from the possibility of Design, we will then owe it to ourselves (and to the integrity of our underlying research program) to honestly say so; but by the same token, if these findings happen to point toward the notion of Design, we will by all means want to take full notice of it.

We will begin our examination of the evidence with a brief examination of the historical background of modern science. We will then take a detailed look at the origin of our life-supporting universe, with particular emphasis being made on the relationship between Murphy's Law and the known trajectory of cosmic evolution. From there we will proceed to examine the growing evidence for design in the fascinating area known as "anthropic cosmology." This evidence will ultimately be recruited into a compelling probabilistic proof for the existence of God, which itself will be based on the various empirical attributes of our Goldilocks Universe.

We will also be taking into consideration a variety of competing theories as well, including Everett's Many Worlds interpretation of quantum mechanics and Lee Smolin's theory of cosmological natural selection. At this point, we will attempt to explicate a naturalistic theory of Divine Action that is based on the religious notion of miracles. This will be followed by an attempt to infer the various Divine Attributes using *only* the empirical evidence of modern science as our interpretive guide. We will then turn our attention toward elucidating the proper role of supernatural agency in the modern scientific method. And last, we will attempt to use the empirical evidence for design to demonstrate why it makes sense to be hopeful about our existence as human beings, even though the world we live in seems hopeless in so many ways.

Notes

1. Although many theorists no longer accept the universal applicability of the Principle of Sufficient Reason due to the putative acausal nature of certain quantum phenomena, this doesn't necessarily mean that this principle is invalid in these quantum-related instances. It doesn't follow that a sufficient reason for these quantum phenomena doesn't exist simply because one hasn't been discovered yet. As physicist David Bohm has pointed out, there are many "hidden variables" at the quantum level of reality, any one of which could contain the sufficient reason for a particular quantum outcome. Moreover, the overall physical matrix out of which quantum events occur can itself be considered to be a sufficient reason for their occurrence, since it provides the essential structural framework upon which these "uncaused" quantum events can take place. It therefore isn't really accurate to say that a particular quantum outcome is "uncaused." It is, to the contrary, caused by a preexisting quantum field, which provides the essential structural backdrop upon which these quantum events can take place. From this point of view, the Principle of Sufficient Reason can indeed be seen to apply at the quantum level of reality after all.

2. John D. Barrow and Frank J. Tipler, *The Anthropic Cosmological Principle* (Oxford: Oxford University Press, 1986), 288.

3. John D. Barrow, *The World within the World* (Oxford: Oxford University Press, 1990), 228.

CHAPTER TWO

The God of the Philosophers

The very order, changes, and movements in the universe, the very beauty of form in all that is visible, proclaim, however silently, both that the world was created and also that its Creator could be none other than God whose greatness and beauty are both ineffable and invisible.

—St. Augustine

Given the nontheistic bias of modern naturalistic science, it is tempting to think that most scientists and philosophers throughout the past have either been atheists or agnostics. I say this for the following reason: If the weight of the empirical evidence is solidly against the existence of an Intelligent Designer, as we have previously been led to believe, then one would suppose that most intellectuals throughout recorded history would have come to a similar conclusion about the likely nonexistence of such a Being.

To the contrary, though, the vast majority of thinkers throughout history have come out strongly in *favor* of a Supreme Being, including the original founding fathers of modern experimental science themselves. In fact, astronomer John D. Barrow has gone so far as to conclude that it was their devout belief in a divine Lawgiver that led the original architects of the modern scientific movement to look for the existence of law and order in the cosmos in the first place. So, far from being antithetical to the development of empirical science, classical theism was actually one of the principal guiding factors that led to the development and expansion of modern science.

However, with the advent of Charles Darwin's theory of evolution by natural selection, the central role of theism in the development of modern science began to be overshadowed by the prospect of an entirely naturalistic origin to the biosphere. But even Darwin himself continued to believe in the existence of a more "distant," naturalistic God to the very end of his life.[1] Darwin's "deistic" Creator differed from classical descriptions of the Deity in one important respect: He opted to create the world gradually, using natural cause and effect processes, instead of instantly by miraculous fiat. And while there have been important differences concerning the nature of this Deity in the years since Darwin's publication of *The Origin of Species*, most thinkers throughout recorded history have nevertheless agreed that some type of Divine Being *must* exist.

The list of historical figures who have come out in support of some form of theism is seemingly endless. Anaxagoras of Clazomenae (500–428 BC), for instance, was probably the first Western thinker to attribute the obvious order in the universe to a larger plan or design. Working on the Greek island of Ionia during the fifth century BC (which was where Western science also had its origin), Anaxagoras came to the conclusion that the existence of order in the universe must be the direct result of some form of cosmic "Mind."

Both Socrates (470–399 BC) and his student Plato (427–347 BC) followed Anaxagoras' lead in concluding that some form of cosmic Mind must necessarily exist. Plato came to this conclusion by developing the first Cosmological Argument for the existence of God. In his timeless genius, Plato realized that matter is incapable of causing motion in and of itself. Therefore, since matter is currently in motion, he reasoned that there had to have been an Unmoved Mover who would have originally set it in motion long ago.

A more recent version of Plato's Cosmological Argument states that everything in existence has a cause. But if this is so, then this means that the universe itself must also have a cause, which of course can only be God.[2]

A possible hitch in this form of the Cosmological Argument is that the entire universe isn't a "thing" in the same sense that the other objects within it are things. It is, rather, a *collection* of things. Therefore, it has been argued, we can't generalize from the existence of specific objects within the universe to the nature of the entire universe itself. For instance, even though every member of a basketball team has a mother, this doesn't mean that the basketball team itself has a mother.

While this may be so, it still doesn't necessarily invalidate the Cosmological Argument for the existence of God, because there are clearly *some* specific intrauniversal properties that *can* be generalized to the nature of the entire universe itself. For instance, every coherent object within the universe clearly possesses the property of existence as such, but then again, so does the entire universe. This is obviously true. The proponent of the Cosmological Argument simply believes that his particular generalization from "cosmic part" to "cosmic whole" is also true in a similar fashion. On this point, he appears to be on firm ground because no universal principle seems to be more fundamental than the idea that everything in existence needs a cause, including the universe itself. Plato himself would have agreed wholeheartedly with this conclusion, as we just saw.

The Cretan philosopher Diogenes (400–325 BC) was also deeply influenced by the degree of order in the natural world. He was impressed by the various global cycles, such as the yearly progression of seasons, and he believed that such a fortunate arrangement could not have been possible without the Creative Intelligence of a Higher Power.

The greatest Greek philosopher to have ever lived, though, was undoubtedly Plato's student Aristotle (384–322 BC). For Aristotle, the ingenious structural and functional design that is displayed by all life forms was itself *proof* of an "intelligent natural world that functions according to some deliberate design." Not surprisingly, then, Aristotle regarded the prospect of an accidental world as blatantly ridiculous and therefore in stark contradiction to the observed facts.

Aristotle postulated the existence of a larger "end," or *telos*, to which all events are magnetically attracted. He believed that it was this end or purpose that gave every universal object its ultimate meaning and significance in the grand cosmic scheme.

Consequently, Aristotle opposed the idea that a thing can be fully understood when one simply learns what it is made of. Rather, Aristotle believed that in order to understand the true meaning of any given object, three other causes besides this "material cause" had to be identified: (1) the "efficient cause," which was the object or process that produced the object in question, (2) the "formal cause," which was the intrinsic pattern or form of the object that distinguished it from all other objects, and (3) the "final cause," which was simply the final purpose for which the object itself was created.

It was here in his goal-directed thinking that Aristotle revealed his true genius. He saw the underlying design of the universe as being conceptually self-evident. Consequently, he came to the conclusion that the best way to understand the ultimate meaning of a thing is by identifying its "final cause" or the purpose that it happens to serve in the larger cosmic scheme.

Moving on, we find that one of Aristotle's associates, Tyrtamus of Eresos (372–287 BC), opted to challenge Aristotle's emphasis on final causation, because he saw many things in the world that seemed to have no discernible purpose at all, such as hurricanes, earthquakes, and disease. Indeed, many people continue to cite these natural evils as evidence against a positive goal-directed purpose in the world. "How," it is wondered, "could a good and loving God allow such tragedies to happen on the earth, especially when so many innocent men, women, and children suffer needlessly as a consequence? If God is even partly good, He[3] would want to prevent these evils, and if He is all-powerful, He would in fact be capable of preventing them; yet they still occur on a regular basis. Therefore, either God isn't totally good, or else He isn't all-powerful."[4]

This is a shortsighted, two-dimensional view of the problem of evil, because the possibility remains that these "acts of God" may in fact be a logically necessary feature of human life. If this is true, then we couldn't abolish evil without simultaneously abolishing human life altogether.[5] We therefore shouldn't be so arrogant as to assume that a given feature of life has no higher purpose, simply because no purpose is immediately apparent, or because it produces a seemingly negative short-term effect in the world.

The Stoic school of philosophy, begun by Zeno of Citium (334–262 BC), would have largely agreed with the above view, since the Stoics believed that everything that happened in the world was for the good of all concerned, even if it didn't superficially appear to be so at first glance. The Stoics were staunch supporters of the traditional Design Argument, so they adopted a human-centered (or anthropocentric) view of the cosmos in which humans were the very pinnacle of creation. Everything else, they believed, was created for humanity's overall benefit.

Nevertheless, many sensitive thinkers have continued to allow the fact of evil in the world to impede their belief in a personal Creator. Albert Einstein, for instance, found it difficult to believe in the existence of a personal Creator because there is so much human suffering in the world. A good God, he reasoned, would never allow this to happen. Therefore, Einstein concluded such a Being couldn't possibly exist.

Instead, Einstein believed in Spinoza's God, who was an impersonal Being who revealed His power in the orderly workings of nature. An impersonal God, Einstein thought, wouldn't know or care about human suffering on this planet, so this would explain why He doesn't seem to do anything to get rid of it.

What Einstein didn't seem to realize, though, is that it is possible for evil and a personal God to coexist together, at least for a time. This would be true if such a Being allowed evil to exist for a Higher Purpose, such as the ultimate betterment of human life.

This is precisely what the German mathematician and philosopher Gottfried Leibniz (1646–1716) believed. In fact, Leibniz went so far as to conclude that when all things are duly considered, this must be the *best* of all possible worlds after all, even if its *prima facie* appearance seems to be otherwise. Leibniz was able to reach this remarkable conclusion because he believed that God, being both all good and all-powerful, was therefore morally compelled to create the best of all possible worlds for human habitation.

Leibniz's Principle of Radical Optimism, as it has also been called, has been severely criticized over the years, most notably by Voltaire's character Dr. Pangloss. The basic idea behind this criticism is that this can't possibly be the best of all possible worlds because of all the evil that regularly transpires here.

The problem with this conclusion is that it focuses almost exclusively on the "macro" level of human existence. There is, however, a deeper level of reality in which our world does indeed appear to be the best of all possible worlds after all, at least in terms of the underlying structural conditions that give us the ability to exist as coherent beings in the universe. This is due to the fact that no other combination of physical constants could possibly have produced a life-sustaining world such as our own. This is an extremely important realization that we will be examining in more detail in chapter 8. It is important because it finally makes traditional theism, with its all-powerful and all-loving Creator, believable again. For even though evil may exist on this planet, this is still the best of all possible worlds in the sense that no other world would have been capable of supporting human life.

It is also possible that this is the best of all possible worlds in a moral sense as well. For even though moral evil clearly exists, it could be argued that the removal of moral evil through the elimination of human freedom would quickly bring about the greatest evil of them all, namely, the destruction of human character.

Interestingly enough, Gene Roddenberry, the maker of the old *Star Trek* series, seems to have been aware of this important metaphysical relationship between human character and moral evil, since one of his classic episodes, called "The Return of the Archons," deals with this very issue. In this marvelous science fiction drama, a master computer named Landru decides to eliminate evil once and for all on its planet by externally controlling the minds and wills of all the planet's humanoid creatures. While this outrageous act of control succeeds in getting rid of all the moral evils on the planet, it does so at far too high a price, because it ends up transforming the "people" there into lifeless sheep.

Heroically, though, Captain Kirk convinces the computer—which has been programmed to bring about only good for the people—that it is *not* acting in the best interests of the planet's inhabitants by controlling their wills.

The computer responds by proclaiming its actions to be "good," since they have eliminated all moral evil on the planet. Kirk, however, responds by convincing the computer that it has committed a far greater evil by destroying the character and creativity of all the planet's citizens with its relentless control of their minds and wills. This internal contradiction causes the computer to self-destruct, which in turn allows the people on the planet to instantly return to normal.

The crew of the *Enterprise*, of course, are delighted to see moral "evils" return to the planet, because it is a sign that the people are finally regaining control of their own lives. Spock, however, is intrigued by Landru's "success" at eliminating moral evil, so he asks the Captain why the clever people of Earth, who have suffered terribly for thousands of years at the hands of moral evil, have never tried to implement Landru's seemingly ingenious "solution" to the problem of evil. Kirk replies that they were probably just lucky.

This penetrating statement at once reveals our world to be a far better place than is superficially apparent, precisely because the *only* logically possible alternative to the existence of moral evil (besides complete nonexistence for humanity) is *far* worse overall, namely, the death of free-willed human character. Hence, as long as we humans wish to remain in control of our lives, this world does indeed appear to be one of the best of all possible worlds after all, not in terms of the number of evils that occur regularly here, but rather in terms of the underlying metaphysical conditions that allow us to be fully human and therefore fully in control of our lives. Leibniz was very much aware of this important distinction, as he seems to have based his Principle of Radical Optimism not on the number of evils that occur daily in the world, but rather on the underlying metaphysical conditions that are necessary for human existence as such.

The God of the Scientists

Given the widespread popular belief that science has somehow disproven the existence of God, one might be tempted to believe that most scientists throughout the past have been atheists. Such a belief, however, would be false. To the contrary, modern science was essentially *founded* by strongly committed theists such as Newton and Kepler. These devout men were driven to look for order and rationality in the cosmos because they first believed in the existence of a divine Lawgiver, whom they thought would have given the physical universe its rational nature. Without this overarching faith in an Intelligent Designer, they would have had little reason to believe in the existence of an orderly cosmos.[6]

Take Nicholas Copernicus (1473–1543), for instance. Copernicus is the scientist who is credited with discovering the heliocentric (or sun-centered) nature of the solar system. Prior to Copernicus' landmark finding, it was believed that the earth, and not the sun, was the geographical center of the cosmos. And even though this discovery has subsequently been utilized to debunk the biblical idea that humans are the central focal point of the Creation, it is an historical fact that Copernicus himself was a deeply committed theist, despite his bold assertion that the sun, and not the earth, exists at the center of the solar system. Indeed, it was Copernicus' conviction that God would have created the solar system in a certain mechanistic fashion that led him to discover its basic heliocentric configuration in the first place.

In fact, Copernicus went to great lengths to show that his sun-centered view of the solar system is still compatible with the theistic idea that human beings are important to God. This is surprising, because Copernicus' work is usually associated with the scientific *removal* of humanity from the center of the universe. We aren't told in the scientific literature that Copernicus was actually a devout believer in God and that he used his goal-oriented ideas to place the earth in its proper cosmic perspective in relation to God. We're simply led to believe that Copernicus removed humankind from *any* privileged position in the cosmos simply because he removed the earth from the geographical center of the solar system.[7]

Likewise, we're also led to believe that Charles Darwin was a dedicated atheist who conceived of his theory of evolution in order to get rid of God forever. In reality, Darwin—who actually studied theology at Cambridge and not science—was a committed deist who believed that God initially created the entire physical universe, along with the self-organizing power of atoms and molecules. Indeed, without his belief in a transcendent Creator, Darwin would have had little basis for developing his famous theory of evolution by natural selection. His chief aim was thus not to remove God altogether from his evolutionary theory; it was merely to show that God did not create the biosphere in its final form by miraculous fiat.

Darwin's central message was simply to demonstrate that God had utilized "secondary" (or natural) causes to generate the biosphere. Yet we continue to read about how Darwin was a dedicated atheist and how our modern theory of evolution has totally disconfirmed the creation account in Genesis. In fact, nothing could be further from the truth. Darwin merely wanted to argue that God was the cause of the various secondary or natural causes in the world, but this is far from being an atheistic point of view, because even the book of Genesis points out that the *earth itself* brought forth living creatures (Gen. 1:24). This momentous realization flies in the face of most "modern" views on this subject. In fact, most people mistakenly believe that the creation account in Genesis is directly antithetical to the theory of evolution by natural selection, but this simply isn't the case. The opposite of evolution is most definitely *not* the six-day creation story in Genesis; it is an instantaneous creation by fiat that takes no time at all. On this view, any type of stepwise creation event that takes more than a split second is itself "evolutionary" by its very nature, since evolution by its very nature is merely "change with respect to time." This being the case, the Genesis account turns out to be just as "evolutionary" as modern Darwinian theory, insofar as it describes a stepwise process of creation that took place in six major stages or "days."

Thus, the true issue here isn't the character or number of evolutionary stages that led to humanity. It is whether or not a larger Designer was actually involved in the evolutionary process. And since most people (including most scientists) mistakenly associate atheism with evolution and God with Genesis, they can't seem to fathom that the biblical creation account could *itself* be evolutionary in nature, just as they also find it hard to believe that God could ever be the cause of the evolutionary process itself.

A similar rationale can also be applied to the common belief that humans descended from apes. Most religious individuals are deeply offended by such rhetoric, but the Bible itself tells us that God created humans out of the moistened dust of the earth (which is mud), and surely mud is much lower on the ontological scale of being than any ape! Accordingly, the true question that is at issue here isn't the underlying medium that we were created out of, but whether or not God had anything to do with it. If God is involved, it doesn't seem to matter *what* He fashioned us out of, but if God is left out of the equation, many people will tend to be offended even if we're told that humans descended from a superhuman race of extraterrestrials.

What we're finding is that many of the historical facts of science have been skewed in favor of a nontheistic view of reality. The unsuspecting student of science isn't generally told that the modern scientific movement was initially founded by devout believers or that there can be no such thing as natural laws without a Divine Lawgiver to create them. Instead, he or she is quietly duped into believing that scientific truth has nothing at all to do with the existence of a Divine Creator.

For the most part, this subtle form of brainwashing has been remarkably successful. That is, until now—because for the first time in human history, we finally have at our disposal a genuine scientific *proof* for the existence of God (see chapter 12). This is due to the fact that the theistic explanation for the Big Bang accounts for the known scientific facts much better than any type of nontheistic explanation.

Indeed, this evidence is so compelling that one prominent researcher has blatantly declared, "If you're religious, it's like looking at God." A great many other scientists have openly shared this sentiment. Sir Fred Hoyle, the physicist who discovered the mechanism by which carbon is generated inside the stars, has even gone so far as to say that the existing physical evidence reveals the tinkering of a "Supercalculating Intellect," who has clearly "monkeyed" with the basic features of chemistry and physics. In fact, Hoyle believes that this conclusion is inescapable:

> I do not believe that any scientist who examined the evidence would fail to draw the inference that the laws of nuclear physics have been deliberately designed with regard to the consequences they produce inside the stars. If this is so, then my apparently random quirks have become part of a deep-laid scheme. If not then we are back again at a monstrous sequence of accidents.[8]

This confession is all the more remarkable because Hoyle was once a committed atheist who openly admitted that his Godless theories were designed to explain God away once and for all. Other scientists are beginning to follow suit. The British author and physicist Paul Davies, for instance, has openly admitted to believing in a grand "cosmic blueprint," and in his most recent book, *The Mind of God*, he concludes that the evidence for Intelligent Design is truly overwhelming. Even John Gribbin and Martin Rees have gone so far as to ask the following "heretical" questions on the back of their book, *Cosmic Coincidences*: "Was the universe made for man?" and "What was in the mind of God 15 billion years ago?"

The great Stephen Hawking, whom many consider to be the most gifted physicist since Einstein, openly admitted that his goal is to "know the mind of God." Of course, one can't know the mind of a being that doesn't exist, so Hawking must also be counted amongst those scientists who believe in some type of Creator.

Now, it doesn't take a genius to see that the evidence must be *overwhelmingly* in favor of an Intelligent Designer in order for so many scientists to be openly talking about Him. Indeed, lengthy discussion about the possible existence of God can be found in many otherwise nontheistic treatises, such as those written by Richard Dawkins or Stephen Jay Gould. But why would these individuals devote even a single page to a being whose possible existence they believe is absurd? Again, it's because the scientific evidence for Design is truly *that* compelling.

In the pages that follow, we will be taking a closer look at the latest empirical evidence for Intelligent Design in the universe. In the process, we will be setting the stage for an all-encompassing probabilistic proof for just such a Designer, for it is by engaging in this form of argument that we will hopefully be able to gain a better understanding of our "just right" universe. For insofar as such a Being exists after all, we will never be able to understand the true nature of the cosmos if we continue to exclude Him from our theories.

Notes

1. Although Darwin was never an atheist himself, his views have nevertheless been exploited by atheists to help demonstrate the supposed ability of the natural world to produce complex designs without the aid of a larger Designer.

2. Thomas Aquinas similarly referred to God as being the original "uncaused Cause" of the entire universe.

3. I use the male personal pronoun to refer to the Deity for the sake of literary simplicity and existing convention. I do not mean to imply that God is a male or to show any disrespect for feminist theology.

4. For an excellent treatment of the problem of evil, please refer to John Hick, *Evil and the God of Love* (New York: Harper and Row, 1977).

5. M. A. Corey, *Evolution and the Problem of Natural Evil* (Lanham, Md.: University Press of America, 2000), 191–258.

6. David C. Lindberg, "Science and the Early Church," in *God and Nature*, ed. David C. Lindberg and Ronald L. Numbers (Berkeley: University of California Press, 1986), 19–48.

7. This type of slanting of the facts in the scientific literature suggests a deep antitheistic bias on the part of many scientists who tend to show a pervasive tendency to interpret the existing facts in a nontheistic manner.

8. Sir Fred Hoyle, *Religion and the Scientists* (London: SCM, 1959).

~

CHAPTER THREE

A Brief History of Our Goldilocks Universe

I want to know how God created the world. I am not interested in this or that phenomenon, in the spectrum of this or that element. I want to know His thoughts, the rest are details.

—Albert Einstein

In the Beginning

By far the most important piece of evidence supporting the existence of a Divine Creator is the relatively recent scientific discovery of a definite beginning to the universe. This beginning is thought to have occurred approximately 15 billion years ago in a sudden flash of heat and light known as the Big Bang.

Prior to this discovery, many scientists believed in the so-called Steady-State theory of the universe, which says that there was no beginning to the universe because it is eternal. However, now that the infamous Big Bang theory is accepted as fact throughout the scientific community, scientists have been forced to concede that the universe did in fact have a violent beginning sometime in the distant past.[1]

Modern science's discovery of the birth of the cosmos began in 1913, when American astronomer Vesto Melvin Slipher accidentally discovered that the light coming from several distant galaxies was strongly displaced toward the red, or lower frequency, end of the electromagnetic spectrum. This famous "red shift" is the result of the Doppler Effect, in which objects that are moving away from us have—by virtue of their own receding motion—their light spectra shifted toward the red end of the visible spectrum. Like an ambulance siren whose pitch gets lower as it moves away from us, the frequency of light coming to us from distant galaxies also gets lower because these galaxies are moving away from us (and each other) at tremendous velocities, up to two million miles per hour.

In 1913, however, no one knew what this galactic red shift actually meant. Nevertheless, when Slipher reported his findings to the American Astronomical Society in 1914, his audience spontaneously stood up and cheered, even though they weren't exactly sure what they were cheering about! Evidently they were able to sense the profound importance of Slipher's discovery for the up-and-coming science of cosmology.

Then, in 1915, Albert Einstein completed his general theory of relativity, which is concerned with the nature of gravitation. Much to Einstein's initial dismay, the simplest solution to his equations revealed an expanding universe, which was something he did not believe in and had not anticipated (largely because an expanding universe implies a beginning, and a beginning implies a personal Creator). To the contrary, Einstein believed in a static and unchanging universe, which is what most astronomical observations up to that point had indicated. As a consequence, Einstein devised an addition to his equations, which he called the *cosmological constant*, which enabled them to reflect a nonexpanding universe. He later called this the greatest mistake of his career.

The purpose of Einstein's cosmological constant was to counteract the pull of gravity, so that the entire universe could be maintained in a static state. In retrospect, Einstein should have realized that such a precarious state of cosmic balance could never have survived for long. Like a gigantic house of cards, it would have collapsed back in on itself just as soon as the slightest degree of gravitational imbalance would have presented itself. This, of course, would have made any sort of life impossible, because stable planetary orbits themselves would have been impossible, and stable planetary orbits are absolutely necessary before life can exist anywhere for very long. No wonder Einstein called this addition of the "cosmological term" to his equations the greatest mistake he ever made.

In the same year that Einstein went public with his static model of the universe (1917), the Dutch astronomer Willem de Sitter solved Einstein's equations and also came to the conclusion that the universe was expanding. Five years later, in 1922, the Russian mathematician Alexander Friedmann discovered a simple algebraic error in Einstein's equations which, when corrected, clearly showed the universe to be expanding.

At first Einstein protested. He simply couldn't believe that the universe was really expanding in this manner, because it meant that the universe had to have had a beginning after all. A universal beginning, of course, implies a Beginner, but Einstein found this conclusion to be unacceptable because, again, he didn't want to believe in the existence of a personal Creator.

As we saw earlier, Einstein didn't believe in a personal God because of the tremendous amount of evil that exists in the world. A personal God, Einstein thought, would surely never have allowed such horrific evils as the Bubonic Plague to happen in the first place. Therefore, he concluded, a personal God can't possibly exist.

Instead, Einstein believed in "Spinoza's God," an impersonal Deity who only revealed Himself in the orderly workings of nature. In Einstein's mind, such an impersonal Creator could conceivably have allowed these worldly evils to happen, either because He wouldn't have known about them, or else because He wouldn't have cared about them. This explains his initial reluctance to believe in the Big Bang, because he couldn't bring himself to acknowledge the existence of a personal Creator.

Then, in 1929, Milton Humason and Edwin Hubble showed once and for all that the entire universe is expanding rapidly in all directions. This was concrete astronomical evidence that Einstein simply couldn't ignore, so he publicly rejected his cosmological constant and begrudgingly accepted the Big Bang.

Still more evidence supporting the notion of a concrete universal beginning was found in the Second Law of Thermodynamics, which basically states that the total amount of disorder in the universe can never decrease. Another way of saying this is that the universe is running down like a clock. If it is running down, it must have been "wound up" at some point in the distant past. It is this initial "winding up" period that corresponds to the thermodynamic beginning of the cosmos.

Yet, despite all the evidence indicating an actual beginning to the universe, there were still those who weren't convinced. Finally, in 1965, two Bell Laboratory employees, Arno Penzias and Robert Wilson, accidentally discovered a faint ($3°$ K) microwave background that was permeating the entire universe. Scientists soon identified this microwave background as a relic of the Big Bang itself. The Russian-American physicist George Gamow had predicted the existence of this background radiation back in 1948 on the basis of his "hot" model of the universe, but few took his prediction seriously until it was actually confirmed by direct observation.

Based on his calculations regarding the Big Bang, Gamow also predicted that approximately 25 percent of all the matter in the universe should be helium, with the other 75 percent or so being made up of hydrogen. Gamow was again vindicated when it was later discovered that hydrogen and helium do indeed comprise approximately 75 percent and 25 percent of the universe respectively.

It remained for an English mathematician named Roger Penrose and the legendary Cambridge physicist Stephen Hawking to demonstrate once and for all that the Big Bang was physically necessary, given certain basic assumptions about the universe. Interestingly enough, they found the proof they needed in the peculiar properties surrounding collapsed stars, also known as "black holes."

Stars are normally comprised of a delicate balance between a gravitational pull inward, which is exerted by the matter contained within the star, and an explosive push outward, which is produced by the nuclear explosions that are constantly going on inside the star's fiery core. When a star begins to run out of nuclear fuel, however, the gravitational forces within it begin to take precedence over the decreasing amount of explosive force being generated in the star's nuclear furnace. Once this critical balance point is surpassed in a dying star, the matter within it spontaneously begins to collapse in upon itself at a steadily increasing rate of speed. If the star's total mass happens to be less than a certain critical amount—known as the Chandrasekhar limit—the collapsed star will eventually reach a point where its inward pull of gravity will be just offset by the outward push generated by the Pauli Exclusion Principle, which forces atomic particles away from one another.

There is, however, a limit to the amount of outward force that can be generated by the Pauli Exclusion Principle—it is the amount of force that would be capable of accelerating particles within the star's interior to the speed of light (which is the cosmic speed limit according to Einstein's theory of relativity). Thus, in a sufficiently dense star that exceeds the Chandrasekhar limit, the inward pull of gravity will eventually be able to overwhelm the outward push exerted by the Pauli Exclusion Principle, with the result that the star itself will begin a calamitous period of runaway contraction. This period of contraction continues unabated until a point of zero size and infinite density—known as a singularity—is eventually reached. A singularity of this type is termed a black hole because its gravitational pull is so great that not even light itself can escape from it.

Interestingly enough, Einstein's theory of general relativity states that the entire universe itself also began as a singularity, a point of zero size and infinite density in which all the matter and energy in the universe is said to have been concentrated. For some unknown reason, this "cosmic egg" is thought to have exploded with just the right degree of vigor to ensure the development of a life-supporting universe several billion years later.

The Belgian priest and mathematician Georges Lemaître had anticipated the discovery of the Big Bang singularity back in 1927 with his publication of the first expanding universe model. But Lemaître went even further. Whereas other scientists were forcing themselves to reject the notion of a concrete universal beginning (again because of its profound religious implications), Lemaître went straight to the heart of the matter and made the first scientific prediction of a Big Bang singularity. He reasoned that if the entire universe was presently expanding, there must have been a time in the past when it was much closer together. Extrapolating back to the very beginning, he concluded that the primordial universe itself must have been very dense indeed, perhaps even infinitely so. Lemaître called his prophetic vision of the cosmic egg "the primordial atom," and its massive explosion "the big noise." Several years later the British astrophysicist Fred Hoyle, who at the time was openly antagonistic to the idea of a singular creation event, sarcastically called it "the big bang," and the name stuck.

It is interesting to note how the first expanding universe model was made not by a physicist or cosmologist, but by a Belgian *priest*. The very notion of an expanding universe, as we have seen, is fraught with profound religious implications, so it is easy to see how a theorist would need the right theological background in order to be able to come up with an accurate conceptual model. For just as the founding fathers of the modern scientific movement were directed by their religious beliefs into looking for law and order in the cosmos, so too did Georges Lemaître allow his faith in God to direct him into devising the first working model of the Big Bang.

This inclusion of religious belief into the scientific struggle for knowledge is anathema to most scientists. Yet, it cannot be denied that it was the religious faith of the first working scientists that played the predominant role in the development of modern science. For as we have seen, it was their relentless belief in a Divine Creator that led the founding fathers of the modern scientific movement to search for order and rationality in the cosmos in the first place. The moral of this story is that while it may be "proper" to exclude God from empirical laboratory science because of His nonphysical nature, He *cannot* be excluded from the working scientist's overall worldview without severe consequences resulting.

It should be pointed out, though, that a theistic interpretation of the Big Bang is *not* absolutely committed to the existence of a Big Bang singularity at the beginning of space and time (otherwise known as space-time). It is only unreservedly committed to the general idea of the universe as a divine creation, which of course leaves room for any and all physical mechanisms that God might have employed in the service of cosmic evolution. Strictly speaking, theism isn't even committed to the notion of time itself having a beginning, since it is possible that an eternal God could have been maintaining the universe for all of eternity.

Nevertheless, the modern scientific belief in a concrete universal beginning still strongly supports the biblical doctrine of creation. For as long as the universe did in fact experience a definite beginning at some point in the distant past, there *had* to have been a sufficient reason for the universe to begin as it did. Moreover, these cosmic initial conditions are now known to have been *incredibly* fine-tuned in support of life, as we have seen. The point is simply that there *had* to have been a sufficient reason for such a well-orchestrated cosmic beginning, and it is this sufficient reason to which we now owe our very lives.

Significantly, though, science will evidently never be able to probe back to the very beginning of space-time, because the very laws of science themselves totally break down as one nears the moment of creation (otherwise known as the "Planck Time," when the universe was but a mere 10^{-43} seconds old). It appears, then, that the ultimate cause of the Big Bang must remain forever shrouded beyond the reach of science, as astrophysicist Robert Jastrow has so eloquently described in his popular book *God and the Astronomers*:

> At this moment it seems as though science will never be able to raise the curtain on the mystery of creation. For the scientist who has lived by his faith in the power of reason, the story ends like a bad dream. He has scaled the mountains of ignorance; he is about to conquer the highest peak; as he pulls himself over the final rock, he is greeted by a band of theologians who have been sitting there for centuries.[2]

It would seem, then, that the moment of creation—and with it the possible role of a Divine Creator—will forever be protected from probing scientific minds. All that can safely be said at this point is that the universe did indeed experience a concrete beginning sometime in the distant past. But this, in turn, raises the question of who or what could have served as a sufficient reason for the Big Bang itself. This question becomes all the more perplexing when we take into consideration the apparent creation of the universe out of nothing (*ex nihilo*), along with the simultaneous fine-tuning of its many life-supporting characteristics. On this score, the age-old notion of a Divine Creator seems to be the most sensible explanation of them all. Whittaker agrees:

> When the development of the system of the world is traced backwards by the light of laws of nature, we arrive finally at a moment when that development begins. This is the ultimate point of physical science, the farthest glimpse that we can ob-

tain of the material universe by our natural faculties. There is no ground for supposing that matter . . . existed before this in an inert condition, and was in some way galvanized into activity at a certain instant: for what could have determined this instant rather than all the other instants of past eternity? It is simpler to postulate a creation *ex nihilo*, an operation of Divine Will to constitute Nature from nothingness.[3]

This is why we can say that belief in God is strongly supported by the notion of a concrete beginning to space-time (even though it isn't absolutely dependent upon it). Accordingly, anything that points *away* from an infinitely old universe and toward a concrete universal beginning sometime in the distant past can be said to support the believer's overall case.

Fortunately for the theist, several intriguing scientific observations have effectively ruled out a universe of infinite size and age. For one thing, the night sky is essentially dark, but this isn't at all what we would expect if there were an infinite number of stars in the heavens. As Thomas Digges first pointed out in 1576, a universe with an infinite number of stars should produce a bright night sky. Edmund Halley reiterated this same paradox in 1715.

For a time it was thought that Heinrich Olbers had solved the paradox in 1823, through his suggestion that a significant proportion of light in an infinite universe would be absorbed by interstellar dust clouds. In 1879, however, Josef Stefan showed that radiant energy isn't just absorbed by these dust clouds; it is also radiated *outward* at a definite proportional rate. According to this finding, Olbers' proposed interstellar medium would eventually reach a temperature where it would radiate out as much energy as it was receiving.[4] This would especially be true in an infinitely old universe, since in this case interstellar dust clouds would have had an infinite amount of time to absorb and reradiate this energy back out into space. In an infinite universe with an infinite number of stars, then, the night sky would have to be much brighter than the one we currently observe. Therefore, the universe probably does *not* contain an infinite number of stars after all.

In addition, one would expect that an infinitely old universe would contain many stars that are at or near their natural age limit. However, no stars have ever been discovered that are older than 17 billion years or so, even though some stars are capable of reaching an upper age-limit of around 80 billion years! This seems to be clear evidence against an infinitely old universe.

Indeed, according to Hugh Ross, *all* galaxies are middle-aged.[5] No newly formed or extinct galaxies have ever been discovered. Therefore, all galaxies were probably formed a finite time ago. This hypothesis is supported by the most recent models of galaxy formation in an expanding universe, which predict a narrow window following the Big Bang in which galaxy formation could have possibly taken place. Beyond this point, matter would have been too dispersed because of the ceaseless universal expansion to have been able to condense into coherent galaxies. Moreover, galaxies look progressively younger as one looks further out into space. In an infinite universe, though, one would not expect such an age–distance relationship to hold.[6]

A few scientists have tried to escape the idea of a beginning by employing the notion of an oscillating universe, in which the universe oscillates back and forth between successive cycles of expansion and contraction. With this superficially clever theoretical maneuver, it is possible to believe in a whole series of big bangs and yet still not be held to a concrete universal beginning.

In fact, several scientists have actually used an oscillating universal model to explain the many improbable coincidences that have led to the rise of life. On this view, if there were indeed an infinite number of oscillations in the cosmic past, then one of these oscillations could have accidentally produced all of the basic qualities that are necessary for the existence of life; and, of course, we would then inevitably find ourselves living within one of these lucky oscillations.

Three pieces of evidence, however, strongly discredit any notion of an oscillating universe. To begin with, cosmologists are by no means certain that our present universe will *ever* collapse back in on itself. According to applied physicist and theologian Gerald L. Schroeder, author of the book *Genesis and the Big Bang*, the latest evidence indicates that we actually live in an "open" universe, which means that the present universal expansion will probably continue forever.[7] Schroeder argues that there simply isn't enough matter in the universe to ever cause it to collapse back in on itself, since current measurements indicate that our universe contains only 10 to 20 percent of the amount of matter that would eventually be needed to halt the present cosmic expansion.[8] This critical amount of matter is known to cosmologists, appropriately enough, as the *critical density* of the universe. While it is possible that nonluminous "dark matter" could be the missing element that would give the universe this critical density, many consider this possibility to be unlikely, given the enormous amount that would be required for the task.

In addition, sophisticated computer analyses of Doppler shift data indicate that the present universal expansion will probably continue forever.[9] That is to say, the rate of slowing of the various galaxies around us does not appear to be sufficient to ever cause them to halt their present expansion. But if our universe is destined to go on expanding forever, it obviously could not be involved in a never-ending pattern of expansion and contraction.

However, the most convincing evidence against an oscillating universe is thermodynamic in nature. Each cycle of expansion and contraction in an oscillating universe must produce an overall increase in cosmic disorder, or entropy.[10] This increase in entropy would reveal itself as a proportionate increase in the number of photons, or light particles, relative to those particles with a rest mass. Accordingly, with each successive oscillation, there should be an *increase* in the ratio between photons and nuclear particles. It follows, then, that an infinite number of oscillations:

> would, according to thermodynamics, have raised the ratio of photons to nuclear particles to infinity. Because the number of photons is finite, for the ratio to equal infinity, the number of particles must equal zero. Zero particles means that there would be no material universe. But our very existence attests that this is not the case. There is a material universe and we are part of it.[11]

This evidence from thermodynamics is so persuasive that even atheistic physicist Steven Weinberg was compelled to admit, "It is hard to see how the universe could have previously experienced an infinite number of cycles."[12]

But even if we assume that there is enough matter in the universe to eventually halt its present expansion, it does *not* necessarily follow that the ensuing contraction will result in another Big Bang type of explosion or "bounce." For one thing, there is no known physical mechanism[13] that is capable of reversing a cosmic contraction.

Hugh Ross builds on this conclusion by noting that the universe is by far the most entropic (i.e., disorder-producing) phenomenon known.[14] As a consequence, even if the universe were to eventually collapse back in on itself, it "would *not* produce a bounce. Far too much of the energy of the universe is dissipated in unreclaimable form to fuel a bounce. Like a clump of wet clay falling on a carpet, the universe, if it did collapse, would go 'splat.'"[15]

But if we do not live in an eternal, oscillating universe, we are left with the conclusion that the Big Bang was in all likelihood a unique event, which of course is another way of saying that there was an actual beginning to the universe some 15 billion years ago. Such a conclusion is enormously significant, because it compels us to come up with a realistic explanation for the sudden, perfect appearance of this primordial explosion.

However, because the familiar chain of cause and effect abruptly terminates as we approach the beginning of the Big Bang (at a temporal limit known as "Planck's Wall"), we will never be able to use our mathematical formulas to probe back to the absolute beginning. It would appear, then, that this mystical point will forever be beyond our reach. It is this transcendent Original Cause that a growing number of thinkers now consider to be God.[16]

Robert Jastrow agrees:

> Now we see how the astronomical evidence leads to a Biblical view of the origin of the world. The details differ, but the essential elements in the astronomical and Biblical accounts of Genesis are the same: the chain of events leading to man commenced suddenly and sharply at a definite moment in time, in a flash of light and energy.[17]

This statement is all the more remarkable because Jastrow himself is a self-avowed agnostic.

In order to learn more about the initial conditions surrounding the birth of the universe, physicists take their cosmological equations that describe our expanding universe and run them backwards until the beginning of time is reached. In the process, an impressive amount of information regarding the early stages of the universe is generated.[18]

In fact, so much information has been produced in this manner that it is sometimes tempting to believe that we will one day be able to come up with an all-encompassing "theory of everything," which will supposedly enable us to unify the four forces of physics[19] so that we can actually predict the values of nature's fundamental constants. We shouldn't get too excited about our chances for discovering such a theory, however, because it is clear that we have *not* been given all of the keys that would lead to a total understanding of the cosmos. The limitations that are posed by (1) our human intellect, (2) our measuring apparatus, and (3) the intrinsic uncertainty of quantum reality itself, all conspire together to make this virtually impossible. Worse still, all our equations break down at Planck's Wall, when the universe was but a mere 10^{-43} seconds old, and for good reason, because the temperature of the primordial universe beyond this point was so high that the four fundamental forces of physics were all dissolved, presumably in the form of a single all-encompassing force. This, in turn, has made it essentially impossible for any direct information about the universe's beginning to survive intact. Planck's Wall thus seems to represent:

> the universe's ultimatum: There will be no further hedging of equations, no more jumping over points too complex or obscure to understand. This is where all your calculations and all your thinking must be brought together in the clearest statement in the history of mankind about the cosmos before you will know how it began. And still you may never know—exactly.[20]

Is the Rate of Cosmic Expansion Increasing?

Because of the natural "braking" action of gravity, cosmologists have long assumed that the rate of cosmic expansion has gradually been decreasing throughout the millennia. A few individuals, such as Tulane University's Frank Tipler, even believe that the universe will eventually stop expanding altogether sometime in the distant future, at which point it will then supposedly begin to collapse back in on itself, eventually leading to what has been called the "Big Crunch."

Recent groundbreaking research, however, from the Hubble Space Telescope has suggested that the universe may actually be *speeding up* over time. Images of distant supernovae taken by Hubble have enabled scientists to calculate the rate of cosmic expansion to an unprecedented degree of accuracy, and the most recent results are nothing short of astounding. For instead of gradually slowing down, as was previously believed, the universe actually appears to be speeding up over time. In the words of UC Berkeley's Adam Riess, "We're speeding to infinity, and we're in a hurry to get there."

"It's tantalizing," says astrophysicist Michael Turner of the University of Chicago. "If the results hold up, it's really magical." But what force or power could possibly enable the universe to continue expanding against the pull of gravity at an ever-increasing rate of speed? Surprisingly, this force appears to be a natural part of the vacuum of "empty" space, in which the vacuum somehow pushes against itself and thus creates a curious repulsive force.

As we saw in the previous section, Albert Einstein originally added this imaginary antigravity force to his relativity equations in order to keep the universe in a static state. He called it the "cosmological constant," and he later discarded it as a mistake when Edwin Hubble demonstrated in 1929 that the universe is expanding after all. But now, thanks to the Hubble Space Telescope, the cosmological constant is making a bold comeback, for it seems to be the only force that could possibly cause the vacuum of "empty" space to expand at an ever-increasing rate.

The importance of this new finding is that it finally enables us to make sense out of one of the most confusing aspects of the Big Bang. For prior to this discovery, cosmologists believed that the universe was expanding at a significantly slower rate of speed, which in turn made the universe itself seem younger than some of the stars contained within it. This striking discrepancy turned the field of cosmology on its head, because it seemed to suggest that something was terribly wrong with the traditional Big Bang scenario. But now that we know that the universe is expanding at a progressively greater rate of speed, it follows that the universe itself is significantly older than was previously believed, which in turn means that there are no stars in existence that are older than the universe itself. Once again, the traditional Big Bang scenario turns out to be vindicated after all, because it is still the best explanation for the known facts.

Notes

1. Of course, there are holdouts to this consensus view, but they are relatively few in number and their objections to the Big Bang almost always fly in the face of accepted empirical data.

2. Robert Jastrow, *God and the Astronomers* (New York: Warner, 1978), 125.

3. Taken from John D. Barrow, *The World within the World* (Oxford: Oxford University Press, 1990), 227.

4. Herman Bondi, *Cosmology* (Cambridge: Cambridge University Press, 1960), 21.

5. Hugh Ross, *The Fingerprint of God* (Orange, Calif.: Promise Publishing, 1991), 91.

6. Ibid.

7. Gerald L. Schroeder, *Genesis and the Big Bang* (New York: Bantam, 1990), 78–79.

8. Ibid., 78.

9. Ibid.

10. Ibid., 80.

11. Ibid., 81.

12. Ibid., 80.

13. Hugh Ross, *The Fingerprint of God*, 104–105.

14. Ibid., 105.

15. Ibid.

16. This is an example of the Cosmological Argument for the Existence of God, which attempts to trace the chain of cause and effect in the universe back to an original Uncaused Cause.

17. Jastrow, *God and the Astronomers*, 13–14.

18. Einstein's equations are able to describe both the current expansion of the universe as well as its beginning using only mathematics and the insight of an incomparable genius. Such a prodigious accomplishment seems to conclusively indicate that the science of mathematics really does describe the inner workings of the universe itself, instead of just the individual peculiarities of human thought.

19. The four fundamental forces of physics are gravitation, electromagnetism, and the strong and weak nuclear forces.

20. John Boslough, *Stephen Hawking's Universe* (New York: William Morrow, 1985), 104.

CHAPTER FOUR

~

The Universe
According to Murphy's Law

The most incomprehensible thing about the universe is that it is comprehensible.

—Albert Einstein

Virtually everyone is familiar with Murphy's Law. It says that anything that can go wrong *will* tend to go wrong eventually. This is unquestionably one of the most fundamental laws of our world. Things go wrong for us every single day of our lives, and as we all know, they're more likely to go wrong the more that they inherently *can* go wrong. For instance, if your car isn't in the best of shape, you can bet that something is going to go wrong with it soon enough. The same thing can be said of computers, musical instruments, and even the events in our own personal lives. Things invariably tend to go wrong to the proportionate extent that they *can* go wrong, and that's just the way life is.

But why should this be so? Why should Murphy's Law be true? The answer seems to be related to the fact that there are vastly more disordered states possible in the universe than ordered states. And since things need to be very highly ordered before they can go right, it follows that things will tend to go wrong far more often than they will end up going right, simply because of the sheer preponderance of disordered states to ordered ones.

It is this natural tendency for things to become more disordered over time that comprises the essence of the Second Law of Thermodynamics. Technically speaking, the Second Law states that energy tends to become less usable with the passage of time. But if this is true, it means that a great deal of effort must be expended in order to make things go right, because some sort of constraining force inherently must be applied to halt this natural descent into disorder. Otherwise, a higher state of order will rarely, if ever, tend to result.

The overall effect of the Second Law, however, isn't entirely negative. To the contrary, it paradoxically possesses a very positive function in human life as far as the developmental process itself is concerned. For by giving us a constant barrage of potential disorder to contend with, it compels us to grow more responsible and mature in our innermost lives so that we can hopefully limit the actualization of this disorder and bring about more order in our lives. Clearly, then, if the Second Law were to ever be replaced by its functional opposite, we'd quickly grow more complacent and irresponsible as a result, since we wouldn't have to exert any effort at all in order to see an overall increase in the amount of order in our lives.

The Second Law is also a vital prerequisite for any type of meaningful action in the world, as the French physicist Poincaré successfully showed. For in a world where the total amount of disorder went down instead of up, it would be impossible to make intelligent predictions regarding future states of affairs since one would no longer be able to count on a steady increase in disorder to base one's actions on. It would thus be impossible to anticipate the future with any appreciable degree of accuracy in this sort of world, so one's capacity for free-willed behavior would inevitably be compromised as a result. Friction, for instance, would be a destabilizing force rather than a dampening one in this type of world, so any mechanism that uses friction to slow things down (such as the brakes in one's automobile) would subsequently be both unreliable and unpredictable.[1] It would therefore be very difficult to anticipate the immediate future with any degree of accuracy in such a world, so intelligent behavior would become impossible. Paradoxically, then, the pervasive rise in disorder that is generated by the Second Law tends to lead to a *more* predictable state of affairs in the realm of human behavior.

But what does all this have to do with the nature of the universe and the possible existence of an Intelligent Designer? Actually, the Second Law has everything to do with this issue, because we have good reason to believe that Murphy's Law applies just as much to the entire universe as it does to our own individual lives. But if this is true, then we are compelled to find a sufficient explanation for why the universe was capable of bringing about the stupendous complexity of human life, despite this natural cosmic tendency toward greater levels of disorder.

Again, the Second Law of Thermodynamics tells us that in the absence of some type of external constraining influence, things should have gotten more disordered in the universe with the passage of time, and not less. This is particularly true when it comes to the initial amount of usable energy in the universe, which was the highest that it's ever been at the Big Bang, in direct contradiction to the Second Law.[2] Murphy's Law builds upon this inviolable principle by stating that things should have gone more and more wrong in the universe over time, especially as far as the existence of life is concerned. This is due to the fact that, without an external constraining influence to act upon matter, there would have been no reason for things to suddenly start going right with respect to life. This is all the more true because of the many profoundly complicated steps that had to have all gone right before life could have ever arisen here.

In fact, we can go so far as to say that there were *infinitely* more ways for the universe to have gone wrong in the past than for it to have gone right. There are two reasons for this: (1) because there were an infinite number of possible values that could have been chosen for each of the nature's fundamental constants and (2) because there are an infinite number of ways in which these fundamental interactions between the constants could have themselves gone wrong. Yet, despite this infinity of possible errors, the universe repeatedly chose the "correct" value each time it had to do so as far as our own existence is concerned. Mathematicians tell us that the probability for this happening is zero. Yet we are here.

Surely this is a fact of tremendous significance, because there *had* to have been a sufficient reason for all of these variables to repeatedly go right in the universe on the way to life, particularly in the face of the Second Law.

In other words, had things been capable of significantly going wrong on the way to life, they almost certainly *would* have, and we would not be here. But we *are* here. Therefore, things must not have been capable of going significantly wrong on the way to life. But the only way this could have possibly been the case is if a supreme constraining influence would have deliberately acted to make it so.

Clearly, we're not talking here about just any type of constraining influence. We're talking about one that could have repeatedly acted in direct opposition to the Second Law of Thermodynamics, even to the point of producing the unfathomable complexity of the human brain. In this case, the enormous time frame postulated by neo-Darwinism for the rise of life is actually a "plus" as far as our argument for Design is concerned, because all this extra time greatly magnifies the number of ways that the universe could conceivably have gone wrong on the way to life.

Most nontheistic scientists will want to reject this conclusion on the premise that living creatures are "thermodynamically open systems," which means that they are capable of growing more complex without contradiction to the Second Law. This is because the local increase in order is "paid for" by a larger increase in the overall amount of disorder that surrounds the biosphere. While this may be true, it is *not* germane to our Argument from Murphy's Law, because what we're actually looking for here is a *sufficient* reason for why the entire universe should have evolved in direct opposition to the Second Law. The fact that order *can* evolve in thermodynamically open systems does not constitute a sufficient explanation as to why it actually *does* so. Some sort of larger constraining influence is needed for that, as Paul Davies points out:

> Biosystems are not closed systems. They are characterized by their very openness, which enables them to export entropy into their environment to prevent degeneration. But the fact that they are able to evade the degenerative (pessimistic) arrow of time does not explain how they comply with the progressive (optimistic) arrow. Freeing a system from the strictures of one law does not prove that it follows another.
>
> Many biologists make this mistake. They assume because they have discovered the above loophole in the second law, the progressive nature of biological evolution is explained. This is simply incorrect. It also confuses order with organization and complexity. Preventing a decrease in order might be a necessary condition for the growth of organization and complexity, but it is not a sufficient condition. We still have to find that elusive arrow of time.[3]

In the next chapter we will focus our attention on the many different ways that things had to have gone right in the universe before intelligent life could have arisen on this planet. This, in turn, will greatly strengthen the persuasiveness of our Argument for Design from Murphy's Law.

Notes

1. The temperature of initially uniform bodies would also be subject to spontaneous change without notice as well.

2. The "cosmic clock" has been running down ever since. This means that some type of order-building force in the universe had to have wound up the cosmic clock to begin with. It is in this fashion that the Second Law of Thermodynamics points decisively in the direction of Intelligent Design.

3. Paul Davies, *The Cosmic Blueprint* (New York: Simon and Schuster, 1989), 113.

CHAPTER FIVE

~

Goldilocks and
the Anthropic Principle

What is a man, that the electron is mindful of him?

—Carl Becker

In the popular children's story "Goldilocks and the Three Bears," Goldilocks ventures into the three bears' home when they're out for a while and helps herself to some porridge. When she tries the papa bear's porridge, she finds that it is too hot, and when she tries the mama bear's porridge, she finds that it is too cold. But when she tries the baby bear's porridge, she finds that it is just right, so she digs right in.

After she is done eating, Goldilocks feels tired, so she tries out the papa bear's bed, but it is too hard. She then tries the mamma bear's bed, but it is too soft. Fortunately, the baby bear's bed is just right, so she decides to take a little nap on it.

Believe it or not, the universe in which we live is remarkably similar to the experience of Goldilocks, except for one thing—the universe had to make many more "just right" choices than Goldilocks ever dreamed of. Basic features like the size of the gravitational force, the rate of cosmic expansion, and thousands of other important structural features all had to be "decided" upon right away.

Unlike the Goldilocks story, though, the universe had far more than three possible options to choose from with respect to each individual choice. In fact, it had *infinitely* more options to consider for each of these choices, since each of its basic features could have occupied an infinite number of possible

41

values. Yet, like Goldilocks, the universe repeatedly chose the value that was "just right" as far as the future existence of intelligent life was concerned, even though the probability for this happening, as we have seen, is essentially zero.

There is, however, another important difference between the Goldilocks story and the way in which our universe came into being. In the fairy tale, Goldilocks first had to try out a couple of unsuccessful alternatives before she was able to find the "right" one. This is the process of trial and error in its simplest form, and it is widely believed that the universe itself also had to undergo a lengthy process of trial and error before it was able to settle on the "right" structural values for the existence of life. Such a belief, however, has now been found to be in error. For as Barrow and Tipler have pointed out, the nascent universe didn't have to undergo a time-consuming process of trial and error before it could settle upon the "right" structural values for the existence of life. Instead, the universe exploded into being with the "right" values already factored in!

> There has grown up, even amongst many educated persons, a view that everything in Nature, every fabrication of its laws, is determined by the local environment in which it was nurtured—that natural selection and the Darwinian revolution have advanced to the boundaries of every scientific discipline. Yet, in reality, this is far from the truth. Twentieth-century physics has discovered that there exist invariant properties of the natural world and its elementary components which render inevitable the gross size and structure of almost all its composite objects. The size of bodies like stars, planets, and even people is neither random nor the result of any progressive selection process, but simply manifestations of the different strengths of the various forces of Nature. They are examples of possible equilibrium states between competing forces of attraction and repulsion.[1]

What this means is that the various structural parameters of our universe did *not* gradually evolve by a trial-and-error process of selection before they were able to find the right life-supporting values. Instead, they emerged from the Big Bang with the right values already programmed in. This is what the term "invariant" means—it means that these structural values were never otherwise, which itself can only mean that these structural parameters emerged from the Big Bang in precisely the right format to promote the existence of life several billion years later.

This is undoubtedly one of the most breathtaking findings in all of modern science, yet it has scarcely been commented upon in the technical literature. It is remarkable because it means that we now have to find a sufficient explanation for how and why these extraordinarily complex structural parameters could have been able to "pop" into existence with precisely the right life-supporting values already determined. It would have been different had these values emerged from the Big Bang in a random format with respect to the existence of life. One could then have argued that these parameters subsequently evolved through a random trial-and-error process of selection until the "right" life-supporting values were finally chosen.

But this isn't what happened at all. To the contrary, the sudden appearance of the correct biocentric parameters "out of nothing" is essentially tantamount to a miracle, because there is evidently no other way to account for this perfect life-giving format by random processes alone.

A brief example may help to clarify my point. Imagine a small bomb detonating in the middle of a field. Imagine further that the shrapnel that is produced by the bomb mysteriously comes together immediately after the explosion to form a coherent statue of former President Clinton. Anyone observing such a thing in real time would conclude that the bomb itself had been rigged or prearranged to do such a thing, since random processes alone are simply incapable of performing such a feat. But the universe itself did something far more impressive than this, since it not only spontaneously emerged out of nothing with the "right" structural parameters for life already factored in, it was also able to generate conscious, intelligent observers from this unique combination of building blocks several billion years later.

There is, however, yet another intriguing aspect to this miraculous cosmic phenomenon. The specific values of nature's fundamental constants all had to have been "fine-tuned" with respect to their many complex interactions with one another, so that the phenomenon of life could eventually be realized.

Take the relationship between electromagnetic and gravitational forces, for instance. These values are perfectly balanced with one another so as to facilitate the formation of stable stars like our sun. The gravitational force itself is far weaker than the electromagnetic force, so it plays essentially no role on the microscopic level of existence, yet it simultaneously dominates the macroscopic level of reality "hands down." Indeed, if gravity were any weaker than it presently is, stars would have subsequently been much bigger, since more mass would have been required to generate a sufficient amount of gravitational pressure in their cores to support nuclear fusion. If, on the other hand, gravity were any stronger, stars would have subsequently been smaller, with much shorter life spans. For instance, had gravity been 10^{26} times weaker than the electrical force, stars would have only been a millionth of a billionth of the sun's mass, and they would subsequently have had life spans of only a year or so. In this case, life forms would have never had enough time to arise on this planet, and even if they did, they would have been much smaller than the sizes we're familiar with, since the effects of gravity would have been overwhelming in this particular instance. Indeed, even the slightest alteration in this ratio between the electromagnetic and gravitational forces would have transformed all stars into red giants or dwarfs, and there would have been no life-supporting main sequence stars like our sun.

The value of the strong nuclear force is also perfectly suited for stellar evolution. Had it been any stronger, then a nuclear structure known as the diproton (which is comprised of two protons stuck together) would have been stable, because the strength of the electromagnetic force would have been insufficient to prevent their union. The result would have been a lack of free protons in the universe to form the element hydrogen, and this would have had a catastrophic effect on the formation of stars like our sun, which rely on pure hydrogen for fuel. At the same time, though, had the strong force been any weaker, then the complex nuclei upon which life depends would not have been capable of forming, and we would have thus been stuck with a universe that is comprised mostly of hydrogen. The cumulative effect of this fine-tuning, according to one writer, is such that "if we could play God, and select values for [nature's fundamental constants] at a whim by twiddling a set of knobs, we would find that almost all knob settings would render the universe uninhabitable."

This is a breathtaking realization that surely smacks of some form of Intelligent Design, because the scope and degree of this fine-tuning extends to *all* of nature's fundamental constants *simultaneously* since they all interact with one another, either directly or indirectly, in a wide variety of different ways. In order to reach this mind-boggling degree of fine-tuning with so many different parameters, the Creator's "aim" had to have been very accurate indeed. According to Penrose, it had to have been accurate to within one part in 10 to the 10^{123}, and this is a number so vast that it can't be written on a piece of paper the size of the entire visible universe!

This is why we can say that the sudden appearance of these life-supporting values in the Big Bang is tantamount to a miracle. It is a miracle in three distinct ways: (1) the sudden appearance of the Big Bang "out of nothing" is itself an inexplicable miracle that can be likened to pulling an entire universe out of an infinitely small hat (because the entire universe is thought to have emerged from an infinitely small "singularity"; (2) the spontaneous emergence of the "right" fundamental parameters out of the Big Bang is also a miracle, because such a finely-tuned orchestration toward a highly complex end product is inherently incompatible with random processes alone; and (3) the stupendous degree of fine-tuning that instantly existed between these fundamental parameters following the Big Bang reveals a miraculous level of micro-engineering that is simply inconceivable in the absence of a "supercalculating" Designer.

The nontheistic scientist has no explanation for these curious phenomena. He has no idea why the universe repeatedly chose the "right" value for each of its basic structural features immediately following the Big Bang. He simply notes that, given our existence, we couldn't possibly have observed a different kind of universe.[2]

This type of self-evident reasoning has become known as the Weak Anthropic Principle. It is one possible interpretation of the more generalized Anthropic Principle, which attempts to explain the nature of our universe in terms of the various requirements for human existence.

The term "Anthropic Principle" comes from the Greek word *anthropos*, meaning "man." The Anthropic Principle is thus the "human-centered principle." It refers to the surprising scientific realization that the entire universe seems to cater to the needs of humanity in a very deep and profound way. For instance, the entire universe possesses just the "right" amount of matter and is expanding at just the "right" velocity to enable human life to exist. Were either of these two parameters even slightly different, we would not be here to discuss the fact.

The Anthropic Principle thus stands in stark contrast to the Principle of Mediocrity, which states that there is nothing special or unique about human existence as such. According to this widely held perspective, we are nothing more than biochemical accidents who happen to live in a very average solar system. We will be rejecting this so-called Copernican Principle throughout the remainder of this book because it stands in direct contradiction to the known facts. Our planet, for instance, isn't typical or ordinary by any stretch of the imagination. It is, instead, exceptionally well adapted to the needs of life; so much so, in fact, that scientists are beginning to realize that complex life forms may actually be a rarity in the cosmos.[3] The startling fact of the matter is that there is indeed something very special about the human race after all, because the entire cosmos is now known to cater to our existence in hundreds of different ways.

It was this stunning realization that led physicist Brandon Carter in 1974 to propose the Anthropic Principle to account for the increasingly "anthropic" nature of the cosmological data. The central point behind Carter's Anthropic Principle is that while human life may not be privileged in *every* way from a cosmic point of view, it can nevertheless be privileged in some ways. And indeed it is. For we now know that the entire universe, from the smallest reaches of subatomic reality to the farthest reaches of the heavens, is permeated with the same structural parameters that are necessary for the existence of human life. This is the chief sense in which the universe can be said to "cater" to the needs of humanity.

For instance, the gravitational force is now known to extend to the furthest reaches of the heavens and is also known to possess the same value of 6.67×10^{-11} at all places and at all times. But this is the very same value that is necessary for the existence of human observers, and the same thing can be said for the remainder of nature's fundamental constants as well. So in this sense, the entire universe does indeed "cater" to the needs of humanity after all, insofar as it is permeated with the very same structural specifications that are necessary for human existence. Moreover, since each of these fundamental parameters is cooperatively interacting with all of the others, the actual degree of complexity that is represented by this interplay is strictly unimaginable. These cosmic "coincidences" between distant branches of physics are so compelling, in fact, that many scientists are actually coming forward and admitting that "something must be going on behind the scenes."

Pioneer quantum physicist John Wheeler, for instance, has wondered whether or not the actual subatomic particles *themselves* are somehow tied into making human life possible, since "the physical world is in some deep sense tied to the human being. . . . We are beginning to suspect that man is not a tiny cog that doesn't make much difference to the running of the machine but rather that there is a much more intimate tie between man and the universe than we heretofore suspected."[4] Physicist Freeman Dyson, author of *Infinite in All Directions* and a recent recipient of the Templeton Prize in Religion, has come to a similar conclusion:

> As we look out into the universe and identify the many accidents of physics and astronomy that have worked together to our benefit, it almost seems as if the universe must in some sense have known that we were coming.[5]

The Different Forms of the Anthropic Principle

In the years since Carter first limited the Copernican dogma, scientists have formulated several versions of the Anthropic Principle. The "weak" form, known as the Weak Anthropic Principle (or WAP), can be stated as follows:

> WEAK ANTHROPIC PRINCIPLE: Given the reality of human life, the physical universe must contain areas that are compatible with our own existence as observers.

In other words, the WAP tells us that we never could expect to observe a universe significantly different from our own, because our existence depends on the prior existence of just such a universe. The WAP thus doesn't try to explain how or why our universe actually came to be life supporting. It simply notes that while the universe is the way it is for unknown reasons, given our current existence it couldn't have been otherwise.

Most people don't find the WAP to be very satisfying because it doesn't tell us anything that we don't already know. We want to know why the universe is the way it is, but the WAP is incapable of answering this question. For this we need a stronger form of the Anthropic Principle, which Carter has appropriately dubbed the Strong Anthropic Principle, or SAP.

The SAP can be stated in the following manner:

STRONG ANTHROPIC PRINCIPLE: The universe must have those properties which allow life to develop within it at some stage in its history.

The key term in the SAP is clearly the word "must." It means that the universe *had* to have been life-supporting at some point in its history. Unfortunately, the conventional SAP doesn't attempt to explain *why* the universe must be capable of supporting life. It simply states *that* this must be so.

Clearly, the SAP comes very close to positing the existence of a grand cosmic Designer. This is because there doesn't seem to be any other intelligible way of explaining why the universe *had* to have become life-supporting at some point in its history. Indeed, the late physicist Heinz Pagels once quipped that the SAP is "the closest that some atheists can get to God."

Actually, one interpretation of the SAP explicitly states that the universe is the way it is because it was deliberately designed to be that way by an Intelligent Power. We can call this the Design-Centered Anthropic Principle, or DCAP. It can be stated in the following manner:

DESIGN-CENTERED ANTHROPIC PRINCIPLE: The universe possesses a life-supporting configuration because it was deliberately infused with these properties by a higher Power.

A second version of the SAP is derived from the findings of modern theoretical physics. Dubbed the Participatory Anthropic Principle (PAP) by John Wheeler, it states the following:

PARTICIPATORY ANTHROPIC PRINCIPLE: Observers are necessary to bring the universe into being.

The PAP follows from the popular scientific idea that some sort of living consciousness is needed to make atoms and molecules "real." This strange notion originates in the paradoxical science of subatomic particles known as quantum mechanics. When scientists study these submicroscopic bits of matter, they don't seem to find anything definite until an actual measurement is made. Without this act of observership, reality seems to be held in a paralyzing state of indecision. Some have even argued that life itself is necessary to give the universe a concrete existence.

The third and final version of the SAP has been dubbed the Final Anthropic Principle, or FAP, by Barrow and Tipler. It can be stated as the following:

> FINAL ANTHROPIC PRINCIPLE: Intelligent life must come into existence in the universe, and, once it comes into existence, it will never die out.[6]

In the words of John Casti, the FAP states that "Once life is created, it will endure forever, become infinitely knowledgeable, and ultimately mold the universe to its will."[7] The FAP thus has an obvious religious quality to it, because it states that there is a positive universal purpose to human life that cannot be thwarted by any possible power. In this sense, it is more or less analogous to the basic tenets of traditional Christian theology, particularly in its affirmation of an "afterlife," in which intelligent beings continue to live on forever. Once again, though, the FAP doesn't tell us *why* intelligent life will continue to endure forever. It merely asserts *that* it will continue to endure forever.

The SAP in all its forms tries to explain the improbable nature of nature's many "coincidences" by asserting that the universe *had* to have been capable of admitting life at some point in its history. It rightly concludes that the odds for these "coincidences" to have independently happened by chance are so vanishingly small that they must have been in some sense deliberate. The FAP even goes so far as to claim that intelligent life will eventually grow to the point of becoming almost godlike!

Overall, the SAP implies a strong sense of necessity as far as the existence of life is concerned. This is due to its claim that the universe *must* contain those properties that are essential for life. It is very difficult to see how this could have possibly been the case in the absence of a Supernatural Creator. This is because there seems to be no other way to guarantee the existence of intelligent life.

Although it is possible to view this universal Creator in impersonal terms, as some Hindus have done, it is hard to see how or why an impersonal creative force could have possibly given rise to beings that are so much more conscious or personal than itself. It therefore makes more sense to view the Creator in the way that theists have traditionally done: as a personal God who has deliberately chosen to create finite "children" in His own spiritual image.

Of course, the opposing atheistic camp could argue that there is no reason to make "personhood" such an important quality in the universe. But the fact remains that personhood is an extremely important characteristic in its own right. Indeed, in terms of its inherent degree of complexity, it is by far the most complicated phenomenon in the entire known universe. It is this quality that has enabled the human race to create art and to walk on the moon, and on this score it can't even be approached by any known power.

So, the quality of personhood is very special indeed and we should be overjoyed and humbled by the fact that we have been blessed with this priceless gift. Without it, we'd be little different from chimpanzees or orangutans, and this is a possibility that we don't even want to contemplate at the present time!

Retrodictive Reasoning

One of the most interesting aspects of the Anthropic Principle is that it reverses the pattern of logic typically employed in scientific reasoning. Normally, scientists begin with an initial situation and the various laws of nature and then come to predict a future state of affairs from it. Anthropic reasoning, on the other hand, proceeds in the opposite direction, in the sense that it begins with the final observed state, which is the present condition of the universe, and then acts to constrain or limit the initial conditions of the Big Bang in such a way that they are consistent with our own existence as observers. This is the same type of "retrodictive reasoning" that is used in the various historical sciences. One attempts to reconstruct historical causes or conditions by inferring backwards from present-day facts or clues.[8]

Not all thinkers, however, are impressed by the various "anthropic" formulations that we have explored. Martin Gardner, for instance, was so disgusted by Barrow and Tipler's grandiose claims regarding the Final Anthropic Principle that he renamed it "the completely ridiculous anthropic principle, or CRAP!"[9] Although it is easy to sympathize with Gardner's exasperation regarding some of these formulations, there is nevertheless a great deal of truth to be found in this kind of "anthropic" thinking.

Surprisingly, though, very few people have tried to work out a precise statement of the Anthropic Principle in the years since it was first proposed. Astrophysicists have apparently wanted to leave a little flexibility in its formulation so that its deeper significance might become more apparent in the future.

Many commentators on the Anthropic Principle have intuitively felt that it has something important to say about our overall position in the cosmos, but most have been unable to suggest what it might actually be. In the following pages, we will be exploring the many "hidden recesses" of the Anthropic Principle so as to determine what it can possibly tell us, if anything, about our role in the universe.

Notes

1. John D. Barrow and Frank J. Tipler, *The Anthropic Cosmological Principle* (Oxford: Oxford University Press, 1986), 288.

2. While this is obviously true, it doesn't really explain anything, because the true question that is at issue here concerns why the universe was able to spontaneously take on such an impressive life-supporting arrangement immediately following the Big Bang.

3. Peter D. Ward and Donald Brownlee, *Rare Earth* (New York: Copernicus, 2000), xxi–xxiv.

4. John A. Wheeler, interviewed by Florence Helitzer, "The Princeton Galaxy," *Intellectual Digest*, no. 10 (June 1973): 32.

5. Freeman Dyson, *Disturbing the Universe* (New York: Harper and Row, 1979), 250.

6. Barrow and Tipler, *Anthropic Cosmological Principle*, 23.

7. John L. Casti, *Paradox Lost* (New York: William Morrow, 1989), 482.

8. Stephen C. Meyer, "The Methodological Equivalence of Design and Descent," in *The Creation Hypothesis*, ed. J. P. Moreland (Downers Grove, Ill.: Intervarsity Press, 1994), 90.

9. See Martin Gardner, "WAP, SAP, PAP, and FAP," *New York Review of Books*, vol. 33 (May 8, 1986): 22–25.

CHAPTER SIX

~

Humanity's Role in
Our "Just Right" Cosmos

The eternal mystery of the world is its comprehensibility. . . . The fact that
it is comprehensible is a miracle.

—Albert Einstein

Since the beginning of recorded history, people have assumed that the universe was made for humanity. To our distant ancestors, just about everything in human experience provided conclusive evidence for this belief, because people have been able to exploit so many natural objects for their own ends. Things like vegetables, fruits, cows, and even the weather all work together for the good of humans (most of the time), so it isn't surprising that our ancestors considered them to be specially designed for human benefit.

But then Nicholas Copernicus came along and discovered that the sun, and not the earth, is the geographical center of the solar system. Of course, this astronomical fact in and of itself has nothing at all to do with humanity's overall degree of importance in the cosmos. Even so, many scientists took it to mean that humans are an insignificant, and therefore unimportant, part of the larger universal scheme. This atheistic conclusion is doubly ironic because Copernicus himself was a devout theist, as we saw in chapter 2.

History, however, has now come full circle once again, because modern scientists, with the aid of the Anthropic Principle, have now come to realize that humans are an indispensable part of the cosmic *status quo*. In fact, we can go so far as to say that, in at least three important ways, the human race *really does* exist at the "center" of the universe after all.

51

We can say this, first of all, because of the validity of the Principle of Universality, which states that the entire universe possesses the same underlying structural features that apply locally in our own solar system, such as the strength of gravity and the size of the proton. This is why these fundamental parameters are called "constants" in the first place—because their values never change. But if this is so, it means that the entire universe is actually based on the same physical "recipe" that applies specifically to human beings. The reason for this, once again, is because the entire universe is now known to be permeated with the very same structural parameters that are necessary for human existence. Everything from the strength of the electromagnetic force to the value of the fine structure constant is now known to have somehow been "determined" by the physical requirements for our own existence. It is in this underlying structural sense that the universe can indeed be said to revolve around the needs of human beings after all.

It is hard to see how this could have been just another mindless coincidence, especially given the trillions of independent cosmic factors that had to have been set "just right" before life could have ever existed here. The findings of modern quantum physics support this surprising realization, because many physicists now believe that human observers are necessary in a deep, fundamental sense in order to give the universe its physical reality. This is the essence of Wheeler's Participatory Anthropic Principle (PAP) that we discussed earlier.

Physically speaking, then, it is a fact that the universe caters to the structural needs of human existence. Predictably, though, most atheistic scientists have been quite bothered by this "anthropic" realization. Physicist George Greenstein has even admitted that the very thought of God as Creator makes him squirm in his seat!

On the one hand, it is very hard to see how we, of all creatures, could possibly reside at the "center" of the universe in any meaningful sense. After all, we've repeatedly been told by some of the best scientists in the land that we are nothing more than insignificant globs of protoplasm who happen to have evolved on a faceless piece of rock in a very average solar system, which is itself a member of a very typical galaxy. This position seems to be supported by the utter smallness and fragility of human life in the grand scheme of things.

There is, however, one thing that nontheistic scientists have very conveniently neglected to tell us about ourselves. While we may be physically small in comparison to the size of the universe, we are the largest things we know of in one important respect: structural complexity. Nothing modern science has yet discovered comes even close to the awesome "abyss of complexity" that is displayed by the human mind. In this important sense we are the "biggest" things we know of, yet for some reason we are still being told that there is nothing special about us at all!

It is a matter of common everyday knowledge that complexity and importance tend to go hand in hand in the world. The immensely complicated Space Shuttle, for instance, is far more important to us than a relatively simple pencil sharpener, and this importance is a direct function of its inner degree of structural complexity. Yet, scientists are still wanting us to believe that there is no relevant connection between our inner complexity and our overall degree of importance in the cosmos.

Think of it! The lowliest beggar in the street is nevertheless one of the most complicated physical objects in the entire known universe (along with all of the other people in the world). This is an utterly astonishing realization in and of itself that compels us to look at ourselves in an entirely different light.

And this, in turn, raises a very important question. Could it really be a coincidence that the most complicated objects in the entire known universe also happen to contain within themselves the same structural specifications that permeate the entire known universe? Could it be a coincidence that the needs of humanity have simultaneously determined the specific nature of the universe's own evolution? It is hard to see how this could ever be the case. The importance of this realization cannot be overstated because it seems to suggest that our existence must indeed be vitally important in the larger scheme of things.

However, there is yet another factor at work here that really drives this point home. The unprecedented complexity of the human brain isn't simply a static marvel of bioengineering. To the contrary, this extreme degree of complexity exists for a specific reason—to make the miracle of human consciousness possible. My use of the word "miracle" here is entirely appropriate, for not only is the phenomenon of human consciousness almost totally inexplicable from a scientific point of view, it also constitutes the single most impressive functional quality that we've ever witnessed. Nothing in the entire known universe even *approaches* the profound functional sophistication of human consciousness.

While researchers may be able to unravel some of the neurological mechanisms by which human consciousness operates, it doesn't follow from this that they have even approached a genuine scientific understanding of what consciousness is in itself. It is one thing to figure out some of the neurological pathways by which human consciousness operates, and quite another to claim that this limited understanding somehow translates into a bona fide explanation for consciousness itself! This is why books such as Daniel Dennett's

Consciousness Explained are utterly misleading. When someone works out a genuine explanation for the phenomenon of human consciousness, it will surely be hailed as one of the greatest scientific discoveries of all time.

At the present time, we don't even know whether the ultimate locus of human consciousness is to be found in a nonphysical human soul or whether it is contained entirely within the physical nature of the human brain itself. If the former possibility turns out to be the case, then the brain would simply function as the physical interface between the human body and the non-material soul. Although many respected neurologists believe that the ultimate explanation for consciousness will turn out to be entirely physical in nature, many others, such as Nobel laureate Sir John Eccles, believe that human consciousness is ultimately rooted in a nonmaterial soul.[1]

The most fascinating research to date in this important area has been carried out by Roger Penrose and Stuart Hameroff. They have identified a structural component of the neuron, known as the "microtubule," as the most likely place for the origin of human consciousness, based on the neurophysiology of anesthesia and various quantum mechanical considerations.[2] But even if the microtubule turns out to be the "seat" of our subjective consciousness after all, it still isn't clear whether it merely functions as the physical interface between the brain and a nonmaterial soul or whether it is unilaterally responsible for generating the subjective experience of human consciousness.

My point is simply that the marvel of human consciousness continues to be the most complex functional reality in the entire known universe. Moreover, when we add this unprecedented degree of complexity to the extreme functionality of human consciousness, as well as to the cosmic ubiquity of our own structural requirements, a clear pattern begins to present itself. *How could all three of these factors have possibly been obtained if human beings weren't vitally important in the overall scheme of things?* From this point of view, the universe caters to the needs of humanity precisely *because* humans represent the absolute pinnacle of cosmic evolution. This possibility is further enhanced by the realization that the entire universe is indeed based on the very same "structural recipe" that applies to human beings themselves.

Moderate Anthropocentrism

The type of worldview that we are espousing here is called *moderate anthropocentrism*. It is moderately anthropocentric because it means that we are only *one* of the most important races of beings in the universe. This leaves room for the possible existence of other intelligent beings like ourselves somewhere else in the cosmos. And while even this moderate degree of anthropocentrism has been severely frowned upon in our modern culture, it nevertheless continues to qualify as the single most ambitious concept ever conceived, as the Australian researcher Michael Denton has pointed out.[3] Moreover, it is a conceptual position that has yet to be disconfirmed by a single empirical observation.[4]

Of course, it is always "possible" that human beings could have developed their unprecedented degree of inner complexity by pure chance. According to the latest scientific wisdom, though, the odds against this kind of accidental evolution are nothing short of astronomical. Roger Penrose, for instance, has calculated these odds to be 1 in 10 to the 10^{123}!

As if these unbelievably remote odds weren't small enough, the odds for the accidental evolution of the human genome are also inconceivably small, on the order of 1 in 10^{243}. Similarly, the odds against the evolution of intelligence are now known to be so astronomically huge that the world's leading nontheistic evolutionists have actually come out and openly admitted that we are probably the only race of intelligent beings in the entire visible universe.[5]

This is undoubtedly one of the greatest concessions ever made by the orthodox evolutionary establishment. For if the evolution of intelligence is so extremely improbable that it probably can't be found anywhere else in the entire visible universe, then by all accounts it shouldn't exist here either! But it obviously does exist here. Accordingly, there almost certainly had to have been some type of larger Power at work in the early universe that would have enabled us to come into existence in the face of such overwhelming odds to the contrary.

Modern science, in fact, is actually founded upon probability theory, because absolutely nothing in the physical universe can be totally understood. In quantum theory, for instance, it is impossible to say for a certainty what a given electron will do in the immediate future. The most that quantum physicists can do is to indicate the relative probabilities of what the electron *might* do and then go from there. If they truly want to predict where it will actually go, then the best thing that they can do is to pick the location that is associated with the highest probability. More often than not, this manner of "going with the odds" works out remarkably well, because the odds are usually greatly in favor of certain highly predictable electronic positions.

Scientists are therefore compelled to align themselves with recognized probabilities in the universe, and not with astronomical long shots. This in itself would seem to invalidate the atheistic theory of human origins, because of the astronomically remote chance that it is actually true.

Returning to a Biblical Conception of Humanity

I never cease to be amazed at how far we have been deluded by the atheistic rhetoric emanating from certain segments of the scientific community. Millions upon millions of people around the world have been systematically brainwashed into thinking that there is nothing truly special about humanity in the grand cosmic scheme. Vast population centers have been led to believe that we are nothing but human worms in an uncaring and amoral universe and that the only thing that ultimately matters in the end is dying "with the most toys."

Most surprising of all, though, is the fact that this brainwashing has taken place not through religious or political means, but through the respected hand of *modern science!* People have been deluded by the technological miracles of the twentieth century into thinking that science has all the answers when it comes to our position in the larger universe. Accordingly, when the "high priests" of modern science tell us that we are nothing but human animals who happened to evolve in a heartless universe, millions of people end up coming to the conclusion that it must be true.

No wonder our world is in such a convoluted mess. As psychologists routinely tell us, genuine happiness can only result when a person has a positive self-image. It is very difficult, though, to feel good about ourselves as long as we believe that there's no fundamental difference between ourselves and apes (or nematodes, for that matter). As psychologist Otto Rank and anthropologist Ernest Becker have gone to great pains to show, we all want to feel that there is truly something special about our lives. Indeed, our mental health absolutely *depends* on it. It isn't surprising, then, that depression, crime, and war are at epidemic levels all around the world. It is hard to be a happy and productive member of society when one possesses a false and demeaning self-image!

This is why the study of anthropic cosmology is so important to us today, because it is the one branch of science that is telling us the truth about ourselves. For as we have seen, we *really do* exist at the "center" of the universe after all, in the following three ways: (1) because of our unprecedented level of inner complexity, (2) because of our unmatched degree of high-level functionality, and (3) because of the cosmic centrality of our own structural requirements. This being the case, it is no longer appropriate for us to look at ourselves in a shameful, derogatory manner, because we are truly far more than just "intelligent animals." We are, to the contrary, the most complex and impressive entities in the entire known universe!

This realization is directly in line with the biblical view of humanity, which regards us as the crowning achievement of God's miraculous Handiwork. For as the Bible repeatedly tells us, each individual human being is of paramount importance in the eyes of God. And now, at long last, modern science is finally beginning to corroborate the Bible's timeless words.

Notes

1. John Eccles and Daniel N. Robinson, *The Wonder of Being Human* (Boston: Shambhala, 1985).

2. Roger Penrose, *Shadows of the Mind* (Oxford: Oxford University Press, 1994), 357–377.

3. Michael Denton, *Nature's Destiny* (New York: Free Press, 1998), 3–4.

4. Ibid., 4.

5. John D. Barrow and Frank J. Tipler, *The Anthropic Cosmological Principle* (Oxford: Oxford University Press, 1986), 133.

CHAPTER SEVEN

~

Science and the Design Argument

If we can accept that the day-to-day actions of living organisms are direct consequences of the molecules that make them up, why should it be any more difficult to see that similar principles are behind the *evolution* of those organisms? If the Creator uses physics and chemistry to *run* the universe of life, why wouldn't He have used physics and chemistry to *produce* it, too?

—Kenneth Miller

The Nature of the Design Argument

The traditional design argument for the existence of God has had a long and distinguished history, beginning in ancient Greece and carrying through St. Thomas to the present day. However, prior to our modern era, the design argument was only weakly empirical at best, since it was based more on real-world inferences to design than on any kind of hard experimental data as such.

By far the most influential design argument during this time period was promulgated in the early part of the nineteenth century by William Paley. According to Paley, any complex natural object that accomplishes a purpose *must* have a Designer, as his now famous Watchmaker Argument makes clear:

> In crossing a heath . . . suppose I had found a watch upon the ground, and it should be inquired how the watch happened to be in that place. . . . For this reason, and for no other, viz. That when we come to inspect the watch, we perceive . . . that its several parts are framed and put together for a purpose.[1]

When Paley introduced this line of argument with the publication of his highly influential *Natural Theology* in 1802, it was thought to represent the very height of scientific sophistication, because Paley made extensive use of nature's inherent complexity to get his point across. Then came the Darwinian revolution of 1859, which all but destroyed the scientific and philosophical credibility of Paley's design argument. For once Darwin showed how the complexity of the biosphere could have evolved primarily through chance processes (*via* the supposedly mindless process of natural selection), Paley's appeal to an Intelligent Designer as the best explanation for natural complexity quickly became *passé*, because Darwin seemed to show how these highly complex objects could have evolved entirely through random processes alone.

To his great credit, though, Paley actually devised a second form of the Design Argument, not around biological adaptations as such, but rather around the optimal design of nature's fundamental laws. And as it turns out, it is this second form of his Design Argument that actually carries the most weight, since there are no known natural processes that could have fine-tuned the laws of nature to such an extraordinary degree of accuracy.

This alternate form of the Design Argument went largely unnoticed in Paley's era. However, with the explosion in scientific knowledge that took place in the twentieth century, Paley's ideas are making a bold comeback. For once scientists learned that there are certain invariant aspects of the natural order that make evolution possible, it quickly became clear that these structural building blocks couldn't have been formed by natural selection alone. The reason for this has to do with the fact that evolution cannot take place in a complete structural vacuum. Instead, there has to be an underlying physical foundation for the process of replication to transpire in, otherwise no form of replication at all—and hence no process of evolution by natural selection—could have ever taken place.

The important point here as far as the design theorist is concerned has to do with the fact that this underlying physical foundation for the natural order *did not gradually evolve by the process of natural selection into its present biocentric format*.[2] Instead, this foundation of life-supporting laws and constants emerged out of the Big Bang, perfectly fine-tuned and ready for action. This realization has to qualify as one of the greatest discoveries of twentieth-century science, because it means that some *other explanation* besides Darwinian evolution has to be found for the perfect setup of nature's fundamental constants.

I can't emphasize the momentousness of this realization as far as natural theology is concerned. For up until recently, it was believed that *all* of nature's fundamental parameters had gradually evolved through a Darwinian process of natural selection. This view, however, turned out to be much too simple, as Barrow and Tipler have pointed out:

> There has grown up, even amongst many educated persons, a view that everything in Nature, every fabrication of its laws, is determined by the local environment in which it was nurtured—that natural selection and the Darwinian revolution have advanced to the boundaries of every scientific discipline. Yet, in reality, this is far from the truth. Twentieth-century physics has discovered that there exist invariant properties of the natural world and its elementary components which render inevitable the gross size and structure of almost all its composite objects.[3]

What this means, in a nutshell, is that the underlying structural foundation of our life-supporting universe didn't gradually evolve by a process of natural selection into its present biocentric format. Instead, it somehow popped into existence *instantaneously* at the Big Bang, perfectly calibrated and ready for action. Moreover, it is precisely *because* of this biocentric foundation that life was eventually able to unfold on this planet.

My use of the word "unfold" here carries with it a deeper meaning that is especially relevant for our purposes here. The word "evolution" is ultimately derived from the Latin word *evolutio*, which means to gradually unfold, in the same way that one might unravel a folded scroll. Technically speaking, this makes the evolutionary process much more consistent with design rather than chance, because the only way the "scroll of evolution" could possibly be unraveled is if it were somehow folded up to begin with.

Now, insofar as there is a connection between the original meaning of the word "evolution" and the actual evolutionary process itself, it means that the entire edifice of evolution was somehow programmed into the primordial seed of the universe at the Big Bang. The Darwinian process of evolution, by contrast, has nothing at all to do with the unraveling of a predesigned cosmic egg; it is, instead, simply the result of a complex interplay between random chance and physical necessity.

But not even this form of Darwinism is self-sufficient, because it begs the much deeper question that is ultimately at issue here, which is this: where did the laws of nature *themselves* ultimately come from? We can't simply assume the prior existence of these natural laws in an axiomatic manner, because it is the *origin* of these life-supporting laws that we're ultimately trying to account for here. Of course, given the prior existence of these laws, it is much easier to imagine some form of evolution occurring as a direct consequence of their activity.

By contrast, *no* form of evolution would have been possible without the prior existence of a suitable metaphysical foundation, which itself would have been comprised of the "right" natural laws and fundamental constants. What this means, in a nutshell, is that until the nontheistic evolutionist is able to account for the origin of these laws and constants in an entirely naturalistic manner, the nontheistic theory of evolution will continue to be insufficient as a valid means of explaining the origin of life. Why? Because it isn't the rise of life *per se* that the evolutionist is ultimately trying to explain here; it is the origin of those natural laws and constants that make evolution possible in the first place. For just as no modern scientist can claim to know anything at all about the natural world without first standing on the shoulders of all those scientists that came before, so too is the Darwinian evolutionist incapable of explaining the rise of the biosphere without first explaining the rise of those natural laws and constants that make evolution possible.

Hence, to simply assume the prior existence of these biocentric laws in an axiomatic manner is to explain precisely nothing, because such an explication turns out to be question-begging, and therefore fallacious, by its very nature. This is the fallacy of circular reasoning in one of its most subtle forms, because the conclusion that the nontheistic evolutionist is looking for in this case (e.g., the origin of the universe's biocentric laws) is hidden within one of the argument's underlying premises.

This is a fatal error in reasoning that many nontheistic evolutionists regularly commit, because there is little choice here but to assume the prior existence of a suitable structural foundation for the evolutionary process itself. But it is precisely here that the natural theologian can drive a lethal wedge into this nontheistic form of modern evolutionary theory, because we now know that no form of evolution could have occurred in the absence of the right constellation of fundamental laws and constants. Yet, modern-day evolutionists haven't even approached a plausible explanation for this fine-tuned biocentric foundation. As a consequence, their nontheistic "explanation" for the rise of life turns out to be a nonexplanation after all.

Of course, one could always counterargue that we just haven't had time to discover the supposed naturalistic origins of the evolutionary process and, moreover, that it is inappropriate to credit God for this present void in our empirical knowledge because someday in the future we probably will discover it. This "God of the gaps" explanation has been severely ridiculed in recent years, because it seems to be invoked only when we can't find a naturalistic explanation for the phenomenon in question. And for the most part, this God of the gaps criticism has been valid because our steadily increasing knowledge of the physical universe has progressively shortened the size of the gaps in our understanding.

It is one thing, however, to use this God of the gaps style of argument to explain discrete physical phenomena, and quite another to use it to explain the underlying ground of being itself, upon which *all* physical events intimately depend. For whereas we can expect to fill the various gaps in our knowledge at some point in the future when it comes to understanding discrete physical phenomena, we probably will never be able to find a naturalistic explanation for the metaphysical ground of being itself, because this sort of knowledge is of a different order of being altogether, since it is the foundation upon which all other physical events so intimately depend. As such, it appears to be different *in kind*, and not just in degree, from all other physical phenomena.

Accordingly, when scientists resort to a God of the gaps criticism to defuse the validity of the theist's emphasis on God as the ground of being, they unknowingly appear to be making a severe category mistake between two utterly different categories of being. The first ontological category applies to all the discrete objects and events that exist throughout the physical universe, whereas the second ontological category applies to the underlying *ground of being* itself, which affords existence to these objects and events. It would therefore be naïve in the extreme to expect to utilize similar types of explanations for both of these ontological categories, yet modern nontheistic scientists routinely engage in this sort of mistaken reasoning.

Another way of saying this is that nontheistic scientists tend to implicitly assume the prior, unexplained existence of an adequate ground of being for the physical universe itself. And while they obviously need to do so in order to be able to do good science (since one has to start from somewhere in order to be able to learn anything at all), they are actually extending the frontiers of their quest from empirical science itself to the underlying ground of being that makes empirical science possible in the first place. They do so because they implicitly believe that an entirely naturalistic explanation will eventually be found for this metaphysical ground of being. And while theistic scientists routinely allow for "naturalistic" cause and effect explanations throughout the physical realm, they also assert that these naturalistic explanations *cannot* by their very nature be extended to the underlying ground of being itself.

Surely this is the question that is ultimately at issue between theists and nontheists, for if an entirely naturalistic explanation can eventually be found for the metaphysical ground of our being, then the existence of God will have been obviated once and for all. The metaphysical "buck" thus seems to stop at the nature and origin of this underlying ground of being. This is why the astronomer Robert Jastrow could assert that the modern scientific quest for knowledge ends like a bad dream, since even at the very peak of our empirical understanding scientists nevertheless have to give way to a "band of theologians" who have been pondering these issues for centuries.[4]

We must therefore be exceptionally careful to distinguish between those forms of explanation that depend on this underlying ground of being for their very existence and those forms of explanation that attempt to explain the origin of this metaphysical ground itself. If, for instance, one were trying to explain the ultimate origin of automobiles, one would be seriously amiss to focus one's attention exclusively on the dynamics of dealer showrooms. Why? Because one cannot hope to explain the ultimate origin of cars by simply assuming, in an axiomatic sense, the prior, unexplained existence of automobiles. Instead, one would need to go straight to the heart of these auto plants in order to understand where cars come from. This much is obvious, but what isn't so obvious is that virtually all nontheistic evolutionists regularly commit the very same sort of logical error. For by focusing their attention exclusively on the "biological showroom" of evolution by natural selection, they conveniently ignore those underlying laws and constants that make evolution possible in the first place. These laws and constants make up the structural "factory" that ultimately enables evolution to take place. It is therefore just as fallacious to think that one can explain life's origin without reference to these foundational parameters as it is to think that one can explain the ultimate origin of automobiles without reference to automobile factories.

Moreover, since this crucial structural foundation for life is now known to have spontaneously come into existence at the Big Bang, perfectly fine-tuned and ready for action, we find that we can actually push our case for the existence of God back to the very birth of the universe itself. In this revised form of the traditional Design Argument, God created the life-supporting foundation for our universe at the Big Bang *via* the perfect calibration of nature's fundamental laws and constants. This is the basic thrust of the "fine-tuning" argument for the existence of God, since these laws and constants are now known to have been fine-tuned to a truly incredible degree of accuracy, not gradually through a random process of natural selection, but *instantaneously* at the Big Bang itself. This is a breathtaking realization that all but destroys Richard Dawkins' "blind watchmaker" argument, because as we just saw, one cannot simply assume the prior existence of a life-supporting foundation for the evolutionary process without committing the fallacy of circular reasoning.

Dawkins tries to get around this fatal blow to his theory by asserting that our biocentric universe itself is just as likely of being self-existent as God Himself is. Therefore, why not simply posit the universe as its own creator "and be done with it?"[5] It is this particular conclusion that leads Dawkins to brand the natural theologian's argument as being "transparently feeble."[6]

The problem with this conclusion is that it commits the fallacy of "misplaced concreteness." That is, it assumes that it is possible for something other than God to be self-existent by its very nature. However, by long-standing definition, only God alone can possibly possess the miraculous property of *aseity*, or self-existence.[7] Accordingly, if the universe itself were self-existent, it would actually *be* God, but this clearly seems absurd. Indeed, there is absolutely nothing about the physical universe that leads us to believe that it could possibly be self-existent by its very nature. To the contrary, the very contingency of the universe and everything that is in it would lead us to believe the exact opposite, namely, that the entire universe is a contingent collection of objects. The fact that the universe had a concrete beginning in the Big Bang strongly supports us in this contention. It is very hard to see how a physical collection of objects that had a formal beginning some 15 billion years ago could nevertheless be self-existent by its very nature. The idea of self-existing God, on the other hand, doesn't seem self-contradictory or absurd at all.

This is why Dawkins' charge against the natural theologian is *itself* transparently feeble, because he is trying to make our contingent universe itself to be God. However, one cannot arbitrarily assign the property of self-existence to material objects, or even to the universe itself, whenever one pleases. One can only do so with an object or being that is inherently worthy (and hence deserving) of such an attribution, and this, according to long-standing convention, can only be said of God Himself.

Many working scientists have openly acknowledged both the logical and empirical validity of this revised form of the traditional Design Argument. Indeed, given the instantaneous appearance of a perfectly calibrated set of natural laws and constants at the Big Bang, there is only one way to escape the conclusion of Intelligent Design: by proposing a naturalistic origin to this perfect foundation before the Big Bang. Cosmologist Lee Smolin has done precisely this by postulating an evolutionary process of selection prior to the Big Bang.[8]

There is, however, not a shred of empirical evidence to support such an idea, as we shall see in more detail in chapter 11. To the contrary, the only way Smolin's theory can get off the ground is by denying the mountain of empirical evidence that points to the Big Bang as the absolute beginning of space, time, and matter. From this point of view, his theory is not only empirically groundless, it is positively antiempirical in nature, since it is the consensus position of virtually all working astronomers that the universe *did* indeed have a formal beginning some 15 to 20 billion years ago. And, going one step further, if space, time, and matter all had their origin in the Big Bang, there could not have been a gradual evolution of nature's laws and constants prior to the Big Bang. This illustrates how far scientists have to go in order to deny the revised form of the traditional Design Argument.

An Important Distinction

It is commonly believed that modern neo-Darwinism presupposes metaphysical naturalism. The Berkeley lawyer and anti-Darwinist Phil Johnson, for instance, has repeatedly made this point in his various writings, as have numerous other proponents of Intelligent Design. However, as William Lane Craig has aptly pointed out, it isn't Darwinism itself that presupposes naturalism, it is the *inference* to Darwinism as the best explanation that presupposes it:

> In inferring to the best explanation, one chooses from a limited pool of live options which explanation of the data is the best. Phil's complaint is that the Darwinist is able to claim that Darwinism is the best explanation only by excluding from the pool of live options theistic or design explanations. This can be done only by gratuitously presupposing the truth of naturalism. . . . His claim is that once you admit to the pool of live options theistic or design accounts, then it is far from obvious that Darwinism is the best explanation. Thus, it is a mistake, both philosophically and strategically, for us to say that Darwinism is incompatible with the existence of God or with His having designed the world. Rather our claim should be that the inference that Darwinism is the best explanation of biological complexity presupposes naturalism. Darwinism doesn't presuppose naturalism; it is the *inference* to Darwinism as the best explanation that presupposes naturalism.[9]

This distinction should not be dismissed as needless hair-splitting, because it is the validity of Craig's point that makes it possible for evolution to be logically compatible with the existence of God. For if all forms of Darwinism are predicated upon metaphysical naturalism, then any form of evolution must be dismissed out of hand by the theist as being incompatible with the existence of God. However, if it is merely the *inference* to Darwinism as the best explanation that actually presupposes naturalism, we can say that this inference to Darwinism is not the best explanation for the data at hand. This being the case, we can then draw an inference to other possibilities as the best explanation for the evolutionary data, including the activity of an Intelligent Designer. There is thus no logical incompatibility between evolution and theism; it is only the inference to Darwinism as the best explanation that is incompatible with theism, since it is indeed predicated upon metaphysical naturalism.

This is no small point, because it is possible to demonstrate that evolution is actually far more consistent with theism than it is with metaphysical naturalism. We can do this by first pointing out that the Darwinian paradigm itself is question-begging, and therefore conceptually inadequate, by its very nature, since it assumes the prior, unexplained existence of those crucial underlying conditions that make Darwinism possible in the first place. I am referring here to the prior existence of: (1) a life-supporting world and universe, (2) a stable biochemistry, and (3) the biochemical machinery of replication and genetic variation.

Darwinian evolutionists simply assume, in a strong axiomatic sense, the prior existence of these underlying conditions for Darwinism, as we have seen. However, these are precisely the types of things that most Darwinists are trying to explain. Therefore, their arguments are question-begging, and hence fallacious, by their very nature.

This is where the superiority of theism comes into play as a valid explanation for the evolutionary data, because only the doctrine of Intelligent Design is able to provide a plausible explanation for the various laws of nature that make evolution possible in the first place. In reality, then, the phenomenon of evolution actually presupposes an Intelligent Designer, and not naturalism *per se*, because God is presently the best explanation we have for why our world is so ideally suited to the "evolution" of new life forms.

Darwinism can only presuppose naturalism if it can also explain the ultimate origin of all those underlying structural conditions that make evolution possible in the first place. But Darwinists are light years away from actually doing this, as we saw in the previous chapter, because we now know that nature's fundamental constants did *not* gradually evolve over billions of years into their present life-supporting format. Instead, they have possessed this remarkable biocentric configuration from the very beginning, and this largely disqualifies Darwinism as a valid explanation for these underlying constants.

This being the case, the traditional Darwinist has little choice but to assume, in an axiomatic sense, the prior existence of the "right" underlying structural conditions that make evolution possible. But since this is ultimately the very same question that is at issue here, her argument turns out to be inherently fallacious by its very nature.

The Providential Evolutionists of the previous century were well aware of this profound limitation of Darwinian theory, and it is for this reason that they were able to use the phenomenon of evolution to actually *support* the existence of God, and not *vice versa*. We would do well to return to their timeless wisdom.

Notes

1. William Paley, *Natural Theology* (1802; reprint, London: Baldwyn, 1819), 8–9.

2. John D. Barrow and Frank J. Tipler, *The Anthropic Cosmological Principle* (Oxford: Oxford University Press, 1986), 288.

3. Ibid.

4. Robert Jastrow, *God and the Astronomers* (New York: Warner, 1978), 125.

5. Richard Dawkins, *The Blind Watchmaker* (New York: Norton, 1986), 141.

6. Ibid.

7. M. A. Corey, *The Natural History of Creation* (Lanham, Md.: University Press of America, 1995), 200–201.

8. Lee Smolin, *The Life of the Cosmos* (Oxford: Oxford University Press, 1997).

9. William Lane Craig, in an unpublished letter for the Phylogeny List.

~

CHAPTER EIGHT

The Scientific Evidence for Intelligent Design

The most miraculous thing is happening. The physicists are getting down to
the nitty gritty . . . and the last thing they ever expected to be happening is
happening. God is showing through.

—John Updike

The scientific evidence for contrivance in the universe is truly overwhelming. It is so compelling, in fact, that even die-hard atheistic scientists are
stepping forward and admitting that they now believe in some form of
Design.

It is now time to turn our attention to the underlying nature of this evidence for Design.

Big Bang Ripples: The "Holy Grail" of Cosmology

On April 23, 1992, one of the most important discoveries in the history of
science was announced to the world. George Smoot's astronomical team
working at Berkeley released the latest findings from the Cosmic Background
Explorer (COBE) satellite, which they had been carefully analyzing for over
a year. Remarkably, these findings have essentially proved the validity of the
traditional Big Bang theory.

Needless to say, once the story broke it immediately made front-page
headlines around the world. Stephen Hawking, who holds the same chair of
physics at Cambridge that Isaac Newton once held, was quoted as saying that

it is "the discovery of the century, if not all time." University of Chicago physicist Michael Turner even went so far as to proclaim that "We have found the Holy Grail of cosmology." However, it was COBE project leader George Smoot who delivered the most astounding quote. He said, "What we have found is evidence for the birth of the universe. If you're religious, it's like looking at God."

These are very big words to come from the mouths of ordinarily conservative scientists, but they are very much deserved. For as scientific historian Frederic B. Burnham pointed out in the *Los Angeles Times*, these findings regarding the Big Bang make the theistic explanation for the birth of the universe "a more respectable hypothesis" today than at any time in the last century.

So what is everyone so excited about? What could possibly merit such a euphoric response from ordinarily conservative scientists? The answer has to do with the nature of the microwave background that we discussed earlier. This background radiation is a relic of the Big Bang itself. It came into existence at the moment of creation and has lingered about ever since.

The important thing about this radiation is that it is so incredibly smooth, down to one part in 10,000. The problem with this profound degree of uniformity is that it also reflects a similar degree of smoothness in the initial distribution of matter in the universe. This is because ordinary matter strongly interacts with radiation. But if this is so, then it is hard to see how galaxies and clusters of galaxies could have ever formed out of such an incredibly smooth arrangement of matter. Galaxy formation requires a significant degree of unevenness in the very early universe, which gravity can then act upon to cause matter to condense into galaxies. This is why the extreme smoothness of the microwave background has posed such a problem to Big Bang theorists.

But not any more. Because of the amazingly precise measurements made by the COBE satellite, we now know that there are indeed irregularities in the microwave background that reflect a similar degree of unevenness in the initial distribution of matter in the universe. These irregularities—otherwise known as "ripples"—are the cosmic "potholes" around which the galaxies appear to have condensed. They are as large as one part in 100,000, which amounts to a mere 30 millionths of a kelvin, but this is nonetheless big enough to represent the earliest stages of matter-clumping in the universe.[1]

Taken together, these fluctuations comprise the largest and most ancient structures ever observed: extremely thin clouds or ripples that stretch across two-thirds of the known universe. These ripples date back to when the universe was 300,000 years old, and they contain the earliest known precursors to the present universal configuration.[2] In this sense, they are like cosmic fossils, which together make up the primordial blueprint for the structure of the entire universe.

Further confirmation for the Big Bang was obtained from the COBE satellite's measurement of the spectrum of the microwave background. The simplest model of the Big Bang predicts that the radiation produced by this primordial explosion should have the characteristics of a perfect blackbody, which is to say that it should trace out a perfectly smooth spectral curve. Amazingly, this is the very same spectrum that the COBE satellite detected in the microwave background!

In order for this particular Big Bang model to work, though, another form of matter must also exist in the universe. This additional form of matter is known as "exotic" or "dark" matter, and it is needed because it doesn't interact strongly with radiation the way ordinary matter does. This is the one feature that would allow galaxies and clusters of galaxies to form out of the observed degree of irregularity in the early universe. Roughly nine times as much exotic matter as ordinary matter is needed to allow this to happen.

Interestingly enough, this is also the amount of exotic matter that is needed to make our universe "flat." To say that our universe is "flat" is simply to assert that it is expanding at precisely the critical rate that would enable it to *just* avoid an eventual collapse. Like a bullet that is fired up in the air with just enough velocity for it to avoid ever falling back to Earth, a "flat" universe will go on expanding forever, but just barely.

This flatness is important because it means that ordinary Euclidian geometry—in which the sum of a triangle's three angles is 180 degrees—can be "true" or valid in this kind of universe. There are also a number of reasons to believe that life is only capable of existing in this kind of "flat" universe.[3] This lends further support to the conclusion that there is roughly nine times as much exotic matter in the universe as ordinary matter.

Exotic matter is nonluminous, so it can't be seen through ordinary astronomical techniques. It can only be detected through other, more indirect means. One of the most effective ways of detecting it is through a marvelous astronomical technique known as *gravitational lensing*. Gravitational lensing works because objects with a large mass are known to bend light rays, the way Einstein originally predicted with his general theory of relativity. Therefore, if large quantities of dark matter actually exist within the universe, they should be capable of bending light rays coming from distant galaxies. And indeed they do. Precise measurements that have been made through this gravitational lensing technique indicate that there is roughly nine times as much dark matter as ordinary matter in the universe. Not coincidentally, this is the same figure that has been derived from the latest COBE satellite measurements.

No wonder there is so much euphoria in the scientific community! The chief mystery behind the traditional Big Bang theory—namely, how galaxies were able to form out of such an initially smooth distribution of matter—has now been dispelled once and for all.

But it isn't as if these findings from the COBE satellite were absolutely necessary in order to confirm the Big Bang theory. Other legitimate mechanisms for mediating galaxy formation have also been proposed recently, and they don't require nearly the same degree of irregularity in the microwave background to be valid.

String theorists, for instance, believe that incredibly massive cosmic strings could have provided the gravitational condensation point for galaxy formation, instead of ordinary matter. A cosmic string is an exceedingly tiny (about 10^{-33} cm across), one-dimensional crack in the fabric of space-time that is thought to be capable of producing all of the particles and forces of nature. This process is believed to be mediated by a progression of different string vibrations or "tones." In the same way that different vibrations of a guitar string produce different notes, different vibrations of a cosmic string are believed to produce the various aspects of physical reality that we now observe. Remarkably, the actual pattern of galaxies in the night sky bears a striking resemblance to the way cosmic strings ought to behave if they actually exist.[4] Unfortunately, there doesn't appear to be any way of proving just yet whether or not cosmic strings actually exist or whether they were actually involved in the process of galaxy formation.

Prior to the COBE satellite's findings, it was thought that primordial field defects known as *textures* might have been responsible for building the large-scale structure of the universe. However, texture theory predicts the existence of a few very large temperature fluctuations, which were not found by the COBE satellite. As a result, texture-based cosmologies have now been effectively ruled out.

The Music of Creation

In April 2001, three independent teams of researchers confirmed the COBE findings by making the most precise measurements to date of our nascent universe. Using a variety of technological breakthroughs that were unheard of just a few short years ago, the research teams probed back through space and time to take very precise readings of light that originated approximately 400,000 years after the Big Bang.[5] This was the point in cosmic evolution where light first emerged from the opaque plasma of charged particles that permeated the very early universe.

By looking as far back as possible with light—approximately 14 billion years—the researchers were effectively able to "see" the various types of sound waves that were generated shortly after the Big Bang. According to Paolo de-Bernardis, the Italian leader of the BOOMERANG research team, this was made possible because the primordial cosmic soup "is full of sound waves compressing and rarefying matter and light, much like sound waves compress and rarefy air inside a flute or trumpet." By measuring variations in the background radiation as fine as 50 millionths to 100 millionths of a degree of temperature, researchers have been able to uncover a "harmonic series" of primordial reverberations, which they have dubbed "the music of creation."

These primordial sound waves were also found to contain an intriguing series of "acoustic peaks," which in turn provided researchers with an exciting new method for calculating the composition of the early universe. For by comparing the heights of the respective peaks, researchers were able to demonstrate that ordinary "luminous" matter constitutes a mere 4.5 percent of the mass of the entire universe. Of the remainder, 30 percent was found to be comprised of dark matter, while an astonishing 65 percent was found to be comprised of a mysterious form of "dark energy."[6] The researchers were even able to provide striking evidence of the universe's perfect degree of geometric "flatness" (in the form of a single acoustic peak or "ripple").

Remarkably, all three research teams came up with essentially the same findings, even though they were all working independently of one another. This "stunning" degree of empirical concurrence, according to MAXIMA project leader Paul Richards, greatly substantiates the validity of these findings and provides "strong confirmation that, overall, we're using the right model to describe the universe." The end result of this cosmological windfall, according to astrophysicist Michael Turner of the University of Chicago, is that both Einstein's theory of gravity and the Big Bang theory itself are now "on much firmer footing" than they ever were before.

The "Just Right" Roughness Parameter

From the preceding discussion, it is clear that the initial distribution of matter in the universe could not have been perfectly smooth, otherwise, matter wouldn't have been capable of congealing together into galaxies and life would have had no place in which to evolve. At the same time, though, too much cosmic "roughness" would have caused the universe to either collapse back in on itself early on or develop into a vast sea of black holes, which would have been separated by mostly barren space. In either case, life as we know it would have never been able to evolve.

In order for the universe to be capable of supporting life, then, the degree of roughness within it must be very precipitously balanced between near infinite extremes on either side. Interestingly enough, the value of the "roughness parameter" can be expressed in terms of a pure number: 10^{-5}. Had the value of this parameter been even slightly different, life could never have evolved here because galaxies would have been incapable of forming.[7]

This fact is all the more remarkable when we consider the infinite range of possible values that this parameter *could* have occupied. Yet, against all the odds, the one value that was essential for the evolution of life is the one that was actually "picked." Surely this cannot be just a coincidence. But if it wasn't a coincidence, then the specific value of this roughness parameter had to have somehow been deliberately chosen.

The Amount of Matter in the Universe

One of the most important "coincidences" in the history of our life-supporting universe concerns the overall amount of matter in existence. Cosmologists have long recognized that there had to have been a precisely determined amount of matter produced by the Big Bang or else our present biocentric universe could never have formed. Too much matter and the gravitational pull would have been enough to counteract the explosive force of the Big Bang, thereby causing the entire universe to collapse back in on itself like a gigantic black hole. Too little matter and there would not have been enough attractive gravitational force to cause the matter to bunch together into galaxies and solar systems.[8]

It is extremely unlikely that a random explosion of the "cosmic egg" would have just happened to produce the precise amount of material density to make our present biocentric universe possible. Indeed, given the infinite range of possible densities that could have been produced by the Big Bang, it seems far more likely that there was a larger principle at work from the very beginning that would have ensured the production of just the "right" amount of matter for our own eventual appearance.

The Big Bang also had to explode with just the right degree of vigor or else our present biocentric universe could never have formed. Too little velocity and the universe would have collapsed back in on itself shortly after the Big Bang because of gravitational forces; too much velocity and the matter would have streaked away so fast that it would have been impossible for galaxies and solar systems to subsequently form. Indeed, as Hawking has pointed out, this balance between universal collapse and eternal expansion is so precise

that scientists have not yet been able to decide on which side of the divid-
ing line our universe actually lies. As a consequence, we still do not know
whether the universe will continue to expand forever or whether it will
begin to contract someday in the future, leading eventually to the "Big
Crunch."

The large-scale properties of the universe also depend on a uniform expansion rate. Specifically, the coherence of light depends on the universe
doubling in size at a uniform rate. As the universe expands, the space between the galaxies is continually stretching, which in turn "stretches" light
rays traveling in the interstellar medium, producing light of longer wavelengths. This is the origin of the famous "red shift," which Slipher first detected in 1913 and which Hubble utilized in 1929 to deduce that the galaxies are receding from one another at tremendous velocities.

However, as space continues to expand and light rays continue to stretch,
the possibility arises that they might stretch to an infinite wavelength,
thereby making it impossible for the constituent light rays to carry any useful information. It turns out that the only way light can avoid getting
stretched to an infinite wavelength in an expanding universe is if the universe expands at a precisely uniform rate. Given the infinite number of possible expansion rates, it is nothing short of remarkable that our present universe is expanding at *precisely* a uniform rate. Even more remarkable,
though, is the fact that our own existence as observers is intimately tied to
this large-scale uniformity. However, the only possible way that the universe
could be capable of such a uniform expansion rate is if the amount of matter produced by the Big Bang was perfectly balanced with the subsequent
rate of cosmic expansion.

Another way of looking at this seemingly lucky "accident" involves the
energy density of matter p, which determines the gravitating power of the entire universe. A higher density causes a greater gravitational force, and vice
versa. Now, there is a critical value, known as p_{crit}, above which gravity would
beat the force of the cosmic expansion and cause the entire universe to collapse back in on itself. Thus, in order for there to be a minimum degree of
stability in the universe, the rate of cosmic expansion has to just beat the inward force of gravity, which means that the value of p has to be exceedingly
close to p_{crit}. Fortunately for us, nature has caused the difference between p
and p_{crit} to vary by less than one part in 10^{60} at the Planck time, when the
universe was a mere 10^{-43} seconds old. Like a bullet that is fired into the sky
with just enough velocity for it to avoid being pulled back to earth by gravity, the entire universe itself is also expanding with just enough velocity for
it to avoid collapsing back in on itself.

Another fortunate consequence of the universe expanding at close to the critical rate has to do with the general geometry of space-time. An expansion rate that is close to critical produces a "flat" universe that approximates the "normal" geometry of Euclid, in which the sum of a triangle's three angles equals precisely 180 degrees.[9] Had the universe expanded at a significantly different rate, the geometry of space-time would have been curved, with the strange result that the sum of a triangle's three angles would have either been more or less than 180 degrees.

Given the incredible amount of fine-tuning that was necessary to allow the universe to expand at precisely this critical rate (accurate to within one part in 10^{60}), many scientists are understandably stunned and amazed. In the words of Paul Davies:

> We know of no reason why p is not a purely arbitrary number. Nature could apparently have chosen any value at all. To choose p so close to p_{crit}, fine-tuned to such stunning accuracy, is surely one of the great mysteries of cosmology. Had this exceedingly delicate tuning of values been even slightly upset, the subsequent structure of the universe would have been totally different. If the crucial ratio had been 10^{-37} rather than 10^{60}, the universe would not even exist, having collapsed to oblivion after just a few million years.[10]

Davies goes on to explain how the "natural" value that describes the curvature of the universe, which is represented by a natural relation between the gravitational constant, Planck's constant, and the speed of light, is 10^{60} times greater than the actual curvature value "chosen" at the beginning of the Hubble expansion. Incredibly, had nature chosen this "natural" curvature value, the universe would have only been able to survive a mere 10^{-43} seconds, after which it would have either collapsed into nothingness or else exploded into oblivion. As Davies concludes:

> To achieve a universe with a longevity some 60 orders of magnitude longer than the natural fundamental unit of cosmic time t_p requires a balancing act between p and p_{crit} of staggering precision.[11]

The implications here are truly astounding. We are being asked to believe that nature somehow chose a universal expansion rate—itself comprised of a critical interaction between three distinct physical parameters—that was over 60 orders of magnitude smaller than the "natural" value that these constants would have ordinarily produced on their own. The result of this "unnatural" choice is that our universe has expanded at *precisely* the proper rate to ensure the evolution of intelligent observers. *Isn't this glaring evidence of Intelligent Contrivance in the universe?*

Cosmologist John Gribbin and astrophysicist Martin Rees are also impressed by the incredible precision of the Hubble expansion rate, since it makes the flatness parameter

> the most accurately measured number in all of physics, and suggests a fine-tuning of the universe, to set up conditions suitable for the emergence of stars, galaxies, and life, of exquisite precision. . . . If this were indeed a coincidence, then it would be a fluke so extraordinary as to make all other cosmic coincidences pale into insignificance. It seems much more reasonable to suppose that there is something in the laws of physics [God?] that requires the universe to be *precisely* flat. After all, the critical density for flatness is the *only* special density; no other value has any cosmic significance at all. It makes more sense to accept that the universe had to be born with *exactly* the critical expansion rate than to believe that by blind luck it happened to start out within 1 part in 10^{60} of the critical value.[12]

It is nothing short of amazing to realize that a "mere" change of one part in 10^{60} in the density parameter, in either direction, would have made the universe completely uninhabitable. It strains credulity to the breaking point to believe that such a perfect degree of balance could have ever happened by chance, especially when we realize that our lives were made possible by this unbelievable act of cosmic precision.

According to George Greenstein, though, the further back one goes in the history of the universe, the closer the difference between p and p_{crit} had to have been in order to keep the universe from collapsing back in on itself instantaneously.[13] For instance, when the universe was a year old, it was 0.00003 percent denser than critical, but it was 0.00000008 percent denser than critical when it was just an hour old. At this profoundly sensitive stage, the slightest perturbation would have caused the universe to recollapse, yet the cosmic expansion continued on without a hitch.

Remarkably, the further back in time one probes, the more perfect the adjustment between p and p_{crit} automatically becomes, so that when one reaches the unsearchable moment of creation itself, the adjustment between p and p_{crit} wasn't one part in a billion; it was one part in infinity. As Greenstein declares, creation was perfect.[14]

This level of perfection completely defies the laws of chance because the odds for a particular value to be chosen out of an infinity of possible choices are precisely *zero*! Accordingly, it seems infinitely unlikely that the "choice" of the universe's actual density could have ever been made by blind chance alone.

> In principle, the Universe could have had any density. A billionth, or a billion times, the critical density, or anything in between, or even anything outside that range. Why should it lie so close to the *only* special density that comes into the cosmological equations of relativity? Surely this cannot be a coincidence—and surely, some cosmologists have speculated, if this is *not* a coincidence then the density of the Universe must be precisely the critical density?[15]

What cosmic power could have possibly accomplished this monumental feat? What power could have possibly ensured that the density of the universe be *precisely* the critical density? Since blind chance alone couldn't possibly have performed such an unprecedented balancing act, there appears to be only one other Alternative to choose from. It is for this reason that more and more scientists are becoming sympathetic to the religious point of view.

The Role of Dark Matter in Our "Just Right" Universe

Precise measurements of the present density of the universe reveal a curious fact: there is approximately ten times less visible matter in existence than is necessary to make the universe "flat." At the same time, though, it is also known that the universe is very nearly flat on the largest possible scale of measurement. These observations have led cosmologists to postulate the existence of nonluminous "dark matter" throughout the universe, which would supply the missing mass needed to make the universe flat. All sorts of possible candidates for this missing mass have been suggested in recent years, but as yet nothing definite has been discovered.

However, while we are still uncertain about the identity of this missing mass, we are fairly clear about how much of it has to exist in the universe: it is precisely the amount that is needed to give the universe its all-important critical density. Since life can only exist in a universe whose energy density is close to critical, the quantity of dark matter in the universe works out to be yet another "cosmic coincidence" upon which we owe our very lives.

Dark matter is also necessary for the evolution of life in yet another way, for without it galaxies and solar systems would probably never have been able to form. It is believed that clouds of dark matter originally functioned as cosmic "potholes," around which the galaxies themselves eventually came to be condensed.[16] The problem with this conceptualization is that it is hard to see how these nonluminous irregularities could have possibly formed in a universe as smooth and homogeneous as our own. Evidently, other processes were also involved in galaxy formation, the cumulative effect of which was to allow galaxies to form in spite of the incredibly smooth distribution of matter in the early universe.

One of the primary reasons why astronomers believe in the existence of dark matter has to do with their observations of spiral galaxy rotation patterns. Normally in such a spiral rotational pattern, the outer edges would be expected to move much more slowly than the inner regions of the spiral, as is true of the planetary orbits in our solar system. With spiral galaxies, however, the outer regions move at precisely the same velocity as the inner regions. This would be impossible without the existence of a "halo" of dark matter outside the boundary of the galaxy to equilibrate the overall rotational velocity. Because all spiral galaxies seem to rotate in this manner, we are led to postulate that the amount and distribution of dark matter in the universe must be incomprehensibly precise, not just for each galaxy individually, but also for the entire visible universe as a whole.

In order for the rotational velocity of any given spiral galaxy to be absolutely uniform across the entire range of its diameter, the halo of dark matter that surrounds it must be very precisely positioned with respect to the stars inside the galaxy in order to be able to counterbalance the pull of gravity from within the spiral.[17] Given the number of stars in each spiral galaxy, along with the number of spiral galaxies in existence, this is a cosmic balancing act of outrageous, unprecedented precision.

Scientists are at a complete loss to explain why the amount and distribution of this halo of dark matter should exactly counterbalance the expected fall-off in rotational velocity from the center of each galaxy. This is known as the "Halo Conspiracy," and it seems to be completely insoluble in the absence of some form of Intelligent Design.[18]

When scientists extrapolate backwards from the orbits of the stars in each spiral galaxy, they are able to get a pretty good estimate of the amount of dark matter that probably exists in the universe. According to the most recent estimates, there is at least 10 times as much dark matter in the universe as visible matter. This renders over 90 percent of the universe nonluminous.[19]

Tony Tyson, a physicist working at AT&T Bell Laboratories, has recently obtained further evidence for the existence of dark matter in the universe. Using the sophisticated technique of gravitational lensing—in which the light from a background curtain of visible galaxies is distorted into an arc by the gravitational pull of invisible matter—Tyson found that the light from many of these distant galaxies is indeed being distorted by the presence of dark matter.[20]

Significantly, Tyson's calculations have shown that this dark matter is some 9 to 10 times more prevalent (or 9 to 10 times more massive) than the "normal" luminous matter we can see. Remarkably, this is approximately the same quantity of dark matter that is needed to make the universe flat and explain spiral galaxy rotation patterns. Numerical convergences like these are what help to make cosmologists so confident about the overall validity of their theories.

Galaxy Formation in Our Goldilocks Universe

One of the greatest problems associated with the process of galaxy formation has to do with the narrow time frame in which galaxies could have possibly formed. On the one hand, galaxies could never have formed before atoms themselves formed, since atoms are the primary constituents of "baryonic" (i.e., normal) matter. However, atoms were unable to form in significant numbers until the universe was approximately 500,000 years old, due to the powerful interaction between radiation and the plasma that is thought to have preceded the formation of coherent atoms. Beginning at the 100,000-year mark, though, radiation began to decouple, or separate from, this embryonic plasma, with the result that solid atoms were finally able to form in appreciable numbers. Atom formation continued on until approximately the million-year mark, at which point essentially all of the initial plasma had condensed into atoms.

The problem with the above time frame is that it does not leave much time for galaxy formation to occur. In order for galaxies to form, matter must be close enough together to condense around a gravitational focal point. However, given the perpetual Hubble expansion, by the time there were enough atoms in existence to condense into galaxies, they would have already become far enough apart to make any type of gravitational condensation extremely unlikely.

As a result, there is a very narrow window between the time atoms actually arrive on the scene and the critical point where matter becomes too sparse to be able to condense into galaxies. It is apparently in this small window that galaxies did indeed form, albeit through processes that are still largely unknown at the present time.[21]

This conclusion is all the more remarkable because the process of galaxy formation is dependent on a long list of *other* fine-tuned cosmic parameters, each of which had to have been set just right before they could all work together to produce coherent galaxies. The "coincidence" here is that all of these separate parameters did in fact conspire together, against all the odds, to make a home suitable for human beings.

An Abyss of Complexity

It is a widely acknowledged fact in the scientific community that our universe is *infinitely* complex in a wide variety of different capacities. Researchers working with mathematical objects known as *fractals* have come to the astonishing realization that even relatively "simple" things like the length of a coastline are infinitely complex in terms of their basic structure. The closer you look, the more complex these natural objects continue to get, *ad infinitum*. This endless degree of complexity is now known to pervade the entire natural realm. It can be found within the DNA molecule and even within the very structure of atoms and molecules themselves.

It can also be found in the way that the different components of the natural realm all cooperate with one another to produce a life-supporting universe.[22] Like an infinitely complex spider's web, in which all of the web's threads interconnect with one another in an infinitely complex matrix, each of the universe's building blocks cooperates with all of the others in a *profoundly* intricate fashion, and the miracle of life is the direct result of this stupendous cooperative effort. This is why life would be impossible if any of nature's fundamental constants were altered even a tiny bit, because it would seriously destabilize this vast intercooperative effort. Indeed, some physicists are so persuaded by this overwhelming degree of cosmic cooperation that they actually believe that only one type of life-supporting universe is logically possible.

> It is clear that for nature to produce a cosmos even remotely resembling our own, many apparently unconnected branches of physics have to cooperate to a remarkable degree. . . . All this prompts the question of why, from the infinite range of possible values that nature could have selected for the fundamental constants, and from the infinite variety of initial conditions that could have characterized the primeval universe, the actual values and conditions conspire to produce the particular range of very special features that we observe. For clearly the universe is a very special place: exceedingly uniform on a large scale, yet not so precisely uniform that galaxies could not form; extremely low entropy per proton and hence cool enough for chemistry to happen; almost zero cosmic repulsion and an expansion rate tuned to the energy content to unbelievable accuracy; values for the strengths of its forces that permit nuclei to exist, yet do not burn up all the cosmic hydrogen, and many more apparent accidents of fortune.[23]

Most amazing of all, though, is the fact that this perfect degree of cooperation has existed from the very birth of the universe itself. The constants[24] didn't achieve their values through a trial-and-error process of cosmic natural selection, as we have seen. Rather, they were *perfect* from the very beginning, and we are alive today because of it.

It is very difficult to see how this initial degree of perfection could have come about purely by chance. Chance processes intrinsically require a lengthy process of trial-and-error intermixing before they can even *begin* to form anything interesting, and this is assuming the prior existence of a realm in which these chance interactions can actually occur. Hence, the initial perfection of our universe automatically seems to rule out any type of chance origin.

The notion of Intelligent Design is perfectly consistent with this initial cosmic perfection as far as the existence of life is concerned. It is, in fact, precisely what we would expect in a universe that has been deliberately designed to support the existence of carbon-based life forms. The very idea of a chance origin, on the other hand, is completely at odds with this initial perfection. For this reason alone it is far more reasonable to believe in Design than not to, because it is far more consistent with the known facts.

The Cosmological Constant

When Einstein first conceived of his theory of relativity, he believed that the heavens were static in nature; that is, he believed that the universe was neither expanding nor contracting. This was the predominant scientific view at the time, and it was supported by astronomical photographs of the night sky, which seemed to show that the stars were firmly anchored in their positions.

Curiously, though, Einstein's equations showed the precise opposite; namely, that the universe was in a dynamic state of expansion. This Einstein found to be immensely disturbing, because it seemed to him to indicate that the universe had experienced a concrete beginning sometime in the distant past. If it had a beginning, Einstein thought, then there must have been a personal Creator to originally set it in motion.

As we saw in chapter 2, Einstein found this scenario disturbing because of his conceptualization of the Divine Being. Einstein clearly did not believe in a personal theistic Creator, because he found the reality of evil in the world far too menacing to be compatible with such a view. He was unable to fathom any possible reason why a perfectly good and all-powerful Creator would deliberately allow evil to exist, so he concluded that there mustn't be any such Being in the first place. Instead, Einstein opted for the impersonal God of Spinoza, who amounted to little more than the unconscious "soul" of the physical universe.

Indeed, Einstein was so opposed to the idea of a personal God, and to the parallel idea of concrete universal beginning, that he decided to insert an additional "cosmological term" into his relativity equations in order to produce a static, nonexpanding universe. Einstein intended this "cosmological constant" to balance out the inward pull of gravity, so that the entire universe could then be maintained in a static state, thereby avoiding the religious problems associated with an expanding universe.

This is one of the greatest examples in the history of science where a prominent scientist's religious prejudices led to a false scientific conclusion. For as Edwin Hubble discovered in 1929, Einstein's equations were right the first time around. The universe *really is* expanding after all, which means that it must indeed have had a concrete beginning sometime in the distant past. It is for this reason that astrophysicist Robert Jastrow has concluded that the astronomical evidence actually "leads to a Biblical view of the origin of the world," whether we like it or not.[25]

When Einstein learned of Hubble's revolutionary discovery, he promptly recognized his error and deleted the cosmological term from his equations. Ironically, though, Einstein's cosmological constant has made a startling comeback in recent years. For physicists now recognize that the empty vacuum of space isn't really empty at all. Instead, it is a bustling arena of quantum activity where "virtual particles" pop into and out of existence on a regular basis.[26] Physicists now understand the dynamics of this quantum vacuum so well that they have actually assigned a definite amount of energy to it, which they also call the *cosmological constant.*

Oddly, though, the expected value of the cosmological constant has turned out to be some 46 orders of magnitude *smaller* than it was "supposed" to be, based on the so-called Standard Model of particle physics.[27] This is an immensely important point that clearly shows some form of contrivance in action, yet this feature of the cosmological constant has hardly been given any attention at all by the scientific and lay communities.

Although the details behind the value of the cosmological constant are exceptionally difficult and involved, the main ideas can be boiled down to a few relatively simple points. Theoretical physicists believe that the physical universe is made up of a large number of "free parameters," or distinct structural components, that work together to make up our coherent universe. Yet, because the Standard Model explicitly rejects any type of Intelligent Design in the nature of these components, scientists believe that they are all completely independent of one another. Accordingly, they believe that all of these components originated totally apart from one another, which in turn means that it was only by the most unlikely of accidents that these components were later able to work together to form a coherent universe.

Based on this assumed independence of the universe's most fundamental building blocks, physicists have calculated the "proper" size for the cosmological constant, and what they found is nothing short of amazing. They came up with a value that is over 10^{46} times *larger* than the value that they actually measured! This is of paramount significance, for if the cosmological constant were truly this large, the geometry of space-time would have been so warped that no form of life could have existed in the universe. Therefore, our lives intimately depend on this unexpectedly small value for the cosmological constant, yet scientists are at a complete loss to explain why it should be so incredibly small.

As physicist Larry Abbot of Brandeis University explains:

> The stupendous failure we have experienced in trying to predict the value of the cosmological constant is far more than a mere embarrassment. Recall that the basic assumption we used to obtain our estimate *of the value of the cosmological constant* was that there are no unexpected cancellations among the various terms in the sum determining the total energy density of the vacuum. This expectation was based on the assumed independence of the free parameters of the Standard Model. Clearly, this assumption is spectacularly wrong. There must in fact be a *miraculous conspiracy* [emphasis mine] occurring among both the known and the unknown parameters governing particle physics, with the result that the many terms making up the cosmological constant add up to a quantity more than 46 orders of magnitude smaller than the individual terms in the sum. In other words, the small value of the cosmological constant is telling us that a remarkably precise and totally unexpected relation exists among all the parameters of the Standard Model of particle physics, the bare cosmological constant and unknown physics.[28]

This is an extraordinary observation that suggests a hidden level of cooperation—which Abbott calls a "miraculous conspiracy"—between the many different structural components that make up the physical universe. This cooperation appears to be directed toward making the cosmological constant small enough to be compatible with the existence of a biocentric cosmos.

Researchers have also recently cited a positive cosmological constant as being the most probable reason why the universe's expansion rate appears to be accelerating with time. In order for this to actually be the case, though, the cosmological constant[29] must be fine-tuned to within one part in 10^{120}. This degree of accuracy is more than ten trillion trillion trillion trillion trillion trillion trillion trillion times more precise than anything human engineers have been able to accomplish thus far.[30]

This conclusion is greatly strengthened by a related aspect of our cosmic history. In order for our nascent universe to have been able to expand at precisely the "right" rate to ensure galaxy formation millions of years later, the antigravity effect of the cosmological constant had to have been precisely counterbalanced against the gravitational pull emanating from the mass of the entire universe, which itself had to have been fine-tuned to within one part in 10^{60} to make life possible.[31] This is a mind-boggling degree of accuracy in and of itself, but when we couple it to the far greater level of accuracy (to within one part in 10^{120}) that must *simultaneously* be displayed by the cosmological constant before life can exist in the cosmos, we can see that some type of "Supercalculating Intellect" must indeed have been responsible for calibrating it all.

This degree of fine-tuning is virtually unthinkable in an undesigned universe, as researchers Idit Zehavi and Avishai Dekel imply in the following passage from the science journal *Nature*:

> This type of universe, however, seems to require a degree of fine-tuning of the initial conditions that is in apparent conflict with "common wisdom."[32]

The "common wisdom" that is being referred to here is the naturalistic scientist's presumption that the universe has *not* been designed by an Intelligent Power. Fine-tuning to this remarkable extent is simply not something that we would *ever* expect to observe in an undesigned universe. And since most working scientists openly subscribe to this sort of nontheistic metaphysical bias, they have little choice but to gasp in amazement at the incredible degree of fine-tuning that our universe seems to have required.

Indeed, this appears to be why particle theorists were originally so far off base in their initial prediction of the cosmological constant's value. Due to their private assumptions regarding the random origin of the universe, they were naturally expecting the "free" parameters of the Standard Model to be totally independent of one another with respect to their contribution to the overall value of the cosmological constant. As it turns out, though, this just doesn't appear to be the case at all. To the contrary, there appears to be an *extremely* intimate degree of hidden cooperation between these physical parameters that functions to make the value of the cosmological constant some 10^{46} orders of magnitude *smaller* than would otherwise be expected without this cooperation.

This kind of multilevel cooperation between so many seemingly "independent" factors is just what we would expect to observe if an Intelligent Power deliberately designed the universe. I say this for three different reasons: (1) because of the number of distinct parameters that are involved, (2) because of the many complex interconnections that exist between these parameters, and (3) because of the overall purpose of this grand cooperative scheme (that of making space-time "flat" so that it can be conducive to life).

It follows, then, that had particle theorists initially assumed the prior existence of some degree of cooperative interdependence between the basic building blocks of the universe, their prediction of the value of the cosmological constant would have likely been *much* more accurate.

Needless to say, it would stretch credulity beyond the breaking point to even *suggest* that the physical parameters that gave rise to the cosmological constant were random in origin. There are simply far too many of them—and far too much cooperative interaction between them aiming for a single unified end—to *ever* be the result of chance processes alone.

To his credit, Abbott doesn't even *attempt* to attribute this interdependence to chance; rather, he openly *assumes* a nonaccidental origin to the cosmological constant, because this is the only conclusion that is consistent with the existing evidence. This is what he means when he asserts that there is a "miraculous conspiracy" going on between the fundamental parameters of particle physics. But if this is so, then we are immediately led to a far more significant conclusion, namely, that the larger universe, which encompasses the cosmological constant, cannot be an accident, either.

Creation out of Nothing?

As we have just seen, one of the most startling revelations of the new physics is that the vacuum of "empty" space isn't really empty. It is, rather, a dynamic, energy-filled environment in which pairs of so-called virtual particles spontaneously arise seemingly out of nowhere and then disappear. This energy density of the vacuum, also known as the cosmological constant, is extremely intriguing, because it seems to imply that real world objects can arise "out of nothing."

Although this idea of something from "nothing" is new to the scientific establishment, it has been around for centuries as part of traditional theological dogma. Theologians have long maintained that God created the world out of nothing (or *ex nihilo*), and it now appears as though modern science has finally corroborated this ancient belief.

One possible means of interpreting the vacuum of "empty" space is in terms of a metaphysical interface between the physical universe, on the one hand, and the hypothetical existence of a Divine Creator, on the other. To be sure, if God does in fact exist, and if He is in fact responsible for creating our world, then it makes sense to suppose that His Creative Activity might interface with the physical universe at the level of the quantum vacuum itself. If so, then God Himself would in some sense be responsible for producing the observed energy density of the vacuum.

The fact that empty space can indeed give rise to "virtual particles" strongly supports this theistic interpretation, because it implies that there is Someone or something on the other side of this metaphysical interface that is channeling a certain amount of energy into it. On this view, the "spontaneous" appearance and disappearance of virtual particles from this quantum field would be due to the activity of God in some fashion.

The science of modern physics, however, is not free to openly attribute this kind of phenomenon to the activity of a hypothetical Creator. As a consequence, it simply accepts the idea of a dynamic cosmic vacuum as a raw given, without taking the "unnecessary" extra step of invoking an unseen supernatural Agency to "explain" it.

A few scientists have even tried to explain the need for God away by arguing that the entire universe could have spontaneously "popped" into existence out of nothing as a huge quantum fluctuation. There is, however, a severe problem with this type of atheistic contention. Spontaneous quantum fluctuations don't really take place in genuine nothingness. Rather, they take place in a larger *quantum field* that enables these things to happen in the first place. But a quantum field can in no way be described as genuine nothingness. It is, instead, a metaphysical entity of unsearchable order and complexity.

In order to be able to explain, then, how the universe could have been able to pop into existence "out of nothing" without a larger Designer, nontheistic scientists first need to explain where the primordial quantum field *itself* could have originally come from. And, as you might have guessed, they are nowhere near doing *that* at the present time.

Cosmic "Coincidences" and the Existence of a Designer

The evidence for Intelligent Design in the cosmos goes far beyond any specific scientific measurements or observations *per se*. Rather, it extends all the way to the very *heart* of our life-supporting universe, and it involves just about every one of its underlying structural features. Indeed, we now know that life is only possible because of a long list of "cosmic coincidences" that just happened to occur in unison with one another during the long course of universal evolution. Without each and every one of these "coincidences," we would not be alive to discuss the fact. It's as simple as that.

For instance, consider the strength of the gravitational force. Although it is by far the weakest of the four physical forces, it is nevertheless powerful enough to have determined the large-scale structure of the entire visible universe. Indeed, had the gravitational constant differed from its present value by a mere one part in 10^{50}, the structure of the entire universe would have been radically different.[33]

The precise value of the gravitational constant is also intimately related to the types of stars that can form in the cosmos, and this in turn is one of the most important factors for the existence of life. Had the gravitational constant been a tad larger than it is, most stars would have been "blue giants," whose life cycles are so brief that they would have died long before any kind of life could have arisen. Similarly, had the gravitational constant been even slightly smaller, far fewer stars would have formed, and the majority of these would have been "red dwarfs," which do not produce enough heat to support life. As it turns out, life can only exist around stable "main sequence" stars like our own sun, which alone are capable of burning hot enough and long enough to support life. Amazingly, though, in order for main sequence stars to form in any appreciable numbers, the gravitational constant could only have occupied its present value.

The gravitational constant, however, doesn't work alone in determining the types of stars that can form in the universe. It works in concert with two other physical parameters, the electromagnetic fine structure constant and the ratio between the mass of the electron and the proton, to ensure that the majority of stars that are formed will be "main sequence" stars like our own sun. As Paul Davies has pointed out, this seemingly fortuitous relation between three independent physical constants is all the more remarkable because in order for typical stars like our sun to be able to form in any appreciable numbers, both sides of the inequality which relates these fundamental values must come very close to the huge number 10^{-39}. This is because the danger of convective instability within a star puts a stringent limitation on the values these constants can possess if stars like our sun are to be able to routinely form.[34] Given this very narrow convective window in which stars like our sun can form, along with the requirement that the strength of gravity, on the one hand, and the product of the electromagnetic fine structure constant and the electron/proton mass ratio, on the other, must both add up to approximately 10^{-39}, one might initially suppose such a feat to be next to impossible, especially in a genuinely accidental universe. Fortunately, the strength of the gravitational force in the above-stated inequality works out to be 5.9×10^{-39}, while the product of the electromagnetic fine structure constant and the electron/proton mass ratio works out to be 2.0×10^{-39}. This inequality is sufficiently close to unity to allow the majority of stars that form to be "main sequence" stars like our own sun.

> Nature has evidently picked the values of the fundamental constants in such a way that typical stars lie very close indeed to the boundary of convective instability. The fact that the two sides of the inequality . . . are such enormous numbers, and yet lie so close to one another, is truly astonishing. If gravity were *very* slightly weaker, or electromagnetism *very* slightly stronger, or the electron slightly less massive relative to the proton, all stars would be red dwarfs. A corresponding tiny change the other way, and they would all be blue giants.[35]

The value of the strong nuclear force, which binds atomic nuclei together, is also critical to the present structure of the universe. Had it been slightly stronger, protons and neutrons would have tended to bind together more frequently and more firmly. This would have had the disastrous effect of making hydrogen, which is the only element in existence that contains a single proton, a rare element in the universe. Not only would this have spelled catastrophe for stars like our own sun, which depend on an abundance of hydrogen for their primary nuclear fuel, it also would have vastly reduced the cosmic supply of elements heavier than iron, upon which life so intimately depends. In either case, life would have been impossible.

Moreover, had the strong nuclear force been slightly stronger in relation to the electromagnetic force, reality would have largely been comprised of a strange entity known as the diproton, which consists of two protons bound together. This would have been catastrophic to the nuclear reactions that fuel our sun, since they would have quickly become so powerful that the sun itself would have exploded.

Similarly, had the strong nuclear force been slightly weaker, multiproton nuclei would not have been able to hold together, so hydrogen would have been the only element in existence. This would have made the existence of life strictly impossible, because life depends on the plentiful existence of many elements heavier than hydrogen.

A second consequence of a slightly less energetic strong force would be that the nucleus consisting of one proton and neutron, known as the deuteron, would have been unable to form inside of stars. This would have been catastrophic to the chain of nuclear reactions that power the stars, because deuterium is the nuclear fuel that "jump-starts" embryonic stars into existence. Thus, the long-term stability of stellar fusion is dependent on the specific value of the strong nuclear force.

Stellar fusion is also dependent on the relative sizes of protons and neutrons, which are the two fundamental building blocks of atomic nuclei. As it stands now, the neutron outweighs the proton by a mere tenth of 1 percent. While this minuscule weight difference may seem to be relatively unimportant, it is actually of paramount significance for beings like ourselves, who depend upon it for our very lives. Had the proton outweighed the neutron by even the tiniest amount, the proton would not have been a stable particle; it would instead have spontaneously decayed into neutrons. This would have made it impossible for hydrogen—which consists of a single stable proton—to exist, which in turn would have proved fatal to everything made of hydrogen, including hydrogen-burning stars and water. But without stars like our sun and without a miracle solvent like water, no form of life even remotely resembling our own could have ever existed.

This mass difference between the proton and the neutron is all the more incredible when one considers the fact that protons and neutrons themselves are made out of even smaller particles known as *quarks*, which themselves had to have been exactly the right size to ensure a mass difference between protons and neutrons of precisely 10^{-3} of the proton mass. If this mass difference were only one-third of its present value, then neutrons could not have decayed to produce protons, because they would not have had enough mass to form an electron. Similarly, if the neutron's mass were only 0.998 of its actual value, free protons would probably decay into neutrons by a process known as positron emission. If this were the case, there would probably be no atoms at all in the universe.[36]

As Davies points out, the above relation between the relative sizes of protons and neutrons is itself derived from a seemingly "accidental" relation between the strength of gravity, the strength of the weak force, and the mass difference between protons and neutrons.[37] Had this not been the case, virtually all the nuclei in existence would have been either protons or neutrons. Either way, the complex chemistry upon which life depends would have been impossible.

Yet another example of near perfect balance in the subatomic realm can be found in the ratio of protons to electrons, which establishes the role of gravity in relation to the electromagnetic force.[38] Fortunately for us, the number of protons and electrons that were able to survive the primordial annihilation between matter and antimatter at the Big Bang was equivalent to within one part in 10^{37}. As Ross has pointed out, had this primordial balance between protons and electrons been any different, the electromagnetic force would have so completely dominated the gravitational force that stars, galaxies, and people would have never been able to form.[39]

Another instance of perfect calibration involves the mass of neutrinos, which are the smallest (5×10^{-35} kg) and most abundant particles in the known universe. Although they are far smaller than electrons, the huge number of neutrinos in existence could easily work together to exert a significant gravitational effect on the rest of the universe. Indeed, had the neutrino been just a tiny fraction bigger, the entire universe would have collapsed back in on itself shortly after the Big Bang because of the neutrinos' cumulative gravitational effect.[40]

The neutrino also figures prominently in the process of galactic motion. Because of their tremendous numbers, neutrinos are able to exert a significant viscous drag on galactic motion, such that had the mass of the neutrino been any larger or smaller, present-day galactic structures would have been impossible.[41]

Still another source of wonder in the subatomic realm can be found in the respective electrical charges of protons and electrons. Although the proton is many orders of magnitude larger than the electron, it possesses exactly the opposite quantity of electrical charge. As a consequence, equal numbers of protons and electrons cancel one another out, producing a net charge of zero. This is vitally important for the existence of biological life forms, because this perfect degree of electrical balance in the atom is a vital prerequisite for the complex biochemistry upon which life so intimately depends.

Indeed, had the electron's charge not been perfectly offset by the charge of a proton, our world would have never had the chance to form at all, since atoms and molecules would have been so unstable that they never would have been able to endure the test of time. In fact, if this perfect degree of electrical balance were to be altered by as little as one part in 100 billion, our bodies would instantaneously explode.[42]

With this in mind, how are we to explain the perfect degree of electrical balance between the proton and the electron? It obviously cannot be a function of mere size, as we might suspect at first glance, because the proton is so much larger than the electron. One could conceivably posit a type of natural selection between subatomic particles, in which an entire range of charged protons and electrons would originally exist, but in which only those particles whose charges were perfectly balanced with one another would be allowed to continue to exist. The problem with this conjecture is twofold: (1) there is no evidence that this could have ever been the case, as we have no good reason to believe that protons or electrons ever existed with even a slightly varying amount of electrical charge; and (2) even if there originally had been such a wide range of charged protons and electrons in existence, we still would have to explain where the correctly charged particles themselves originally came from, and how they subsequently could have come to be the only particles in existence.

A far simpler and more satisfying way to explain this perfect electrical balance between protons and electrons is to assert that they were deliberately designed to be this way by a Larger Power. This hypothesis has the added value of being consistent with all the other explanations being offered in this chapter for the many cosmic coincidences in our universe.

The strength of the electromagnetic coupling constant, which determines how strongly electrons are bound to protons in atoms, is also intimately related to the existence of biological life forms.[43] As you may recall from an earlier study of chemistry, complex molecules are formed by the spontaneous interaction between the electrons of different atoms. The behavior of these electrons, in turn, is directly determined by the strength of the electromagnetic coupling constant. Had this constant been slightly smaller, relatively few electrons would have been able to remain in "orbit" about nuclei. Had it been slightly stronger, covalent bonding—in which atoms share electrons with one another—would not have been possible. In either case, the complex chemistry upon which life depends would have been strictly impossible.

Digging deeper, we find two other principles at work at the subatomic level that function to stabilize atomic interactions, thereby guaranteeing the stability of all matter and, as a consequence, enabling complex chemistries to result. The first stabilizing force, known as the Pauli Exclusion Principle, acts to guarantee that no more than one particular kind of particle and spin can occupy a single quantum state at the same time. If this Exclusion Principle did not apply, all electrons would occupy the lowest quantum state, since it is the orbital with the lowest energy. This would have had two disastrous effects: (1) The various positively and negatively charged particles in an atom would spontaneously rearrange themselves so that interactions between their nearest neighbors would predominate. This would result in the spontaneous collapse of the entire atomic structure into a single particle of enormous density, thereby destroying any further possibility for complex chemical interaction. (2) By destroying the multiple shell structure of heavier atoms, upon which most of the known chemical properties of the elements absolutely depend, the vast majority of these properties would disappear. This would make any type of complex biochemistry impossible, with the result that no carbon-based life forms at all would have been able to exist on this planet.

As Barrow and Tipler point out, it is possible to imagine a world where the Pauli Exclusion Principle did not apply, but it would be a very different world containing superdense objects that would possess no capacity at all for complex organization.[44] Our very lives thus depend on the existence of the Pauli Exclusion Principle, yet we have no idea where it comes from or why it functions the way it does. All we know is that it does indeed work and that it is this very functionality that has enabled life to form.

The second stabilizing force at the subatomic level is the quantization of electronic energy levels. As Bohr originally showed in 1913, electrons can only exist at discrete levels about the nucleus, which amount to multiples of Planck's universal quantum of energy. The great benefit of this quantum nature of the atom is that it allows for all atoms of a particular atomic number and weight to be both identical and stable in the face of a continual bombardment of energy from without. In a nonquantum atom, electrons could possess all possible energy states and therefore all possible orbital distances from the nucleus. This, of course, would render all atoms different from one another and would allow electrons to continually change their energy levels in response to the slightest amount of incoming energy, be it in the form of photons, cosmic rays, or whatever. This, in turn, would make a given atom's chemical properties subject to change at a moment's notice, thereby making any stable form of chemical interaction absolutely impossible. Fortunately, the existence of discrete quantum states greatly stabilizes each individual atom, because an entire quantum of energy is needed to alter a given electron's particular energy level.

As Barrow and Tipler point out, the atomic stability that is created by quantization ironically flies in the face of the popular perception of quantum theory, which sees it as being the very essence of randomness and indeterminism. In reality, though, quantization forms the physical basis for much of the stability and fidelity that is regularly observed in the natural world.[45]

Another important source of atomic stability is the stability of the proton itself, which is one of the primary constituents of atoms and molecules. Indeed, this stability of the proton turns out to be absolutely essential for the evolution of life, for had the proton been significantly less stable, life-destroying doses of radiation would have been a much more common occurrence in matter. Similarly, had protons been significantly more stable (i.e., less easily formed and less susceptible to decay), less matter would have been produced in the Big Bang, and, as a consequence, life—which intimately depends on the current amount of matter in the universe—would have been impossible.[46]

A "Just Right" State of Cooperation

Perhaps the most remarkable thing about nature's fundamental constants is that they do not work in isolation from one another. Instead, there is a deep level of cooperation in nature between the different physical forces such that, in the absence of this cooperation, our present world could not exist. For instance, if the gravitational constant were just a wee bit stronger in relation to the strong nuclear force, the universe would have been a good deal smaller and faster than it presently is, with the result that stars like our own sun would have been much smaller and would have only lasted for about a year. On the other hand, if gravity were any weaker in relation to the strong force, then the various galaxies and solar systems in the cosmos would never have been able to form in the first place. Either way, life would have been impossible.

Similarly, had the electromagnetic force been slightly stronger in relation to the strong force, the heavier elements that are so important to life would have been nonexistent. If the strong force is held constant, we learn that the fine structure constant must be less than approximately 0.1 in order for heavier elements such as carbon to be able to exist.[47]

A delicate "coincidence" also seems to have been at work between the gravitational interaction and the weak nuclear force at the very beginning of the Hubble expansion, for it was this "coincidence" that produced the hydrogen and helium which in turn made the evolution of life possible. As it turns out, the primordial nuclear reactions that produced these elements are only possible within an exceedingly narrow range of universal temperatures (around 5×10^9 kelvins) and universal ages (anywhere between 0.04 seconds and 500 seconds). Had these reactions taken place at any time prior to 0.04 seconds, all incipient nuclei would have been instantly photodisintegrated; but had they taken place at any time after approximately 500 seconds, the reacting nuclei would have possessed too little energy to overcome electrical barriers to the nuclear force.

Fortunately, by virtue of the intimate cooperation between the gravitational and weak interactions, sufficient matter to produce a biocentric universe was indeed formed in the initial nucleosynthesis "window" of the cosmic expansion—75 percent in the form of hydrogen and 25 percent in the form of helium. Had this cooperation not occurred, the universe would have been comprised of either 100 percent hydrogen or 100 percent helium, if indeed any atoms at all would have been capable of forming. While there does not seem to be any "anthropic" problems associated with a primordial universe containing 100 percent hydrogen, life would have been impossible in a universe consisting of 100 percent helium. This is because hydrogen would not have been available to form compounds essential to life, such as water; in addition, exclusively helium-burning stars would have been far too short-lived to allow sufficient time for the evolution of life.

Remarkably, the gross properties of all atomic and molecular structures can ultimately be traced to the specific values of only two dimensionless physical parameters: the fine structure constant and the electron-to-proton mass ratio. We clearly owe our lives to the specific values of these fundamental parameters, for had either one been even slightly different, we wouldn't be here to discuss the fact.

A commonsense interpretation of the evidence suggests that a larger Creative Principle was probably at work in the early universe coordinating events so as to make the later evolution of life possible. Davies agrees:

> The nature of the physical world depends delicately on seemingly fortuitous cooperation between distant branches of physics. In particular, accidental numerical re-

lations between quantities as unconnected as the fine structure constants for gravity and electromagnetism, or between the strengths of nuclear forces and the thermodynamic condition of the primeval universe, suggest that many of the familiar systems that populate the universe are the result of exceedingly improbable coincidences. . . . Turning to the subject of cosmology . . . we encounter further cosmic cooperation of such a wildly improbable nature, it becomes hard to resist the impression that some basic principle is at work.[48]

Nuclear Stability

The temperature of nuclear stability in the universe—which marks the point at which radiation began to decouple from embryonic matter—is highly significant from a biocentric point of view. Had this temperature of approximately 10^9 kelvins been even slightly different from its present value, our biocentric universe could never have formed. As Gerald L. Schroeder explains:

> If $10^{10°}$ K. was the temperature of stability, then stability would have been reached at approximately one second after the Big Bang. The composition of the universe at that time was approximately 25 percent neutrons and 75 percent protons and the particle plus energy density of the universe was some 400,000 times that of water. This high density would have caused rapid fusion among particles and therefore rapid building of heavier nuclei. . . . How would this affect us? First of all, we probably would not be here. Immediately, the composition of the universe would have shifted from its present 75 percent hydrogen and 25 percent helium to a 50–50 ratio as the abundant free neutrons joined with protons to form helium. The high particle density would have changed more, perhaps all, of the hydrogen into nuclei of heavier elements. Little or no hydrogen would have remained. No hydrogen means no significant solar radiation. The stellar furnaces would not have burned as they do today, because the energy of stars is fueled almost entirely by the fusion of hydrogen into helium. Those elements heavier than helium, which life now gleans from the residues of supernovas, would have been abundant. But the hot spots of the universe, which we call stars, would not be there to provide life-giving energy.

Had nuclear stability been delayed until the universe temperature cooled to $10^{3°}$ K., then instead of having an abundance of heavier elements and a dearth of hydrogen, as we saw in the previous scenario, there would be hydrogen and not much else in the universe. Approximately 300 minutes had elapsed before the expansion of the universe had lowered the temperature to $10^{3°}$ K. Although neutrons bound in a nucleus are stable and do not decay radioactively, free neutrons are radioactive. They decay with a 15-minute half-period. The 300 minutes that elapsed before reaching $10^{3°}$ K. would have allowed almost total decay of all free neutrons. Nuclear synthesis requires neutrons. A universe with no neutrons means a universe composed of hydrogen and no other elements. There is no place for life in such a universe.[49]

In short, the biocentric nature of the universe extends to the very origin of the physical realm itself. Prior to this discovery, who would have thought that such a tiny change in the temperature of nuclear stability could have had such a huge effect on the later evolution of life? This fact in itself is strongly indicative of Intelligent Design. For had the evolution of life been dependent on recent, local factors only, such as the arrangement of atoms on a planet, we might have been able to argue more persuasively for a possible random origin of life. However, now that we know that the biocentric nature of the cosmos dates back to the very origins of the universe itself, and extends to each and every one of the foundational parameters that comprise physical reality, it is hard to see how it could have been produced by anything *but* Intelligent Design.

The Color of Sunlight

Another remarkable cosmic "coincidence" involves the surface temperature of the sun and its relationship to the particular needs of life on earth. In order for the life-generating process of photosynthesis to take place, in which plants remove poisonous carbon dioxide from the air and replace it with oxygen, the spectral temperature of sunlight must be very near the molecular binding energy of around 1 Rydberg.[50] If it exceeded this value, all life on earth would either be sterilized or completely annihilated. If it were significantly below this value, the crucial photosynthetic reactions that recycle carbon dioxide into oxygen would proceed much too slowly to be of any benefit to the rigid demands of life.

In other words, sunlight must be of the right color in order for photosynthetic reactions to occur in an optimal fashion. However, it would be wrong to assume that had sunlight been of a different overall color, another type of molecule besides chlorophyll would have evolved to take advantage of it. The fact is, due to the specific quantum states that are common to all the elements, *all* molecules absorb light of approximately the same color. Thus, given this necessary requirement of all molecular structures, the sun's spectral temperature (and hence its color) had to have been just right or else photosynthetic reactions would have never occurred on this planet. Fortunately, due to a separate series of nuclear coincidences at work in the stars themselves, our sun not only possesses the right spectral temperature to fuel earth-based photosynthetic reactions, it is also sufficiently long-lived to give carbon-based life forms enough time to evolve and prosper on this planet.

The Transition to a Nontoxic, Oxidizing Atmosphere

In order for green plants to be capable of producing oxygen via the process of photosynthesis, light must be capable of reaching the surface of the earth in sufficient quantities. However, the primeval atmosphere of the earth was much too opaque to allow for the unrestricted passage of light through it.[51] Much of this opaqueness is thought to have been due to the presence of large quantities of methane and ammonia—which are biotoxic poisons in their own right—in the atmosphere. Hence, before life could have ever been capable of evolving on the surface of the earth in any appreciable quantities, a way had to be found to transform the earth's toxic, opaque atmosphere into a nontoxic, translucent one.

This global transformation was necessary for yet another reason: it enabled the earth's atmosphere to be converted from a reducing one—in which elements tend to combine with hydrogen—to an oxidizing one, in which elements tend to combine with oxygen. An oxidizing atmosphere is absolutely essential for the development of life for two reasons: (1) routine metabolic processes require a certain minimum amount of oxygen in the atmosphere and (2) life cannot evolve without an ozone shield to block out the sun's harmful ultraviolet radiation, and ozone is comprised of three oxygen atoms.

In order for life to evolve, then, the earth's toxic, reducing atmosphere had to have somehow purged itself of its high ammonia and methane content, so that the way could be paved for the transformation to a translucent, oxidizing atmosphere. At the same time, though, it also had to retain almost all of its water vapor, because water is an absolutely essential ingredient for all earth-based life forms.

It is generally thought that this selective loss of methane and ammonia occurred through a process of atmospheric evaporation; the methane and ammonia evaporated into outer space, while the water vapor was selectively retained within the earth's atmosphere. However, as Hugh Ross[52] points out in *Genesis One: A Scientific Perspective*, this process of atmospheric evaporation had to have been very finely balanced indeed, because the molecular weights of these three substances are so close to one another. Methane, for instance, has a molecular weight of 16, ammonia has a molecular weight of 17, and water vapor has a molecular weight of 18. Hence, the climatological forces that facilitated this process had to have been just strong enough to allow for the selective evaporation of methane and ammonia, but not quite strong enough to allow for the evaporation of water vapor. This undoubtedly qualifies as one of the most remarkable events in the earth's entire history, because water vapor is heavier than ammonia by a mere factor of one atomic unit.

In order for *any* molecule to be capable of evaporating from the earth's atmosphere, though, a complex quantity known as its *escape time* must add up to a certain minimum amount. This quantity is comprised of a number[53] of discrete cosmic factors: (1) the mass of a planet, (2) the square of the planet's radius, (3) the square root of both the molecule's mass and the atmospheric temperature of the planet, and (4) the individual temperature gradient for each of the different layers in the planet's atmosphere. As far as the primeval earth itself was concerned, this latter factor was greatly influenced by a series of other factors, including: (1) the gradual increase in the sun's luminosity (which we will discuss in more detail later on in this chapter), (2) the gravitational "mopping up" of interplanetary debris by the sun and other gravitational bodies, and (3) the steady decrease in the earth's volcanic activity.

It is astonishing to realize that all of these causally distinct factors had to have worked together to a very high degree of accuracy to have allowed for the selective evaporation of methane and ammonia, while simultaneously allowing for the selective retaining of water vapor in the earth's early atmosphere.[54] Considering the very close proximity between the molecular weights of methane, ammonia, and water vapor, this would seem to be the result of an exceedingly clever Intelligence.

Of course, there will always be those who insist on seeing such remarkable events as being purely accidental. However, in light of all the other cosmic "coincidences" that we've discussed in this chapter, it just doesn't seem credible to believe that they *all* could have happened by chance alone.

Many scientists, of course, like to attribute our existence to a mere selection effect, in which we can't help but find ourselves living in that part of the universe that just happens to be capable of supporting our existence. While it is necessarily the case that we can't help but observe ourselves living in such a world, this self-evident observation can never be used as a *sufficient* explanation for our own existence, because it doesn't explain how the universe originally came to occupy its present biocentric character in the first place.

A Case of Perfect Timing

As Gerald L. Schroeder explains in *Genesis and the Big Bang*, most stars in the early stages of their evolution are observed to lose tremendous amounts of matter in a single convulsive outburst.[55] This explosive period is known as the T-Tauri Phase of stellar evolution. In all likelihood, our own sun experienced just such a violent outburst early in its history, during which time it probably expelled the equivalent of two or three solar masses.

Indeed, according to Schroeder, the sun produced such a powerful solar wind during its T-Tauri Phase that it probably blew all residual interplanetary gases straight out of the solar system.[56] The devastation, however, affected far more than just these interplanetary gases; it also blew away the atmospheres of the various planets as well. This of course presented a potentially catastrophic threat as far as the life-supporting capacity of the earth was concerned, for had the sun's T-Tauri wind occurred *after* the basic atmosphere of the earth had already formed, it would have blown away these precious gases once and for all, with the result that life would have never been able to evolve here.

On the other hand, had the sun's T-Tauri wind occurred *before* the aggregation of matter into planets, all the potential water for our world—which originally clung to the surfaces of interstellar dust particles as frost—would have been instantly vaporized by the massive radiation.[57] This would have produced an earth without water, which of course would have made it impossible for life to arise here. It is also possible that an "early" T-Tauri wind would have blown many of the uncongealed precursors of the earth straight out of the solar system as well, which of course would have made it impossible for our planet to form in the first place.

It is thus the timing of the sun's T-Tauri wind, in relation to the appearance of the earth's atmosphere, that becomes the all-important factor as far as the life-supporting capacity of our planet is concerned: it had to have occurred *after* the congealing of matter into planets, but *before* the creation of the earth's atmosphere (which is thought to have occurred via the outgassing of volcanoes). Fortunately for us, this appears to have been precisely what happened.

Goldilocks and a Brighter Sun?

If the universe were merely an undesigned accident, we would never expect there to be a high level of cooperation between different parts of the universe that have never communicated with one another. For instance, we would never expect solar events that do not causally impinge on the earth to be intimately coordinated with events happening on this planet, especially if they are found to be working together to produce something interesting. For if there is no larger cosmic meaning and no coordinating Designer to tie these causally distinct events together, we would never expect to see any significant degree of cooperation between them, especially if it had the fortunate effect of enabling life to evolve here.

Incredibly, though, in one of the most startling instances of cooperative change ever to occur during the history of our planet, it turns out that the sun experienced a significant change in its luminosity at *precisely* the same time that certain life forms were appearing on the earth. These lifeforms were themselves capable of compensating for these extreme solar changes in such a way as to keep the earth's overall temperature relatively constant. As astronomer Owen Gingerich explains, this transformation qualifies as a genuine scientific miracle:

> From what astronomers have deduced about solar evolution, we believe that the Sun was perhaps 25 percent less luminous several billion years ago. Today, if the solar luminosity dropped by 25 percent, the oceans would freeze solid to the bottom, and it would take a substantial increase to thaw them out again. Life could not have originated on such a frozen globe, so it seems that the Earth's surface never suffered such frigid conditions. As it turns out, there is a very good reason for this. The original atmosphere would surely have consisted of hydrogen, by far the most abundant element in the universe, but this light element would have rapidly escaped, and a secondary atmosphere of carbon dioxide and water vapor would have formed from the outgassing of volcanoes. This secondary atmosphere would have produced a strong greenhouse effect, an effect that might be more readily explained with a locked car parked in the Sun on a hot summer day than with a greenhouse. When you open the car, it's like an oven inside. The glass lets in the photons of visible light from the Sun. Hot as the interior of the car may seem, it's quite cool compared to the Sun's surface, so the reradiation from inside the car is in the infrared. The glass is quite opaque for those longer wavelengths, and because the radiation can't get out, the car heats up inside. Similarly, the carbon dioxide and water vapor partially blocked the reradiation from the early Earth, raising its surface temperature above the mean freezing point of water.
>
> Over the ages, as the Sun's luminosity rose, so did the surface temperature of the Earth, and had the atmosphere stayed constant, our planet would now have a runaway greenhouse effect, something like that found on the planet Venus; the Earth's oceans would have boiled away, leaving a hot, lifeless globe.
>
> How did our atmosphere change over to oxygen just in the nick of time? Apparently, the earliest widely successful life form on Earth was a single-celled prokaryote, the so-called blue-greens, which survive to this day as stromatolites. Evidence for them appears in the Precambrian fossil record of a billion years ago. In the absence of predators, the algaelike organisms covered the oceans, extracting hydrogen from the water and releasing oxygen to the air. Nothing much seems to have happened for over a billion years, which is an interesting counterargument to those who claim intelligent life is the inevitable result whenever life forms. However, about 600 million years ago the oxygen content of the atmosphere rose rapidly, and then a series of events, quite possibly interrelated, took place: 1) eukariotic cells, that is, cells with their genetic information contained within a nucleus, originated, which allowed the invention of sex and the more efficient sharing of genetic material, and hence a more rapid adaptation of life forms to new environments; 2) more complicated organisms breathing oxygen, with its much higher energy yield, developed; and 3) the excess carbon dioxide was converted to limestone in the structure of these creatures, thus making the atmosphere more transparent

in the infrared and thereby preventing the oceans from boiling away in a runaway greenhouse effect as the Sun brightened. The perfect timing of this complex configuration of circumstances is enough to amaze and bewilder many of my friends who look at all this in purely mechanistic terms—the survival of life on Earth seems such a close shave as to border on the miraculous. Can we not see here the designer's hand at work?[58]

Carbon's Amazing Birthplace

One of the most important prerequisites for the development of organic life is, of course, the element carbon. Unbeknownst to most people, though, virtually all of the carbon in our universe—including the carbon in our bodies—was manufactured billions of years ago in the fiery interiors of dying red giant stars. We are quite literally, then, made of recycled star stuff.[59]

However, if it weren't for a series of wildly improbable "coincidences" involving the ambient heat energy of a star and a peculiar nuclear property known as *resonance*, there would be virtually no carbon in the universe at all. This is a truly astonishing realization that figures prominently in the "cosmic conspiracy" to evolve life that we have been discussing throughout this chapter. For this reason, we shall devote a particular amount of attention to this all-important cosmic phenomenon.

There are two possible ways in which carbon can be manufactured inside of stars. The first mechanism involves the simultaneous fusion of three helium nuclei into a single carbon nucleus. The reaction rate, however, for this simultaneous triple collision is much too slow to enable a significant quantity of carbon to be formed in this manner. Something else needs to occur to enable this reaction to proceed at a more favorable rate, otherwise virtually no carbon at all would be synthesized within dying stars.

As it turns out, two helium nuclei are able to fuse together to produce a beryllium intermediate at a much faster rate. Once this beryllium intermediate is formed, an additional collision with a single helium nucleus is then able to produce the desired carbon product in appreciable numbers.

However, before this two-step reaction can take place, two nuclear factors need to exist to help the process along. First, the beryllium intermediate needs to be relatively long-lived, in comparison with the helium + helium reaction that gave rise to it. This is so as to allow the beryllium intermediate a sufficient amount of time to react with a helium nucleus before it decays.

However, this mechanism is complicated by the fact that the beryllium intermediate, which is necessary in the first stage of this process, is not the normal form of beryllium found in nature (which possesses one more neutron).

To the contrary, it is the most wildly unstable isotope (or form) of beryllium known, which is only stable for a mere 0.000000000000001 of a second, after which point it flies apart.[60] Therefore, some other factor had to exist to compensate for this exceedingly short lifetime; otherwise, there wouldn't be enough of the beryllium substrate produced inside of these dying red giant stars to allow for the generation of sufficient quantities of carbon.

The discovery of this crucial additional factor came in 1953 when Cornell University astrophysicist Edwin Salpeter found that the beryllium intermediate inside these stars possesses just the right nuclear *resonance* level to help facilitate the production of sufficient quantities of carbon.

The term "nuclear resonance" refers to the natural vibration frequencies of atomic nuclei. Just as electrons are known to occupy different energy levels in an atom, so too are the nuclei themselves capable of occupying different energy levels, which are known as *resonance energies*. Resonance becomes a factor when two nuclei collide, for if the nuclear resonance of the composite structure (the potential product) matches the combined mass-energy of the two reactants, the two nuclei "resonate" with one another when they collide, with the effect that there is a much greater chance that they will stick together to form a new product.

In other words, just as all physical objects naturally possess a sympathetic vibrational frequency, so too do all atomic nuclei. This sympathetic vibrational frequency of an atomic nucleus is known as its nuclear resonance level, and all nuclei possess a coordinated mixture of them. Nuclear reactions, in turn, are either facilitated or hindered by the specific resonances of reacting nuclei in the following manner: if the sympathetic vibrational frequency of one of the reactants happens to "resonate" with the energy of an incoming nucleus, the two nuclei are more likely to fuse together; if no resonance at all occurs, they are more likely to "bounce off" one another and remain separate.

It is the phenomenon of nuclear resonance that enables the essential beryllium intermediate to be produced in appreciable quantities inside dying red giant stars, in spite of its extremely short lifetime. Fortunately for us, the reacting helium nucleus resonates with the beryllium intermediate in such a fashion that the latter substance is able to be produced in much greater quantities than would have otherwise been the case. This additional factor compensates for the unusually brief lifetime of the beryllium intermediate and allows for its production in sufficient quantities to facilitate the eventual synthesis of carbon.

It is instructive to note at this point that there is a deeper "reason" for the radical instability of the beryllium intermediate: it is crucial for the development of the *other* heavy elements upon which life so intimately depends. As

Hugh Ross has pointed out, if this beryllium intermediate were even a tad bit more stable, the production of heavier elements would proceed so rapidly that violent stellar explosions would inevitably result, and this would effectively short-circuit the stepwise fusion of the heavier elements that are so crucial to life.[61]

In order for carbon-based life forms to be capable of existing, then, it was necessary for the lifetime of the beryllium intermediate to be balanced on a knife-edge between two extremes, both of which, had they obtained, would have made the evolution of life impossible. On the one hand, the lifetime of the beryllium intermediate had to have been short enough to slow the process of fusion down sufficiently in stars, so as to prevent catastrophic intrastellar explosions from occurring. On the other hand, it also had to have been long enough to allow enough time for a third helium nucleus to hit home so that a precious carbon-12 nucleus[62] could be generated. Needless to say, the actual lifetime of this beryllium intermediate is precisely what it needs to be in order to allow for the production of carbon-based life forms such as ourselves.

Even so, the lifetime of the beryllium intermediate *still* isn't long enough by itself to allow for the production of significant quantities of carbon. Yet another nuclear factor has to intervene before this can take place. It was precisely here that British astrophysicist Sir Fred Hoyle made an incredible anthropically motivated discovery. Reasoning backwards from the existence of life, Hoyle knew that carbon *had* to have been formed in sufficient quantities in dying red giant stars (otherwise we wouldn't be here), so he doggedly set about looking for a suitable mechanism that would have been responsible for producing it. Hoyle expanded upon Salpeter's original discovery and proposed that a *second* nuclear resonance must be at work between helium, the reacting beryllium, and the final carbon product.

At first, Hoyle was unsuccessful in locating this second resonance level. In an impressive display of anthropically motivated faith, however, Hoyle persisted, because he knew that nuclei typically possess not one but *many* resonances. Working at Caltech with physicist Willy Fowler, he eventually found the nuclear resonance frequency he was looking for, which turned out to be precisely the 7.6 MeV energy level that he had originally predicted. As a direct consequence of this second resonance level, helium and the already facilitated beryllium intermediate are able to come together to form significant quantities of carbon when they wouldn't have otherwise been able to do so.

Going one step further, we find that the thermal energy of the nuclei in a typical star is almost exactly equivalent to the nuclear resonance level of the carbon nucleus. This further facilitates the production of carbon, as it ensures that the thermal energy of the reacting helium nucleus is almost exactly the same as the nuclear resonance level of the desired carbon product. The result of this happy "coincidence" is that the helium and beryllium nuclei are encouraged to stick together to form carbon, and this, in turn, ensures that relatively large quantities of carbon are regularly formed inside of dying red giant stars.

As if that weren't enough, there is a *third* resonance at work inside dying red giant stars that prevents the newly synthesized carbon from reacting with another helium nucleus to form oxygen. At it turns out, the oxygen nucleus possesses a resonance level that actually *discourages* its production from the fusion of carbon and helium nuclei. We owe our lives to this lucky "coincidence," for had a more favorable resonance level existed between carbon, helium, and oxygen, most of the carbon that is essential to life would have quickly been transformed into oxygen, and we would not be here to wonder about it.

Overall, then, it is safe to say that given the utter precision displayed by these nuclear resonances with respect to the synthesis of carbon, not even *one* of them could have been even *slightly* different without destroying their precious carbon yield. Had this change in the cosmic *status quo* actually occurred, carbon would have probably been an exceedingly rare element in the universe, and we in all likelihood would not be here.

In an intriguing essay entitled "Let There Be Light: Modern Cosmogony and Biblical Creation," astronomer Owen Gingerich explains how these unique nuclear properties have conspired together to facilitate the intrastellar production of carbon:

> Carbon is the fourth most common atom in our galaxy, after hydrogen, helium, and oxygen, but it isn't very abundant; there are 250 helium atoms for every carbon atom. A carbon atom can be made by merging three helium nuclei, but a triple collision is tolerably rare. It would be easier if two helium nuclei would stick together to form beryllium, but beryllium is not very stable. Nevertheless, sometimes before the two helium nuclei can come unstuck, a third helium atom strikes home, and a carbon nucleus results. And here the details of the internal energy levels of the carbon nucleus become interesting: it turns out that there is precisely the right resonance within the carbon that helps this process along. Without it, there would be relatively few carbon atoms. Similarly, the internal details of the oxygen nucleus play a critical role. Oxygen can be formed by combining helium and carbon nuclei, but the corresponding resonance level in the oxygen nucleus is *half a percent too low* for the combination to stay together easily. Had the resonance level in the carbon been 4 percent higher, there would be essentially no carbon. Had that level in the oxygen been only half a percent higher, virtually all of the carbon would have been

converted to oxygen. Without that carbon abundance, neither you nor I would be here tonight.[63]

As a direct consequence of this harmonious, teleological interplay between four distinct nuclear structures and three distinct nuclear resonances, carbon was able to be produced in stellar interiors in sufficient quantities to allow for the subsequent existence of carbon-based life forms. In order for this to have happened, though, the nuclear resonance levels of beryllium, carbon, and oxygen nuclei had to have been meticulously fine-tuned to better than accuracy. This, in turn, required additional fine-tuning between the relative strengths of the nuclear and electromagnetic interactions, as well as between the relative masses of nucleons and electrons. The cumulative effect of this fine-tuning is that, against all the odds, carbon was able to be manufactured in sufficient quantities inside stellar interiors to make our lives possible.

It is very hard to escape the impression that each stage of this carbon-making process was deliberately calibrated with all the others "in Mind"; otherwise, they almost certainly would have never been able to cooperate with one another in such a precise and meticulous fashion so as to ensure the production of sufficient quantities of carbon. In addition, we mustn't forget that a high degree of cooperation between several distinct structures for a common end product is *itself* indicative of intelligent design.[64]

The elucidation of this relationship between organic life and nuclear resonance levels has to be one of the greatest discoveries in the history of modern science, for it provides yet another powerful reason to believe that our physical universe has indeed been contrived by some sort of Divine "Superintellect," whose long-term goal was to create carbon-based life forms. There are simply too many "coincidences" at work here to allow for any other reasonable conclusion.[65]

Indeed, Hoyle was so persuaded by his findings that he has since come to the radical conclusion that they were probably the work of a Supernatural Contriver. For Hoyle, this meticulous fine-tuning of nuclear resonance levels is direct evidence of a kind of "put-up job" in the universe. In reference to the precise positioning of these nuclear resonances, Hoyle has written the following:

> If you wanted to produce carbon and oxygen in roughly equal quantities by stellar nucleosynthesis, these are the two levels you would have to fix, and your fixing would have to be just about where these levels are actually found to be. Would you not say to yourself, "Some supercalculating intellect must have designed the properties of the carbon atom, otherwise the chances of my finding such an atom

through the blind forces of nature would be utterly miniscule"? Of course you would. . . . . A common sense interpretation of the facts suggests that a superintellect has monkeyed with physics, as well as with chemistry and biology, and that there are no blind forces worth speaking about in nature. The numbers one calculates from the facts seem to me so overwhelming as to put this conclusion almost beyond question. (Emphasis mine)[66]

The significance of this statement from Hoyle cannot be overemphasized, not only because of its obvious theological content, but also because of Hoyle's blatant atheistic background. At one time, Hoyle was a strong proponent of the Steady State theory of the universe (which he helped to formulate), not because of the persuasiveness of the scientific evidence *per se*, but because of its freedom from any need for a Divine Creator. Indeed, throughout his early writings Hoyle proclaimed himself to be a firmly entrenched atheist and openly admitted that his cosmological theories were explicitly designed to support his nontheistic worldview.

It is against this atheistic background that Sir Fred's admission of a "Supercalculating Intellect" at work in the universe is nothing short of remarkable. It also says something about the intrinsic persuasiveness of the cosmological data, for as Hoyle correctly points out, the numbers one calculates from the facts are indeed *so overwhelming* as to put the theistic hypothesis virtually beyond question.

The Role of Supernovae in Our "Just Right" Universe

In order for carbon and the other heavy elements that are essential for life to become available for the formation of planets and ultimately people, they must find a way to become dispersed throughout the interstellar medium. This function is served by the magnificent explosions of dying red giant stars known as supernovae, which release so much radiant energy into the heavens that for a time they are brighter than anything else in the night sky.[67] When these spectacular cosmic events take place, they spew out into space billions of tons of carbon, oxygen, and all the other heavy elements that are essential for life, which are then made available to form planets and ultimately people.

However, had the weak nuclear force—which mediates radioactive decay—been any weaker, the neutrinos that cause supernova explosions would not have had sufficient power to do so.[68] Similarly, had the weak force been much stronger, the same neutrinos would have been hopelessly trapped within the cores of these dying stars.[69] Either way, the heavier organic elements that are so essential to life would have never been made available to the rest of the universe.

As we saw earlier, the strength of the weak force also determines how much hydrogen is converted into helium at the Big Bang. This dual role of the weak force strictly limits the possible values that it can possess and still be conducive to life. As Gribbin and Rees put it:

> The weak force seems to be just about as weak as it can be in order to avoid all the original hydrogen being converted into helium. Supernovae might still work (exploding by a different mechanism) if the force were a little stronger, but if the force were weaker the neutrinos could not drive any kind of explosion; the Universe would be even more comfortably dominated (baryonically speaking) by hydrogen if the force were a little stronger. But the window of opportunity for a universe in which there is *some* helium, *and* exploding supernovae, is very narrow.[70]

It is a mind-boggling thought to realize that all of nature's fundamental parameters possess multiple functions throughout the universe, and moreover, that they cross-interact with one another on a wide variety of different levels, despite their fixed status. In order for this to have been possible, though, each of these parameters had to have been calibrated and fine-tuned from the very beginning with the specific values of *all* the other parameters "in mind." This is a fantastically complicated requirement by anyone's standard, since each of these parameters clearly had to have been tweaked to a near-infinite degree of precision, not only along a single functional pathway, but along several different functional pathways *simultaneously*.

What cosmic power could have possibly carried out this stupendous feat? An important clue can be found here in the spatio-temporal positioning of this fine-tuning, since it had to have taken place at the general time of the Big Bang, long before there was a coherent universe in existence. This means that the cosmic power we are in search of couldn't possibly be physical in nature. This greatly simplifies the nature of our question, because there is only one nonphysical Being imaginable who could have possibly predated the Big Bang and who would have *also* had enough intelligence and power on hand to fine-tune the fundamental properties of the universe in such a manner as to naturally generate life several billion years later.

Notes

1. Corey S. Powell, "The Golden Age of Cosmology," *Scientific American*, vol. 267, no. 1 (July 1992): 17–22.

2. Ibid.

3. John D. Barrow and Frank L. Tipler, *The Anthropic Cosmological Principle* (Oxford: Oxford University Press, 1986), 410–412.

4. John Gribbin and Martin Rees, *Cosmic Coincidences* (New York: Bantam, 1989), 175–201.

5. Kathy Sawyer, "Calculating the Contents of the Cosmos," *Washington Post*, 30 April 2001.

6. This enigmatic "dark energy" is causing galaxies to rush apart at an ever-accelerating rate of speed.

7. Gribbin and Rees, *Cosmic Coincidences*, 92–93.

8. Barrow and Tipler, *Anthropic Cosmological Principle*, 376–379.

9. "Flatness" in this sense corresponds to a rate of cosmic expansion that just equals the inward pull of gravity.

10. Paul Davies, *The Accidental Universe* (New York: Cambridge University Press, 1982), 90.

11. Ibid.

12. Gribbin and Rees, *Cosmic Coincidences*, 26.

13. George Greenstein, *The Symbiotic Universe* (New York: Cambridge University Press, 1988), 134–135.

14. Ibid., 135.

15. John Gribbin, *The Omega Point* (New York: Bantam, 1988), 43.

16. Gribbin and Rees, *Cosmic Coincidences*, 53.

17. Gribbin, *Omega Point*, 139–140.

18. The Halo Conspiracy will probably remain insoluble in the absence of Intelligent Design, even if natural processes are eventually discovered that happen to mediate this particular effect in the universe, because in this case we would then need to find a sufficient explanation for these natural processes. The fecundity of natural processes thus does not eliminate the need for an Intelligent Designer in the universe.

19. James Trefil, *The Dark Side of the Universe* (New York: Doubleday, 1988), 90–91.

20. Sam Flamsteed, "Probing the Edge of the Universe," *Discover*, vol. 12, no. 7 (July 1991): 43–47.

21. Trefil, *Dark Side of the Universe*, 62.

22. Since everything in existence is infinitely complex in one way or another, it is highly unlikely that we will ever be able to reach a point where we can say that we understand everything there is to know.

23. Davies, *Accidental Universe*, 111.

24. Barrow and Tipler, *Anthropic Cosmological Principle*, 288.

25. Robert Jastrow, *God and the Astronomers* (New York: Warmer, 1978), 13–14.

26. This very fact alone seems to indicate the existence of an unseen Spiritual Power on the other side of the quantum "fence," who is regulating the existence of our physical universe through mechanisms that are totally beyond our comprehension at the present time.

27. The Standard Model of particle physics attempts to describe all known elementary particles and their interactions in terms of fields.

28. Larry Abbott, "The Mystery of the Cosmological Constant," *Scientific American*, vol. 3, no. 1 (1991): 78.

29. Hugh Ross, "Einstein Exonerated in Breakthrough Discovery," *Facts and Faith*, vol. 1, no. 3 (1999): 2–3.

30. Ibid.

31. Ibid.

32. Idit Zehavi and Avishai Dekel, "Evidence for a Positive Cosmological Constant from Flows of Galaxies and Distant Supernovae," *Nature*, vol. 401, no. 6750 (September 16, 1999).

33. Davies, *Accidental Universe*, 107.

34. Ibid., 73.

35. Ibid.

36. Davies, *Accidental Universe*, 62–64.

37. Ibid., 63–64.

38. Hugh Ross, *The Fingerprint of God* (Orange, Calif.: Promise Publishing, 1991), 123.

39. Ibid.

40. Davies, *Accidental Universe*, 61.

41. Ibid., 61–62.

42. Greenstein, *Symbiotic Universe*, 63–65.

43. Ross, *Fingerprint of God*, 123.

44. Barrow and Tipler, *Anthropic Cosmological Principle*, 303.

45. Ibid., 305.

46. Ross, *Fingerprint of God*, 125.

47. Barrow and Tipler, *Anthropic Cosmological Principle*, 289–305.

48. Davies, *Accidental Universe*, 77.

49. Gerald L. Schroeder, *Genesis and the Big Bang* (New York: Bantam, 1990), 119–120.

50. Greenstein, *Symbiotic Universe*, 95–97.

51. Hugh Ross, *Genesis One: A Scientific Perspective* (Sierra Madre, Calif.: Wisemen Productions, 1983), 6–7.

52. Ibid.

53. Ibid., 6.

54. Hugh Ross has estimated the odds for such a coordinated series of events to be far less than one in a billion (see Ross, *Genesis One*, 7).

55. Schroeder, *Genesis and the Big Bang*, 122–123.

56. Ibid., 122.

57. Ibid.

58. Owen Gingerich, "Modern Cosmogony and Biblical Creation," in *Is God a Creationist?*, ed. Roland Mushat Frye (New York: Scribner's, 1983), 132–133.

59. This is good news for aspiring actors and actresses who desperately want to become international stars. While they may never achieve this lofty goal here on earth, the surprising fact of the matter is that they have been star stuff all along!

60. Greenstein, *Symbiotic Universe*, 40.

61. Ross, *Fingerprint of God*, 126.

62. Carbon-12 is the normal, nonradioactive form of carbon that is used in most biochemical processes.

63. Gingerich, "Let There Be Light: Modern Cosmogony and Biblical Creation," in *Is God a Creationist?*, ed. Roland Mushat Frye (New York: Scribner's, 1983), 134.

64. Please refer to Errol E. Harris, *Cosmos and Anthropos* (Atlantic Highlands, N.J.: Humanities Press International, 1991), for an excellent philosophical analysis of functional holism and its relationship to the concept of design.

65. It is interesting to note that many of the physicists who write about these cosmic coincidences enclose the word "coincidence" in quotation marks, as I do. This would appear to signify the intuitive realization that these events are probably not coincidental after all.

66. Fred Hoyle, "The Universe: Past and Present Reflections," *Engineering and Science* (November 1981): 8–12.

67. Many theistic researchers believe that the famous Star of Bethlehem was actually a supernova explosion. On this view, the terrific brightness of this explosion was sufficient to guide the three wise men to the baby Jesus.

68. Davies, *Accidental Universe*, 68.

69. Ibid.

70. Gribbin and Rees, *Cosmic Coincidences*, 254.

CHAPTER NINE

~

More Evidence of Design

God never wrought miracle to convince atheism, because his ordinary works convince it.

—Francis Bacon

The Size of Our Goldilocks Universe

Another intriguing characteristic of the present cosmic order is the overall sparseness of matter in the universe, a property that was originally thought to represent evidence *against* deliberate design.[1] On this view, perpetrated by the philosopher Bertrand Russell, the vast reaches of uninhabitable emptiness in the universe couldn't possibly serve a constructive function for an Intelligent Designer; therefore, according to Russell, such a Being probably doesn't exist.

At first glance, this argument appears to be persuasive. If life really is important to a Grand Designer, then why would He put it on such a small "speck of dust" in such an unfathomably large and ancient universe? Moreover, as Russell has asked:

Why should the best things in the history of the world *such as life and mind* come late rather than early? Would not the reverse order have done just as well? . . . Before the Copernican revolution, it was natural to suppose that God's purposes were specially concerned with the Earth, but now this has become an unplausible hypothesis. If the purpose of the Cosmos is to evolve mind, we must regard it as rather incompetent in having produced so little in such a long time.[2]

Recent cosmological research, however, has yielded a fascinating explanation for this nagging problem. The universe is as big and old as it is because if it were any younger or smaller, it would have been incapable of producing any carbon-based life forms at all. There is a minimum cosmological time that it takes to produce a world where intelligent (and nonintelligent) life forms can develop through standard evolutionary pathways. These pathways are themselves divided into three separate cosmic epochs: (1) an initial stellar synthesis epoch, in which the heavier organic elements that are essential to life are synthesized deep within stellar interiors, over approximately 10 billion years of time; (2) an intermediate epoch, in which these heavy elements are spewed into space by huge supernova explosions, and are then allowed to crystallize into concrete solar systems; and (3) a final biosynthesis epoch, in which life gradually evolves into progressively more complex forms over billions of years of organic evolution.

When the minimum times for these major cosmic epochs are calculated, we find that the *minimum* age for the development of intelligent life is approximately 12–15 billion years, which is also the estimated age of our present universe! Ironically, then, when we take into account the universal expansion rate during this entire time period, we find that our incomprehensibly large universe is nevertheless the *smallest possible one* that would allow for the existence of life in this manner. It follows, then, that the vast reaches of empty space which characterize our present universe are *absolutely necessary* for the evolution and continued existence of all carbon-based life forms.

The upshot of this astonishing realization is that the immense size and age of the universe can no longer be used as evidence against a Grand Designer, for as we have just seen, ours is the smallest and youngest universe that could possibly produce life through natural evolutionary pathways. If anything, then, the size and age of the universe can be used as evidence *for*, and not against, the existence of a Grand Designer for the following reason. If the evolution of life were merely a random event, one would never expect it to happen just as soon as it possibly could. The random shuffling of atoms inherently requires an enormous amount of time to produce anything of value (if indeed such a thing can happen at all), so the random evolution of life would naturally be expected to take many billions of years *longer* than the minimum possible time frame for such a complex occurrence. Yet, life evolved just as soon as it possibly could on this planet, despite truly overwhelming odds to the contrary. Can we not see the Hand of God at work here, designing the universe in such a way as to facilitate the rise of life at the earliest possible moment?

The incredible sparseness of matter in the universe is also a necessary feature of our biocentric universe as well. This life-supporting function has to do with preserving the orbital integrity of planets like our own earth against potentially disturbing gravitational influences from other celestial bodies. Had the universe been any more compact, the immense gravitational power of wandering stars and other large gravitating objects would have jerked the earth out of its delicate orbit about the sun long before life ever got a chance to evolve here. This, of course, would have forever destroyed the life-supporting capacity of our planet.[3] Alternatively, had life been lucky enough to evolve here before the appearance of such a disturbing gravitational influence, it would have only been a matter of time until one would have come close enough to the earth to knock it out of its orbit about the sun.

Even worse, a wandering star could have come close enough to our own sun in a significantly smaller universe to become trapped by the sun's immense gravitational field. This would have quickly rendered the earth uninhabitable, either through a direct collision of the earth with the vagabond star, or through the severe climatic disruptions that would have inevitably resulted from the star's additional heat input. But even if the star's presence in our solar system didn't immediately exterminate all life here, it would have only been a matter of time until a collision between the wandering star and our own sun would have incinerated the entire solar system.

A collision between the two stars, however, wouldn't have to actually happen in order for all life on earth to be destroyed, nor would the earth have to be completely jerked out of its orbit by a wandering star in order for its entire ecosystem to be wiped out. These same ominous events would have also transpired if a distantly passing star succeeded in pulling the earth out of its nearly concentric orbit about the sun. We mustn't forget that the stability of the earth's climate is absolutely dependent on the reception of a near constant amount of heat energy from the sun. In order for this to occur, the earth must remain more or less the same distance from the sun at all times. This is "why" the earth's orbit is anomalously circular, when the orbits of most of the other planets in the solar system are elliptical—because a circular orbit ensures that the earth will be bathed in a more or less constant amount of heat energy from the sun.

The extreme sensitivity of the earth's ecosystem to the strength of incoming solar radiation is well illustrated by the seasonal variations in temperature that are caused by the earth's 23.27 degree tilt on its axis of rotation. This relatively small amount of tilt varies the angle, and hence the strength, of the sun's incoming rays sufficiently to alter the earth's surface temperature by as much as 175 degrees Fahrenheit in different regions, and this is while the earth's distance from the sun remains more or less constant. Given this extremely delicate balance of the earth's climate with its overall distance from the sun, it clearly would not take much of a change in this distance to render the earth either too hot or too cold to be able to support the delicate needs of life.

Thus, even if a wandering star were to pass within only a few million miles of our solar system, it would nevertheless be close enough to induce a significant change in the earth's orbital radius and hence in its climatic stability, and this would be enough to render the earth uninhabitable forevermore. Fortunately, though, due to the vast reaches of empty space throughout the cosmos, along with the fact that all stars are rapidly moving away from one another, it is exceedingly unlikely that any star will ever pass close enough to our planet to affect its orbital integrity. Indeed, the nearest star to our solar system, Proxima Centauri, is over four and a half light years away from us. It is this tremendous degree of sparseness in the universe that virtually guarantees that the earth's orbit will remain undisturbed by any passing stars for the remainder of our sun's lifetime, at which point *it* will be the sole cause of the earth's eventual demise. Fortunately for us, this point lies billions of years in the future.

We are also protected from the gravitational influences of distant stars by the fact that the gravitational force happens to vary by the inverse square of the distance between any two gravitating bodies. This means that the force of gravity declines sharply as the distance between gravitating objects is increased. Had this Inverse Square Law occupied another value, it is conceivable that we would have been much more susceptible to the gravitating influences of distant stars, with the result that our planet's orbital integrity would have been greatly jeopardized.

The fact that our universe exists in precisely three spatial dimensions further protects the orbital integrity of the earth in two separate ways: (1) the Inverse Square Law is only possible in a universe of precisely three spatial dimensions and (2) a three-dimensional universe provides the maximal degree of stability for all planetary orbits.

Now, how is it that the universe happens to exist in precisely the right number of spatial dimensions to guarantee the maximal degree of stability for all planetary orbits? How is it that the gravitational force between two bodies happens to vary at precisely the right rate to protect the orbital integrity of the earth from the disruptive gravitational effects of distant stars and galaxies? And how is it that our universe has precisely the right degree of sparseness to guarantee the earth's orbital integrity over the billions of years of life's gradual evolution? Of course, one could argue that these are just colossal cosmic coincidences, whose haphazard occurrence accidentally allowed life to evolve. However, this alternative "possibility" becomes more and more remote with each successive instance of fine-tuning that we are able to document in the universe.

The Specific Entropy of the Universe

All forms of work require the prior existence of a usable amount of energy before they can take place. Once work is performed, though, a less organized form of energy is dissipated back into the environment, where it is inherently less capable of performing additional work.

This difference in energy quality is known as entropy, and it refers to the amount of disorder or unusable energy that is present in a system. The *specific entropy* of a system is yet another thermodynamic property of an energy-containing system that refers to the rate of energy degradation within it. The higher the specific entropy of a system, the more efficient we can say it is at dissipating energy and vice versa. A candle, for instance, has a specific entropy of two, while the universe, by contrast, has a specific entropy of one billion, which is many orders of magnitude greater than any other known system. This simply means that the universe is very efficient at producing unusable quantities of heat energy, and this turns out to be very important for the existence of life. For had the specific entropy of the universe been any greater, it would have dissipated energy far too efficiently to have been compatible with the existence of life. On the other hand, had the specific entropy of the universe been much less, it would have trapped energy more efficiently and stars and galaxies would have never been able to form.

The upshot of this realization is that the specific entropy of the universe is *precisely* what it needs to be if carbon-based life forms are to be capable of existing on this planet. Not surprisingly, then, our very existence tells us that the specific gravity of the universe *must* be big enough to support the existence of life, otherwise we wouldn't be here. This of course is the Weak Anthropic Principle in its purest form, but such a tautologous explanation doesn't really do anything to explain *why* the universe has the specific entropy it does. It merely tells us that we couldn't possibly hope to observe another type of universe with a different specific entropy since there is no possible way that we could live in such a universe.

In order to find a sufficient explanation for the perfect specific entropy of our universe, then, we must resort to a more robust class of explanation, namely, that of the Strong Anthropic Principle, which states that the universe *must* be life-supporting at some stage in its history. The challenge here is to find out why this might be so.

Large Number Coincidences

One of the hallmarks of an intelligently designed system is the recurrence of the same numbers or equations in different areas of the system itself. For instance, electronic capacitors, which have the formula xyz, are used repeatedly throughout the electrical circuits that are designed by humans. In the same way, if the universe is indeed the product of Intelligent Design, we would expect to see the same numerical patterns exemplified throughout the creation.

And indeed we do. For as it turns out, the very large number 10^{40} can be found in several highly disparate areas of the physical realm. For instance, the number 10^{40} is mathematically related to the gravitational fine structure constant, the number of charged particles in the universe, the ratio between the Hubble time and the Planck time, the ratio between the proton's Compton wavelength and the Planck time, the ratio between the strengths of electrical and gravitational forces in a hydrogen atom, and the ratio between the present epoch and the time it takes light to travel across the proton's Compton wavelength.[4] It is also mathematically related to the weak fine structure constant, the cosmic photon/proton ratio, and both the number of stars in a galaxy and the number of galaxies in the universe. Given the extremely large magnitude of this number, there is no *a priori* reason why it should keep cropping up in so many different, and seemingly unrelated, branches of physics, that is, unless there is a deeper level of Intelligent Design at work in the universe than is superficially apparent.

The most famous of the large number coincidences was studied intently by the British physicist Paul Dirac, who noted how the age of the universe in nuclear units is very close to the square root of the number of particles in the universe and to the square of the ratio between the electrical and gravitational forces, all three of which are represented by that magic number 10^{40}. Of this mysterious relationship, Dirac wrote "Such a coincidence we may presume is due to some deep connexion in Nature between cosmology and atomic theory."[5]

The "anthropic" significance of this coincidence lies in the fact that the age of the universe is always changing. Therefore, our choice of the "present" epoch is clearly related to our own existence as observers.

That is to say, the fundamental question at issue here centers on why the age of the universe in nuclear units should be related numerically to both the number of particles in the universe and to the relative strengths of gravity and electromagnetism. Dirac attempted to explain this remarkable coincidence by suggesting that perhaps the gravitational constant may not really be a constant at all, but may always be changing, so that the strength of the gravitational constant will always be related to the overall age of the universe and to the overall number of particles in existence. There is, however, no evidence whatsoever that the value of the gravitational constant has ever varied from its present value throughout the entire history of the cosmos.

In 1961, the American physicist Robert Dicke proposed a novel solution for this cosmological curiosity. Dicke reasoned that the present cosmic epoch is itself intimately related to those larger cosmic processes that are themselves necessary for the existence of life. We know, for instance, that carbon-based life forms can only exist in a universe that is at least as old as one stellar generation, because carbon and the other heavy elements upon which life depends are actually *formed* within dying stars. Hence, we *can't help* but observe the present universal age, because it is the only one (within a few orders of magnitude) that is consistent with our own existence as observers. The present universal age, in turn, determines the number of particles that we can detect in the observable universe, due to the ongoing expansion of the universe and the subsequent widening of the particle horizon.[6] Hence, the number of particles in the observable universe is in fact related to the age of the universe, which itself is determined by the necessity that it be consistent with our own existence as observers.

Furthermore, the ratio of the electrical force to the gravitational force inside the hydrogen atom has a direct influence on the lifetime of stars.[7] This, in turn, is related to the present age of the universe, which is approximately equal to the lifetime of a typical star (due to the need for carbon, which is dispersed when dying stars explode as supernovae). Hence, all three aspects of Dirac's large number coincidence—the present age of the universe, the relative strengths of gravity and electromagnetism, and the number of particles in the universe—can be "explained" by the requirement that they be consistent with our own existence as observers.

The significance of Dicke's explanation lies in the fact that "a *biological* explanation of a fundamental feature of our world has succeeded where theoretical physics has failed."[8] Although Dicke was unable to explain all of the large number coincidences, he nevertheless succeeded in showing that the existence of life on earth cannot be considered to be unrelated to the structure of the universe as a whole.

The "Just Right" Nature of Carbon, Nitrogen, and Phosphorous

Carbon is uniquely qualified to be the structural backbone upon which the biochemistry of life can be based. Being situated in the first row of the Periodic

Table, carbon is able to form multiple bonds extensively with its four available outer-level electrons. This gives it the structural flexibility that is so important in the building of complex biochemical structures which are essential for life.

Carbon is required in a wide range of biological processes. For instance, carbon is a major ingredient of carbon dioxide, which is one of the most important organic compounds in the biosphere. Since carbon dioxide is both an essential nutrient for plant photosynthesis and one of the most important products of cellular respiration, it provides a continuously renewable form of energy that is completely recyclable. The importance of this one feature should not be underestimated, for it is what has enabled our world to remain viable for billions of years, in spite of the constant production of vast quantities of organic waste.

Carbon dioxide is able to serve a variety of important biological roles because of its ingenious structural configuration, which enables it to experience very little attraction to other carbon dioxide molecules. This allows carbon dioxide to be a gas within the range of temperatures that can support biological life. This is important, because it allows carbon dioxide—which is the final waste product of animal metabolism—to be removed from the body quite easily.

Moreover, carbon dioxide is unique among all known compounds in the fact that its concentration in air is essentially the same as its concentration in water. This allows carbon dioxide to freely move from air to water and from water to air, another property that makes the removal of carbon dioxide from the body (via the blood) relatively easy.

Carbon dioxide also has the marvelous ability to react with water in the body to form carbonic acid, which can then be broken down to form carbonate and bicarbonate. This allows carbon dioxide to act as a powerful acid (or pH) regulator within the body, since both bicarbonate and carbonate can neutralize excess acidity in the blood quite effectively.

Carbon dioxide's life-supporting role even extends beyond its many activities in supporting animal metabolism. As Barrow and Tipler point out, carbon dioxide also plays a critical role in maintaining the earth's surface temperature within a range that is favorable for life. It is able to do this because it acts as a barrier to prevent heat from escaping from the earth's surface. This "greenhouse effect" raises the earth's surface temperature tens of degrees higher than it otherwise would have been.[9]

Some have argued that silicon, being positioned just below carbon on the Periodic Table, could possibly have taken carbon's place as the backbone of organic chemistry. Recent work by Sidgwick and others, however, has shown that this is unlikely.[10] For one thing, silicon is unable to form double bonds like carbon can, and double bonds are absolutely essential to any form of complex biochemistry. Silicon compounds are also not nearly as stable over time as carbon compounds are. The unusual stability of carbon encourages the formation of long molecular chains, which play an important role in the maintenance of life.

Moreover, the heat of formation for carbon compounds is typically quite small, which means that the amount of energy that is needed to promote a reaction between carbon and other elements also tends to be small. This enables many carbon compounds to form spontaneously, a feature that is crucial to the spontaneous evolution of life as well as to the support and maintenance of normal body metabolism.

Carbon is also blessed with the ability to store a maximal amount of information in its various compounds, due to its capacity to form a wider variety of compounds than almost any other element. As Barrow and Tipler point out, it is the information-carrying capacity of living organisms, which is made possible by this unique property of carbon, that defines them as "living." Consequently, carbon compounds are now recognized to be "uniquely fitted to serve as the basis of life."[11]

However, carbon isn't alone in this vital life-supporting capacity. Nitrogen is also extremely important in the formation and maintenance of life, because it is a defining component of the various amino acids and proteins that make life possible. It is also a fundamental ingredient in the nitrogenous bases that comprise the all-important genetic code. It is the unique structure of the nitrogen molecule that enables it to be so effectively utilized by both proteins and nucleic acids. No other element could possibly take its place, and indeed, if the molecular properties of nitrogen were only slightly different, proteins and nucleic acids could never have formed.

The same thing can be said of phosphorous compounds, which are utilized extensively by the cellular machinery of the body to produce energy through the breaking of high-energy bonds. Adenosine triphosphate, or ATP, is the central energy producer of the cell. It releases energy when its high-energy phosphate bonds are broken; this energy then goes into the driving of other important life-supporting reactions.

Interestingly, the cell is unable to directly utilize the energy that is produced when sugars are oxidized, because too much energy is typically produced to be directly utilized by the cell. However, by harnessing this energy in the form of high-energy phosphate bonds, it becomes much more available over the long term for the cell's constant energy needs.

Water—The Ultimate Goldilocks Compound

Although the existence of ordinary water is indispensable for the sustenance of life, most people tend to take it for granted. From a molecular and biochemical standpoint, however, the various properties of water are nothing short of miraculous, as no other compound even comes close to duplicating its many life-supporting properties. Indeed, if it weren't for these unique and anomalous properties of water, life as we know it would be absolutely impossible.

The unique properties of water immediately set it apart from all other similar hydride compounds. For instance, if the boiling points of all compounds similar to water are graphed as a function of their atomic weight, a simple extrapolation to the expected boiling point of water would produce a temperature of −100 degrees Celsius. This, of course, is 200 degrees less than water's actual boiling point of +100 degrees Celsius. If water did not have such a high boiling point, life as we know it would be impossible. It is this particular property, for instance, that enables water to be the most effective coolant by evaporation ever discovered. Animals naturally exploit this unique property through the process of sweating.

However, when we analyze the various water-like hydride compounds, we instantly see that water is an isolated and special substance that does not reflect the properties of other similar compounds, as we would naturally expect if an Intelligent Power didn't specifically design the realm of organic chemistry. Thus, the anomalous character of water can be seen to be related to its capacity to support life and it is this relationship that seems to point decisively in the direction of Intelligent Design.

Of course, there is a structural explanation for water's anomalously high boiling point. It has to do with the electrochemically unbalanced structure of the water molecule itself, which in turn is related to the asymmetrical way the water molecule is constructed. On one side of this "polar" molecule lies an oxygen atom, while on the other side two hydrogen atoms exist. This results in one side of the water molecule being more electronegative than the other, and vice versa. This electrochemical polarity enables the positive end of one water molecule to be attracted to the negative end of an adjacent molecule. It is this process of "hydrogen bonding" that produces the anomalously high boiling point of water, since the additional attractive force between water molecules that is produced by hydrogen bonding must be overcome before the actual boiling point can be reached.

However, water has other anomalous properties that are just as amazing. It is the only known substance, for instance, whose solid phase (ice) is less dense than its liquid phase. This is why ice floats in water. The advantage of this strange property is that it has prevented the earth's oceans and lakes from freezing over, since ice now forms at the top of these bodies of water instead of at the bottom, which in turn allows it to melt away during the summer. This process also protects marine life from additional cooling.

Water also has an unusually high specific heat, higher in fact than almost all other organic compounds. The specific heat of a substance is the amount of heat that is required to raise its temperature one degree Celsius. Having such a high specific heat enables water to retain heat longer, which in turn helps to stabilize the temperature of the global environment. The fact that water also has a higher thermal conductivity than the majority of other liquids also makes it an optimal temperature stabilizer for the environment as well.

Water also has an unusually high surface tension, which causes certain compounds to aggregate near the surface. This, in turn, enables biochemical reactions to proceed at a much faster rate than would have otherwise been the case. Indeed, were it not for this one property of water, existing rates of metabolism in living organisms would be impossible to maintain for very long.

Another anomalous feature of water is its unusually high dielectric constant, which is a measure of a substance's ability to dissolve ionic compounds into their respective ions. It is water's anomalously high dielectric constant that enables it to dissolve salt and other ionic substances so easily.

Water's high dielectric constant also allows it to spontaneously ionize itself into its constituent hydrogen and hydroxide ions; indeed, at any one time, 10^{-7} water molecules are dissociated because of this constant. This effect is exceedingly important in biochemical reactions since it furnishes a ready supply of the hydrogen and hydroxide ions upon which so many reactions depend. This, in turn, has the effect of greatly speeding up reaction rates in living organisms.

Water molecules also exhibit an important characteristic known as the *hydrophobic* (or water-repelling) effect, again because of water's unique molecular structure. It is this hydrophobic effect that gives water the unique ability to shape proteins and nucleic acids into their biologically active configurations. Without this shaping effect, the enzymes upon which life depends could not function properly because their biochemical activity is directly elicited by their three-dimensional configurations in space.

Another important result of this hydrophobic effect is that it seems to have played an important role in the formation of cell walls and cell membranes. Water has the ability to cause the nonpolar ends of molecules to aggregate together, which happens to be the first step in the formation of cell walls and membranes. Indeed, the origin of life itself seems to have been dependent on this hydrophobic characteristic of water, since the initial primordial cell could not have formed without first having a cell wall to protect it and to differentiate it from the rest of the world.

Given the absolute dependence of life on the water molecule's many anomalous properties, where did the structure of the water molecule itself ultimately come from? Science itself is unable to provide an adequate answer to this question. However, since life is absolutely dependent on water's many anomalous properties, and since water stands alone in this life-supporting capacity, it seems to follow that the water molecule was probably designed on purpose to be the medium through which life could evolve and sustain itself.

The alternative view, of course, is that water first existed by chance and that life later evolved to take advantage of it. However, it is the water molecule's many *anomalous* properties that seem to legislate decisively against this possibility. For if water's molecular properties were truly the result of chance alone, we would naturally expect it to be qualitatively similar to other natural substances of similar structure and atomic weight. But this isn't the case at all, for as we have seen, water is absolutely unique in terms of its ability to support the life process. And since it is the water molecule's many anomalous features that turn out to be crucial to the well-being of life on earth, it seems to follow that the water molecule was somehow engineered with this one important biocentric effect "in Mind."

The great Harvard biochemist Lawrence J. Henderson was one of the first scientists to recognize the many biocentric properties of "ordinary" matter. Working in the early 1900s, Henderson came to the momentous conclusion that the specific properties of matter seem to be a kind of teleological "preparation" for the existence of life. For Henderson, the traditional notion of chance as an explanation for these seemingly tailor-made properties was simply untenable:

> The chance that this unique ensemble of properties should occur by "accident" is almost infinitely small. The chance that each of the unit properties of the ensemble, by itself and in cooperation with the others, should "accidentally" contribute a maximum increment is also almost infinitely small. Therefore, there is a relevant causal connection between the properties of the elements and the "freedom" of evolution.[12]

Henderson went even further. He argued that the absolute dependence of biological life on the physical properties of matter is strongly indicative of the existence of a biocentric universe:

The properties of matter and the course of cosmic evolution are now seen to be intimately related to the structure of the living being and to its activities; they become, therefore, far more important in biology than has previously been suspected. For the whole evolutionary process, both cosmic and organic, is one, and the biologist may now rightly regard the universe in its very essence as biocentric.[13]

Henderson thus came very close to crediting an Intelligent Designer for the creation of this biocentricity. This is remarkable, given his professional status as a respected physical scientist.

Indeed, given the many complex physical properties that are required by living systems, it is hard to escape the notion that atoms and molecules have the chemical properties they do because of the unique requirements of biological life. Atheistic scientists, however, simply believe that our particular type of matter just happened to exist in the universe purely by accident. On this view, biological life naturally evolved to take advantage of the "natural" properties of matter. But what are the odds that undesigned atoms and molecules could have accidentally fulfilled all of the many complex requirements for life? If there were truly an accidental relationship at work here, we would perhaps expect that *some* of the properties of matter would have been sufficient for the development of life, but certainly not *all* of them. Moreover, it is a well-known assumption in the scientific community that had the properties of matter been significantly different, life almost certainly would have never been able to arise here. This again appears to point decisively in the direction of Intelligent Design.

A Goldilocks World

In *Other Worlds*, physicist Paul Davies[14] cites seven essential prerequisites that must be satisfied if life is to be capable of existing on this planet:

1. There must be an adequate supply of the elements that comprise our bodies, such as carbon, oxygen, hydrogen, phosphorus, and calcium.
2. There must be little or no risk of contamination by other poisonous chemicals, such as would be found in an atmosphere of methane or ammonia.
3. The climatic temperature must remain within the narrow range of 5 to 40 degrees Centigrade, which is a mere 2 percent of the temperature range found within the solar system as a whole.
4. A stable supply of free energy must exist, which in our case is provided by the sun.

5. Gravity must be strong enough to keep the atmosphere from escaping into space, but it must also be weak enough to enable us to move freely about on the earth's surface.
6. A protective screen must exist to filter out the sun's harmful ultraviolet rays, which in our case is provided by a delicate layer of ozone in the upper atmosphere.
7. A magnetic field must exist in order to prevent cosmic subatomic particles from raining on the earth.

There are a number of additional prerequisites that must also be satisfied if life is to be capable of existing here. For one thing, the earth's orbit about the sun must be very nearly circular if the earth is to have a climate that is hospitable to life. As it stands now, the earth's orbit about the sun is nearly circular, varying by only a relatively small 3 percent.[15] In this respect the geometry of the earth's orbital trajectory is quite anomalous, since the orbits of most of the other planets in our solar system are much more elliptical in nature. Mars, for instance, varies in its distance from the sun by a whopping 50 million kilometers, as compared to a variance of only 4.5 million kilometers for the earth.[16] If the earth's orbital trajectory were to experience this degree of change, everything on the surface of the earth would be incinerated once a year (during January, when the earth is closest to the sun). Indeed, as Schroeder points out, if our distance from the sun were only 7 percent less, the atmosphere would be so hot that water vapor would be incapable of condensing.[17] Oceans, lakes—and ultimately people—would be nonexistent in such a world.

In order to be capable of supporting biological life, then, the earth must be close enough to the sun to be bathed in a sufficient degree of warmth, yet it can't be *too* close, otherwise it would be bombarded with an excessive amount of life-destroying ultraviolet radiation from the sun.[18] Indeed, even at its current distance from the sun, too much ultraviolet radiation exists to allow for the flourishing of life without an additional means of protection. Fortunately for earth-based life, this extra protection exists in the form of an ozone layer high in the atmosphere.

Other forms of deadly cosmic radiation are deflected from the earth's surface by a powerful magnetic field, which is generated by the motion of molten iron deep in our planet's seething radioactive interior. A precise balance of this radioactivity is absolutely essential if life is to be capable of surviving here.[19] On the one hand, it is the heat generated by this radioactivity that is ultimately responsible for producing the earth's magnetic field (by causing the earth's iron core to remain fluid enough to flow). On the other hand, an excessive amount of radioactivity would render the surface of the earth uninhabitable, as it was some 4.5 billion years ago.

The severity of volcanic activity on the earth is also vitally important for the existence of life.[20] Too little volcanic activity and there wouldn't have been enough water liberated by volcanic explosions to fill the world's oceans, lakes, and rivers. (Liquid water is thought to have originated when water dissolved in molten rock escaped into the atmosphere in the form of steam during volcanic eruptions.)

Volcanoes are also known to be an important factor in the maintenance of a suitable atmospheric temperature for life through the much-talked-about greenhouse effect. Volcanoes are now recognized[21] to be a significant source of atmospheric carbon dioxide, which is an important greenhouse gas (since it enables the earth's atmosphere to trap sufficient quantities of solar radiation to significantly increase its surface temperature). Without this additional input of carbon dioxide from volcanoes, there probably wouldn't have been enough carbon dioxide in the earth's atmosphere to maintain a life-supporting range of environmental temperatures.

Too much volcanic activity, on the other hand, and the earth's surface would have been too violent and unstable to support the gradual evolution of life; it also would have caused the earth's atmosphere to be so dark and sooty that a nuclear-type winter would have ensued.

A similar degree of balance exists in the amount of seismic activity found on the earth. A certain amount must exist so that nutrients that have been channeled to ocean floors through river runoff can be recycled to the continents through a phenomenon known as tectonic uplift.[22] Yet, too much seismic activity would spell catastrophe for many forms of life, so it appears as though the earth possesses just the right degree of seismic activity to make it a viable place for biological habitation.

Hugh Ross documents the existence of several other finely tuned parameters which strictly limit the capacity of our planet to support life. For instance, if our solar system contained more than one star (which many systems do), tidal effects would severely disrupt the earth's orbit, rendering it either too hot or too cold to support life.[23]

The sun's date of birth and overall age are also intimately related to the earth's capacity to support life. If the sun were significantly younger, it wouldn't have had time to reach a stable burning phase, which means that its luminosity would have been subject to a life-devastating change in the future. On the other hand, if the sun were significantly older, its luminosity would have either been subject to changing too quickly, or else it would have been in danger of running out of fuel and completely burning out.[24] Indeed,

Brandon Carter has shown that the lifetime of G-type stars like our sun provides a clearly defined upper bound on the length of time life can evolve on a planet.

The strength of the earth's surface gravity, which in turn is directly related to the earth's size and mass, is also very finely balanced between two competing extremes. On the one hand, the earth must be sufficiently large to ensure that a life-supporting atmosphere of oxygen, nitrogen, carbon dioxide, and water vapor is gravitationally bound to the planet's surface.[25] On the other hand, the earth mustn't be too large, because the resulting increase in the pull of gravity would have caused the atmosphere to retain too much poisonous ammonia and methane to have been conducive to life.[26] It would have also generated destructive tidal effects in living bodies.[27] Moreover, a significantly larger earth would have generated too much internal heat to have been compatible with the fragile needs of life.[28]

The earth's degree of axial tilt is also an important part of the biocentric equation, for if it were greater or less, surface temperature differences on the earth's surface would have been too extreme to support the existence of life.[29]

Similarly, the earth's period of rotation is also subject to a strict upper and lower bound if it is to be hospitable to life. A longer rotational period would have generated diurnal temperature differences that would have been too great, whereas a shorter rotational period would have caused atmospheric wind velocities to be too extreme.[30]

The earth's gravitational interaction with the moon is also very delicately balanced as far as life is concerned. If it were any greater, the resulting tidal effects on the earth's atmosphere, oceans, and rotational period would have been too great. Yet, if it were less, orbital obliquity changes would have caused severe climatic instabilities throughout the earth's various ecosystems.[31]

Even the thickness of the earth's crust is related to its capacity for supporting life. A thicker crust would have caused too much oxygen to be transferred from the atmosphere to the crust, whereas a thinner crust would have caused volcanic and tectonic activity to be too frequent and too violent for the fragile needs of living organisms.[32]

The albedo parameter—which compares the amount of light reflected off the earth to the amount falling on the earth's surface—is also vitally important for the needs of life. If it were much greater, a runaway ice age would have developed in the past, but if it were much less, a runaway greenhouse effect would have occurred.[33] Either way, life would have never been able to exist here.

The oxygen to nitrogen ratio in the atmosphere is also important for life, for had it been much greater, advanced life functions would have transpired too quickly. On the other hand, had it been much less, these same biochemical functions would have transpired too slowly for the needs of life.[34]

A similar degree of balance exists in the combined amount of carbon dioxide and water vapor in the earth's atmosphere. If it were much greater, a runaway greenhouse effect would have developed sometime in the past, but if it were much less, there wouldn't have been *enough* of a greenhouse effect to keep our planet sufficiently warm for the evolution of life.[35]

The amount of oxygen in the atmosphere also appears to be optimal for the existence of life. Had it been much greater, plants and other combustible materials would have burned too easily, but had it been less, animals wouldn't have had enough oxygen to breathe.[36]

The same thing can be said of the amount of ozone in the atmosphere. Had it been much greater, the earth's surface temperature would have been too low. On the other hand, had it been significantly less, the earth's surface temperature would have been too high, and there would have been too much harmful ultraviolet radiation at the surface.[37]

Even the atmospheric discharge rate appears to have been fine-tuned for the benefit of life. Had it been any greater, terrestrial fires would have started much too easily. Yet, had it been significantly less, an insufficient quantity of nitrogen would have been fixed in the atmosphere to have been conducive to life.[38]

And then there are the extraordinarily complex recycling mechanisms that the earth uses to convert waste products into usable forms of matter and energy. Thousands of exceedingly complex structures and mechanisms are known to cooperate with one another so that no unrecyclable forms of waste are ever produced anywhere in the world (except by humans). This has enabled the earth to be maintained in its precious life-supporting mode for millions of years.

By contrast, we humans excel at producing unrecyclable waste products. Despite the many impressive technological achievements of the twentieth century, we are still producing trillions of tons of unrecyclable toxic waste every year, and there doesn't appear to be any realistic solution to this problem in sight.

This brings to mind a very interesting question. Why is it that the earth has been able to successfully recycle *all* of its toxic waste products over the millennia, but *we* cannot? One would think that if the earth's ecosystem had truly evolved by chance alone, it would never have been able to reach this extreme level of technological sophistication. But it has, and not even our most brilliant engineers have been able to come close to duplicating this perfect level of recycling efficiency.

Put another way, why should a mindless evolutionary process succeed where intelligent humans have repeatedly failed? It doesn't help to say that our world couldn't have survived to the present day without such a high degree of recycling efficiency. For while this may be so, it doesn't explain *why* it is so. This is the chief difficulty behind all theories of natural selection, for while the selective process may explain why certain forms and structures have been able to survive to the present day, it doesn't explain *where* this initial survival capacity *itself* originally came from. For this we have to look somewhere deeper.

This is why all nontheistic evolutionary theories are ultimately unsatisfactory, because natural selection is only capable of explaining the process of differential survival amongst self-replicating species; it can't explain where the initial capacity for self-replication *itself* originally came from. Evolutionists thus beg the true question that is at issue here when they try to explain our current existence by means of natural selection. For while the selective process may help to explain why certain groups, and not others, have been able to survive the test of time, it doesn't tell us a thing about where the original survival capacities *themselves* originally came from. For this we have to look somewhere else—to a creative power that is entirely capable of producing self-replicating objects like living organisms.

Nevertheless, many nontheistic evolutionists insist on crediting natural selection for bringing about the phenomenon of life, despite the severe *category mistake* that is involved in this line of reasoning. They routinely mistake one category of explanation, namely, that of differing survival rates amongst self-replicating objects, for a very different category of explanation, which concerns the original generation of self-replicating properties. These two categories of explanation are both ontologically and causally distinct from one another, so there is very little, if any, realistic chance that the first category of explanation could ever substitute for the second. Nevertheless, many nontheistic evolutionists still spend their entire careers trying to do this very thing.

This is an important point that can perhaps be better illustrated by means of an analogy with automobiles. It is a well-known fact that certain car models are able to survive the test of time in the marketplace from year to year, while others are not. The models that are "lucky" enough to survive do so because they fulfill a dual criterion of fitness: they are popular with the public and they are profitable for the parent company.

However, it would be ludicrous to suppose that this popularity and profitability somehow explains the ultimate origin of the various car models themselves. For while it may be true that corporate executives are aiming for maximum profitability when they initially choose to take certain car models to market, the existence of this financial goal still does not explain the ultimate origin of the car models themselves. For this, we have to look beyond the dual intentions of popularity and profitability to the tremendous *ingenuity* of the automobile designers and engineers.

In the same way, the fact that certain groups of living creatures can survive better than others in the wild doesn't explain where this original capacity for survival *itself* came from. For this, we have to look beyond the selective process to an underlying Creative Power that is sufficient to the task.

Nontheistic evolutionists, however, do not believe this. They are instead convinced that the self-replicating process could have come into being by pure chance in the form of a relatively simple primeval replicator. Over time, they believe that these simple chemical replicators could have accidentally developed into increasingly complex forms, primarily through the agency of natural selection acting upon random variations. Eventually, these successful variants are thought to have developed into plants, animals, and ultimately people.

Significantly, the overall trajectory that has been traced out by the evolutionary process has consistently been in the direction of increasingly greater levels of organic complexity. While the ascent of each major zoological group is known to have taken place through a highly contingent process of repeated fits and starts, the overall trend has nevertheless been toward increasingly greater levels of organic complexity. An analogy can be drawn here with the stock market. In the same way that the Dow Jones Industrial Average can trend upwards in spite of short-term setbacks in the individual stocks themselves, the overall trend of life on this planet, at least as far as biological complexity is concerned, has been upwards.

This trend is so pronounced that Paul Davies has actually defined a new arrow of time in terms of it.[39] As far as Davies is concerned, standard evolutionary theory is incapable of explaining the origin of this trend, because it defines success solely in terms of differential reproduction; the more offspring a species leaves behind, the more successful it is thought to be. However, this definition makes the myriad members of the microbial world the most successful species of all, since they leave behind by far the most offspring. Nevertheless, this unprecedented rate of reproductive success in the various bacterial lines has *not* been accompanied by any significant increase in evolutionary complexity, since most microbes today remain essentially unchanged from prehistoric times. Therefore, according to Davies, reproductive success alone cannot account for the existence of biological complexity as such.[40]

Evidently, another mechanism, intrinsic to the organic replicators themselves, must have been at work fueling the rise toward progressively greater levels of complexity. Natural selection in this case would have functioned in a *secondary* capacity to this internal drive, amplifying and refining it, but in no case substituting for it.

It isn't difficult to see that a replicator's ability to stand the test of time cannot in itself account for this gradual progression toward greater levels of organic complexity. For as Davies has pointed out, just because a replicator's internal degree of complexity enables it to survive the test of time without contradiction to the Second Law of Thermodynamics doesn't mean that its complexity is *explained* by its ability to survive.[41] Freedom from the constraining influences of the Second Law cannot explain why this trend toward greater complexity occurs in the first place:

> Biosystems are not closed systems. They are characterized by their very openness, which enables them to export entropy into their environment to prevent degeneration. But the fact that they are able to evade the degenerative (pessimistic) arrow of time does not explain how they comply with the progressive (optimistic) arrow. Freeing a system from the strictures of one law does not prove that it follows another.
>
> Many biologists make this mistake. They assume because they have discovered the above loophole in the second law, the progressive nature of biological evolution is explained. This is simply incorrect. It also confuses order with organization and complexity. Preventing a decrease in order might be a necessary condition for the growth of organization and complexity, but it is not a sufficient condition. We still have to find that elusive arrow of time.[42]

Davies' identification of the arrow of time with this trend toward greater organic complexity elevates this trend to the level of a *fundamental cosmic principle*. But how could this trend have ever reached the status of a bona fide cosmic principle if it were merely the result of the differential process of survival? Such a "possibility" seems very remote indeed, because something much more direct and fundamental seems to be necessary for that.

Indeed, if natural selection alone were the sole arbiter of this trend toward greater complexity, life probably would have never evolved to begin with because natural selection in all likelihood would have never had anything to select *from*. We mustn't forget that the phenomenon of self-replication is *itself* a fairly sophisticated property, which inherently requires a substantial level of complexity in order to be operational. But if there is no drive toward self-organization inherent in matter, then the property of self-replication probably would have never come into being in the first place, and we would not be here.

In other words, the process of natural selection *presupposes* a significant degree of self-organization in matter. This is due to the fact that the only objects that natural selection can possibly select from are self-replicators, and self-replication is a sophisticated form of complexity that requires the prior existence of self-organizing atoms and molecules. Hence, natural selection in all probability could not have been responsible for generating the property of self-replication, since natural selection couldn't possibly have taken place before self-replication ever existed.

It follows, then, that the twin properties of self-organization and self-replication are necessarily *prior* to the property of being subject to natural selection, which in turn means that there *had* to have been a sufficient cause for matter to have originally become self-replicating in the first place; otherwise, natural selection almost certainly would have never had anything to select *from*. This sufficient cause was in all likelihood a self-organizing drive internal to matter, because chance processes alone do not seem to be capable of generating the extreme degree of quantum sophistication that is required for even the simplest structures to be self-replicating.

This argument can be reduced to the following:

1. Matter must be self-replicating before natural selection can act upon it.
2. Self-replication is a highly sophisticated property that requires an impressive level of material complexity in order to be operational.
3. If no tendency toward greater levels of complexity is intrinsic to matter, then the property of self-replication in all likelihood would have never evolved, because chance processes alone are inherently incapable of generating this critical degree of subatomic order (which necessarily includes both the Pauli Exclusion Principle and the Principle of Quantization).
4. This in turn means that matter would have almost certainly remained in the simplest form possible.
5. The simplest conceivable forms of matter are not self-replicating by their very nature, because of (2). Furthermore, the simplest forms of matter are known to be *incapable* of self-replication.
6. Therefore, even the simplest forms of self-replication require the prior existence of an impressive level of material complexity.
7. Natural selection can only act upon matter that possesses a certain minimum level of complexity, which is the level that would enable it to be self-replicating.

8. It is next to impossible for natural selection alone to have initially created this extreme level of material complexity because prior to this point, matter *could not* have been self-replicating by definition, since there would have been nothing for natural selection to select from.

9. If no tendency toward greater levels of complexity exists in matter, and if natural selection can only operate upon substantially complex self-replicators, it follows that matter should exist in its simplest form only, which, by virtue of its very simplicity, is not subject to natural selection because it is not self-replicating.

10. Natural selection, however, is a fact.

11. Therefore, something internal to matter must have caused it to become complex enough to become self-replicating, because chance processes alone do not seem to be capable of generating the extreme level of material complexity that is required for the process of self-replication to become actual.

The only way the nontheistic evolutionist can escape from this bind is to assert that matter could have *accidentally* acquired the property of self-replication with no outside help. However, it is very hard to see how this could have ever been the case, especially if it is asserted that no natural tendency toward self-organization exists in matter (apart from the action of natural selection) and if it is further acknowledged that natural selection is nonfunctional at this simple level of organization. Davies agrees:

> Since the work of Boltzmann, physicists have appreciated that microscopic random shuffling does not alone possess the power to generate an arrow of time, because of the underlying time symmetry of the microscopic laws of motion. On its own, random shuffling merely produces what might be called stochastic drift with no coherent directionality. The biological significance of this has recently been recognized by the Japanese biologist Kimura who has coined the phrase "neutral evolution" to describe such directionless drift.[43]

Implicit in the above argument is the assumption that even the simplest self-replicators require an underlying degree of fidelity and stability at the subatomic level before they can be actual. For without a stable subatomic foundation to rely on, no coherent self-replicators could possibly exist for more than a few seconds. The first structural prerequisite for this stability, as we have seen, is the Pauli Exclusion Principle. If this inordinately complex Exclusion Principle did not apply, all electrons would occupy the lowest quantum state, since it is the orbital with the lowest energy. And this, in turn, would eventually result in the spontaneous collapse of the entire atomic structure into a single particle of enormous density, thus destroying any further possibility for self-replication to become actual.

The second stabilizing force at the subatomic level is the quantization of electronic energy levels. Electrons can only exist at discrete levels about the nucleus, as we have seen, and it is this quantum nature that allows for all atoms of a particular atomic number and weight to be both identical and stable in the face of a continual bombardment of energy from the outside world. In a nonquantum atom, electrons could possess all possible energy states and therefore all possible orbital distances from the nucleus. This would render all atoms different from one another, and it would also allow electrons to continually change their energy levels in response to the slightest amount of incoming energy. And this, in turn, would make a given atom's chemical properties subject to change at a moment's notice, thereby making any stable form of self-replication absolutely impossible. Fortunately, the existence of discrete quantum states greatly stabilizes each individual atom, because an entire quantum of energy is needed to alter a given electron's particular energy level.[44]

In order for atoms and molecules to have accidentally stumbled upon the property of self-replication, then, the atom first had to have discovered a reliable means of employing the Pauli Exclusion Principle within itself, and second, it had to have discovered a means of operating in a quantum fashion only. It is unlikely to the highest degree that atoms and molecules could have accidentally stumbled upon these two discoveries by chance alone, again due to their overwhelmingly complex internal nature. Indeed, these stabilization mechanisms are so profoundly complex that we humans haven't even *begun* to understand how they actually operate at the subatomic level. Consequently, if these two properties are so complex that our best minds continue to be baffled by them, then mindless natural processes almost certainly would have never been able to discover a means of employing them purely by accident. And this, in turn, means that matter in all likelihood did not acquire the twin properties of self-organization and self-replication by chance alone.

The Rapidity of Life's Evolution

According to nontheistic scientists, life was only able to evolve on this planet after a long series of chance molecular combinations happened to produce the right organizational structures for life. This assumption is based upon the belief that the trial-and-error networking of a vast number of molecules will eventually produce a living cell. Like a thief who tries to open a lock by first attempting to go through all possible numerical combinations, so too is the nontheistic scientist convinced that life could have accidentally evolved by eventually stumbling upon the "right" biochemical configuration of particles. Hence, for the incredible complexity of even the "simplest" living cell to become actual, many billions of years of chance rearrangements had to have first transpired before life could have ever had a chance of getting off the ground.

The historical fact of life's evolution, however, is totally at odds with this nontheistic belief. For instead of taking billions of years to evolve, the first living cell came into being just as soon as it possibly could, when the newly formed earth became cool enough to support it.[45] This is perhaps the most significant "coincidence" of them all, and it is very much at odds with the predictions of nontheistic evolutionary theory. For if life evolved just as soon as it possibly could, then chance processes alone, which inherently require vast amounts of time, could never have produced it.[46] If, on the other hand, the universe were intelligently designed after all, we would naturally expect life to have evolved just as soon as it possibly could. And since this is precisely what happened, the theistic explanation for the origin of life is to be preferred over the nontheistic explanation, since it is the one that is most consistent with the available evidence.

The nontheistic evolutionist, of course, is at a complete loss to explain how life could have arisen so quickly on this planet. Since random concatenations of order inherently take vast amounts of time, she cannot fall back on the "cosmic accident hypothesis" to explain the origin of life, so she really has little choice but to "abandon ship" and look for a better solution.

The Fifth Miracle

In his book *The Fifth Miracle*, Paul Davies posits an internal drive in matter that makes the evolution of life virtually inevitable, given the right conditions.[47] This hypothesis has the great advantage of being totally consistent with all of the known facts surrounding the appearance of life, but it begs a much deeper question that is really at issue here. For if atoms and molecules do indeed possess such a profound degree of fecundity, we must then ask ourselves where they obtained this marvelous quality to begin with.

As far as the Theistic Evolutionist is concerned, this amazing property was somehow designed into matter at some point in the past by the creative Hand of God Himself. And while this may seem like just another God of the gaps "cop-out," it really isn't, for the following reason: the metaphysical "buck" has to stop *somewhere* in our cosmological past, otherwise we'd have an endless series of question-begging causes and nonexplanations to contend with. It is at this hypothetical point that we can properly invoke the activity of an Intelligent Designer without being guilty of resorting to yet another empty God of the gaps explanation. The challenge is simply to find an appropriate place for locating this metaphysical endpoint.

Many thinkers have tried to locate this ontological endpoint at the epistemological "dead end" of our existence known as Planck's Wall, when the universe was but a mere 10^{-43} seconds old. They want to do so because our theories and calculations inherently break down at this point, but we can actually go back further still, to the very origin of the Big Bang itself, since it was in this primordial event that space, time, and matter all had their beginning long ago. This is the most logical place for us to locate our cosmic metaphysical endpoint, especially since we can also trace the self-organizing power of atoms and molecules back to this singular point. We can do so because it was at this point that the life-giving properties of matter were ultimately bequeathed to the universe long ago. It is precisely here that we can credit God for giving matter these self-organizing propensities without falling victim to yet another God of the gaps fiasco.

The Ingenuity of Nature

Although human engineers are admittedly quite clever when it comes to the types of machines they have been able to devise, they are no match for the incredible engineering capacity of the natural world. Indeed, the living cell is vastly more complicated than anything human engineers have been able to come up with at the present time. On this score, the humble little amoeba runs circles around the Space Shuttle in terms of its underlying degree of structural complexity.

In one of the most memorable scientific passages ever written, Michael Denton describes the miraculous inner workings of a living cell:

> To grasp the reality of life as it has been revealed by molecular biology, we must magnify a cell a thousand million times until it is twenty kilometres in diameter and resembles a giant airship large enough to cover a great city like London or New York. What we would then see would be an object of unparalleled complexity and adaptive design. On the surface of the cell we would see millions of openings, like the port holes of a vast space ship, opening and closing to allow a continual stream of materials to flow in and out. If we were to enter one of these openings we would find ourselves in a world of supreme technology and bewildering complexity. We would see endless highly organized corridors and

conduits branching in every direction away from the perimeter of the cell, some leading to the central memory bank in the nucleus and others to assembly plants and processing units. . . . We would wonder at the level of control implicit in the movement of so many objects down so many seemingly endless conduits, all in perfect unison. We would see all around us . . . all sorts of robot-like machines. We would notice that the simplest of the functional components of the cell, the protein molecules, were astonishingly complex pieces of molecular machinery, each one consisting of about three thousand atoms arranged in highly organized 3-D spatial conformation. We would wonder even more as we watched the strangely purposeful activities of these weird molecular machines, particularly when we realized that, despite all our accumulated knowledge of physics and chemistry, the task of designing one such molecular machine . . . would be completely beyond our capacity at present and will probably not be achieved until at least the beginning of the next century.

What we would be witnessing would be an object resembling an immense automated factory, a factory larger than a city and carrying out almost as many unique functions as all the manufacturing activities of man on earth. However, it would be a factory which would have one capacity not equaled in any of our most advanced machines, for it would be capable of replicating its entire structure within a matter of a few hours. To witness such an act at a magnification of one thousand million times would be an awe-inspiring spectacle.[48]

Significantly, Denton rejects the idea that this structural perfection could have been due to chance alone:

It is the sheer universality of perfection, the fact that everywhere we look, to whatever depth we look, we find an elegance and ingenuity of an absolutely transcending quality, which so mitigates against the idea of chance. Is it really credible that random processes could have constructed a reality, the smallest element of which—a functional protein or gene—is complex beyond our own creative capacities, a reality which is the very antithesis of chance, which excels in every sense anything produced by the intelligence of man? Alongside the level of ingenuity and complexity exhibited by the molecular machinery of life, even our most advanced artifacts appear clumsy. We feel humbled, as neolithic man would be in the presence of twentieth-century technology.

It would be an illusion to think that what we are aware of at present is any more than a fraction of the full extent of biological design. In practically every field of fundamental biological research ever-increasing levels of design and complexity are being revealed at an ever-accelerating rate. The credibility of natural selection is weakened, therefore, not only by the perfection we have already glimpsed but by the expectation of further as yet undreamt of depths of ingenuity and complexity.[49]

But it isn't as if matter needs to be alive in order for its internal degree of complexity to be impressive. The atom also displays a level of complexity that far outstrips anything in the human repertoire of engineering. For instance, the very fact that all atoms of a particular element are identical to one another is itself a marvelous property that speaks directly of Intelligent Design. The physicist James Clerk Maxwell—whose study of electromagnetic phenomena led directly to Einstein's special theory of relativity—recognized this stunning property of the atom, and he even went so far as to conclude that it gave the atom "the stamp of the manufactured article."

Maxwell also recognized that the immutability of both the atom and the molecule could not be explained in terms of a theory of evolution by natural selection:

> No theory of evolution can be formed to account for the similarity of molecules, for evolution necessarily implies continuous change, and the molecule is incapable of growth, or decay, of generation or destruction. None of the processes of Nature, since the time when Nature began, have produced the slightest difference in the properties in the operation of any of the causes which we call natural . . . the molecules out of which these systems are built—the foundation stones of the material universe—remain unbroken and unknown.[50]

This is a fascinating realization that has been all but ignored in our "modern" era. The atom's remarkable stability has also gone unheralded. For although we have identified some of the physical principles that "explain" why atoms are so stable (modern quantum theory and the Pauli Exclusion Principle), we have no idea *how* these fundamental principles work or where they originally came from. All we know is that without them, we wouldn't even have a chance of existing.

Self-organization is yet another property that is essential to life. For some mysterious reason, atoms and molecules are able to spontaneously organize themselves into higher degrees of order "on their own." Indeed, many nontheistic scientists like to use this self-organizing capacity to obviate the creative activity of God altogether. "If atoms and molecules can organize themselves into things like mountains and people," they say, "why bring God into the equation at all?"

The problem with this pseudo-explanation is that it fails to address the single most important question of them all as far as this particular issue is concerned, which is this: where did atoms and molecules originally get this capacity to self-organize in the first place? Since evolution itself is incapable of accounting for this miraculous property, we are left with one other alternative, namely, that some form of Cosmic Intelligence must have deliberately designed this self-ordering capacity into atoms and molecules long ago.

The Role of the Moon in Our "Just Right" Solar System

Another important cosmic factor that facilitates the existence of life on earth, according to French astronomer Jacques Laskar, is the unusually large size of our moon. As a direct consequence of this anomalously large size, the moon is able to exert a strong stabilizing influence on the earth's axis of rotation, thereby enabling it to avoid wobbling out of control. This is a vitally important effect as far as the existence of life is concerned, because it prevented the earth from experiencing extreme climatic fluctuations in the distant past that would have been utterly devastating to any fledgling life forms.[51]

Laskar utilized computer simulations of the earth's rotational integrity in the hypothetical absence of the moon to arrive at this remarkable conclusion.[52] The basis of this finding can be traced to the earth's equatorial bulge, which results from the fact that the earth spins on its axis. As it turns out, the various constituents of our solar system exert a significant gravitational pull on this bulge, which can be traced to the many different areas of gravitational influence that are constantly impinging on the earth from all points in the solar system. Without the moon to stabilize these gravitational influences, the earth's axis would have gyrated slowly throughout the cosmic past. And this, in turn, would have eventually caused the earth's spin axis to oscillate wildly in an intrinsically unpredictable fashion, yielding a spin axis that could have ranged anywhere between 0 to 85 degrees.[53] This would have been catastrophic for fledgling life forms on land because they almost certainly wouldn't have been able to survive the climatic extremes that would have necessarily ensued.[54]

Luckily, however, we have a satellite circling our planet that is *precisely* the right size to cancel out these gravitationally induced gyrations in our planet's spin axis. This is very fortunate indeed, for without this gravitational safety valve, life almost certainly would have been incapable of evolving here, due to the extreme fluctuations in climate that would have inevitably resulted from such extreme changes in our planet's spin axis.

What are the odds for this happening by chance alone? How likely is it that our moon would have been *just* big enough to cancel out the many different gravitational influences on our planet, so that we could subsequently enjoy a relatively stable global climate for the evolution of life? A closer investigation reveals that this is an *exceedingly* delicate balancing act indeed, since it is one that had to have been fine-tuned in conjunction with a vast number of other gravitational influences upon the earth that are constantly changing by virtue of the incessant motion of the various gravitating bodies in our solar system.

In view of this astonishing fact, it would seem to be next to impossible for our moon to have assumed *precisely* the "right" size and orbital relationship to our planet by chance alone. Fine-tuned balancing acts like these don't happen by accident, especially when they turn out to be essential for the development of inherently valuable things, like living organisms. And while it is conceivable that this perfect gravitational relationship could have merely been the result of a selection effect, in which life would have spontaneously evolved around the only type of planet capable of supporting its existence (which would necessarily entail the simultaneous existence of an ideally sized companion satellite), this alternative seems far less likely when it is viewed in conjunction with the many *other* cosmic coincidences that are known to have been necessary for the rise of life. Indeed, according to Laskar, if all planets must possess the right-sized moon before they can be capable of supporting organic life, the number of these biologically friendly planets—and hence the potential number of intelligent life forms—throughout the universe must be far smaller than we ever dreamed.[55]

This conclusion dovetails nicely with recent work carried out by geologist Peter D. Ward and astronomer Donald Brownlee. Upon noting the extreme precariousness of the planetary conditions that are necessary to support higher life forms, Ward and Brownlee have come to the momentous conclusion that complex living organisms such as *Homo sapiens* may actually be a rarity in the universe—if indeed they exist anywhere else at all.[56]

Ward and Brownlee's ideas blend in perfectly with the long-standing consensus position of the world's leading evolutionary scientists, such as Ayala and Mayr, concerning the odds for the evolution of intelligence elsewhere in the universe. According to this consensus position, the odds for the evolution of intelligence are *so* astronomically remote that no other form of intelligence is likely be found anywhere else in the entire visible universe.[57]

Solar Eclipses and the Size of the Moon

Total solar eclipses have been an important part of the distinctly human experience for thousands of years. They have been used both as a cosmic reference point for human time-keeping purposes as well as for the spiritual enrichment of humanity's collective unconscious.

A total solar eclipse occurs when the moon temporarily blocks out the sun from an earthbound point of view. This breathtaking phenomenon happens every few years or so, when the moon happens to pass directly between the earth and the sun.

Interestingly enough, though, a total solar eclipse is only possible because of the intimate cooperation between two independent cosmic factors: (1) the size of the moon, which is 400 times smaller than the sun and (2) the moon's orbital radius about the earth, which is 400 times smaller than the earth's orbital radius about the sun. Another way of saying this is that solar eclipses are able to happen because the moon, which is 400 times smaller than the sun, just happens to be precisely 400 times closer to the earth than the sun is. As a consequence of these two independent factors, the moon is able to completely block out the sun from an earthbound point of view whenever their orbital trajectories bring them in line with one another.

Computer studies have also shown that our solar eclipse is a unique phenomenon amongst all the known satellites in the solar system.[58] With this in mind, how are we to explain this remarkable coincidence? How are we to explain the fact that the moon is both 400 times smaller than the sun, and yet also 400 times closer to the earth than the sun is? Out of the millions of possible values that these two independent variables could have conceivably possessed, both happen to have precisely the same value: 400, and it is precisely this equality that makes total solar eclipses possible from an earthbound point of view.

While one could simply attempt to dodge this vexing issue by attributing it to blind chance, it is hard to resist the feeling that something more is going on here. Could it be merely a coincidence that the only planet in the entire solar system with intelligent life—and hence the capacity to perceive the significance of solar eclipses—*also* just happens to possess a moon of just the right size and proximity to earth to make total solar eclipses possible?

In order to visualize the implicit implausibility of this scenario, let us consider the following thought experiment. Imagine that there is a rock formation on the moon that just happens to be arranged in the form of a coherent English sentence. Imagine further that it is the only satellite in the solar system that happens to possess this curious feature. Now, insofar as this were actually the case, would anyone in their right mind suppose that these intelligible rock formations would be merely the result of chance alone? Probably not, since in this hypothetical case the moon would belong to the only planet in the solar system that would be inhabited by beings who would be capable of reading these messages.

In the same way, we can use the meaningfulness of total solar eclipses in human life to justify the positing of a *transcendent causal connection* between the intelligibility of eclipses, on the one hand, and the precise size and orbital location of the moon, on the other. While there is no way to prove the truth of this speculative hypothesis, its general character of contrivance is consistent with all of the other cosmic "coincidences" that we have discussed previously. And this, in turn, would seem to afford it an additional degree of plausibility overall.[59]

Indeed, we mustn't forget that as far as the size of our moon is concerned, we're talking about two *entirely independent* coincidences with respect to earthbound observers. The first coincidence concerns the size necessary to stabilize the earth's axis of rotation, while the second concerns the size necessary to enable the occurrence of total solar eclipses. Now, the odds for either one of these coincidences to have occurred by accident are small enough, but when one considers the likelihood that *both* of them could have simultaneously occurred by chance alone, it becomes readily apparent that something more must be going on here. Moreover, when we factor in all of the other cosmic "coincidences" that have turned out to be essential for life, we can safely conclude that some form of Design *must* be at work here. After all, the very essence of rationality dictates that at some point, fortuity must give way to deliberate design. It is the contention of the Theistic Evolutionist that this "design threshold" has indeed been exceeded as far as the character of the underlying evidence itself is concerned.

The Size of the Human Body

The final cosmic "coincidence" that we are going to discuss in this chapter has to do with the relative size of the human body in the cosmic hierarchy of objects. In order to make this determination, we are going to make use of a physical relation called the *geometric mean*, which is used to compare objects of widely varying size. It is obtained by first multiplying the lengths or diameters of the objects being compared and then taking the square root of the product.

When we do this, the size of a human being turns out to be the geometric mean between the size of a planet and the size of an atom, whereas the size of a planet turns out to be the geometric mean between the size of an atom and the size of the entire universe.[60] This seems to place humanity squarely in the middle of the cosmic hierarchy of objects.

Interestingly enough, the nature of this positioning doesn't at all seem to be accidental, because we need to be just about as big as we are in order to be able to move about with ease and to keep from hurting ourselves when we fall. If we were much smaller in relation to the rest of the world, we wouldn't be able to move about in our environment nearly as efficiently. On the other hand, if we were much bigger, we would severely injure ourselves every time we fell down. Whales can be as big as they are simply because of the buoyant effect of water, which helps to support their tremendous weight. We humans, on the other hand, have no such luxury, so there are very strict limits on how big we can safely be in the world. Not surprisingly, our current size turns out to be just right for us.

As if this weren't enough, astrophysicists also tell us that human life appeared on the earth at approximately the halfway point in our sun's life cycle. Of course, there is no way to tell for a certainty whether or not this is a genuine series of coincidences (and therefore the product of mere chance) or whether these curious facts reveal the actual creative purpose of an Intelligent Designer. Even so, one can't help but feel a nagging sense of suspicion about these intriguing relations, especially when they are considered alongside the many other "coincidences" that we have explored in this chapter.

That is to say, could it be merely a coincidence that the most sophisticated and complex objects in the entire known universe (human beings) also happen to be poised midway between the smallest known objects (atoms) and the single largest macroscopic object (the entire universe)? Could it be a coincidence that we are just about as big as we need to be to be able to carry on with our lives in a constructive fashion? And finally, could it also be a coincidence that we just happened to make our appearance at approximately the halfway point in our sun's life cycle? Common sense dictates that there is probably more going on here than just a mindless series of happy accidents.

The Marvel of Organic Biochemical "Engineering"

If we take a moment to think about it, a human being is quite literally a miracle of physio-chemical engineering. This isn't philosophical speculation; it is a self-evident fact. Even if we remove the possible existence of the soul from our consideration, a human being is nevertheless an engineering feat of quite literally *miraculous* proportions, and as such, could only have been produced by a larger Intelligence of unfathomable power.

The issue itself is refreshingly simple and to the point: What degree of engineering power and know-how would be required to produce an intelligent, self-conscious, and ambulatory creature that functions on the same level as a bona fide human being? The degree of engineering power, of course, vastly— and perhaps infinitely—exceeds anything that we're capable of on planet earth. As such, it represents a totally different kind of creative intelligence than the type we're familiar with in human society.

As one simple illustration of this, just consider the phenomenon of self-replication in the biochemical realm. Both microscopic cells and their biochemical constituents are able to self-replicate repeatedly with remarkable precision and fidelity as far as the original structures themselves are concerned. Our best engineers, by contrast, haven't even approached the ability to produce self-replicating structures of supreme complexity.

The reason for this, it would seem, is that the degree of technological sophistication that is inherently required to create a self-replicating machine vastly exceeds the level that we're capable of achieving as human beings. This would seem to imply that a superhuman level of technological sophistication is naturally required to produce this type of self-replicating molecular machine, as the following quote from Denton makes clear:

> Molecular biology has shown that even the simplest of all living organisms on earth today, bacterial cells, are exceedingly complex objects. Although the tiniest bacterial cells are incredibly small, weighing less than 10^{-12} gms, each is in effect a veritable micro-miniaturized factory containing thousands of exquisitely designed pieces of intricate molecular machinery, made up altogether of one hundred thousand million atoms, far more complicated than any machine built by man and absolutely without parallel in the non-living world. . . . The recently revealed world of molecular machinery, of coding systems, of informational molecules, of catalytic devices and feedback control, is in its design and complexity quite unique to living systems and without parallel in the non-living world.[61]

Why Evolution?

People often wonder why an all-powerful Designer would have resorted to the time-consuming and wasteful process of evolution by natural selection to create the biosphere, when He presumably could have done so instantaneously by miraculous Fiat. There are two reasons we can offer as to why the evolutionary process might have been preferable to God, all things considered.

The first reason has to do with the underlying specifications for our own existence as human beings. For as I explained at length in *Evolution and the Problem of Natural Evil*, one of the essential properties of the Human Definition appears to require that all human beings experience a birth from the simplest possible starting point, which would correspond to the profound ontological immaturity of the nascent human spirit.[62] This initial immaturity appears to be an essential requirement of the human ontological makeup, because it affords us the luxury of building our own minds and personalities for ourselves. This, in turn, is vitally important because it seems to translate into a more robust form of free will, since an agent's degree of freedom appears to be directly proportional to the extent to which it has acquired its own inner programming for itself.

A robot, by contrast, is considered to be relatively unfree because it has been preprogrammed by an external programmer, and it is logically impossible to be significantly free if an entity is merely responding to programming that has been "downloaded" into it. Genuine freedom thus necessitates that an agent act in accordance to knowledge that has been self-acquired. But if this is so, then we can see why God would have wanted us to begin our lives at the earliest possible starting point: so that we could obtain the most robust form of freedom possible, by self-acquiring as much of our own knowledge as possible.

In order for this ontological goal to be realized, though, it was ostensibly necessary for the entire universe to be structured, at least in part, around the necessary nature of the Human Definition.[63] To the extent that this is so, it follows that the entire universe had to have begun its existence from the earliest possible starting point as well (the Big Bang singularity).

This principle would also seem to apply with equal force to the rise of life on this planet. If true, this would necessitate a similar type of evolution for the entire biosphere. In this case, life would begin at the smallest possible starting point, only to gradually evolve by natural cause and effect processes into progressively more complex life forms, in much the same way that infantile humans also tend to steadily grow more mature in response to natural causal processes.

According to this speculative hypothesis, God created the entire biosphere through natural evolutionary pathways because this is the same general pattern of development that necessarily applies to the genesis of human beings. And while it is possible that God could have utilized a different creative mechanism to instantiate the world, the demands of structural and functional unity seem to have required the use of similar evolutionary mechanisms throughout the cosmos.[64]

There is, however, a second reason why God might have wanted to create the biosphere through natural evolutionary pathways. It has to do with the *epistemic distance* stipulation between God and humanity, which we briefly discussed in the introduction. The basic idea here is that God couldn't have created a world in which His existence was obvious to everyone and *still* have allowed us to have a significant amount of personal autonomy over our lives. For to the extent that we could directly perceive the Divine Reality in all of its magnificent glory, we would probably be *so* overwhelmed that our freedom to act in this world would essentially be negated as a result, particularly in relation to God.

A quiet bit of reflection reveals that there is only one way around this problem. The Divine Reality must be temporarily hidden behind the natural course of events in this world so that the reality of God's existence can then become ambiguous to us. For this is the only way that we can be genuinely free in the world, particularly in relation to God. This remarkable idea has been promulgated in recent years by the British philosopher John Hick:

> In creating finite persons to love and be loved by Him God must endow them with a certain relative autonomy over against Himself. But how can a finite creature, dependent upon the infinite creator for its very existence and for every power and quality of its being, possess any significant autonomy in relation to that creator? The only way we can conceive is that suggested by our actual situation. God must set man at a distance from Himself, from which he can then voluntarily come to God. But how can anything be set at a distance from One who is infinite and omnipresent? Clearly spatial distance means nothing in this case. The kind of distance between God and man that would make room for a degree of human autonomy is epistemic distance. In other words, the reality and presence of God must not be borne in upon men in the coercive way in which their natural environment forces itself upon their attention. The world must be to man, at least to some extent, *etsi deus non daretur,* "as if there were no God." God must be a hidden deity, veiled by his creation.[65]

The logic behind this train of thought is clear, and it leads to the following realization when it is applied to the evolution of life on this planet. If God had acted to bring about the biosphere instantaneously by miraculous fiat— that is, without the use of a protracted evolutionary process that is dominated by the law of cause and effect—then this fact would surely have been visible to virtually all human beings, especially those who have been trained in the physical sciences; and this, in turn, would have significantly jeopardized the freedom of human beings by reducing or even eliminating the necessary epistemic distance between God and the human race. As it stands now, the evolutionary process itself is *already* highly suggestive of an Intelligent Designer, so it stands to reason that the sudden creation of all life forms by miraculous fiat would have probably made the creatorship of God far more obvious to everyone, because it would have removed any hint of a possible naturalistic origin to life. And this, in turn, would have caused us to be so heavily influenced by God's transcending magnificence that our freedom to act in this world would have been significantly compromised as a result.

Of course, God could have avoided this problem by instantaneously creating the biosphere to look *as if* it had been gradually produced by natural processes over billions of years. The problem with this purported solution, however, is that it involves needless deception on the part of the Creator, and willful deception isn't generally acknowledged to be one of the intrinsic attributes of the Deity.

This being the case, the only legitimate alternative appears to be the gradual creation of the living world by natural processes alone (via the process of evolution by natural selection), because this is the only possibility that would have enabled God to remain substantially hidden from the world so that human freedom could be preserved in the process. Far from constituting evidence against God, then, we see that the evolutionary process paradoxically ends up *serving* the Divine Purpose in the end, through the indirect facilitation of human freedom.

Notes

1. Bertrand Russell, *Religion and Science* (New York: Oxford University Press, 1968), 216.

2. Quoted in John D. Barrow and Frank J. Tipler, *The Anthropic Cosmological Principle* (Oxford: Oxford University Press, 1986), 169.

3. George Greenstein, *The Symbiotic Universe* (New York: William Morrow, 1988), 18–21.

4. Paul Davies, *The Accidental Universe* (New York: Cambridge University Press, 1982), 82.

5. Ibid., 81.

6. John D. Barrow, *The World within the World* (Oxford: Oxford University Press, 1990), 358.

7. Davies, *Accidental Universe*, 55.

8. Ibid., 114.

9. Barrow and Tipler, *Anthropic Cosmological Principle*, 548.

10. Ibid., 545–546.

11. Ibid., 547.

12. Lawrence J. Henderson, *The Order of Nature* (Cambridge, Mass.: Harvard University Press, 1917), 191.

13. Lawrence J. Henderson, *The Fitness of the Environment* (Glouster: Peter Smith, 1970), 312.

14. Paul Davies, *Other Worlds* (New York: Simon and Schuster, 1980), 143.

15. Gerald L. Schroeder, *Genesis and the Big Bang* (New York: Bantam, 1990), 123.

16. Ibid.

17. Ibid.

18. Ibid., 124.

19. Ibid., 125.

20. Ibid., 126.

21. Corey S. Powell, "Greenhouse Gusher," *Scientific American*, vol. 265, no. 4 (October 1991): 20.

22. Hugh Ross, *The Fingerprint of God* (Orange, Calif.: Promise Publishing, 1991), 131.

23. Ibid., 129.

24. Ibid.

25. Ibid., 130.

26. Ibid.

27. Errol E. Harris, *Cosmos and Anthropos* (Atlantic Highlands, N.J.: Humanities Press International, 1991), 52.

28. Ibid.

29. Ross, *The Fingerprint of God*, 130.

30. Ibid.

31. Ibid.

32. Ibid., 131.

33. Ibid.

34. Ibid.

35. Ibid.

36. Ibid.

37. Ibid.

38. Ibid.

39. Paul Davies, *The Cosmic Blueprint* (New York: Simon and Schuster, 1989), 112–113.

40. Ibid., 112.

41. Ibid., 113.

42. Ibid.

43. Ibid.

44. Barrow and Tipler, *Anthropic Cosmological Principle*, 305.

45. Schroeder, *Genesis and the Big Bang*, 157–158.

46. Ibid., 158.

47. Paul Davies, *The Fifth Miracle* (New York: Simon and Schuster, 1999), 20–21.

48. Michael Denton, *Evolution: A Theory in Crisis* (Bethesda, Md.: Adler and Adler, 1986), 328–329.

49. Ibid., 342.

50. Quoted in Barrow and Tipler, *Anthropic Cosmological Principle*, 88.

51. Robert Naeye, "Moon of Our Delight," *Discover*, vol. 15, no. 1 (January 1994): 72–74.

52. Ibid., 72.

53. Ibid.

54. Peter D. Ward and Donald Brownlee, *Rare Earth* (New York: Copernicus, 2000), 223–227.

55. Naeye, "Moon of Our Delight," 74.

56. Ward and Brownlee, *Rare Earth*, xx–xxiv.

57. Barrow and Tipler, *Anthropic Cosmological Principle*, 133.

58. M. Mendillo and R. Hart, "Resonances," *Physics Today*, vol. 27, no. 2 (February 1974): 73.

59. There are a large number of other lunar "coincidences" that also seem to point in the direction of Intelligent Design. For instance, the moon's stable orbit, capacity to

evoke tides, anomalously large size relative to the earth, and tremendous reflective capacity are all precisely suited for an optimal degree of functionality on this planet. If the moon's composition, size, and location were all a matter of chance alone, we would never expect for all of its properties relative to the earth to be so beneficial to human life.

60. John Gribbin and Martin Rees, *Cosmic Coincidences* (New York: Bantam, 1989), 67.

61. Denton, *Evolution*, 250, 271.

62. M. A. Corey, *Evolution and the Problem of Natural Evil* (Lanham, Md.: University Press of America, 2000), 93–124.

63. Ibid., 94–102.

64. Ibid., 122–124.

65. John Hick, *Evil and the God of Love* (New York: Harper and Row, 1977), 281.

CHAPTER TEN

~

Is It All a Coincidence?

Although we talk so much about coincidence we do not really believe in it. In our heart of hearts we think better of the universe, we are secretly convinced that it is not such a slipshod, haphazard affair, that everything in it has meaning.

—J. B. Priestley

What are we to make of the many remarkable "coincidences" discussed in the previous two chapters? Canadian philosopher John Leslie has suggested an appropriate analogy to better illustrate the central question that is at issue here. Imagine a condemned man who is about to be executed before a hundred-man firing squad. As the command to fire is given, each rifle spontaneously misfires, with the result that the condemned criminal is subsequently allowed to remain alive.

On one level, of course, this orchestrated misfiring represents nothing mysterious. No physical laws are actually violated; each rifle simply experiences an ordinary mechanical malfunctioning. However, even though the odds for a single misfiring are finite enough, almost no one would be satisfied with the contention that *each* of the hundred rifles had misfired *purely by chance*. The very fact that all the rifles misfired *simultaneously* in Leslie's example appears to indicate that an underlying "conspiracy" was probably at work to coordinate the misfiring. Otherwise, at least one of the rifles would have fired properly and the condemned man would have been executed. This is why it is eminently rational to conclude that some type of unifying principle was probably at work to coordinate the misfiring.

Similarly, by all "natural" accounts we shouldn't have ever had the opportunity to exist on this planet, since there are far too many disorganizing influences at work in the universe to ever allow such a coordinated masterpiece of engineering to transpire purely by chance. However, due to the huge number of cosmic "coincidences" throughout our cosmological history, these potential roadblocks to our own evolution have somehow been bypassed, against all the odds. As a consequence, life did indeed have the opportunity to arise on this planet after all.

The challenge, of course, is to find a suitable explanation for these "coincidences." Asserting that they were merely the result of a colossal cosmic accident doesn't seem to constitute a sufficient explanation because, once again, their very coordination toward a common goal seems to suggest an overwhelming degree of deliberateness, and hence contrivance. It therefore isn't a question of whether or not such a "miraculous conspiracy" actually exists in the universe—it is, rather, a question of how and why this cosmic conspiracy could have come to exist in the first place.

The Probabilistic Significance of These "Coincidences"

We have seen that there are a large number of stunning "coincidences" in distant branches of physics that have conspired together to make life possible on this planet. These "coincidences" involve the intimate cooperation of so many finely tuned physical parameters that it is hard to see how one can avoid the conclusion that something mysterious is going on "behind the scenes" to make life possible. The evidence is so compelling, in fact, that many respected scientists, including Sir Fred Hoyle and Paul Davies, have openly admitted that some type of "supercalculating intellect" must have been at work to make our biocentric universe possible.

Nevertheless, there are two possible ways to interpret the meaning of these "coincidences." The first is the method employed by the scientific agnostic: it is simply to note that since "something had to happen" in the universe, that something might as well have been our own biocentric universe. As paleontologist Stephen Jay Gould of Harvard University has put it:

> Any complex historical outcome—intelligent life on Earth, for example—represents a summation of improbabilities and becomes thereby absurdly unlikely. But something has to happen, even if any particular "something" must stun us by its improbability. We could look at any outcome and say, "Ain't it amazing. If the laws of nature had been set up just a tad differently, we wouldn't have this kind of universe at all."

Does this kind of improbability permit us to conclude anything at all about that mystery of mysteries, the ultimate origin of things? Suppose the universe were made of little more than diprotons? Would that be bad, irrational, or unworthy of spirit that moves in many ways its wonders to perform? Could we conclude that some kind of God looked like or merely loved bounded hydrogen nuclei or that no God or mentality existed at all? Likewise, does the existence of intelligent life in our universe demand some preexisting mind just because another cosmos would have yielded a different outcome?[1]

There are two ways to respond to this serious attack. First, it is far from obvious that "something had to happen" in the universe. Indeed, if Thomistic philosophy is correct, then *nothing at all* could have ever happened in a universe devoid of any Supernatural Power. The reason for this, of course, is that by long-standing convention only God Himself is capable of acting as the First Cause for any contingent chain of existence. Without this First Cause, nothing else is presumably capable of reaching the level of true ontological being.

The Principle of Sufficient Reason supports us in this contention, as it demands that everything which occurs in the universe must have a sufficient reason for its occurrence. Traditionally, this adequate reason has been understood to be God, who has been defined as the very ground of all being. On this view, there couldn't possibly be anything at all in existence if it weren't for the deliberate existence-sustaining power of God Himself. As a consequence, we can't just flippantly conclude that "something had to happen" in the universe, because such an assertion isn't apparent by any means.

On a deeper level, it simply isn't true that the existence of a concrete life-supporting world can even be *partially* explained by Gould's "something has to happen" argument. Such a bare assertion commits the well-known fallacy of circular reasoning in which the conclusion is implicitly contained within one of its underlying premises. For while it may be true that "something has to happen" in the world, this is only true in a functional world that *already* exists. But it is precisely the origin of our world that we are trying to explain here! One can't simply observe the current reality of worldly events and then conclude that things are the way they are because "something had to happen." Before the birth of the universe some 12 to 15 billion years ago *nothing at all* was evidently happening. What's more, scientists have no good explanation as to why anything *ever* happened to begin with. To be sure, given the existence of absolute nothingness, we would *never* expect a highly organized universe such as our own to suddenly spring into existence out of nowhere, that is, without some Larger Power intervening in this nothingness and orchestrating the whole affair.

Indeed, science itself is based on the conviction that nothing ever happens in the universe without a sufficient prior cause, and this assumption necessarily includes the birth of the universe itself.[2] But if this is true, then it becomes very difficult to explain the sudden creation of matter out of absolute nothingness apart from the creative activity of some type of "disembodied Power." The perfect symmetry of absolute nothingness, and therefore of perennial nonexistence, would likely be the cosmic *status quo* in such a Mindless scenario, because there would be no compelling reason for anything concrete to happen in the first place.[3]

But even if, for the sake of argument, we assume the prior existence of an unexplained material realm, it still doesn't follow that all events are equally impressive or meaningful just because "something had to happen." If this were so, then Beethoven's Ninth Symphony would be no more significant or noteworthy than the sounds that are randomly generated when an orchestra warms up.

In short, some events are, by virtue of their internal degree of order, far more impressive than other, less ordered events. A straight flush, for instance, is far more impressive than a pair of twos during a poker game, and the fact that some combination of cards had to be dealt does not diminish this inherent degree of impressiveness in the least.

Our present biocentric world, with its plethora of life-supporting physical parameters, represents the ultimate example of just such a complex historical outcome. Each and every one of the many variables that went into making it happen seem to have been deliberately contrived to enable life to evolve here, yet the combined improbability of all these events isn't diminished in the least by the suggestion that "something had to happen." In terms of Leslie's firing squad analogy, the prisoner's astonishment at having survived a 100-man firing squad also isn't diminished in the least simply because "something had to happen." In the same way, our astonishment at finding ourselves in a perfectly designed world shouldn't at all be diminished simply because "something had to happen."

One of the problems with Gould's reasoning concerns the critical *perspective* from which he draws his radical conclusion. There are two possible perspectives that can be taken here: an *a priori* perspective, which is situated *before* the occurrence of the event in question, and an *a posteriori* perspective, which is situated *after* it occurs. Gould is clearly taking the latter perspective in the above passage, since he is looking *back* at the event and noting the number of "improbable" things that went into making it happen. From this point of view, it is true that most complex historical outcomes are exceedingly "improbable" to one extent or another, at least insofar as they are all comprised of an intricate combination of events, each of which is unique and "improbable" in its own right. And since a precise duplication of each particular combination will likely never occur again, due to the utter uniqueness of all of its various constituents, there is a sense in which *all* complex historical outcomes are so improbable that they will never be able to happen again in precisely the same way.

In short, complex historical outcomes happen all the time, and insofar as "something has to happen" in the world, it is true that we shouldn't be unduly impressed by most of these functionally trivial outcomes. However, it doesn't follow from this that all complex historical outcomes are functionally equivalent or impressive simply because they'll never be precisely duplicated again.

In speaking about the probability of life's spontaneous origin, though, the natural theologian isn't taking an *a posteriori* point of view at all. He is, to the contrary, taking an *a priori* point of view, since he is convinced that life is so complex and important that it actually existed *before* the specter of the Big Bang in the eternal Mind of God Himself. To the extent that this is so, it follows that the cosmic "blueprint" for life's evolution actually *preceded* the birth of the universe itself, because there is a very real sense in which the individual specifications for life have existed for all eternity. And this, in turn, means that there is a sense in which the evolution of life could have actually been *predicted* in principle before it ever occurred since the underlying requirements for life have been true and self-identical for all eternity.

So, the ultimate significance of our biocentric world isn't to be found from an *a posteriori* point of view, except to the extent that such a perspective redirects us to examine our world from an *a priori* point of view (which takes note of the underlying requirements for our own existence). Accordingly, the ultimate significance of our world is to be found by focusing on two related *a priori* factors: (1) the intrinsic value of human intelligence and (2) the profound unlikelihood that the underlying conditions for life could have ever spontaneously appeared by chance alone.

We can conduct a thought experiment to help clarify this second point. If we imagine ourselves to be disembodied observers who are suddenly projected back in time before the Big Bang, it would be clear to us that the universe hadn't yet come into being. Furthermore, we would know that any future universe would necessarily have to possess a certain constellation of fundamental parameters before it would be capable of supporting *any* type of carbon-based life.[4] It is this timeless specification of the basic parameters for our biocentric universe that constitutes our *a priori* perspective concerning the universe's existence and subsequent evolution.

But we can go one step further. If we were to watch our biocentric universe suddenly explode into being, we would justifiably be overwhelmed, even to the extent that we would be certain that we had just witnessed a genuine cosmological miracle. There are two reasons why we would naturally construe such an event to be miraculous. First, *any* complex historical outcome that is accurately predictable beforehand, when there is no possible causal connection between one's prediction and the actual occurrence itself, seems to be miraculous by its very nature. And second, the miraculous nature of life itself naturally compels us to believe that the ultimate source of life's reality must *also* be miraculous. And while it is conceivable that there was no conscious being in existence prior to the Big Bang to make this momentous prediction, such a prediction would have nevertheless been "made" by the eternally existing requirements for our own existence.

Amazingly, this is the same type of miracle that occurred with the evolution of our biocentric universe. For regardless of whether or not there was a cosmic Mind in existence at the Big Bang, it is nevertheless true that the various requirements for the evolution of our biocentric universe have existed for all eternity. It doesn't ultimately matter whether they had a concrete place in which to exist or not, since the fact remains that a certain series of requirements *had* to have first been met before life could have ever evolved here. It is these perennial requirements that have existed for all eternity. But if this is true, then it is also true that at some point in the past, these eternal requirements for life somehow became actualized when our biocentric universe exploded into being. In this sense, the "prediction" of life that we are referring to here would have been made by the eternally existing requirements for the evolution of carbon-based life forms. Thus, one doesn't even have to be a theist in order to see how the evolution of life was actually "predicted" before it ever occurred. For the theist, however, this affirmation comes a good deal easier, since he can simply place these *a priori* specifications for the existence of life in the eternal Mind of God Himself.

From this *a priori* perspective, it is hard to avoid the conclusion that some form of miraculous contrivance has been at work all along in the evolution of our life-supporting universe. For just as an accurate prediction of 100 straight hands of poker *before* the cards are actually dealt is far more impressive than an *a posteriori* appreciation of their "improbability" *after* each is dealt, so too is the actualization of our biocentric universe infinitely more impressive than the spontaneous appearance of a cosmos whose constitutive entities are viewed as being similarly "improbable" after the fact.

The astronomical improbability of life's evolution, of course, only compounds the impressiveness of our biocentric universe. In the same way that a royal flush is inherently far more impressive than a pair of Queens (due to its inherent value and the greatly increased odds that are involved), so too is the evolution of our biocentric universe vastly more impressive than the evolution of a universe that is comprised merely of diprotons.[5]

Of course, the reason we are so impressed when we are dealt a royal flush is because we have preestablished the importance of this hand in an *a priori* sense by virtue of its inherent degree of order. The evolution of life is precisely the same way, insofar as its importance has been preestablished by its internal degree of order and the intrinsic value of life itself. It follows, then, that when intelligent life came into being long ago, something truly special *really did* happen—a part of the universe actually became *alive* and conscious of itself.

Gould further attempts to downplay the cosmic importance of our world by asserting that any other type of cosmos would have been just as good in the end, all things considered. According to this view, our world is really nothing special because any other cosmos would have been just as acceptable overall. Therefore, we shouldn't be particularly impressed that our universe happens to exist as it does.

This type of argument is easy enough to dismiss because it is undermined by its own propagation. The very act of forming a concrete conceptualization of the universe, so that one can then present a logical evaluation of it to the rest of the world, is *itself* one of the most impressive acts that can possibly be performed by an individual. To the best of our knowledge, no other being or power in the entire universe is capable of performing such a feat. But Gould would have us believe that there is really nothing special about this ability at all, since it would have been just as good overall if only diprotons were in existence. But if there is nothing special about this ability, then there is nothing special about any of its *conclusions* either. Therefore, on Gould's own terms we should downplay the value of his conclusions!

However, the very fact that Gould continues to make such grand, all-encompassing statements about the nature of reality provides strong evidence that, deep down, he *really does* believe that human life is special. It simply would not be possible for him to take such an authoritative position about the meaning of life if he truly believed that humans are no more significant than diprotons.

Coincidence or Contrivance?

In its barest sense, the word "coincidence" refers to the coincidence of two or more distinct events which may or may not be causally related. Although the simultaneous occurrence of two or more such events doesn't *necessarily* mean that the events themselves are causally related, many people like to believe in just such a causal relationship, especially when a higher degree of meaning can be attributed to the "coincidence." Indeed, the Swiss psychiatrist Carl Jung observed such a large number of meaningful coincidences in his career that he actually coined a term—"synchronicity"—to refer to the underlying causal mechanism of the universe that allows these meaningful coincidences to occur.

However, this larger degree of meaningfulness doesn't necessarily guarantee that the coincident events in question are *in fact* causally related; it only seems to make it more likely overall. At the same time, though, there is always the possibility that the events themselves could be merely the result of chance. The highly selective nature of human consciousness significantly increases the likelihood of this latter possibility, since we only tend to notice those things in our lives that have some relevant meaning for us. Indeed, given the trillions of causally unrelated events that occur daily in the world, we would naturally expect a certain small percentage of them to work together by chance to occasionally produce a higher level of meaning for us. And since we only tend to notice those events that are meaningful to us, a selection effect naturally operates in the realm of random events to make certain chance occurrences seem meaningful, when in fact they're not.

We can better illustrate the nature of this selection effect by means of an example. Imagine a person who is allergic to cigarette smoke and who also happens to eat in restaurants several times a week. Over the course of year, this individual will eat out over a hundred times, and during a certain small percentage of these visits she will just happen to be randomly seated by a cigarette smoker, whose smoke then happens to be blown precisely in her direction. (Unfortunately for her, there are no nonsmoking sections available in any of the restaurants that she likes to visit.) Of course, she will tend to notice only those instances in which the smoke is actually blowing her way (which may actually be only 10 percent of the time). As a consequence of this selection effect, she will tend to conclude that the noxious smoke always seems to blow her way, when in fact it only does so approximately 10 percent of the time. It is thus a curious selection effect that makes our allergic individual feel like she's been cursed to always breathe cigarette smoke in restaurants, when in fact this isn't really the case.

In this instance, the selection effect makes a random coincidence *seem* personally meaningful, when in fact it is not, because most of the time the allergic individual is *not* exposed to cigarette smoke. However, since she only notices those times in which she *is* exposed to it, it is a subtle selection effect that makes it seem like an uncanny coincidence, when it's really not.

At the same time, though, it doesn't follow from this that all coincident events are similarly random and ultimately meaningless just because some of them happen to be. A deeper level of discernment is thus required in order to be able to distinguish meaningful coincidences from random, meaningless ones.

Not all ostensibly meaningful coincidences, then, can be said to actually be causally related. However, when the relationship between two or more events seems uncanny (i.e., when the meaningful cooperation between distinct events is judged to be too elaborate to be the result of chance alone), there is a tendency to conclude that such a coincident occurrence *could not* have transpired without a common meaningful cause. The strength of this tendency increases in geometric fashion as additional coincident events are added to the "event pool" in question.

For instance, the coincident occurrence of five or six seemingly separate events, which together hold some larger degree of meaning for us, is generally held to be far more indicative of a common cause than the meaningful co-occurrence of only two or three such events. This is because the cumulative probability that any given coincidence is due to chance vastly decreases as more and more meaningful coincident events are taken into consideration. This is why it is so unreasonable to believe that the misfiring of all 100 rifles in Leslie's analogy could have been a mere chance occurrence—there are far too many distinct events involved to be due to chance alone.

This conclusion is buttressed by the larger degree of meaning that is conveyed by the cumulative rifle failure itself. For it is only because of this cumulative failure that the condemned criminal is allowed to survive, against truly astronomical odds to the contrary. Rationally speaking, this appears to be far too significant a consequence, in light of the laws of probability, to have been due to chance alone.

It is thus the phenomenon of multifaceted cooperation toward a single meaningful end result that compels us to posit a common cause to a series of distinct events. In general, we can say that the larger the number of cooperating events and the greater the extent of cooperation between them, the less likely it is that they could have been due to chance alone. The addition of a final meaningful result makes the conclusion of a common cause virtually irresistible.

When we speak of a common cause behind coincident events, we usually have in mind some sense of underlying deliberateness that is aimed toward a particular result. The more relevant this result is perceived to be, the more likely we are to suspect that some type of deliberate causal mechanism must be behind it, linking the events in question together to form a single meaningful result. This tendency is greatly accentuated by the perceived degree of improbability of the coincident events themselves: the more improbable these events are deemed to be on their own (apart from the activity of an unseen common cause), the more likely we are to conclude that they could not have been due to chance alone. It is thus the conjunction of two distinct characteristics, the personal relevance of a given constellation of events and the perceived unlikelihood of their simultaneous occurrence, that compels us to conclude that they could not have been due to chance alone.

These criteria are implicit in the popular image of a "coincidence," which can be defined as the co-occurrence of two or more distinct events that is judged to be sufficiently remarkable as to warrant special attention. The question of what could be causing the coincidence is thus not directly addressed by this conceptualization. Such an explanation, if one is deemed to be necessary at all, is generally left to the individual's own preconceived view of the world.

While most coincident occurrences can simply be explained away as being mere chance events (especially in scientific circles), most people tend to suspect the activity of a common causal element when the meaning and extent of a particular coincidence is judged to be sufficiently noteworthy. Nowhere is there a more noteworthy coincidence, according to these two criteria, than in the case of the universe itself, where there are literally *dozens* of "coincidences" in existence, each of which is outrageously unlikely in itself, and all of which are coordinated together in an exceedingly precise fashion toward a single end product. Our sense of uncanniness here is further supported by the fact that life as we know it would not be capable of existing if even a single one of these fundamental parameters were altered in the least.

Moreover, when we take a closer look at the cosmological evidence itself, we find additional support for our contention that these "coincidences" could not have been due to chance alone. Five distinct factors can be seen to conspire together to make such a conclusion very compelling:

1. The tremendous number of distinct coincident events that have transpired in the universe.
2. The tremendous unlikelihood that any one of these events could have occurred by chance alone.
3. The intimate degree of cooperation that is displayed by all of these coincident events in their mutual support of life.
4. The intolerance to change of even a single one of these basic parameters.
5. The unprecedented significance of life itself.

By these criteria, it seems apparent that some type of underlying causal relationship does in fact exist behind these cosmic "coincidences." The big question concerns the nature of this causal influence. There appear to be only two possibilities. On the one hand, it is possible that some type of mindless cosmic force could have orchestrated these coincident occurrences. This possibility, however, is significantly weakened by the stupendous degree of intelligence and foresight that is repeatedly displayed by the nature of the "coincidences" themselves. It is hard to see how anything less than a Being of Infinite Intelligence could have possibly been responsible for such a grand cosmic performance, and this type of transcendent Power is clearly more than just a mindless cosmic force.

The obvious inference, then, is that an Intelligent Designer *really did* calibrate the underlying parameters of the universe in such a way as to allow life to evolve on this planet. It is the almost self-evident nature of this inference that explains why so many secular books on cosmology end up mentioning God in one way or another. Even so, most of these nontheistic authors fail to take the required "leap of fact" to openly acknowledge the likely role of a Creator in the genesis of our universe.

Physicist George Greenstein, for example, openly mentions the idea of God several times in his book *The Symbiotic Universe*. After observing that the laws of physics seem to conform themselves to the rigorous demands for life, he wonders whether it was:

> God who stepped in and so providentially crafted the cosmos for our benefit. . . . Do we not see in its harmony, a harmony so perfectly fitted to our needs, evidence of what one writer has called "a preserving, a continuing, an intending mind; a Wisdom, Power, and Goodness far exceeding the limits of our thoughts?"[6]

Remarkably, though, Greenstein still ends up rejecting the whole prospect of Intelligent Design since "God is not an explanation."[7] This conclusion, however, appears to be logically misplaced, for whereas God may not be a typical scientific explanation (since He isn't an empirically measurable entity within the laboratory), it doesn't follow from this that He can't function as a larger metaphysical explanation within the natural sciences. In this case, we wouldn't want to throw the proverbial baby out with the bathwater, because God can still play a vital role in our theories even if He can't be measured in a test tube! Greenstein seems to be aware of this possibility, because he openly admits that the mere thought of a Divine Creator makes him squirm in his seat!

Another "reason" Greenstein uses for rejecting a supernatural explanation for the various anthropic "coincidences" is that it would go directly against the historical tendency of science to oppose religion.[8] The origins of this opposition, though, are easy enough to understand. For centuries the Church persecuted pioneering scientists out of its fear that new scientific discoveries would cast a shadow on its claim to inerrant truth; it even put some, such as Giordano Bruno, to death. Accordingly, the scientific establishment rapidly became conditioned to reject most religious matters out of hand, especially those that attempted to use religious explanations to account for genuine scientific phenomena.

But even though the scientific establishment has a legitimate gripe against the Church, it is utterly fallacious to use this historical feud as objective evidence against a Divine Creator. *Merely human activities in and of themselves have nothing at all to do with how the universe itself came into being or why it operates the way it does.* For just as one would never believe that the science of nuclear physics was a sham simply because a group of religious fanatics happened to organize a cult around it, so too is God's role in the universe not affected in the least by the Church's various improprieties over the years. We must, therefore, sharply distinguish between merely human events, on the one hand, and objective physical reality, on the other. Once we do this, though, it quickly becomes apparent that the historical clash between science and religion has absolutely nothing to do with whether or not God is truly the Author of the physical universe as a whole.

Once we do away with Greenstein's two objections to the use of God as an explanation, we can see that the obvious inference here is that some sort of Designer *had* to have been at work in the genesis of our life-supporting universe. Even Greenstein himself sees the obvious nature of this inference.[9] Even so, he tries to get around this inference by invoking the Participatory Anthropic Principle (PAP). His rationale is as follows. If a living consciousness is actually required in a quantum sense in order to impart reality to the cosmos (as the PAP suggests), then the universe probably designed itself to be life-supporting, so that it could then observe itself into continued existence. For Greenstein, then, a gigantic symbiosis is at work in the universe between life, on the one hand, and the physical machinery of the universe, on the other, since both seem to need each other in order to survive.

However, this speculative hypothesis appears to be fallacious as well. For even if we affirm the quantum suggestion that a living observer is needed to give the universe a bona fide reality, this idea can never coherently be used to explain how the universe *itself* originally came into being or how it first came to exhibit the unique life-supporting characteristics that it now in fact possesses. The reason for this is simple enough. Modern science knows for a fact that there was a definite time in the past before which any life forms at all existed on this planet. This conclusion applies to extraterrestrial life forms as well, because there was a definite time in our cosmic past before which any life forms at all were in existence. For instance, no physical form of life could have possibly existed three minutes after the Big Bang, since coherent atoms and molecules hadn't yet been able to form. Indeed, since all carbon-based life forms *must* contain significant quantities of heavy elements, which are only synthesized inside of dying red giant stars, life couldn't possibly have evolved until *after* the first generation of supernovae had already exploded. And since the lifetime of a typical red giant star is on the order of 10 billion years, this means that approximately 70 percent of the universe's history was probably spent in a state of lifeless cosmic evolution. But if this is so, and if a living consciousness is indeed required to keep the universe in existence, then how could the universe have arisen so many billions of years ago before life itself came into being? This is a fatal contradiction that all but destroys Greenstein's hypothesis of a "symbiotic universe."

There are two ways to get around this problem. To begin with, one can simply reject the PAP altogether and assert that life is *not* necessary to give the universe a concrete existence. This alternative, of course, destroys Greenstein's hypothesis and puts him face to face with the need for a Cosmic Designer. On the other hand, if we accept the validity of the PAP and affirm the need for life to keep the universe in existence (through a mysterious collapsing of the "universal wave function"), we then need to find another kind of life in the universe that would have been in existence from the very beginning of the Hubble expansion. However, the only conceivable form of life that could have possibly been around at the very beginning of space-time is the "Ultimate Observer" Himself, who would have been responsible for observing the entire universe into being at the Big Bang. Ironically, then, Greenstein's heroic attempt to bypass the need for a Creator ends up leading him to precisely the opposite conclusion that he was aiming for.[10]

God, Randomness, and the Laws of Nature

In our attempt to account for the origin of our life-supporting universe, two possibilities immediately present themselves: either the universe was intelligently designed in one way or another, or else it was all a huge—albeit magnificent—accident. Of course, no one yet knows the answer to this question for an absolute, empirical certainty. But we can guess, which is simply to say that we can use our best intuitive sense to reason to the best possible explanation for the given evidence at hand. This form of reasoning is known as abduction, and according to the founder of American pragmatism, C. S. Peirce (1839–1914), it plays an essential role in the development and progression of science.[11]

Abduction is the only type of reasoning that is *ampliative* in nature, since it is able to give us more information than is contained in the premises. As a consequence, it is the only form of reasoning "which can introduce novel ideas differing in kind from those found in the premises or explanandum. This sort of reasoning takes place at the very beginning of scientific inquiry."[12] In fact, Peirce went so far as to claim that "all the ideas of science come to it by way of abduction," or by intuitively reasoning to the best explanation.[13]

We can use this process of abductive reasoning to great advantage in our attempt to find the best possible explanation for the origin of our biocentric universe. In order to do so, however, we must first identify every possible explanation that is even remotely conceivable. Then, using our best intuitive sense, we can proceed to figure out which possible explanation is the most plausible in the real world, given what we already know to be true about the universe.

Now, since there are only two possible explanations for the origin of our biocentric universe, our task is greatly simplified from the very outset, since we only have two diametrically opposed alternatives to choose between. It also vastly improves the odds that we will end up choosing the correct alternative, because we can use our best intuitive sense, coupled with what we already know to be true about the universe, to pick the alternative that is most plausible overall.

But how can we do this? We can take a hint from Peirce's own description of abductive reasoning:

> Upon finding himself confronted with a phenomenon unlike what he would have expected under the circumstances . . . [the scientist or philosopher of science] looks over its features and notices some remarkable character or relation among them, which he at once recognizes as being characteristic of *some conception with which his mind is already stored*, so that a theory is suggested which would explain that which is surprising in the phenomena. (Emphasis mine)[14]

What Peirce is saying here is that we need to find an interpretive yardstick that will help us to determine which explanation of universal origins is the most plausible, given the data at hand. The best way to do this, according to Peirce, is to rely on those explanatory "conceptions" that are already stored in our minds. Another way of saying this is that we need to examine the evidence at hand in light of what we *already* know to be true about the universe, instead of inventing new explanatory principles that have no precedent in the real world. It therefore behooves us to find a previously observed explanatory principle that adequately describes the cosmological data we're considering.

This suggestion has the further advantage of being consistent with the Principle of Theoretical Economy known as Ockham's Razor, which basically asserts that we are not to "multiply causes beyond necessity." Another way of saying this is that the simplest possible explanation is usually the correct one. This admonition has been empirically verified many times over in the history of science, and we have every reason to believe that it will continue to be so in the future. Therefore, since it is metaphysically "simpler" and more in line with the nature of abductive reasoning to stick with known explanatory principles, it follows that we should first draw upon those principles that we are already familiar with in our attempt to explain the origin of the universe, rather than attempt to rely on unknown principles that have no genuine precedent in the real world.

When we do this, we find that the theistic alternative is by far the simplest—and therefore the most plausible—one. This is because of one overarching metaphysical principle that we intuitively know to be true at all times and in all places, namely, that *complex functional mechanisms inherently require a larger designer*. We see this principle at work every day in the real world, and indeed, it is hard to even *imagine* a single instance in which a complex functional design was exclusively the result of chance and chance alone.

This may seem like an overly ambitious statement, especially given the prevalence of "chance processes" in chaos theory, quantum theory, and the history of evolutionary development. However, this isn't the form of chance that I'm referring to here. I am referring instead to a much more radical and all-encompassing form of chance that hasn't yet been found anywhere in the entire universe. In fact, it probably *cannot* be found from our present vantage point, because the cosmic "cards" have *already* been "stacked" in a certain direction. This is the direction that has been defined and directed by natural law.

Moreover, since the laws of nature permeate the entire universe, all the events that transpire within it are profoundly constrained to occur in a certain direction. It is this inherent directionality in matter that is the essence of modern complexity theory. According to this comparatively new branch of science, higher degrees of order can spontaneously arise from putative chaos, not because of chance processes alone, but because of the underlying bias toward order that is an inherent part of the physical universe in which we live. It is this underlying bias that greatly weakens any argument for true randomness in the universe.

We are, therefore, justified in asserting that nothing *ever* happens in our self-organizing universe by *genuine* chance. This is because of the many physical necessities that have been impressed upon matter by natural law, which are themselves the very *antithesis* of genuine chance. And since the laws of nature extend to the very limits of the universe itself, every conceivable event that transpires with it is profoundly biased to occur in a certain non-random direction. Again, this is the very antithesis of true randomness, which we can define here as "physical behavior that is not biased to occur in any predefined direction."

Of course, there are ostensible "chance processes" that transpire under the overall rubric of natural law, but these so-called chance events are nevertheless profoundly constrained by the laws of nature to possess a certain non-random character, just as they are also constrained to occur in a certain non-random direction. In this sense, they aren't truly random at all, which is just another way of saying that they aren't transpiring in response to the forces of genuine, unadulterated chance.

It doesn't necessarily follow from this, however, that true randomness never existed in the universe. It is conceivable—albeit unlikely—that the laws of nature were *themselves* somehow the product of genuine random processes prior to the Big Bang. This is one of the core beliefs, in fact, of genuine atheistic evolutionism, because it is a logically necessary consequence of a nontheistic worldview. For without a Divine Lawgiver to impart the laws of nature to the universe, the only creative "agent" remaining is random chance. The nontheistic evolutionist is thus very strongly committed to a chance-mediated Big Bang event, because there are simply no other conceivable alternatives to choose from in an atheistic universe.

This means that the entire debate between theistic and nontheistic evolution boils down to a single question, namely, can we reasonably believe that the laws of nature were ultimately the result of chance, and chance alone? On a purely intuitive level, the answer to this question would seem to be a resounding "No," because such a belief clearly seems to stretch credulity far beyond the breaking point. Chance processes alone simply do not seem to be capable of producing such an incredibly elaborate, fine-tuned biocentric system, nor has such a thing ever been observed anywhere in the natural world.

More support for this conclusion can be found in the current cosmological consensus that *nothing at all* existed prior to the Big Bang. This conclusion follows necessarily from the Space-Time Theorem of General Relativity, which states that space, time, and matter *all* came into existence at the Big Bang. Now, insofar as this actually turns out to be the case, chance processes alone could *not* have produced the Big Bang, because nothing at all—including chance processes—could have possibly existed prior to it.

This theistic position is further reinforced by yet another empirical finding. For as we have seen, the various laws of nature did *not* gradually evolve into their present life-supporting format over billions of years. Instead, they popped into existence immediately following the Big Bang, perfectly calibrated and ready for action.[15] This finding is absolutely *catastrophic* to the atheistic position on the origin of life, because it is next to impossible to imagine how such an incredibly elaborate system could have spontaneously sprung into existence by chance alone. The very complexity and purposiveness of our biocentric universe seems to legislate decisively against that.

It is for this reason that the atheistic position entails a necessary refutation of the Space-Time Theorem of General Relativity, at least insofar as it postulates a gradual, chance-mediated evolution of laws and constants prior to the Big Bang (since there was no time for them to gradually evolve by natural selection after the Big Bang).

However, there is no such thing as genuine chance processes in the total vacuum of absolute nothingness, so the atheist has little choice but to affirm *some* form of material existence prior to the Big Bang, otherwise there can be no medium at all for chance processes to operate.

This, in turn, means that we now have to make a choice between two competing possibilities: (1) either the Big Bang arose in response to chance-mediated processes that existed prior to the Big Bang, or else (2) the Big Bang itself was the absolute beginning of all material existence, including the existence of all putative chance processes. This appears to be a fairly straightforward question to answer, because virtually all of the empirical evidence strongly favors the latter assertion. The Space-Time Theorem of General Relativity has, after all, been experimentally confirmed many times over to an astonishing degree of accuracy, and the same thing can be said for the existence of the Big Bang itself. By contrast, there isn't a shred of empirical evidence supporting the idea that the Big Bang was produced in response to chance processes alone that somehow existed prior to the Big Bang. We are therefore rationally compelled to align ourselves with the empirical evidence in this particular instance, which, in turn, would seem to invalidate the atheist's belief in chance processes as the ultimate origin for all material existence.

But if chance processes alone couldn't possibly have produced the fine-tuned magnificence of the Big Bang, there can only be one other logical alternative, namely, that it had to have been the result of some type of Intelligent Design. This conclusion is bolstered by a corollary metaphysical assumption that we already know to be true; namely, that all intelligent designs ultimately require an intelligent designer, even if much of the designing work is delegated to physically mediated secondary causes. Conversely, the "universe as accident" hypothesis requires the invention of a totally new metaphysical principle with no correlate at all in the entire known universe—a "chancy" maneuver by any stretch of the imagination. Surely it requires more faith to believe in the "design by accident" hypothesis than it does to believe in the hypothesis of Intelligent Design, because we have no clear reason for believing that order can arise from true randomness.

Neo-Darwinian evolutionists, of course, disagree strongly with this conclusion because they are convinced that there is such a thing as design-by-accident, due primarily to the process of natural selection working on "random" mutations. This position, however, is fallacious, as we have seen, because it begs the true question that is ultimately at issue here, which concerns *why* atoms and molecules are capable of self-organizing to begin with. It is of no help to simply assume the prior existence of this self-organizing power, because again, this is the central question that is at issue here.

But this question, in turn, gets back to whether or not there is truly such a thing as genuine randomness in the universe in the first place. For while there is no doubt that certain functional designs can indeed be the result of seemingly random processes, these "random" events are nevertheless transpiring under the overall rubric of natural law, as we just saw. And since there is no such thing as a material event that has not been influenced by the nonrandom influence of natural law, we are incapable of making any determination at all regarding the possible existence of true randomness in the universe without first going back to the very origin of the laws themselves (a tall order at best).

The best that we can do, in the meantime, is to use our best sense of intuition, in conjunction with the empirical findings of modern science, to work our way to the best possible conclusion.

The Odds Surrounding Life's Evolution

There is an interesting parallel between the "need" for "coincidences" to make life possible, on the one hand, and the actual odds against any sort of life evolving on earth without a Designer, on the other. Roger Penrose, for instance, has estimated[16] that the odds against our present universe forming by chance are an astronomical one in $10^{10000000000000000000000000000000}$. Morowitz, in like fashion, has calculated the odds against life emerging from a primordial soup with all the right ingredients[17] to be a mind-boggling one in $10^{100,000,000,000}$, which is thousands of orders of magnitude above the widely accepted level of statistical nonpossibility.[18] Such observations—and there are many more like them—lead one to believe that there must be an additional creative factor at work here, a "loading of the cosmic dice," if you will;

otherwise, life would have never been able to evolve on this planet.[19] The unifying principle that appears to be applicable here is one of deliberate design by a Higher Power.

With this possibility in mind, the next thing we need to do is to ask ourselves the following question: What are the specific criteria by which we can judge a given artifact to be deliberately contrived? There are several:

1. The existence of a coherent object that is comprised of a complex concatenation of interconnected parts that all work together toward achieving some practical end.
2. A complex degree of cooperative interaction between the various internal components toward a single functional end.
3. An Aristotelian "formal cause," or intelligible design, that can be laid out in a logical, coherent fashion.
4. The exploitation of well-known technological and engineering principles which are utilized for a common, constructive end.

By these criteria, it is evident that the universe has indeed been contrived in some fashion. For one thing, it is hard to question the assertion that the universe itself is a coherent mega-artifact which has the goal of supporting biological life as one of its "intended" functions.

With the advent of modern physics, it has also become evident that there is a complex state of cooperation between the various structures of the universe and their resultant functions. The various cosmic "coincidences" themselves are perhaps the most exquisite illustration of this type of functional cooperation. Moreover, these "coincidences" are known to exploit a wide variety of technological and engineering principles in their mutual cooperation to produce a viable life-supporting universe. Last, it is hard to question the assertion that there exists a larger design, or formal cause, to the universe itself. Indeed, it is the very intelligibility of this design that makes modern empirical science possible in the first place.

As far as Paul Davies is concerned, it is the unique adaptation of the laws of nature to the needs of life that gives the universe the mark of an intelligently designed object:

The essential feature is that something of *value* emerges as the result of processing according to some ingenious pre-existing set of rules. *These rules look as if they are the product of intelligent design. I do not see how that can be denied.* Whether you wish to believe that they really have been so designed, and if so by what sort of being, must remain a matter of personal taste. My own inclination is to suppose that qualities such as ingenuity, economy, beauty, and so on have a genuine transcendent reality—they are not merely the product of human experience—and that these qualities are reflected in the structure of the natural world. (Emphasis mine)[20]

On the other hand, there are those who would argue that the very "naturalness" of the universe *itself* counts against the prospect of Intelligent Design. On this view, a "natural appearance" is held to be functionally synonymous with "uncontrived." But this isn't the attitude that we normally take toward human artifacts.

To the contrary, we typically judge an artist's skill to be inversely proportional to the degree to which the artist's product appears contrived—the more skilled she is, the less likely it is for her creation to appear contrived. But if this is so, then an artifact produced by a Perfect Artist shouldn't appear to be contrived at all! From this point of view, the uncontrived appearance of the natural world *itself* provides one of the strongest arguments for a Perfect Designer.

David Hume's Objection

The Scottish philosopher David Hume would have rejected Leslie's analogy of the misfiring rifles for the following reason. Since the evolution of our present universe was by definition a unique occurrence, we have nothing else to compare it to. However, since we need an objective frame of reference in order to be able to evaluate the relative probability of an event, there would seem to be no coherent way of assessing the underlying probability of the various "cosmic coincidences" that have transpired in the distant past. Moreover, because the character of the universe as a whole appears to be significantly different than any of the individual parts that are contained within it, Hume believed that the natural theologian isn't justified in drawing *any* such analogy to argue for the existence of God:

> Can a conclusion, with any propriety, be transferred from parts to the whole? Does not the great disproportion bar all comparison and inference? From observing the growth of a hair, can we learn anything concerning the generation of a man?
>
> But allowing that we were to take the operations of one part of nature upon another for the foundation of our judgment concerning the origin of the whole (which never can be admitted), yet why select so minute, so weak, so bounded a principle as the reason and design of animals *that are* found to be upon this planet. What peculiar privilege has this little agitation of the brain which we call "thought," that we must thus make it the model of the whole universe?[21]

While it is true that the evolution of our universe is probably a unique event, it doesn't follow from this that we are therefore incapable of ascertaining the relative probability of its occurrence. For while the universe itself may be unique, the individual events that have gone into comprising it are probably *not* unique in terms of their fundamental underlying nature. To the extent, then, that they are similar to events in our own local field of experience, we *can* potentially use them to make certain rational judgments concerning the nature of the universe as a whole.

We can say this because the universe's many building blocks are known to possess their own descriptive laws and behavior patterns that can, in principle, be generalized out to the behavior of the universe as a whole, because they seem to represent basic universal principles that apply at all times and in all places. Indeed, the very nature of cosmology itself is based upon the Principle of Universality, which assumes the universal applicability of the various laws of nature. So by understanding the fundamental patterns that are represented by these laws, we can develop a series of rational expectations that can in principle be extrapolated out to the universe as a whole. In this case, a part of the universe *can* actually tell us a great deal about the whole thing. If this weren't so, both astronomers and cosmologists would be out of a job, since they would be unable to draw *any* significant conclusions about the nature of the larger cosmos.

In fact, with the advent of modern science, we now know that this process of generalizing from a part to its corresponding whole can be exceptionally accurate. Take, for instance, the discovery of the DNA molecule, which is now known to contain the genetic information for the entire body, and not just the genetic instructions for the particular cell it is found in. This empirical fact demonstrates that one can indeed infer the structure of a complex whole (i.e., the genetic information for the entire body) by studying a single microscopic part of it (i.e., the DNA of any given cell). Accordingly, Hume's sarcastic charge that the growth of a hair is incapable of telling us anything about the generation of a man has turned out to be empirically false after all. For we now know that the DNA of a single hair-generating follicle *will* actually yield a complete genetic description of the entire body.

Indeed, if the ideas of quantum physicist David Bohm are correct, all of the information in the *entire universe* is somehow "enfolded" into each of its constituent parts. On this view, each universal particle actually contains a holographic "picture" of the entire cosmos. Accordingly, if we could somehow tap into this underlying "implicate order," we could learn all there is to know about the entire universe, Hume's protestations notwithstanding.

Actually, Hume's dogmatic argument is fatally undermined by its *own* underlying premise. For if it is true that *no* analogies can be drawn to absolutely unique events, then this is a principle that has *itself* been learned from within the overall body of the present universal structure. But if this is so, then by Hume's own admission it cannot be applied to the universe as a whole, because this would also amount to the drawing of an analogy from a part within the universe (the assertion that one cannot draw an analogy to absolutely unique events) to the whole (that the universe itself is beyond analogy). If the universe is truly beyond analogy, then we can never prove it to be so, because in the very act of asserting such a proof we can't help but commit the same cognitive error that we were trying to legislate against in the first place. Hence, not even Hume can utilize a part contained within the universe to help explain the whole.

There is yet another scientific fact that helps to further invalidate Hume's argument against holism. A very high degree of cosmic order is now known to extend not only to the farthest reaches of the observable universe, but to the most distant reaches of time as well. Everywhere we look, an extreme amount of order is found to exist, and this fact remains true on both the macroscopic and microscopic levels of existence. The implication here is that our local observations can indeed be generalized out to the nature of the universe as a whole. And while it might be possible to imagine that the entire universe is merely a small "pocket of order" within a much larger abyss of disorder, there isn't a shred of evidence to be found in support of this possibility.

Hume also questions the appropriateness of thought as a model for the entire universe. He wants to know what "peculiar privilege" this "agitation of the brain" possesses to justify its use as the creative paradigm for the rest of the universe. In point of fact, though, human thought is by far the most advanced and "privileged" faculty of its kind in the entire known universe! For not only can it go back in time to within 10^{-43} seconds of the Big Bang to ponder the universe's origin, it can also construct intelligent space probes that are able to travel beyond the confines of the entire solar system. More ominously, the human mind has also been "privileged" with the ability to unlock the secrets of nuclear power, and this is something that would have never been possible had the human cognitive apparatus not been capable of tapping into the underlying structure of physical reality.

If anything, the faculty of human thought appears to be *one step ahead* of the physical universe in one important respect. For while both are capable of producing spectacular instances of intelligent creation and nuclear destruction, only humans are capable of consciously conceptualizing both the past and the future in a logical and meaningful way. On this score, the "privileged" status of human thought is unrivaled by anything else in the entire known universe.

Notes

1. Stephen Jay Gould, *The Flamingo's Smile* (New York: Norton, 1985), 395.

2. Although it has been claimed that there are events in the quantum world that have no cause, this has yet to be firmly established. All we really know for a certainty is that we can't identify any specific causes in the quantum world, but this is a far cry from saying that no such causes actually exist. In all likelihood, we are probably just ignorant of the true identity of these quantum-level causes. Moreover, while it may indeed be true that some quantum events may not have an immediate discernible cause, there may not need to be any such cause in order for these quantum events to be able to function properly. In this case, the very existence of matter within a larger quantum field would itself be the cause of these "uncaused" quantum events.

3. While some thinkers attempt to get around this problem by positing an eternally existing material realm, which was simply reorganized at the Big Bang, there isn't a shred of scientific evidence for this position. Such a belief also leaves the existence of matter itself unaccounted for, since an eternal material realm would not seem to contain within itself a sufficient reason for its own existence.

4. Although there are other conceivable forms of life that are not centered around carbon, I am focusing here only on those that are carbon-dependent, for three reasons: (1) because we are carbon-based, and we are primarily concerned about a universe that caters to our own existence, (2) because carbon-based life forms are the only kind that we know about for a certainty, and (3) because carbon seems to be the only element that is sufficiently versatile to support any physical kind of life.

5. Our own existence attests to this fact: we are the most impressive objects in the entire known universe, but we are nevertheless only able to exist because of the exceedingly improbable universe that evolved before us.

6. George Greenstein, *The Symbiotic Universe* (New York: William Morrow, 1988), 27.

7. Ibid., 28.

8. Ibid., 126–128.

9. Ibid., 27.

10. Although this type of theoretical evidence for an "Ultimate Observer" in the universe would not exist if one simply rejected the PAP, Greenstein himself actually accepts it, so he does indeed inadvertently end up supporting the existence of God in the end.

11. C. S. Peirce, Harvard Lecture 5, "On Three Kinds of Goodness," vol. 5 (1903): 145.

12. Ibid.

13. Ibid.

14. C. S. Peirce, "Syllabus," vol. 2 (1903): 776.

15. John D. Barrow and Frank J. Tipler, *The Anthropic Cosmological Principle* (Oxford: Oxford University Press, 1986), 288.

16. Barrow and Tipler, *The Anthropic Cosmological Principle*, 448.

17. Ibid., 565.

18. Hugh Ross, *The Creator and the Cosmos* (Colorado Springs, Colo.: NavPress, 1993), 139–141.

19. In saying that God might have "loaded the cosmic dice," I mean to say that God might have increased the inherent probability of life's evolution to the point of being weakly necessary. If true, this would have entailed a self-organizing world in which the evolution of life was a virtual inevitability, given the underlying biocentricity of the universe itself. This doesn't necessarily mean, however, that it was logically mandatory for life to evolve here, particularly since many of the steps on the way to life were contingent to some degree. The overall trend, though, has inexorably been toward the evolution of life. This leads us to speculate that the contingency of the natural order may be confined primarily to small-scale causal interactions. On a larger, holistic scale, however, the universe appears to be strongly goal-oriented, despite its many small-scale contingencies. This appears to be analogous to the random behavior of individual gas molecules in a closed container, which is somehow compensated for in the large scale by the predictable and orderly behavior of the entire group of gas molecules.

20. Paul Davies, *The Mind of God* (New York: Simon and Schuster, 1992), 214.

21. David Hume, *Dialogues Concerning Natural Religion* (London: Penguin, 1990), 58.

CHAPTER ELEVEN

~

Other Explanations
for the Goldilocks Effect

It has been said that the highest praise of God consists in the denial of Him by the atheist, who finds creation so perfect that he can dispense with a creator.

—Marcel Proust

The Strong Anthropic Principle, as we have seen, asserts that the universe *had* to have become life-supporting at some stage of its history. It is this powerful element of necessity that makes the SAP most consistent with the traditional concept of Design. For even though it is possible to conceive of various nontheistic explanations for this strong element of necessity, none are as intrinsically compelling as the standard theistic explanation, because of the extreme degree of intelligence and foresight that clearly would have been required to make life a *necessary* outcome of the laws of nature.

The Weak Anthropic Principle, by contrast, is more often utilized by nontheists in their attempt to explain God away, because it seems to suggest that the biosphere could have been the result of a grand cosmic accident. The basic idea here is that if there are a large number of randomly varying compartments within the universe, then in principle it should have been possible for one of these regions to have the "right" laws and constants entirely by chance. Insofar as this "many worlds" conceptualization is accurate, we would then naturally find ourselves living in one of these biocentric regions by chance alone.

The Weak Anthropic Principle, however, can be utilized within the general context of Design as well. From this theistic point of view, there were an infinite number of possible worlds that God *could* conceivably have instantiated at the beginning of time. Out of this infinite number, God simply would have chosen the one world that was most consistent with the existence of human beings. Our world would have thus been selected out of this infinite range by virtue of its "just right" constellation of fundamental parameters.

The Many Worlds View

The "just right" nature of our Goldilocks Universe is not in serious dispute today. It is, rather, the underlying explanation for this "Goldilocks effect" that is aggressively being debated, because the entire notion of God as Creator actually hinges on the type of explanation that we choose to employ here.

The most popular nontheistic explanation, as we just saw, is the so-called Many Worlds view, which regards the universe as being infinitely large. Within this boundless universe an infinite number of discrete compartments is further imagined, each of which differs from all the others in many important and fundamental respects. In some regions, for instance, the fine structure constant might be twice as large as it is in our own region.

Insofar as this is actually the case, we would naturally expect there to be an infinite number of possibilities expressed throughout the cosmos. Indeed, according to one view, anything that can possibly happen in such an infinite universe *will* happen infinitely often! Therefore, since our present universal arrangement *can* obviously happen, it should come as no surprise that it actually *did* happen, since it is the power of our own living consciousness that would have selected out the "right" cosmic arrangement for us to observe.

This is where the Weak Anthropic Principle comes into play, because it tells us that we *can't help* but observe our present universal arrangement, because it is the only one that is capable of supporting our existence. When this obvious realization is transferred out to an infinitely large universe, we find that intelligent life will only evolve in those regions that happen to be capable of supporting it. Moreover, once this evolution actually occurs, these intelligent beings will automatically select out this life-supporting region for observation by virtue of the underlying conditions for their own existence.

The Strong Anthropic Principle, by contrast, asserts that the universe *must* become life-supporting at some stage in its history. The most sensible way to explain why this might be so, as we have seen, is in terms of a deliberate creation by an Intelligent Designer.

In their book *Cosmic Coincidences*, cosmologist John Gribbin and astronomer Martin Rees use a fitting analogy to illustrate the inherent differences between the Strong and Weak versions of the Anthropic Principle.

Imagine, they say, walking into a clothing store and trying on a suit. If the suit happens to fit you perfectly from the very outset, there are two ways you could account for this. On the one hand, the suit itself could have been tailor-made to fit every part of your body. On the other hand, the store could have contained such a wide variety of different suits that it might have actually been possible for you to accidentally choose the perfect one "off the peg."

The tailor-made suit, of course, corresponds to the tailor-made universe described by the Strong Anthropic Principle. It uses the intelligent "tailoring" capacity of a Grand Designer to explain why the universe is so perfectly attuned to the needs of humanity. The suit that is accidentally chosen "off the peg," on the other hand, describes a single region within an infinite universe that just happens to be selected by our own capacity to observe it. On this latter view, the universe's life-supporting capacity wasn't specifically designed for us, since it is only one out of an infinite range of different regions within a much larger "meta-universe." It isn't surprising, then, that we should find ourselves observing the "right" compartment within this infinitely varying meta-universe, because it is only within this type of region that we could possibly exist.

Two empirical observations, however, effectively legislate against this conclusion. To begin with, it is very difficult to see how the universe could possibly be infinite in spatial extent and yet simultaneously be finite in age. For if the universe began a finite time ago, as the Big Bang theory asserts, it couldn't possibly have expanded to infinite size in a mere 15 to 20 billion years. The fact that the sky is dark at night further supports this conclusion, because if the universe were truly infinite in spatial extent, it would necessarily contain an infinite number of stars; and this, in turn, would translate into a much brighter night sky than the one we presently observe. Therefore, the universe is almost certainly *not* infinitely large after all.

This conclusion is further supported by the naïve absurdity that surrounds one of the chief ramifications of an infinite universe. For insofar as the universe itself is truly infinite in size, it will necessarily contain an infinite number and variety of every possible thing that is capable of existing. An infinite number of Adolf Hitlers, for instance, would exist in such a "multiverse," some which are wicked and others which are good. Most theorists agree, however, that this "possibility" is manifestly absurd. Moreover, since there are numerous empirical observations that further rule out the possibility of an infinite universe, we can safely conclude that our universe is probably spatially finite after all.

Another possible interpretation of the Many Worlds scenario is "inflationary" in nature. MIT's Alan Guth has hypothesized that there may have been a period of extremely rapid cosmic expansion, or "inflation," immediately following the Big Bang. On this view, the area corresponding to our entire visible universe spontaneously inflated from a very tiny region within the primordial "cosmic egg." Within this self-contained region, all of our universe's various constituent parts were in contact with one another before the period of inflation actually began, which explains why they were so well coordinated with one another following this brief period of inflation. Other regions within the cosmic egg, however, may or may not have inflated, and of those that did, most were probably "stillborn," in the sense that they didn't possess the requisite conditions for the support of life. So, insofar as we can imagine many different areas of the cosmic egg randomly inflating to produce regions with different laws and constants, we can see how certain regions could "accidentally" take on the "right" specifications for life purely by chance.[1]

There is yet another Many Worlds theory for us to consider. It goes by the imposing name of "Everett's Many Worlds Interpretation of Quantum Mechanics," and it postulates that every particle in existence is repeatedly "splitting" in a quantum[2] sense into every possible type of "world" simultaneously. In the midst of these "many worlds," we can be imagined to inhabit the one world that just happens to be capable of supporting our existence.

The problem with Everett's Many Worlds interpretation, apart from its complete lack of empirical support, is that it appears to be fundamentally incoherent by its very nature. For if every particle repeatedly splits into every possible quantum outcome simultaneously, it would be intrinsically impossible for any "world" that is formed in this manner to remain structurally coherent for more than a nanosecond or two (if at all). Moreover, since all of these other worlds are inherently unobservable, even in principle, there is no way to falsify Everett's theory. This makes it unscientific by its very nature, for as philosopher of science Karl Popper has pointed out, a theory needs to be falsifiable, at least in principle, before it can claim to be genuinely scientific.

Everett's Many Worlds theory is also unsatisfactory because it can be used to "explain" just about everything. And as Paul Davies has pointed out, this has the unsavory effect of making science redundant, since all the regularities of nature can be "explained" as a mere selection effect.[3] Davies further rejects Everett's Many Worlds theory because "it seems like another case of *ad hoc* or miraculous solutions. Invoking an infinite number of other universes just to explain the apparent contrivances of the one we see is pretty drastic, and in stark conflict with Ockham's razor. . . . I think it's much more satisfactory from a scientific point of view to try to understand why things are the way they are in *this* universe and not to invent invisible universes to do the job."[4]

In short, Everett's Many Worlds theory is far too complicated and burdensome an explanation for life to be taken seriously, especially when we have a vastly simpler and more elegant explanation at our ready disposal; namely, that a Divine Creator is personally responsible for fine-tuning our biocentric cosmos. Oxford University's Richard Swinburne agrees.

> The postulation of God is the postulation of one entity of a simple kind. . . . The postulation of the actual existence of an infinite number of worlds, between them exhausting all the logical possibilities . . . is to postulate complexity and non-prearranged coincidence of infinite dimensions beyond rational belief.[5]

Another way of saying this is that if we apply the Principle of Economy known as Ockham's Razor to the question of life's origin, we find that we must sacrifice the infinitely complicated Many Worlds theory in favor of the infinitely simpler notion of Intelligent Design. No one is more aware of this than the quantum physicists themselves, the majority of whom only give passing lip service to Everett's theory. Almost no one seems to take it seriously. Most physicists instead believe that Bohr's Copenhagen Interpretation of quantum mechanics—in which only one quantum possibility is actually realized at a time—is in fact the correct one.

In order for the Copenhagen Interpretation to be true, however, there must be an outside observer to give reality to a particular quantum state of affairs. This is because any given quantum particle is perpetually in a state of "indecision" until it is forced to make a "decision" by the process of being observed. In the language of quantum mechanics, it takes an act of observation to "collapse the wave function" of any given quantum system, so that it can then become "real."

But if this is true—and the majority of physicists believe that it is—then what type of observer would be required to collapse the wave function of the entire universe? Traditional physics, of course, has no answer to this question. The natural theologian, by contrast, believes that God Himself functions as the "Ultimate Observer" of the entire universe, whose underlying function is to collapse the various wave functions of the universe so that it can cumulatively experience the miracle of concrete existence.

This idea of God as the universe's Ultimate Observer gives new meaning to the traditional theological idea that it is God's Will which is responsible for maintaining the entire universe in a dynamic state of existence. On this view, God Himself acts as the metaphysical ground of all being, since nothing at all could possibly exist without Him. Remarkably, modern science appears to have corroborated this ancient belief.

Shadow Photons and Parallel Universes

In his prize-winning book *The Fabric of Reality*, theoretical physicist David Deutsch compellingly argues for the existence of parallel universes, based on the observed interference patterns of light particles, or photons, when they are passed through various combinations of tiny slits.[6] Using these interference patterns as a guide, Deutsch persuasively demonstrates the existence of a vast, unseen realm of "shadow photons," whose only interaction with normal "tangible" photons is in the form of interference effects.

Deutsch builds on this theme by noting that the tangible realm of atomic particles also seems to have its own corresponding realm of interference-generating shadow particles as well.[7] He concludes from this that all shadow particles "are grouped into parallel universes. They are 'parallel' in the sense that within each universe particles interact with each other just as they do in the tangible universe, but each universe affects the others only weakly, through interference phenomena."[8] Deutsch then proceeds to group these parallel universes into a single comprehensive "multiverse," which he believes contains a great many copies of everything that exists in our own universe.

Deutsch's ideas are clearly an offshoot of Everett's Many Worlds interpretation of quantum mechanics and as such they are also vulnerable to many of the same criticisms that were levied against it in the previous section. However, they can also be used to argue for the random origin of intelligent life, particularly given Deutsch's brilliant analysis of quantum interference phenomena. For as long as an infinite number of worlds is deemed to exist, each differing from all the others to varying degrees, it is possible to imagine that life could have evolved by chance alone in the one part of the multiverse that just happened to be capable of supporting it.

This "possibility," however, fails to hold up under scrutiny. For one thing, to posit, willy-nilly, the existence of even a single parallel universe is to presuppose the prior, unexplained existence of the entire multiverse itself. But this is the very same thing that many of the proponents of Deutsch's ideas are trying to prove. Therefore, one cannot use the hypothetical existence of these parallel universes to account for the rise of life without committing the fallacy of circular reasoning. So even if Deutsch's conception of a shadowy multiverse turns out to be true, one *still* has to account for the origin of the multiverse itself, along with its many biocentric structural features.

The flip side of Deutsch's multiverse is that it may very well be required to make our own "just right" world coherent and operational. That is to say, if shadow photons are required to generate the observed interference patterns of light particles, and if shadow atoms are required to make the tangible atoms of our own world function properly, then an Intelligent Designer may have found it necessary to create all of these parallel universes just to make our own tangible realm function properly. This suggestion isn't as far-fetched as it may initially seem, because we barely have an inkling about the many structural features that are needed to make our free-willed existence on this planet fully operational. For insofar as we choose to take the "just right" status of our Goldilocks Universe at face value, it follows that all of the structural parameters within it *must* be functionally optimal, including the presumed existence of shadow particles and parallel worlds. In addition, the major theistic religions of the world have long asserted the existence of unseen worlds that are populated by invisible beings, so Deutsch's postulation of a multiplicity of parallel universes isn't totally at odds with the tenets of classical theism.

Moreover, it doesn't necessarily follow that there are an infinite number of inhabited worlds in existence similar to our own, simply because there may be a vast realm of shadow particles in existence somewhere else in the multiverse. For even if a vast realm of shadow particles turns out to be a metaphysically necessary ingredient of our own world, this doesn't automatically translate into the simultaneous existence of an infinite number of inhabited worlds similar to our own. This is a speculative hypothesis at best, and *not* an inevitable (or even likely) outcome of known physical laws. These "parallel worlds" therefore don't appear to be *necessarily* entailed by the probable existence of shadow particles as such. We mustn't forget that we're only just beginning to understand how the physical realm actually operates, particularly at the level of quantum mechanics. For all we know, shadow photons and shadow particles may be an essential part of our own tangible universe's structural foundation.[9] Deutsch directly implies this when he asserts that "understanding the multiverse is a precondition for understanding reality as best we can."[10]

It is also possible that this type of multiverse may ultimately be required to make human freedom possible. For insofar as we can freely choose between a multitude of different behavioral alternatives in this world, it must be possible for each of these other "possible worlds" to formally come into existence; that is, it must be feasible for these possible worlds to somehow traverse the metaphysical distance between "potential existence" and "actual existence." A similar process of transformation (from potential existence to actual existence) is also believed to take place at the quantum level of reality by the proponents of Niels Bohr's Copenhagen School. On this traditional view, the act of observation automatically selects a single concrete reality out of a vast number of other quantum possibilities. In this case, though, it is our own free choice that selects out a single possible world for subsequent instantiation, out of a vast number of other possibilities.

But what is the ontological status of these other possible worlds? Might they simply represent the way things *could* have been in our own tangible world had we made other free choices? If so, these other possible worlds could conceivably correspond to Deutsch's concept of parallel universes, except for one important difference—they wouldn't all simultaneously exist *en masse*, as they do in Deutsch's ontology. Instead, they would merely exhibit the distinct *potential* for existence at the quantum level of reality. We would thus be the final arbiters who would ultimately get to decide which of these possible worlds are going to get instantiated and which are not (depending again on the nature of our own free-willed decisions).

Campbell's Criticism of the Weak Anthropic Principle

As we have just seen, one of the ways in which the Weak Anthropic Principle has been utilized to "explain" the existence of our life-supporting world has been in terms of a self-selection principle—out of a multiplicity of possible worlds, we inevitably find ourselves living in the one world that happens to be capable of supporting our existence.

This position has been severely criticized by the UCLA molecular biologist John H. Campbell, whose selection-based criticism is reminiscent of Alfred Russell Wallace's criticism of Darwin's selectionist explanation for the marvel of human intelligence. Campbell notes that if the character of the visible universe were merely dependent on the fact of our existence, we wouldn't expect the exceedingly perfect universe that we presently observe; we would instead expect to observe a barely adequate universe whose qualities are just minimally sufficient to support our existence.

The central premise behind Campbell's argument against the WAP is that our universe is far better than it has to be in order to support human existence. He bases his judgment primarily on the anomalously long lifetime of our present universe, because he doesn't believe that this extra life span was actually necessary to support human life. Instead, Campbell believes that these extra universal years will be used to greatly extend the biological and psychological evolution of the human race, and he even goes so far as to conclude that the purpose of these extra years is partially explained by the needs of our own future evolution.[11]

In order to account for our unexpectedly perfect universe, then, Campbell believes that we have to go beyond the WAP to a higher level of explanation, which itself would be capable of taking the future evolutionary needs of the human race into proper account. Similarly, Alfred Russell Wallace believed that the evolution of the human brain couldn't be explained merely by reference to natural selection, for if selection alone were responsible for generating human intelligence, it would have fashioned a brain that was barely superior to that of an ape, since our survival needs in the wild don't seem to require significantly more intelligence than that possessed by apes. Instead, Wallace noted how the brain of the most rudimentary savage is more or less identical in capacity to the most advanced European brain, so he also concluded that natural selection alone couldn't possibly be responsible for generating the marvel of human intelligence.

Baby Universes?

An interesting variation on this Many Worlds theme has been proposed by cosmologist Lee Smolin, who has envisioned a type of natural selection between entire "baby universes," which Smolin believes may be spawned at the center of black holes in response to ordinary quantum fluctuations.[12]

Smolin's theory builds on the work of quantum physicist John Wheeler. According to Wheeler, it is possible that during the latter stages of black hole formation, part of the matter and energy that is imploding into the black hole may nevertheless be forcefully ejected from it by tiny quantum fluctuations in the space-time geometry around the black hole itself. It is then possible for this freshly liberated bolus of matter and energy to subsequently coalesce into a new "baby universe," which may then be able to expand into a very different type of universe from the "mother universe" that initially gave rise to it. The basic idea here is that the fundamental constants that go into comprising these new baby universes could vary tremendously from offspring to offspring, such that one of them could eventually end up with the "right" biocentric mix by chance alone.

Smolin conceives of these varying constants as being analogous to the random genetic variations that are produced in the offspring of procreating animals. Hence, as each successive baby universe is spawned out of a black hole, Smolin envisions a process of universal Darwinian evolution taking place. Those baby universes that happen to be better suited at producing organic life will presumably be more likely to survive and reproduce than other types of baby universes, because the same factors that are thought to be responsible for generating organic life forms (the ability to form coherent stars) are also thought to be responsible for generating baby universes as well (via the process of black hole formation). If this process of universal "reproduction" is repeated often enough, Smolin believes, a coherent life-supporting universe could eventually become a very real possibility.[13]

Smolin even believes that his theory is empirically testable. The test in this case is that the fundamental constants of our own universe should allow for maximal black hole formation.[14] There is, however, an important competing variable for this particular criterion that significantly weakens Smolin's argument. For while Smolin's speculative hypothesis may indeed be supported to a point by the efficacy of nature's fundamental constants in generating black holes, there is another competing explanation for this effect, namely, that the underlying conditions for the existence of life in the cosmos are the *very same conditions* that naturally tend to generate a large number of black holes. This realization casts a shadow of doubt on Smolin's sweeping conclusions, particularly since the phenomenon of life appears to be far more intrinsically valuable than an inanimate black hole could ever be. This being the case, it seems far more likely that the universe would have been "set up" primarily to encourage the rise of life, and not simply to promote the greatest number of black holes, since even the "lowest" life forms are intrinsically more valuable than an entire universe of black holes. On this view, the production of a maximal number of black holes is merely an inevitable side effect to those processes that are required to produce life.

Although much of the remaining science behind Smolin's work appears solid, it is still hard to imagine how a process of cosmic selection could possibly take place in a genuinely Godless universe. For one thing, Smolin doesn't even attempt to account for the origin of the "mother universe" itself, or for its curious propensity for generating functional baby universes. Hence the ultimate cosmological question still remains, which is this: "Why is there something rather than nothing, and why is this 'something' so cleverly attuned to producing baby universes, and through them, the miracle of life?" There seems to be no satisfactory way of responding to this conundrum without resorting to the existence of an Unmoved Mover, which seems to explain why so many of history's greatest thinkers (including Plato) have come to this very same conclusion.

It also seems overly extravagant and wasteful to posit such a huge number of reproducing universes just to explain the existence of our own universe, when a much simpler explanation can readily be formulated. It is far simpler, as we have seen, to simply posit the existence of an Intelligent Designer, who would have deliberately infused the universe with the capacity to bring about life from the very beginning.

As far as where the Creator Himself would have come from, the answer is simply that He has *always* been in existence. Theists believe that the Divine

Existence had no formal beginning, and while this may initially seem to be too difficult a concept to be comfortable with, it really isn't, because we deal with similar beginning-less "things" every day without even thinking about it. I am referring here to the grade school concept of a number line. Like God, the number line also has no formal beginning, because there are an infinite number of negative numbers that are smaller than zero, just as there are also an infinite number of fractions between zero and one. Moreover, in the same way that God Himself is without end, so too is there no formal end to the number line. But if we can deal with beginning-less and endless numbers every day without being overly perplexed, then why shouldn't we feel similarly comfortable about God's lack of a formal beginning or ending?

Many scientific skeptics, however, find this concept of the Divine aseity (or self-existence) to be grossly inadequate, on the rationale that a self-existing physical universe is just as possible as a self-existing Supernatural Being. But is this really true? For one thing, cosmologists are reasonably confident that the entire material realm suddenly exploded into being some 15 billion years ago at the Big Bang. But if this is so, then matter *couldn't* have existed forever.

Of course, it's always possible that matter in some form could have somehow preceded the Big Bang, but there is no empirical way to verify this. Indeed, if the Grand Unifying Theories of modern particle physics are correct, then the proton *necessarily* possesses a finite lifetime, which in turn means that matter as we know it could *not* have existed forever.

The traditional definition of the word "God" supports us in this conclusion, as it necessarily contains self-existence within itself as one of its chief defining properties. The same thing has *not* been said of finite, corruptible matter, for obvious reasons. After all, how could a finite, corruptible substance possibly possess the miraculous property of self-existence? Of course, it is always possible that self-existence is a hidden property of matter. But if this were true, then matter itself would be a "god," because it would have created the entire universe out of its own self-existence! So, there appears to be no coherent way of arguing for the self-existence of matter without simultaneously affirming the existence of some sort of creative deity.

Nevertheless, many theorists like to imagine an eternally existing material realm, which somehow stimulates itself into experiencing all possible spatial configurations over time. If this were so, it could conceivably lead to a spatial configuration that would eventually become hospitable to life. But where would the larger universe itself have come from? It seems deeply unsatisfying to simply assert that it has existed forever, for the aforementioned reasons.

Moreover, it is far from obvious that even a spatially infinite universe will explore all possible configurations over an infinite amount of time.[15]

The assumption is made here that all possible spatial configurations will eventually be explored in an infinite universe. But is this a realistic belief? What about those configurations that have been brought about by human creativity? Will *they* eventually be duplicated totally by chance in an infinite universe? Will Beethoven's Ninth Symphony or Michelangelo's *David* ever be precisely duplicated again at some point in the future, even given an infinite amount of time? It is very hard to see how this could be the case.

This type of argument rests on the assumption that the concept of infinity can somehow make up for the extreme degree of creativity that is displayed by intelligent creatures, but this just doesn't seem to be possible. As Father Copleston once pointed out in his famous debate with Bertrand Russell, if one has an infinity of chocolates, one still has chocolates all the way down! An infinite number of chocolates thus doesn't necessarily entail the eventual production of anything else besides chocolate.

It is important to distinguish, then, between spatial configurations that are only attainable through the vehicle of intelligent design and those that are attainable through random physical motions. Most intelligently designed configurations are, by their very nature, incapable of being spontaneously duplicated by random motions alone, even in an infinite universe. But if this is so, then the concept of infinity is only capable of compensating for those states of matter that are *randomly* possible, and not those that are the product of intelligent design. To the natural theologian, this means that our life-supporting universe is inherently *incapable* of being randomly generated, no matter how much time is allotted to this particular task.

But even if we assume that all possible spatial configurations are repeatedly being explored in our universe, this leads to the nonsensical conclusion that there must be an infinite number of worlds in existence that contain an infinite number of slight variations on the various themes that we are familiar with in our present world. An infinite number of Adolf Hitlers would thus exist in this scheme, as we have seen, with a widely varying array of personal characteristics. Some of these Hitlers would even be kind and loving individuals, because if there are an infinite number of worlds in existence, there must also by definition be an infinite number of gradations on all possible basic themes. But these are clearly ridiculous notions, so the very idea of an infinite universe is probably false.

With all this talk about an infinite universe, one might be tempted to think that there must be *some* concrete physical evidence for one. There isn't. To the contrary, there is a wealth of empirical evidence that points decidedly in the opposite direction, as we saw in chapters 8 and 9. Indeed, the whole point of the Big Bang is that the universe had to have begun a finite time ago from a common point of origination. But if this is so, then the universe must *necessarily* be of finite size, because it is impossible for an infinite amount of space to be created from nothing in a finite amount of time. Moreover, there isn't a shred of evidence that anything besides our present universe exists "out there." Not one speck of evidence has ever been amassed in support of other radically different regions within the larger universe itself, where things might be fundamentally different than they are here. Once again, we seem to be left with some form of Intelligent Design as the best explanation for our Goldilocks Universe.

There is yet another way in which one can conceptualize a random origin to our biocentric universe. It entails the notion of an oscillating universe, which we encountered at length in chapter 3. On this view, our "just right" universe has experienced a countless series of "bangs" and "crunches" in the distant cosmological past, with each successive "crunch and bang" spontaneously producing different values for each of nature's fundamental constants. The basic idea here is that if this oscillating series went on long enough, it is possible that the "right" combination of constants could have resulted by chance alone.

Once again, though, no attempt is made here to explain where this spontaneously expanding and contracting cosmic system could have originally come from in the first place, or how it could have possibly obtained this capacity to cycle back and forth in this manner. These factors are simply taken as axiomatic givens; but this is clearly unsatisfactory, because it is precisely these capacities that we are ultimately trying to explain here.

Indeed, it is by no means clear that our present universe will ever collapse back in on itself. To the contrary, present measurements regarding the density of the universe and its overall expansion rate indicate that it will probably go on expanding *forever*.[16] If this is true, then it automatically invalidates this "cosmic bounce" proposal once and for all.

Other factors legislate decisively against the prospect of an oscillating universe. For as we have seen, thermodynamic considerations make it impossible for our present universe to have experienced a significant number of previous cycles.[17] Hugh Ross builds on this conclusion by noting that the universe is by far the most entropic (i.e., disorder-producing) phenomenon known.[18] As a consequence, even if the universe were to eventually collapse back in on itself, it "would *not* produce a bounce. Far too much of the energy of the universe is dissipated in unreclaimable form to fuel a bounce. Like a clump of wet clay falling on a carpet, the universe, if it did collapse, would go 'splat.'"[19]

But if we do not live in an eternal, oscillating universe, we are left with the conclusion that the Big Bang probably was a unique event, which of course is to say that the universe almost certainly *did* have an actual beginning long ago. A recent barrage of highly sophisticated cosmological data has now empirically confirmed the validity of this theoretical scenario to an unprecedented degree of accuracy.[20] This is significant, because we are now compelled to come up with a realistic explanation for the sudden, perfect appearance of this primordial explosion.

Is Our Goldilocks Universe Self-Sufficient?

We have seen that the most powerful argument for the existence of an Intelligent Designer appeals to the perfect fine-tuning of nature's fundamental constants, which have evidently occupied their present life-supporting values from the very beginning. This state of affairs is virtually inconceivable in the absence of an Intelligent Designer, because there is no time immediately following the Big Bang for a process of natural selection to occur amongst the constants themselves.

Hence, in order for any nontheistic explanation of the universe to succeed, it must provide a plausible mechanism for how the constants could have come to occupy their present life-supporting values by chance alone. Until recently, this appeared to be a near unattainable task, but new findings in quantum cosmology have led to bold new theories about how our fine-tuned universe could have come into being. The most important of these theories utilizes a form of cosmological Darwinism to account for this mysterious fine-tuning, as we saw in the previous section. It was originally conceived by cosmologist Lee Smolin, and it has recently been popularized by John Gribbin in his book *In the Beginning*.

Gribbin begins his version of the argument by calling into question Barrow and Tipler's conclusion that the values of nature's fundamental constants have been invariant for as long as the universe has been in existence.[21] He doesn't question their invariant nature as far as our present universal order is concerned, but he does speculate that the constants could have taken on other values before the Big Bang. As a consequence, Gribbin wants to know what was going on *before* the Big Bang, because he believes that this possible state of affairs holds the key to explaining why the constants are as precisely fine-tuned as they are.

Up until now, these questions have been the near exclusive province of philosophers and theologians, because science by its very nature is prevented from probing back in time before the Big Bang. The reason for this is that the very equations that scientists use to study the universe break down completely when they are projected back to the so-called Planck time, when the universe was a mere 10^{-43} seconds old. The history of the universe before this time is thus forever beyond the reach of empirical science.

As far as the "time" before the Big Bang itself is concerned, most physicists agree that such a question is meaningless from an empirical point of view. This is because the most recent scientific consensus states that there was no such thing as time at all prior to the Big Bang, since time itself is presumed to have come into being during that primordial blast. Hence, Gribbin's questioning about what was going on "before" the Big Bang is very much off base as far as the beliefs of empirical scientists themselves are concerned. Nevertheless, Gribbin persists in this line of reasoning anyway, because he *has* to resort to such extreme lengths in order to do away with the prospect of an Intelligent Designer.

Gribbin wants to argue that there were indeed physical events going on before the Big Bang, because he wants to credit them with the perfect calibration of nature's fundamental constants. He wants to do this because again, this is what *must* be done if the idea of God is going to be expunged from the realm of cosmological theory once and for all. For as long as it is possible to come up with a suitable naturalistic explanation for the specific values of the constants, the need for an Intelligent Designer would then seem to be superfluous.[22]

In order for this goal to be accomplished, though, a way must be found to expose the constants to some form of natural selection prior to the Big Bang, because we now know that the constants themselves have remained unchanged throughout this entire cosmic epoch.[23] This makes Gribbin's goal problematic by its very nature, since our modern understanding of the universe is based, as we have seen, on the presupposition that space, time, and matter all came into existence at the Big Bang.

Nevertheless, we can still assume, for the sake of argument, that some form of existence may have preceded the Big Bang. If we do this, it then becomes possible to posit, as Gribbin has done, the existence of a series of "baby universes" that are able to continually reproduce themselves over time, so that slight variations in the resulting "progeny" can then be amplified by a process of natural selection, just as we see happening in the organic realm. To the extent that Gribbin's assumptions turn out to be valid, it is possible that a self-reproducing series of "baby universes" could have accidentally fine-tuned itself over billions of years to support life by selection alone.

In support of this contention, Gribbin argues that the entire universe is alive, not simply in a figurative or metaphorical sense, but in a completely literal fashion. He draws this conclusion for two reasons. First, certain types of cosmic processes, such as those regulating intragalactic self-maintenance activities, do indeed seem to have much in common with the various processes of life. The most important of these processes as far as Gribbin is concerned is cosmic self-reproduction, because it provides a plausible mechanism for an ongoing process of natural selection. This is why Gribbin wants to believe that the universe is alive in the first place, because it is the capacity for self-reproduction, which is one of the hallmarks of life, that allows for a gradual process of cosmic selection with each successive generation of "progeny."

Gribbin finds support for this belief in the fact that the universe seems to have evolved in a way that is primarily good for it alone. To the extent that this is so, it would seem to indicate that any derivative benefits that we humans have been able to enjoy over the years have ultimately been accidental in nature. Gribbin fully affirms this belief, since he clearly states that humanity is only the incidental byproduct of a much larger cosmic quest for survival and expansion.[24]

Having made this radical point, Gribbin then moves on to wonder what is "being selected for out there in the universe at large?"[25] Since the universe itself has concentrated heavily on the production of main sequence stars and heavy elements—both of which are essential ingredients in our own evolution—he then questions why these things may be "good" for the universe itself.

Gribbin comes up with a plausible answer to this question by showing how both the process of carbon nucleosynthesis in stellar interiors, as well as the release of this newly synthesized carbon via gigantic supernova explosions, are essential for the continued formation of these same types of heavenly bodies. He notes, for instance, that the shock waves produced by supernova explosions are "just the thing to squeeze any nearby *gas and dust* clouds that are on the brink of collapsing to form new stars, setting off a further burst of star formation"[26]

Gribbin goes on to point out that the process of star formation is much more difficult than might initially be expected, because a great deal of gravitational energy is released when clouds of gas and dust begin condensing into stars. This energy heats up the molecules themselves, which in turn produces an outer pressure that acts to oppose the overall condensation process. As a consequence, a way must be found to dissipate this gravitational energy in the form of radiation, otherwise most clouds would never be able to condense to the densities that are needed for star formation. That is to say, when the molecules that are at the center of a condensing cloud reach a certain temperature, they begin radiating a great deal of energy in the form of visible light and ultraviolet radiation. The pressure that is produced by this radiation is so intense that it would end up aborting the process of star formation altogether (by blowing the cloud completely apart), were it not for the existence of tiny carbon grains in the cloud itself, which have the ability to absorb this ultraviolet radiation so it can then be reradiated back out into space again in the form of infrared radiation, which itself is able to escape into space more transparently. This process of reradiation in the infrared has the effect of preserving the integrity of these shrinking clouds, thus making it much more likely that bona fide stars will end up forming in the end.[27] Gribbin further points out that the process of star formation is almost entirely self-regulating as well, insofar as the amount of matter that is incorporated into new stars is very close to the amount that is ejected back to interstellar space by dying stars.

After making this point, Gribbin goes on to show how this process of star formation is intimately dependent on a precise balance between the various forces of nature. He notes, for instance, that the strength of the weak force has to be perfectly calibrated in order to allow supernovae to explode, so that their vital life-supporting contents can then be dispersed throughout interstellar space. He similarly notes how the many coincidences that are known to facilitate intrastellar carbon formation are also simultaneously essential to the complicated process of star-building.

But instead of acknowledging how these star-forming coincidences are clearly beneficial for the human race (which they are), he claims that they were "set up,"

> so that galaxies like our Milky Way can operate as supernova nurseries, producing successive generations of massive, short-lived stars in association with spiral arms. It just happens that these processes require carbon, and the presence of complex organic molecules, and water. So the production of carbon-based organic molecules has evolved as part of the life processes of galaxies. Once that carbon, those organic molecules, and water exist, it was probably inevitable that life-forms like us should evolve. But we are at best seen as a by-product of the processes by which our Galaxy maintains itself in a far from equilibrium state—the processes by which it keeps itself alive.[28]

In other words, Gribbin takes the universe's capacity for self-maintenance as convincing evidence that the universe was somehow responsible for creating itself. He also takes the involvement of natural selection in these processes as further evidence of its random and meaningless origin. Gribbin doesn't seem to realize, though, that a theistic worldview provides a much better explanation for this perfect fit between the present cosmic structure and the various processes of natural selection. For as long as an Intelligent Designer would have wanted to create a stable home for human beings that would itself be capable of persisting for billions of years, it makes sense to suppose that

He would have wanted to create precisely the same sort of self-perpetuating universe that we presently observe. It is, therefore, a mistake to suppose that the close fit between natural selection and the existing cosmic structure *necessarily* means that the universe had to have had a totally naturalistic origin.

On one level of analysis Gribbin's argument appears to be somewhat persuasive. There is also a certain amount of desirability that is naturally associated with being objective and nonpresumptuous, especially when it comes to trying to figure out humanity's overall role in the cosmos. Consequently, when one discovers that a certain set of cosmological circumstances happens to be favored by natural selection, it suddenly seems less puzzling that these circumstances should in fact obtain. In the same way, when one discovers that this is the same set of circumstances that happens to favor the existence of organic life, it is tempting to conclude that one has therefore "explained" the existence of life. And while this view seems to have a lot going for it, it turns out to be much too simplistic when it is viewed from a larger perspective, because the available facts can be shown to openly contradict it.

The problem isn't so much with the idea that the galaxies themselves might be "alive" in some sort of extended biological sense. Indeed, I have argued elsewhere[29] that God seems to have used the basic features of the Human Form as His developmental template for designing the entire cosmos. On this view, the entire universe grows and evolves like a human being because it was originally designed according to the same overall model or pattern. The basic problem, then, with Gribbin's view isn't so much to be found in the specific types of objects or processes that he observes in the universe. It is, rather, to be found in his conceptualization of how the universe itself ultimately originated.

In keeping with his nontheistic view of cosmogenesis, Gribbin believes that the fundamental constants themselves were somehow "set up" (his phrase) to promote stellar evolution and not to promote the existence of human beings as such. The first part of this belief is clearly acceptable to the Theistic Evolutionist, because the universe *had* to have initially been set up to promote stellar evolution in order to allow for *our own* existence. Thus, if the constants weren't fine-tuned to promote the formation of stars, we wouldn't be here to discuss the fact. Even so, Gribbin fails to see it this way, since he believes that our own existence is merely an incidental side-effect to a universe that was somehow "set up" to promote its own self-propagation through time. Gribbin's beliefs are thus clearly antagonistic toward theism, so it isn't surprising that he leaves out even an indirect mention of a larger Creator.

Curiously, though, Gribbin leaves the primary question that is at issue here unaccounted for. He claims that the constants were "set up" in order to promote stellar evolution, but he doesn't even attempt to identify who or what might have been responsible for doing the initial setting up. This is a question-begging deficiency in his argument that undermines it from the very outset. For in the end, it is only an academic distinction as to whether the constants were directly set up for the stars and only indirectly for us or vice versa. What really matters here is *who* ultimately did the setting up in the first place. And since this is clearly the central question that is at issue here, Gribbin can't properly assume the prior, unexplained existence of this "setup" and then turn around and claim to have explained how the constants themselves were originally calibrated! This is the fallacy of circular reasoning, and it totally undermines the validity of Gribbin's conclusion.

In Gribbin's own words, there are only two possible explanations for the way the universe itself has been set up: blind chance or deliberate design.[30] Interestingly, though, Gribbin admits that the latter possibility intuitively seems to be the correct one:

> The more you look at the way our Universe is set up, the more it seems to be set up in a very odd way, to encourage nucleosynthesis and the formation of stars, planets, and people. In his book *Galaxies, Nuclei, and Quasars* (published in 1965), Hoyle says that it looks as if "the laws of physics have been deliberately designed with regard to the consequences they produce inside stars." He has also described the Universe, and the carbon and oxygen resonances in particular, as a "put-up job."[31]

However, Gribbin immediately acts to discredit this intuitive conclusion by arguing that it is

> almost exactly the "argument of design" used, before evolution was understood, as evidence for the existence of God (it still is used, as an alleged refutation of the ideas of evolution, by people who do not—or will not—understand Darwin's theory). . . . The refutation of this *design* argument is that evolution by natural selection does not operate by chance in the way that the argument from design suggests as the only alternative to the hand of God. Variations from one generation to the next—mutations—may indeed occur at random, but the *selection* process, essential to evolution, is not random at all, and involves selection *of the fittest*.[32]

Gribbin's fatal mistake in the above argument rests on his assumption that the evolutionary process is somehow mutually exclusive with the activities of an Intelligent Designer. This is a fallacious presumption that was laid to rest long ago by such theistic evolutionists as Robert Chambers, Asa Gray, Richard Owen, the Duke of Argyll, St. George Jackson Mivart, and even

Charles Darwin himself, who was a self-confessed deist.[33] Indeed, even the text of Genesis One is set up in a stepwise, evolutionary manner (in the sense of representing a logical sequence of universal changes with respect to time), so there is no question that the generic process of evolution itself is consistent with the workings of an Intelligent Designer. Nevertheless, the misguided efforts of many scientific creationists have put a dark cloud over this harmonious relationship between creation and evolution, because these individuals have argued that the process of evolution *in any form* is intrinsically incompatible with the biblical record. Although this assertion can be demonstrated[34] to be false, millions of scientists and laymen have nevertheless been duped into believing it to be true. Therefore, it comes as no surprise that scientific advocates of the neo-Darwinian perspective, such as John Gribbin, Stephen Jay Gould, and Richard Dawkins, continue to presume that any form of creation must be false.

But this isn't necessarily true at all. To the contrary, I have argued elsewhere[35] that the process of evolution *itself* is untenable in the absence of an Intelligent Designer. For not only do we need a Creator to bring the entire universe into being (or to "breathe fire into the equations," as Stephen Hawking has put it), we also need a Creator to account for the many self-organizing powers of atoms and molecules, as well as to explain the perfect calibration of nature's fundamental constants. It doesn't do any good to merely assume the prior existence of a self-reproducing set of galaxies and star systems, because the ultimate question that is at issue here concerns where they originally got *their* self-organizing power.

Natural selection alone clearly cannot be given all the credit for bringing this self-organizing tendency into being, because this still leaves the origin of the selective process *itself* unaccounted for. Hence, in order for any cosmological theory to be plausible, it must first provide a sufficient explanation as to where the selective process itself could have come from, and this seems next to impossible without invoking the activity of an Intelligent Designer. For even though an inorganic process of selection could have conceivably led to the evolution of the first living cell, this still leaves the self-organizing power of atoms and molecules unaccounted for. Not coincidentally, it is precisely this power for atomic self-organization that is by far the most difficult thing for scientists to explain, because it involves a number of profoundly complex subatomic principles, such as the phenomenon of quantization and the Pauli Exclusion Principle, that we are nowhere near understanding at the present time.

Predictably, though, Gribbin chooses to simply take these subatomic self-organizing principles for granted, probably because there doesn't seem to be any conceivable naturalistic explanation for them. But this sort of assumption ends up undermining his entire argument, because it involves the fallacy of circular reasoning or the positing of his conclusion in his beginning premise. For as we have seen, Gribbin is trying to argue that the entire universe is totally self-organizing by its very nature, and moreover, that this self-organizing power is what has been responsible for the remarkable fine-tuning of nature's fundamental constants. However, in order to properly arrive at this conclusion, Gribbin must first provide a plausible explanation for where this self-organizing power itself could have come from. He can't simply take it to be a mere given, because the ultimate question that is being debated here is precisely the *origin* of this self-organizing power. But Gribbin wants to avoid this sticky problem by simply assuming that the universe has *always* had this power to evolve by the power of natural selection. He can't legitimately do this, however, without begging the true question that is at issue here, as we have seen. Until Gribbin can answer this question in a plausible fashion, his argument fails on the weight of this one fallacy alone.

St. Thomas would have agreed with this surmisal, because he realized that one cannot account for the properties of a given material system without accounting for the existence of the larger system itself. This is the basic idea behind the age-old Cosmological Argument for the existence of God. And since the age of the universe is now known to be finite, we can't keep pushing the list of contingent causes back indefinitely. The cosmic "buck" has to stop somewhere, and the only place where it can find a proper resting place is with the "Unmoved Mover" Himself, because God is by definition the only entity who contains within Himself a sufficient explanation for His own existence.

Gribbin claims that it is the nonrandom nature of the selective process that undermines[36] the traditional Argument from Design, but this conclusion is also mistaken. Gribbin correctly states that the chief alternative to the Design Argument is evolution by chance, but he then confuses the nonrandomness of natural selection with the alleged nonrandomness of evolution itself. Having done this, he then concludes that evolution is not the random event that philosophical theists have made it out to be, so he consequently proclaims the Design Argument to be invalid.

This precarious bit of reasoning fails on several counts. First, the nonrandomness of natural selection doesn't necessarily carry over into a nonrandom process of evolution. That is to say, one can have a randomly generated process of evolution and *still* have a nonrandom process of natural selection within it. The distinction that is thus being drawn here is between natural selection, on the one hand, and the cosmic conditions that were necessary to produce it, on the other. But Gribbin doesn't seem to recognize this distinction, because he wants to argue that the nonrandomness of selection automatically carries over into a nonrandom process of evolution in general, but such a conclusion doesn't follow at all, as we have seen, because the very basis of the atheistic position is that life itself is the *accidental* byproduct of cosmic forces that were themselves random and unplanned.

The true issue here thus isn't whether or not the selective process itself is random, but whether cosmic existence in general was ultimately preplanned and therefore designed. This being the case, the purported nonrandomness of selection is irrelevant to the basic question that is being debated here, which in turn means that it has no significant effect on the intrinsic plausibility of the Design Argument.

In other words, even if it turns out to be true that our present cosmic structure was produced by a Godless brand of selection, this doesn't mean that our lives are suddenly nonrandom in a larger metaphysical sense, just because the process of selection itself is supposedly nonrandom. To the contrary, our world would remain just as much a product of chance as ever, no matter how many nonrandom events are known to have taken place within it.

The persistent use of natural selection as a metaphysical explanatory tool also turns out to be self-defeating as well for the nontheist, because we still have to come up with a sufficient explanation for where the selective forces themselves ultimately came from. It is very difficult for any Godless cosmology to do this without appealing to other forms of natural selection, but natural selection alone clearly cannot give rise to itself (in the sense of serving as a sufficient explanation for its own existence), so it is evident that some *other* power or force had to have originally been responsible for bringing the selective process into being.

Indeed, if natural selection alone were the sole arbiter of the trend toward greater complexity, life would have probably never evolved to begin with, because the selective process *itself* would have never come into being. We mustn't forget that the phenomenon of self-replication, which is the very basis of natural selection, is *itself* a highly sophisticated property that inherently requires a substantial amount of complexity in order to be operative. It follows from this realization that matter *had* to have been self-organizing from the very beginning; otherwise, the twin processes of self-replication and natural selection would have never come into being, and we would not be here.

In other words, natural selection *presupposes* a significant degree of self-organization in matter. This is due to the fact that the only objects that natural selection can act upon are self-replicators, and self-replication is a sophisticated form of complexity that requires the prior existence of self-organizing atoms and molecules. Hence, natural selection in all probability could not have been responsible for generating the property of self-replication, since natural selection could not possibly have taken place before self-replication ever existed.

It follows, then, that the twin properties of self-organization and self-replication are necessarily *prior to* the property of being subject to natural selection, which in turn means that there had to have been a sufficient cause for matter to have originally become self-replicating in the first place; otherwise, natural selection almost certainly would have never become operational to begin with. This sufficient cause was probably a self-organizing drive internal to matter, as we saw in chapter 9, because chance processes alone do not seem to be capable of producing self-replicating atoms and molecules, even over immense stretches of time.

The only way the nontheist can escape from this dilemma is to assert that matter could have *accidentally* acquired the property of self-replication entirely by chance. However, it is very hard to see how this could have ever been the case, especially if it is asserted that no natural tendency toward self-organization exists in matter (apart from the action of natural selection), and moreover, if it is acknowledged that natural selection is inoperative in a positive sense at this relatively simple level of organization.

Indeed, in order for matter to have accidentally acquired the property of self-replication, it first had to have discovered a means of becoming stable at the subatomic level. But as any particle physicist will immediately attest, this is a very tall order indeed, because subatomic stability is an *exceedingly* complex phenomenon that is only just beginning to be understood by theorists. It is unlikely to the highest degree that matter could have accidentally stumbled upon the two chief prerequisites for subatomic stability, the principle of quantization and the Pauli Exclusion Principle, by chance alone, again because of their overwhelmingly complicated internal nature. These stabilization mechanisms are so profoundly complex, in fact, that our best minds haven't even begun to understand how they actually operate at the subatomic level. But if these two properties are so complex that our most brilliant scientists continue to be baffled by them, it is exceedingly unlikely that matter could have discovered a means of employing them purely by accident, which in turn means that matter in all likelihood did not acquire the twin properties of self-organization and self-replication by chance alone.

Is Our "Just Right" Universe a Free Lunch?

Gribbin's chief point is that we don't need a supernatural Designer to explain the perfect calibration of nature's fundamental constants, because the very existence of a cosmos evolving by natural selection can explain this calibration in an entirely naturalistic fashion. We have already seen how the process of selection itself cannot be used as a self-sufficient explanatory device, but even if we grant, for the sake of argument, the prior, unexplained existence of a universe evolving by natural selection, Gribbin's point *still* isn't very persuasive, as we shall now see in more detail.

In order to set the stage for his nontheistic argument, Gribbin explains how the various galaxies in the universe have been able to selectively evolve in a strict Darwinian sense toward the "goal" of being entirely self-propagating. They have been able to do this because the traits that regulate this process of self-propagation are selectively preserved by the ongoing process of natural selection itself. Hence, we shouldn't be surprised, according to Gribbin, that "clouds which are 'just right' for the birth of many supernovae produce supernovae which are 'just right' for the production of clouds similar to the ones that gave them birth."[37] For as long as a variety of physical traits are produced during each act of stellar reproduction, it is clear that the only ones that will be capable of persisting for many generations will be those that naturally favor the process of stellar reproduction. This is a process of evolution by natural selection that is exactly analogous to the same process in organic beings because, as we have seen, Gribbin believes that the entire universe itself is actually alive in a strict biological sense. Gribbin therefore doesn't find it surprising that galaxies are able to continue reproducing themselves the way biological organisms do.

Gribbin makes this point in order to move on to the chief argument of his book, which is that the same sort of selective process that gave rise to self-propagating galaxies also gave rise to the entire universe itself. He is able to make this point because of a series of recent developments in the field of quantum cosmology, which indicate that small bubbles of mass-energy can spontaneously form by pure chance in the vacuum of space, due to the phenomenon of quantum uncertainty. While the vast majority of these bubbles will quickly pop back out of existence, it is possible for one to spontaneously inflate to a much larger size, due to the existence of another set of physical laws that promote rapid inflation.[38] It is even conceivable that one of these bubbles could spontaneously grow into a universe that is similar to our own.

MIT physicist Alan Guth has called this theory of cosmogenesis the "ultimate free lunch," because the universe on this view is thought to be able to pop into existence out of nothing at all, due to unpredictable quantum fluctuations. It is important to understand, though, that this sort of quantum fluctuation doesn't take place out of *absolute* nothingness. It takes place out of a larger *quantum field* that apparently underlies all of physical reality. Without this mysterious quantum field, there wouldn't be any such thing as quantum events at all, yet the proponents of this "free lunch" theory have conveniently chosen not to mention it, because it directly contradicts their thesis in two related ways. First and foremost, the very existence of a pervasive quantum field throughout the universe conclusively shows that the universe could not have popped into existence out of *absolute* nothingness. Thus, in order to provide a plausible explanation for the present universal order, quantum cosmologists must first explain the nature and origin of this primordial quantum field; and needless to say, they are nowhere near doing *that* at the present time. This realization would seem to eliminate the free lunch hypothesis from serious consideration.

But there is another serious problem with the free lunch hypothesis that has to do with the property of time. In order for the universe to have been able to pop into existence as a spontaneous quantum fluctuation, there had to have been a sufficient amount of time available for this to happen, as Hugh Ross has pointed out:

> Quantum mechanics is founded on the concept that quantum events occur according to finite probabilities within finite intervals of time. The larger the time interval, the greater the probability that a specific quantum event will occur. This means that if the time interval is zero, the probability for that event occurring is also zero. Because time began when the universe was created, the time interval is zero, eliminating quantum tunneling (i.e., the free lunch hypothesis) as a possible candidate to be the creator of the cosmos.[39]

There is only one way for proponents of the free lunch hypothesis to get around this huge weakness in their theory. They have to assert that time did *not* come into being at the Big Bang, but this presupposition contradicts one of the most hallowed findings of modern cosmology, namely, that both space and time *did* actually come into existence at the Big Bang and therefore could not have existed prior to it. Stephen Hawking, George Ellis, and Roger Penrose are credited with making this epic discovery, called the Space-Time Theorem of General Relativity, which itself is based on a mathematical extension of general relativity to include space and time.[40] Hugh Ross has called it "the most theologically significant theorem of all time," and indeed it is.[41] This is most unfortunate for the free lunch hypothesis, though, since it can't possibly be true as long as the Space-Time Theorem is also true. But the Space-Rime Theorem is one of the most empirically validated theorems ever devised, because it is based on Einstein's general theory of relativity, which itself has been shown to be accurate to within five decimal places.[42] According to the latest findings of modern empirical science, then, the free lunch hypothesis cannot be true.

Nevertheless, let us suppose, for the sake of argument, that time did indeed exist prior to the Big Bang and that a pervasive quantum field also happened to simultaneously exist, so that bubbles of virtual energy were then somehow able to spontaneously form out of this field by chance processes alone. Even if we allow this much, it *still* doesn't provide us with a convincing explanation for our own universe, since there is always the "puzzle of fine tuning" that needs to be accounted for, "because there is no obvious reason why inflation itself should have just the right strength to 'make' a universe like our own out of tiny quantum fluctuation of the vacuum."[43] Indeed, Gribbin fully admits that our biocentric universe is so profoundly complex that it could not "have appeared just by chance out of a random quantum fluctuation of the vacuum."[44] But this is the entire crux of the matter, because everyone agrees that nature's fundamental constants could never have spontaneously taken on their present biocentric values by chance alone, at least not in a sample size of anything less than infinity. But there is no evidence at all that the sample size of our universe exceeds one.[45] Therefore, cosmological theories that are based on an infinite number of different universes are founded upon "a flagrant abuse of probability theory."[46] All we have evidence for is a single universe, which we now know is permeated through and through with the conditions that are necessary for the existence of life. Therefore, we only really need to come up with a plausible explanation for the fine-tuning of our one universe alone.

Not surprisingly, Gribbin has a naturalistic explanation for this, too. For instead of postulating the spontaneous appearance of our biocentric universe in one huge step, Gribbin believes that it slowly made its appearance over vast eons of time, as natural selection worked its magic with successive generations of "baby universes." For as we have seen, it is possible that each of these baby universes could have displayed slight variations in the laws of physics, in which case it may have been possible for there to have been a subsequent process of selection amongst the baby universes themselves. In this case, selection would favor those baby universes that happen to be geared toward the production of additional black holes and baby universes.[47] This process of selection, according to Gribbin, should also favor the production of progressively larger baby universes, because "the number of new universes produced in each generation will be roughly proportional to the volume of the parent universe. There is even an element of competition involved, if the many baby universes are in some sense vying with one another, jostling for space-time elbow room within superspace."[48]

Gribbin goes on to draw the obvious analogy here with selection in the biological realm:

Universes that are "successful" are the ones that leave the most offspring. Provided the random mutations are indeed small, there will be a genuinely evolutionary process favouring larger and larger universes. Once universes start to be big enough to allow stars to form, in succeeding generations of universes there will be a natural evolution of the laws of physics. This will favour a drift in the laws and in properties like the carbon energy resonance and the mass difference between the proton and the neutron, a drift which in turn will increasingly favour the production of stars that will eventually form black holes. . . .

This explains the otherwise baffling mystery of why the Universe we live in should be "set up" in what seems, at first sight, such an unusual way. Just as you would not expect a random collection of chemicals to organize themselves suddenly into a human being, so you would not expect a random collection of physical laws emerging from a singularity to give rise to a universe like the one we live in.[49]

But even though Gribbin seems to fully recognize the tremendous power of the Anthropic Design Argument, he still chooses to reject it! A commonsense interpretation of the facts does indeed suggest that our universe has been intelligently designed after all, as Hoyle has pointed out, but not everyone is open to this type of theistic conclusion.

This sort of behavior is reminiscent of George Greenstein's reaction toward the prospect of a Creator in *The Symbiotic Universe*. After providing a list of the many conditions that had to have been met before life could have evolved here, Greenstein makes the following observation:

As we survey all the evidence, the thought insistently arises that some supernatural agency—or, rather, Agency—must be involved. Is it possible that suddenly, without intending to, we have stumbled upon scientific proof of the existence of a Supreme Being? Was it God who stepped in and so providentially crafted the cosmos for our benefit?[50]

Surprisingly, though, Greenstein also chooses to reject this theistic possibility, because he doesn't believe that a reference to God can explain even a single one of these coincidences.[51] In one fell swoop, then, Greenstein opts to totally dismiss *any* type of theistic alternative.

Greenstein doesn't believe that God is an explanation because "it is no more than a confession of ignorance to give a religious answer to a question pertaining to matters of fact. The lesson of history is plain on this matter: Time and time again people have sought to account for some mystery by reference to God's wishes, and time and time again a purely natural explanation has been found."[52]

Greenstein is actually using a God of the gaps criticism to undermine any type of theistic alternative to the standard evolutionary view. And in a certain limited sense he is right: it is useless to attribute most of the physical phenomena in our universe *directly* to an Intelligent Designer, because secondary causes seem to cause all, or virtually all, of the physical events throughout the cosmos. The fallacy in Greenstein's line of argument, though, lies in its short-sighted conceptualization of the Divine Power, since it assumes that God must be the *direct* or primary cause of most of the events in our experience. But this isn't necessarily the case at all. To the contrary, it is much more expedient to view God in the same way that Charles Darwin's grandfather Erasmus did before him, namely, as the cause of the various causes of events in the universe.

Another way of saying this is that while God may have originally been responsible for creating the various laws of nature, He nevertheless allows these same natural laws to operate on their own power today to produce the various events that we observe in the universe. On this view it would be a serious mistake to try to identify God as the direct or primary cause of virtually *anything* that we can physically observe in the cosmos, because He is much more appropriately conceptualized as the underlying *foundation* of physical reality itself. This is why Greenstein's God of the gaps criticism is a farce—because the true creativity of God isn't to be found in the realm of efficient causation itself; it is, rather, to be found in the underlying system of physical laws that allows for the existence of our self-organizing universe in the first place. Hence, as far as the Theistic Evolutionist is concerned, Greenstein's criticism is totally off-base, because God clearly *can* be a legitimate explanation for the existence of the entire universe, even if He isn't a direct or primary cause of the various physical events that transpire within it.

The Theistic Evolutionist thus fully expects that a legitimate physical cause will eventually be found for *all* of the immediate physical events in our universe, but *not* for the perfect calibration of the fundamental constants or for the laws of nature themselves. Hugh Ross agrees:

> For centuries Christians were criticized for their "God of the gaps." Sometimes that criticism was deserved. Christians tended to use gaps in understanding or data to build a case for God's miraculous intervention. Then, when scientific discoveries offered a natural explanation for the "divine phenomenon," ridicule was heaped not only on those proposing the divine explanation but also on belief in God's existence.
>
> In the twentieth century we see the reverse of the God of the gaps. Non-theists, confronted with problems for which ample research leads to no natural explanations and instead points to the supernatural, utterly reject the possibility of the supernatural and insist on a natural explanation even if it means resorting to absurdity.[53]

So the God of the Theistic Evolutionist can indeed be used as a legitimate explanation within our present universal scheme. Nevertheless, Gribbin still chooses to go to extreme lengths to provide a naturalistic explanation for our fine-tuned universe. He does so, as we have seen, by proposing a gradual process of selection between baby universes that form out of black holes. The advantage of this theoretical maneuver is that it allows for a comparatively simple beginning to the universe itself, which is a situation that would surely need to have been obtained if the universe were merely the product of chance alone. The baby universes that would have followed this comparatively simple point of initiation can then be imagined to have become progressively more complex with the passage of time, due to the cumulative effects of natural selection, until eventually, our own biocentric universe would have come into being, purely by chance! As Gribbin himself explains:

> Before Charles Darwin and Alfred Russell Wallace came up with the idea of evolution, many people believed that the only way to explain the existence of so unlikely an organism as a human being was by supernatural intervention; recently, the apparent unlikelihood of the Universe has led some people to suggest that the Big Bang itself may have resulted from supernatural intervention. But there is no longer any basis for invoking the supernatural. We live in a Universe which is exactly the most likely kind of universe to exist, if there are many living universes that have evolved in the same way that living things on earth have evolved. And the fact that our Universe is "just right" for organic life-forms like ourselves turns out to be no more than a side-effect of the fact that it is "just right" for the production of black holes and baby universes. . . . Although it is now clear that the Universe has not been set up for our benefit, and that the existence of organic life-forms on Earth is simply a minor side-effect of an evolutionary process involving universes, galaxies, and stars which actually favours the production of black holes, nevertheless it is clear that the existence of life-forms like ourselves is an inevitable side-effect of those greater evolutionary processes.[54]

Gribbin implies in the above passage that both Darwin and Wallace were nontheists, but this simply isn't the case. For as I have explained at length elsewhere, both Darwin and Wallace openly acknowledged their belief in *some* type of Creator.[55] Darwin's God was deistic in nature, and he even went so far as to base his entire theory on the underlying presumption that God had originally created the same self-organizing molecules that later evolved on their own power into the entire living world. This is the same sort of deistic Creator that Darwin's grandfather Erasmus believed in, and while the younger Darwin's beliefs were often plagued with doubt, especially concerning the issue of why a benevolent Creator would have employed such a pain-filled natural process to create the biosphere, he nevertheless continued to believe in a deistic Creator throughout most of his career. As for Wallace, he was much more up front with his theistic inclinations, as he publicly stated on numerous occasions that the evolution of human intelligence by natural selection alone was next to impossible, since it would have provided us with a brain that was barely superior to that of an ape.

So both of the founding fathers of modern evolutionary theory believed in the existence of some type of Creator. This basic historical fact renders Gribbin's argument much less convincing, because it is based on the prior assumption that modern Darwinism is intrinsically opposed to *any* form of theistic evolution.

But even if we disregard the God-fearing inclinations of both Darwin and Wallace, Gribbin nevertheless has been much too hasty with his radical conclusion, because there is no way that we can know for a certainty that the universe has not been set up for our benefit, the way he implies. This conclusion isn't justified at all by the mere fact that the process of natural selection in the universe favors the formation of black holes and baby universes, because the same thing would be true for Theistic Evolution as well. A universe that has been set up for our benefit will also maintain the continued reproduction of entire star systems, because we never would have been able to exist without these self-propagating galaxies. This is an important competing variable that Gribbin hasn't taken into account. If anything, the greater amount of intrinsic value that human beings possess, in relation to black holes and baby universes, makes it much more likely that we are the ultimate beneficiaries of this felicitous arrangement. The following quote from physicist Paul Davies supports this contention:

> The essential feature of our universe is that something of value emerges as the result of processing according to some ingenious pre-existing set of rules. It looks *as if* they are the product of intelligent design. I do not see how this can be denied. Whether you wish to believe that they really *have* been so designed, and if so by what sort of being, must remain a matter of personal taste. My own inclination is to suppose that qualities such as ingenuity, economy, beauty, and so on have a genuine transcendent reality—they are not merely the product of human experience—and that these qualities are reflected in the structure of the natural world.[56]

Davies' point is well taken, because human consciousness *is* without question the most complex and sophisticated property in the entire known universe. Indeed, it is this singular fact that leads most anthropically minded cosmologists to conclude that the universe does indeed revolve around human existence in one way or another. In his memorable closing to *The Mind of God*, Davies agrees that it is the remarkable nature of human intelligence that tips the scales in favor of Intelligent Design:

We have cracked part of the cosmic code. Why this should be, just why *Homo sapiens* should carry the spark of rationality that provides the key to the universe, is a deep enigma. We, who are children of the universe—animated stardust—can nevertheless reflect on the nature of the same universe, even to the extent of glimpsing the rules on which it runs. How we have become linked into this cosmic dimension is a mystery. Yet the linkage cannot be denied.

What does it mean? What is Man that we might be party to such privilege? I cannot believe that our existence in this universe is a mere quirk of fate, an accident of history, an incidental blip in the great cosmic drama. Our involvement is too intimate. The physical species *Homo* may count for nothing, but the existence of mind in some organism on some planet in the universe is surely a fact of fundamental significance. This can be no trivial detail, no minor byproduct of mindless, purposeless forces. We are truly meant to be here.[57]

Given the nontheistic bias of modern science, Davies' conclusion is particularly striking. One cannot appreciate the intrinsic nature of human art, for instance, without being continually reminded of the transcendent nature of human consciousness itself. I, for one, cannot help but see a reflection of the Divine when I listen to such musical artists as Jeff Lorber, Al Dimeola, and Elliot Namay. The very intensity of their musical expression automatically transports the avid listener out of the realm of the purely physical, to a world where spiritual purity and higher meaning rule the day. But even if one were to confine oneself to the realm of the physical only, one can *still* see this spark of the Divine just as clearly, because the simple act of moving one's finger to pluck a note is far more complicated, physiologically speaking, than any of us are capable of understanding at the present time.

The real clincher, though, comes when we combine this awesome level of physical complexity with the unsearchable profundity of artistic inspiration itself. When we do so, it quickly becomes apparent that we are beings with a "divine connection," so much so, in fact, that the theological concept of the *Imago Dei* (i.e., that humans were created in the image of God) suddenly takes on a whole new level of meaning. We are much more than we tend to think we are.

Further evidence against Gribbin's nontheistic contention is that it doesn't necessarily follow that just because the universe is set up for the production of black holes, it will *also* be able to fine-tune itself even further to the point of becoming biocentric. This is a *monumental* assumption that has little basis in fact. It also fails to address the question of why this linkage between cosmic and biological evolution is able to occur in the first place:

The linkage between biological and cosmological selection is an attractive feature of this theoretical model, but we can still wonder why the laws of nature are such that this linkage occurs. How fortunate that the requirements of life match those of the baby universes so well. Moreover, we still require the same basic structure of the laws in all these universes in order to make sense of the theory. That this basic structure also permits the formation of life remains a remarkable fact.[58]

Gribbin's argument makes no attempt to account for the underlying laws of nature that permit the supposed evolution of black holes and baby universes into people. For even though he claims that the laws of nature are slightly changed each time they are recycled by imploding black holes into new baby universes, this still doesn't explain where the *original* set of laws would have come from that makes this entire process possible in the first place. This is Davies' main criticism against their theory and it is very much well-deserved, because it is the *origin* of nature's fundamental laws that is the ultimate question at issue here. One simply cannot assume the prior existence of these laws and then attempt to build a coherent theory around them without begging the entire question that is at issue here. This is why the process of natural selection cannot be used to explain its own existence, and it is also why Gribbin's argument turns out to be moot after all.

There is nothing to be gained, as we have seen, by trying to employ a process of natural selection before the Big Bang to explain the ideal arrangement of the constants, because such a maneuver still leaves unanswered the primary questions that are being debated here. Once again, we find ourselves coming up against the full force of the Cosmological Argument, because without a Necessary Being to give impetus to reality, there doesn't seem to be a coherent way of accounting for *anything*. This is why the greatest minds in the history of Western thought, including Plato, Aristotle, Augustine, and Aquinas, have all appreciated the power and logical force of the Cosmological Argument for the existence of God.

In fact, the Cosmological Argument has been deeply strengthened by the recent scientific discovery that our universe actually did have a concrete beginning some 15 to 20 billion years ago in the Big Bang. This is one of the greatest empirical discoveries in the history of modern science, and it strongly supports the Cosmological Argument because it conclusively shows that the historical chain of contingency does indeed come to an abrupt end several thousand million years ago. The Space-Time Theorem of General Relativity provides further support for this interpretation, as it shows that space, time, and matter all had a concrete beginning at the Big Bang.[59] While it is possible that the Space-Time Theorem could turn out to be wrong, the empirical evidence for the Big Bang, along with the extreme accuracy of Einstein's general theory of relativity, strongly legislate against this possibility.

This is why most scientists now believe that time did indeed come into being at the Big Bang. To the extent that this belief is accurate, it renders meaningless all nontheistic theories that posit the existence of time and matter before the Big Bang.

Thermodynamic considerations strongly support this contention, because it is now clear that the energy system of our universe could not be of infinite age; there is far too much usable energy around to allow for this conclusion.[60] It is also why our universe could not have been oscillating back and forth between successive phases of expansion and contraction forever, because the Second Law of Thermodynamics "compels the maximum diameter of the universe to increase from cycle to cycle. Therefore, such a universe could look forward to an infinitely long future but only a finite past. The ultimate moment of creation, at most, could be pushed back only to about a trillion years ago."[61]

Moreover, the very idea of an oscillating or bouncing universe has turned out to be untenable, because the mechanical efficiency of the entire universe is so low (about 0.00000001 percent) that it could never have generated enough energy to produce a bounce; hence, "even if the universe contained enough mass to halt its current expansion, any ultimate collapse would end in a thud, not a bounce."[62] It is this realization that led astrophysicists Alan Guth and Marc Sher to write a scientific paper entitled "The Impossibility of a Bouncing Universe."

Gribbin reminds us of the central flaw in his argument when he repeatedly asserts that the universe was "set up" to promote the formation of black holes and baby universes, and not us. We have seen how this sort of assumption conveniently fails to address the issue of who or what was originally responsible for carrying out this initial "setup," and this, in turn, must be counted as a major weakness in Gribbin's theory.

But even if we assume, for the sake of argument, that Gribbin does affirm the existence of some type of creative force in the universe that would have been responsible for its initial setup, it is clear that such a force or entity *cannot* be the God of traditional theism. To the contrary, it is more like the God of process thought, whose power over the universe is necessarily limited by a number of metaphysical factors over which he has no control, such as the simultaneous coexistence of a self-determining realm of finite actualities. This is why the process God is believed to have been unable to coerce these fundamental universal constituents into taking on a biocentric format long ago. To the contrary, the process deity only has the power to "persuade" these finite actualities into becoming more and more complex with the passage of time. If he is lucky, he may be able to eventually create a number of worlds that contain significant amounts of intrinsic value. On this view, the evolution of humans may have been intended all along by the process deity, but it was by no means guaranteed, since there would have been no way for him to know in advance how the finite actualities themselves would have elected to respond to his creative lure.

To the extent that this process view is accurate, one can imagine the process deity aiming for a self-propagating system of galaxies to begin with. Having accomplished this initial goal, one can then imagine him trying to lure the universe toward the eventual creation of intelligent life forms through natural evolutionary pathways, which could conceivably have taken place through a process of competition between baby universes, much the way Gribbin has conceived. Nevertheless, I believe that the most recent cosmological data is far more consistent with the coercive, all-powerful Deity of traditional theism than it is with the struggling deity of process thought.[63]

Design and the Nature of Photosynthesis

In order to offer further support for the existence of an undesigned universe, Gribbin draws an interesting comparison. He contrasts sunlight with deliberately contrived human lights, and concludes that "there is no doubt that artificial lights . . . were designed for our benefit, with human eyes in mind. But there is no reason at all to think that the Sun was designed to produce light suitable for human eyes. Rather, the light came first and eyes evolved to make use of it."[64]

According to George Greenstein, though, this illustration isn't true at all as far as photosynthetic plants are concerned. For as it turns out, sunlight must be of the right color and wavelength in order to be used for photosynthetic purposes by chlorophyll-containing plants. However, the evidence by no means suggests that sunlight came first, and that plants simply evolved to make the best use of it. To the contrary, it is now known that *all* molecules absorb light of similar wavelengths, so the chlorophyll molecule (or any other one, for that matter) could *not* have adapted to sunlight of a different color. As Greenstein explains:

> One might think that a certain adaptation has been at work here: the adaptation of plant life to the properties of sunlight. After all, if the Sun were a different temperature could not some other molecule, tuned to absorb light of a different color, take the place of chlorophyll? Remarkably enough the answer is no, for within broad limits all molecules absorb light of similar colors. The absorption of light is accomplished by the excitation of electrons in molecules to higher energy states,

and the general scale of energy required to do this is the same no mater what molecule you are discussing. Furthermore, light is composed of photons, packets of energy, and photons of the wrong energy simply cannot be absorbed.[65]

Greenstein goes on to show how "the energy carried by these photons . . . depends upon the color of the light," which itself depends on the temperature of the nuclear reactions that are taking place inside our sun.[66] Fortunately for us, this temperature is precisely what it needs to be in order to produce light that can be absorbed by chlorophyll molecules. And since no other molecules could have evolved to make use of a different color of light, we find that a very precise match really does exist between the temperature of our sun, on the one hand, and the molecular process of energy absorption, on the other. Without this correspondence, life would have never been able to evolve on this planet.

Interestingly, the process of natural selection cannot be used to account for this precise matching between chlorophyll and solar temperature, because photosynthesis could never have taken place with light of a different color and energy. This once again leaves us with two explanatory alternatives to choose from: either chance alone produced this precise matching without the benefit of natural selection, or else the entire situation was deliberately contrived by a Higher Power. The evidence strongly suggests that the latter alternative is in fact the correct one.

Notes

1. It isn't quite right to speak of a Godless universe as being "accidental." An "accident" is normally understood as being a malfunctioning—and therefore unintended—byproduct of a purposive system that has been initiated by some type of intelligent creative force. That is to say, the very concept of an "accident" presupposes a preexisting world of volition where some things happen in a predictable manner, and others do not. It would therefore be correct to say that an individual who had deliberately intended to produce one behavioral outcome accidentally produced an unexpected result unintentionally. With the random origin of the universe, however, we aren't talking about the accidental production of an unintended outcome by a volitional being; we are talking instead about the spontaneous origin of the entire cosmos by pure happenstance. While we may be justified in calling such a hypothetical event a product of chance, we are not justified in calling it a bona fide accident. To do so anyway is to give the word "accident" a meaning that it was never intended to possess.

2. These "splittings" refer to all of the quantum possibilities for all of the subatomic particles in existence.

3. Paul Davies, *The Mind of God* (New York: Simon and Schuster, 1992), 190.

4. Paul Davies, *Are We Alone* (New York: Basic, 1995), 121.

5. Richard Swinburne, "Argument from the Fine-Tuning of the Universe," in *Physical Cosmology and Philosophy*, ed. J. Leslie (London: Macmillan, 1990), 172.

6. David Deutsch, *The Fabric of Reality* (New York: Penguin, 1997), 32–52.

7. Ibid., 46–48.

8. Ibid., 47.

9. If so, this would explain why an Intelligent Designer would have created these vast shadowy realms in the first place.

10. Deutsch, *Fabric of Reality*, 48.

11. These ideas were communicated during a personal meeting between Professor John H. Campbell and me.

12. Thomas R. McDonough and David Brin, "The Bubbling Universe," *Omni*, vol. 15, no. 1 (1992): 85–90.

13. Lee Smolin, *The Life of the Cosmos* (Oxford: Oxford University Press, 1997), 90–106.

14. Ibid., 108–109.

15. This is an assumption that can be traced to the work of the French physicist Henri Poincaré, who showed that "almost any mechanical system with finite potential energy, finite kinetic energy, and bounded in space must necessarily return to any previous initial state." See John D. Barrow and Frank J. Tipler, *The Anthropic Cosmological Principle* (Oxford: Oxford University Press, 1986), 174–175. The key word here is "almost." Poincaré's Recurrence Theorem never showed that all mechanical systems will necessarily return to a previous state.

16. Wendy L. Freedman, "The Expansion Rate and Size of the Universe," *Scientific American*, vol. 267, no. 5 (November 1992): 54–60.

17. Igor D. Novikov and Yakob Zel'dovich, "Physical Processes Near Cosmological Singularities," *Annual Review of Astronomy and Astrophysics*, no. 11 (1973).

18. Hugh Ross, *The Fingerprint of God* (Orange, Calif.: Promise Publishing, 1991), 105.

19. Ibid.

20. Kathy Sawyer, "Calculating the Contents of the Cosmos," *Washington Post*, 30 April 2001.

21. John Gribbin, *In the Beginning* (Boston: Little, Brown, 1993), 176–177.

22. This conclusion is actually false, because even if one could come up with a plausible naturalistic explanation for the values of the constants, one would still have to come up with a suitable explanation for the origin of the universe itself, and this is a question that Gribbin doesn't even attempt to answer.

23. Barrow and Tipler, *Anthropic Cosmological Principle*, 288.

24. Gribbin, *In the Beginning*, 187.

25. Ibid.

26. Ibid., 202.

27. Ibid., 203–204.

28. Ibid., 205.

29. M. A. Corey, *Evolution and the Problem of Natural Evil* (Lanham, Md.: University Press of America, 2000), 115–124.

30. Gribbin, *In the Beginning*, 179.

31. Ibid., 185.

32. Ibid.

33. For a more thorough explanation of Darwin's religious beliefs, please refer to Corey, *Evolution and the Problem of Natural Evil*, 75–83.

34. For a more detailed description of how the creation account in Genesis One is "evolutionary" by its very nature, please refer to M. A. Corey, *The Natural History of Creation* (Lanham, Md.: University Press of America, 1995), 14–83.

35. M. A. Corey, *Back to Darwin* (Lanham, Md.: University Press of America, 2000), 31–230.

36. Ibid., 186.

37. Gribbin, *In the Beginning*, 207.

38. M. A. Corey, *God and the New Cosmology* (Lanham, Md.: Rowman & Littlefield, 1993), 128–133.

39. Hugh Ross, *The Creator and the Cosmos* (Colorado Springs, Colo.: NavPress, 1993), 91.

40. Ibid., 67.

41. Ibid.

42. Ibid., 68.

43. Gribbin, *In the Beginning*, 251.

44. Ibid.

45. Ross, *Creator and the Cosmos*, 92.

46. Ibid.

47. A baby universe that forms in this manner will exist in a space-time that is at right angles to our own space-time, but according to Stephen Hawking, it is also possible for it to hook back up again to our own region of space-time. (See Stephen Hawking, *Black Holes and Baby Universes* [New York: Bantam, 1993], 121–123). Indeed, Hawking believes that this process can alter the apparent values of different physical quantities, such as the amount of electric charge on a given particle. This possibility introduces an element of unpredictability into our own region of the cosmos, because there is no way to know how many baby universes are out there waiting to join forces with our own universe.

48. Gribbin, *In the Beginning*, 252.

49. Ibid., 253–254.

50. George Greenstein, *The Symbiotic Universe* (New York: William Morrow, 1988), 27.

51. Ibid., 28.

52. Ibid., 189.

53. Ross, *Creator and the Cosmos*, 66.

54. Gribbin, *In the Beginning*, 254–255.

55. Corey, *Back to Darwin*, 6–24, 143–144.

56. Davies, *Mind of God*, 214.

57. Ibid., 232.

58. Ibid., 222.

59. Ross, *Creator and the Cosmos*, 67.

60. Ibid., 59.

61. Ibid.
62. Ibid., 60.
63. Corey, *God and the New Cosmology*, 249–256.
64. Gribbin, *In the Beginning*, 186.
65. Greenstein, *Symbiotic Universe*, 96–97.
66. Ibid., 97.

~

CHAPTER TWELVE

Scientific Proof for a "Just Right" Designer

This most beautiful system of the sun, planets, and comets, could only proceed from the council and dominion of an Intelligent and Powerful Being.

—Isaac Newton

The scientific evidence for Intelligent Design is truly overwhelming. It is so compelling, in fact, that on the face of it one would think that we have actually discovered a valid proof for the existence of God. Even scientists with a nontheistic bent, such as physicist George Greenstein, can "see" the extreme persuasive power of the latest scientific evidence for the Divine Being:

> As we survey all the evidence, the thought insistently arises that some supernatural agency—or rather, Agency—must be involved. Is it possible that suddenly, without intending to, we have stumbled upon scientific proof of the existence of a Supreme Being?[1]

Or what about the case of Sir Fred Hoyle, the pioneering astrophysicist who discovered how carbon is synthesized inside the stars? A former proponent of atheism, Hoyle found the empirical evidence for Design to be *so compelling that he has now radically altered his former atheistic position to be consistent with the existence of a "supercalculating intellect" in the universe.*

Now, one would never expect nontheistic scientists—who have been trained from the very outset to reject as "unscientific" all religious considerations—to openly mention God as a possible explanation unless the evidence itself was compelling enough to justify this sort of behavior. Indeed, judging from the many incredible things that these individuals are saying about God's possible relationship to the cosmos, it is likely that deep down many of them actually believe in—and are fascinated by—the idea that God Himself may be behind the marvel of physical reality.

Yet, both scientists and philosophers alike have rejected the idea that a formal scientific proof of God is possible *even in principle*. The chief reason that is given for this rejection has to do with the inherent ambiguity surrounding the origin of life. For every theistic explanation that can be offered by the religious believer, the scientific naturalist can give a competing atheistic explanation. And since there is no way to prove *either* explanation absolutely, the issue is held to be inherently ambiguous. Moreover, since the prospect for an absolute proof of God is deemed to be impossible, due to God's nonempirical nature and the ostensible ambiguity surrounding this issue, the question of God's possible existence has been relegated by most theorists to the domain of faith, and *not* empirical science.

However, just because one lacks absolute proof for a given conclusion doesn't necessarily mean that the conclusion itself is inherently ambiguous. To the contrary, there are numerous "degrees of certainty" that span the range between absolute proof and total ambiguity. For instance, even though I may be unable to prove in an absolute fashion that I am typing on a computer today (for all I know, I could be a mere figment in some extraterrestrial's mind), I'm quite certain that I *am* indeed typing on a computer anyway, even though I can't prove this to be the case absolutely.

My lack of absolute proof here thus does not make this situation inherently ambiguous, for I can be sure *beyond a reasonable doubt* that I am actually sitting here typing this sentence. This means that there is a much greater probability that my typing experiences are true than that they are not. In fact, these relative probabilities are so radically divergent from one another that we can actually construct a valid *probabilistic proof* of the ostensible fact that I really am sitting here typing on a computer. This probabilistic proof would basically state that given the evidence at hand, it is far more likely that my subjective experience of typing is true than that it is not.

Virtually everything in our lives is like this. It is virtually impossible to prove anything absolutely, even in the comparatively straightforward world of arithmetic. For as the brilliant mathematician Kurt Gödel has clearly demonstrated, there will always be arithmetic statements that can never be proven absolutely, no matter how hard we try. While it may be possible to prove that the sum of the angles in a triangle will always equal 180 degrees, one still cannot be *absolutely certain* of this ostensible truth, because one's sense of certainty here could nevertheless be the result of an elaborate extraterrestrial scam, which itself can never be absolutely disproven.

From this point of view, everything we experience in the world is necessarily circumstantial in nature, because we can never know anything in an absolute fashion. That is to say, we can never be sure that we know the identity of *all* the forces in the universe that are causally impinging on our lives. It is because of this crucial epistemic limitation that we may only be experiencing a relatively tiny portion of the many causal influences that actually exist in the cosmos. Moreover, even though we routinely assume that the events in our world are exclusively brought about by local causal influences, we have no absolute proof of this; we have only circumstantial evidence that it is so. This is why we can say that the temporal conjunction between cause and effect that we regularly observe in the world is simply circumstantial evidence of a direct causal relationship that has a very high probability of being true.[2]

Interestingly, though, we are rarely swayed by our lack of absolute proof when it comes to our daily experiences in the world. Take the existence of the moon, for example. While we may be incapable of proving beyond any possible doubt that the moon really exists, we can nevertheless be sure of its existence beyond a reasonable doubt by making use of the strong circumstantial evidence for the moon's existence that we have been amassing for decades. From this point of view, we can be reasonably certain (on a probabilistic basis) that, given the evidence at hand, it is more likely overall that the moon exists than that it doesn't.

Most people are quite comfortable, then, with probabilistic conclusions (or proofs) that are based on strong circumstantial evidence. For some reason, though, very few probabilistic proofs for the existence of God have been proposed over the years. Critics, of course, would have us believe that no such proofs are plausible because it is inherently impossible to prove beyond a possible doubt the existence of any unseen being. While this may be so, it is still throwing the proverbial baby out with the bathwater, because it eliminates *all* types of proofs on the basis of a single unsuitable one.

This is the faulty train of logic that has been used to preempt the development of a valid probabilistic proof for the existence of God. Since absolute proofs are deemed to be impossible, no *other* types of proofs are thought to be possible, either. However, it doesn't follow that no proofs are possible simply because one type is deemed to be impossible. Hence, the impossibility of an absolute proof for God turns out to be an insubstantial Red Herring after all, since there is ultimately no such thing as an absolute proof for *anything* in our limited cognitive environment.

In reality, all we have to go on in this world are *relative probabilities*, and not absolute ones. We can say that we have obtained a relative "proof" for something when the probability of its being true is judged to be far in excess of its probability of being false. This is known in the philosophical literature, appropriately enough, as a *probabilistic proof*, and it is by far the most useful type of proof that we have access to in this world.

Absolute proofs, by contrast, appear to be the exclusive domain of God. This is because the only way that anything can be known or proven absolutely is if one has the ability to survey *all* of the possible explanations for any given state of affairs. But this is impossible, because no mere mortal can simultaneously have access to *all* of the various possibilities pertaining to any given issue, which in turn means that we are inherently incapable of judging in an absolute fashion *which* possibilities are ultimately true and which are false. We clearly would need to be omniscient in order to be able to do this, and only God Himself is in possession of this particular attribute. Therefore, absolute proofs are the sole province of God only. For finite intellects, on the other hand, probabilistic proofs appear to be the best measure of certainty that we can possibly come to in this world.[3]

So it is the notion of probability that enables us to establish the relative degree of certainty of our causal explanations in life. Whenever we are in doubt about the cause of any given state of affairs, we typically weigh the relative probabilities of all the relevant alternatives in order to be able to determine which is the most probable explanation in light of the existing evidence. If the relative probabilities of competing explanations are deemed to be similar to one another, our decision subsequently becomes difficult, because it then becomes hard to distinguish which alternative is likely to be the true one. However, when one alternative is recognized as being far more probable than all of the others, this is the one that is generally regarded as being "true."

This line of reasoning is directly applicable to our goal of finding a suitable explanation for the many "coincidences" that we have examined in this book. These "coincidences" are so numerous, complex, and intrinsically improbable that they seem to push the circumstantial evidence for Design far beyond the critical threshold needed to comprise a reasonable theistic proof.

For Hick, though, the fact that there are two possible interpretations of the cosmological data (naturalistic and theistic) automatically renders both explanations ambiguous. The question of either alternative's inherent probability thus does not enter into the discussion for Hick, because as long as more than one explanation is thought to be possible, it is concluded that the larger issue itself must therefore remain inherently ambiguous. But surely the existence of two possible alternatives does not in itself preclude the possibility that one of the alternatives may in fact be far more probable, and hence far more likely, than the other.

In short, just because one can conceive of two possible explanations for something doesn't necessarily make the resulting choice between them ambiguous. The only way this would be true is if the two alternatives in question could be shown to be similarly probable. But this isn't always the case, because one can easily conceive of a situation where one of the alternatives is overwhelmingly more probable than the other. The fact that there might be two possible alternatives in this instance doesn't seriously detract from the conclusion that one of the alternatives is clearly to be preferred over the other on probabilistic grounds. For example, while it may be possible that Smith is a being from another world, this possibility in and of itself does not make Smith's true identity ambiguous. Rather, it is the immense unlikelihood of Smith's possible extraterrestrial status that makes our determination of his earthbound humanity almost certain.

Of course, people differ in their readiness to accept a given amount of circumstantial evidence as "proof." There are undoubtedly those who would resist even a blatantly obvious conclusion that is based on circumstantial evidence alone. Take, for instance, Leslie's previously mentioned example of a condemned criminal who is lucky enough to survive a hundred-man firing squad because of the simultaneous misfiring of all 100 rifles. Remarkably, there are some people who would resist the conclusion that something had to have been going on "behind the scenes" to make such a thing happen. These individuals are few in number, though, and it is safe to say that most would probably be motivated by reasons other than the weight of the circumstantial evidence itself. Similarly, there are those who continue to resist the conclusion of Intelligent Design, in spite of the growing mountain of scientific evidence to the contrary. It is likely that many of these "theistically resistant" individuals are rejecting the God Hypothesis for reasons other than the weight of the evidence itself.

Causality and Coherent Data Patterns

Before we can use the most recent cosmological evidence to help us construct a probabilistic proof for the existence of God, we must first be able to reasonably establish a direct causal relationship between the various events that led up to the origin of life. We can do this by using the criterion of *data coherence around a central focal point*. For if most of the cosmological events in question can be shown to cohere together into a recognizable pattern, we can safely assume that a common causal element is probably responsible for eliciting it.

A good example of this process can be found in the various global weather patterns that are routinely detected by meteorological satellites. A single photograph, of course, can show the existence of a well-developed weather pattern, but a sequence of photographs over an extended period of time is clearly much more effective in this capacity, since each repetition of the observed pattern through a variety of successive states tends to further reinforce the impression that a single causative agent has in fact been responsible for generating the pattern itself.

A similar situation can be seen to exist in the area of "anthropic" cosmology, where the structure of the entire universe can repeatedly be seen to cohere around the central focal point of living tissue. Two inferences can be drawn from this cosmological fact: (1) that a common causal element is probably responsible for generating this pattern and (2) that the existence of biological life appears to be the implicit aim of this causative force. While these conclusions are not beyond possible doubt (since a variety of nontheistic alternatives can be proposed to account for the same pattern), they nevertheless seem to lead directly to a theistic view of cosmogenesis. The "take home" point here is that given the evidence at hand, the theistic alternative appears to be significantly more probable than the nontheistic one. The statistician Bartholomew agrees:

> Let us set up the hypothesis that there is no directing purpose behind the universe so that all change and development is the product of "blind chance." We then proceed to calculate the probability that the world (or that aspect of it under consideration) would turn out to be as we find it. If that probability turns out to be extremely small we argue that the occurrence of something so rare is totally implausible and hence that the hypothesis on which it is calculated is almost certainly false. The only reasonable alternative open to us is to postulate a grand intelligence to account for what has occurred. This procedure is based on the logical disjunction *either* an extremely rare event has occurred or the hypothesis on which the probability is calculated is false. Faced with this choice the rational thing to do is to prefer the latter alternative.[4]

Constructing a Probabilistic Proof for the Existence of God

Probabilistic proofs for the existence of God take the general form that, given this or that feature of the world, it is more likely that there is a God than that there is not.[5] These arguments make no claim of absolute certitude; they simply state that, given the evidence at hand, it is more rational to believe in God than not to do so.[6]

Actually, next to a direct, first-hand experience of the Deity, this probabilistic style of argument constitutes the next strongest proof of the Divine Being. This is because probabilistic proofs themselves are based on the direct perception of a real world body of facts. And while they do not involve a direct perception of God's own Being as such, they *do* offer a direct perception of the *effects* of God's creative activities, from which it is possible to infer the reality of Intelligent Design.

Probabilistic proofs in the realm of cosmology are based on circumstantial evidence whose existence is hard to refute. It is the conclusion that is inferred from this circumstantial evidence that is open to doubt, because of the dubitable premise that the data in question could not have come about in the absence of Intelligent Design. In this case, the more evidence that one can marshal in support of one's position the better, because the entire issue under consideration here is one of probability, so a greater number of examples typically translates into a greater overall probability for Intelligent Design. This being the case, we now need to ask ourselves whether or not there is enough circumstantial evidence in the cosmological realm to "prove" the existence of a Designer beyond a reasonable doubt.

The answer to this question appears to be an unequivocal Yes! The mountain of scientific evidence pointing in the direction of Design is *so* overwhelming that many of the world's leading scientists have openly acknowledged its extreme persuasiveness as far as the probable existence of a Designer is concerned. Paul Davies, for instance, has pointed out the need[7] for a "selector" or "designer" to choose our exceedingly improbable universe out of an infinity of possible choices. Hawking agrees that, given the infinite number of different universes that could have been born at the Big Bang, "there ought to be some principle that picks one initial state, and hence one model, to represent our universe."[8] Hawking openly admits that God could very well turn out to be the Author of this necessary primordial principle.[9] Indeed, given the *extremely* precise initial conditions that were necessary to generate a life-supporting universe, Hawking has gone so far as to assert that, "It would be very difficult to explain why the universe should have begun in just this way, except as an act of God who intended to create beings like us."[10]

The circumstantial evidence for Intelligent Design *really is* this compelling. But is it so inordinately compelling that it can actually be used to help constitute a valid probabilistic proof for the existence of God? I believe that the answer is yes, because there appears to be more than enough evidence available right now to justify a transition between circumstantial evidence for Design, on the one hand, and circumstantial (or probabilistic) proof of a Designer, on the other. But how can we possibly know this?

We can make this claim by appealing to a *functional criterion* with respect to this particular issue. For just as we tend to judge the goodness of a given thing in terms of how well it serves its intended purpose, we can also judge the adequacy of the evidence for Design in terms of its *functional competence* toward the attainment of its ostensible purpose, which is the support of life. We are compelled to conclude, on the basis of this functional criterion, that the evidence at hand is almost perfectly adequate for this life-supporting function.

Indeed, this is where the Anthropic Principle derives its meaning in the first place, because the various "coincidences" that are at work in the universe are so well coordinated with one another that intelligent life has been able to arise on this planet against all the odds. Surely this is a fact of fundamental significance, because it demonstrates that a very high level of functional *success* has in fact been attained in the cosmos. It is this perfect degree of advanced functional success, in the face of overwhelming odds to the contrary, that compels us to conclude that there is more than enough circumstantial evidence in cosmology to probabilistically prove the covert activity of an Intelligent Designer.

Going with the Odds

The extreme unlikelihood that our biocentric universe could have evolved by chance alone only strengthens the validity of this conclusion, because the odds against the accidental evolution of life are widely acknowledged, even by nontheists, to be nothing short of astronomical.

Take, for instance, the odds against even the simplest living cell spontaneously emerging out of a primordial soup containing all of the right ingredients for life. This probability has been calculated[11] by Morowitz to be a mind-boggling one chance in $10^{100,000,000,000}$. The odds against the accidental evolution of the human genome are also vanishingly small as well, on the order of one chance in 10^{243}, while the odds for the accidental evolution of intelligence have been judged to be so incredibly remote that most nontheistic evolutionists *themselves* believe that we are probably the only race of intelligent beings in the entire galaxy.[12]

According to calculations performed by Hoyle and Wickramasinghe, the odds for the random generation of a simple bacterium work out to be an astonishing one chance in $10^{40,000}$. "This is a number so vast," according to Overman, that "any mathematician would agree that it amounts to total impossibility."[13] There are, after all, only 10^{80} particles in the entire universe!

Hoyle and Wickramasinghe concluded from this that life could never have randomly evolved here, even if the entire universe were made of primeval soup.[14] There is simply too much information packed into living organisms to make this even a remote possibility. It is for this reason that "any theory with a probability of being accurate larger than one in $10^{40,000}$ must be considered superior to random processes. The probability that life was as-sembled by an intelligence has vastly greater probability."[15] Therefore, it is to be preferred on probabilistic grounds alone.

Hubert Yockey, one of the world's leading information theorists, has es-sentially confirmed the basic thrust of these calculations, insofar as he has also come to the mathematically based conclusion that the evolution of life couldn't have been the result of chance processes alone. Yockey endeavored to calculate the probability of a single protein, iso-1-cytochrome c, forming by chance processes alone. The probability he came up with, 2×10^{-44}, con-firms the idea that it is mathematically impossible for life to have evolved by chance forces alone:

> Let us remind ourselves that we have calculated the probability of the generation of only a single molecule of iso-1-cytochrome c. . . . I am using probability as a measure of degree of belief. It is clear that the belief that a molecule of iso-1-cytochrome c or any other protein could appear by chance is based on faith. And so we see that even if we believe that the "building blocks" are available, they do not spontaneously make proteins, at least not by chance. The origin of life by chance in a primeval soup is impossible in probability in the same way that a perpetual motion machine is im-possible in probability. The extremely small probabilities calculated in this chapter are not discouraging to true believers . . . or to people who live in a universe of infi-nite extension that has no beginning or end in time. In such a universe all things not *streng verboten* will happen. In fact we live in a small, young universe generated by an enormous hydrogen bomb explosion some time between 10×10^9 and 20×10^9 years ago. A practical person must conclude that life didn't happen by chance.[16]

Harold Morowitz has furthered this line of argument by calculating the probability of broken chemical bonds in a single-celled bacterium sponta-neously reassembling under ideal conditions. The resulting probability, one in $10^{100,000,000,000}$, is so outrageously small that Morowitz concluded that "the largest possible fluctuation in the history of the universe is likely to have been no larger than a small peptide. Again, we stress in a very firm quantita-tive way, the impossibility of life originating as a fluctuation in an equilib-rium ensemble."[17]

Bernd-Olaf Küppers adds the final "icing on the cake" with respect to this particular issue. Working on the premise that the random formation of pre-defined molecular sequences is reciprocally proportional to the number of all possible combinations, Küppers concluded the following:

> The human genome consists of about 109 nucleotides, and the number of combi-natorially possible sequences attains the unimaginable size of . . . $10^{600\ million}$. Even in the simple case of a bacterium, the genome consists of some 4.106 nucleotides,

and the number of combinatorially possible sequences is . . . $10^{2.4 \text{ million}}$. The expectation probability for the nucleotide sequence of a bacterium is thus so slight that not even the entire space of the universe would be enough to make the random synthesis of a bacterial genome probable. For example, the entire mass of the universe, expressed as a multiple of the mass of the hydrogen atom, amounts to about 10^{80} units. Even if all the matter in space consisted of DNA molecules of the structural complexity of the bacterial genome, with random sequences, then the chances of finding among them a bacterial genome or something resembling one would still be completely negligible.[18]

Time itself cannot be "the hero of the plot," either, because life evolved on the earth just as soon as it possibly could.[19] At most, there might have been 130 million years available for life to form by random processes, but as Overman concludes, "Calculations of mathematical probabilities unequivocally demonstrate that it is mathematically impossible for unguided, random events to produce life in this short period of time."[20]

A number of prominent scientists, including Sir Francis Crick (one of the codiscoverers of the DNA molecule), have assented to this conclusion, namely, that it is mathematically impossible for life to have randomly evolved on earth by chance processes alone. Accordingly, these individuals now believe that the seeds of life were deliberately sent here from somewhere in outer space.[21] This belief is known as *directed panspermia*, but it clearly does nothing to solve the problem of the origin of life. It merely pushes it back an additional step, because it then compels us to ask where these extraterrestrial seeds *themselves* could have originated from.

The directed panspermia hypothesis is about as close as nontheistic scientists are going to get to an explicit admission that earth-based life was intelligently designed by a Higher Power. It is, after all, an admission that the odds for the random evolution of life are so vanishingly small that life therefore *had* to have originated "from outer space." But this is precisely the same line of reasoning that the Intelligent Design theorist uses as well, except for the fact that the concept of God is directly utilized to explain the ultimate source of this "extraterrestrial seeding."

However, it isn't merely life's enormous complexity that makes it impossible for the universe to have been a chance event. It is also the incredible precision that must be displayed throughout the larger universe itself that makes this conclusion a virtual certainty.

Our universe is so precisely built, in fact, that there wasn't room for *any error at all* in its creation. Roger Penrose reaches this momentous conclusion by imagining all of the possible universes that God *could* have created in the beginning. He then imagines the Creator, armed with a pin, trying to pick out the type of universe that He wants to create. Since each positioning of the pin represents a different type of universe, the Creator's aim must be *very* precise indeed.

How precise must it be? Since the universe had to have started out in a very highly ordered state, it must be *extraordinarily* precise, to the tune of one part in 10 to the 10^{123}. Again, this is a number so vast that it couldn't possibly be written on a piece of paper the size of the entire universe!

With odds like these, it is hard to see how anyone could possibly believe that the origin of life was merely a chance event. Indeed, the odds are so overwhelmingly in favor of Intelligent Design that we can actually use these probabilities to construct a genuine probabilistic *proof* for the existence of God. We can formally state this probabilistic proof in the following manner:

1. Carbon-based life forms are so profoundly complex that they inherently require a tremendous degree of order before they can be actual.
2. To be life-supporting, then, the universe has to first be capable of providing this enormous degree of order.
3. For this to be possible, though, the universe had to have been fine-tuned to an extraordinary degree of accuracy—one part in 10 to the 10^{123}.
4. Chance processes alone are inherently incapable of duplicating this enormous structural precision, since the statistical threshold for non-possibility is held to be a comparatively paltry one part in 10^{40}.
5. Even with the prior existence of a biocentric world, life is *still* so inordinately complex that the odds for a simple bacterium to spontaneously reassemble itself under ideal conditions after its chemical bonds have been broken have been calculated[22] to be an astounding one chance in $10^{100,000,000,000}$.
6. Chance processes again are inherently incapable of duplicating these odds.
7. The odds against the accidental evolution of the human genome, even under ideal circumstances, have been calculated to be one in 10^{243}.
8. Again, this is a likelihood that is so incredibly remote that chance processes alone almost certainly could have never duplicated it, even over immense periods of time.
9. There were an infinity of possible values that could have been assigned to nature's fundamental constants. Each time a choice was made, though, it turned out to be "just right" for the evolution of life.
10. The odds for a single functional value to be chosen out of an infinity of possible choices are *precisely* zero.

11. Therefore, chance forces alone could *never* have been responsible for selecting these ideal values, which in turn means that some type of deliberate, nonrandom force had to have been responsible for it.

12. Natural selection is inherently incapable of solving this problem, because the degree of material complexity that is required by the process of self-replication (which is the precursor of selection) vastly exceeds the alleged creative power of chance.

13. The accidental evolution of intelligence is *so* inherently problematic in and of itself that virtually all nontheistic evolutionists believe that intelligent life forms probably won't be found anywhere else in the entire visible universe.

14. Long stretches of time cannot be "the hero of the plot" either, because life evolved on the earth just as soon as it possibly could, thus leaving essentially no time at all for life to form by random processes alone.

15. When all of the prerequisites for the evolution of intelligent life are taken together, it becomes abundantly clear that the overall probability for it to have evolved by chance alone is essentially zero, particularly given the fact that the statistical threshold for nonpossibility is held to be a mere 10^{-40}.

16. Conversely, the overall probability that intelligent life is the result of some form of Design is proportionately huge.

17. Therefore, it is overwhelmingly more likely that the universe is the product of Design, and *not* random chance.

18. This amounts to a compelling probabilistic proof for the existence of God.

We can go one step further and argue that, given the above-stated odds, it is positively *irrational* to believe in an accidental evolution of the biosphere. We can say this because the very concept of "rationality" is based upon an underlying sense of reasonableness in the face of everyday real world probabilities, such that the more a person begins to align himself with statistically improbable events, the less proportionately rational he is said to be. For instance, even though it might be a statistical possibility for a person to witness a live UFO abduction, it would nevertheless be irrational for someone to camp out in the middle of the desert waiting for such a thing to happen. This sort of behavior is irrational because of the deep behavioral commitment that would be given in this instance to such an astronomically remote "possibility." In the same way, though, nontheists have deeply committed themselves to a far *more* remote possibility, namely, the accidental evolution of intelligent life by chance processes alone. Yet, for some reason, we have been conditioned to accept this type of irrational belief structure as "scientific."

Of course, there will always be those who will want to argue that circumstantial evidence alone isn't good enough to prove the existence of God, even from a probabilistic point of view. However, it is very hard to see how this could possibly be the case, because we use circumstantial evidence every single day to great advantage, and the fact that it is "only" circumstantial in nature doesn't seem to detract from its effectiveness in the least. If anything, it is the way that *we* piece together this circumstantial evidence into a meaningful pattern that could potentially create a problem for us, but even so, the resulting problem wouldn't be with the circumstantial evidence itself; it would lie, instead, with our own reasoning ability (or lack thereof).

We can use an example to better illustrate this point. Imagine coming home late one evening, only to find your front door ajar, your clothes strewn all over the floor, and your drawers open and obviously tampered with. Upon further inspection, you find that your diamond watch and notebook computer are missing, along with the DVD player and five hundred dollars in cash. There are also tracks of mud scattered throughout the house. Your first impression, of course, will be to naturally conclude that you have been robbed, because *all* of the circumstantial evidence is highly consistent with this conclusion. Still, you cannot be certain about this spur-of-the-moment conclusion, at least not yet, because there are other possible explanations that are also consistent with the available evidence. So, before you can conclude beyond a reasonable doubt that you have in fact been robbed, you must first consider all of these other possibilities.

Upon deeper reflection, you find that the only other possible explanation for your torn-up house is that your daughter *could* conceivably have flown in from the other side of the country to take possession of these missing items. This explanation also appears to fit the circumstantial evidence, especially because of several arguments that you recently had with her over the proper ownership of some (but not all) of these items. But while this alternative explanation might be possible in principle, it still isn't likely, because you quickly begin to realize that this sort of behavior isn't consistent with your daughter's underlying character, nor is it consistent with the fact that you just had a very pleasant conversation with her two nights previously. It is at this point that you come to the very rational conclusion that you have indeed been robbed by an unknown individual, largely because of the tremendous likelihood of this particular explanation, relative to the extreme improbability of the "daughter hypothesis."

Now, your lack of absolute proof in this instance clearly doesn't detract from your relative degree of certainty about the robbery itself, because the enormous dissimilarity in the respective probabilities involved almost completely compensates for your lack of absolute proof. It is for this reason that we can assert that the circumstantial evidence in this instance proves beyond a reasonable doubt that a robbery did in fact take place in your home.

In fact, given the strength of the circumstantial evidence in this particular example, an absolute proof of the robbery (which would amount to a videotape or a reliable eyewitness) is almost unnecessary. Of course, it is possible that there could still be another explanation for your torn-up house that you haven't yet been able to imagine (such as a disorganizing local disturbance in the quantum field surrounding your home), but such an "explanation" can quickly be seen to be improbable enough to be dismissed entirely in favor of the far more convincing robbery hypothesis.

In the same way, we can say that the recent spate of scientific evidence regarding the various "anthropic coincidences" proves the existence of an Intelligent Designer beyond reasonable doubt. The overwhelming discrepancies between the different probabilities involved make this conclusion almost irresistible. After all, statisticians consider the realm of nonpossibility to be anything smaller than 10^{-40} or so. But as we have seen, the odds for the accidental evolution of life are hundreds of orders of magnitude smaller than this. Statistically speaking, then, it isn't even *possible* for our life-supporting universe to have evolved by chance alone.

Inferring the Existence of God from the Intelligence of Nature

It is possible to add to the weight of our probabilistic proof by inferring the existence of God from the underlying intelligence of the natural world. For it would seem to be a truism that *any system that requires a certain amount of intelligence to understand originally required at least as much intelligence to bring about.* This much appears to be self-evident.

However, to the extent that we accept this relation as true, we find that we must attribute the creation of the universe to an intelligence that is superior to our own, since the intelligence that is exemplified in even the "simplest" atom vastly exceeds our ability to understand it. And since God appears to be the only intelligence superior to our own who could have actually created the present universal order, it follows such a Divine Being probably exists after all.

The Stoic philosopher Chrysippus used a similar argument to prove the existence of God:

> If there is something in the world which human reason, strength and power are incapable of producing, that which produces it must be better than man. But the heavens and everything which displays unceasing regularity cannot be produced by

man. Therefore that by which those things are produced is better than man. And what name rather than God would you give to this?[23]

Paul Davies reaches a similar conclusion in *Superforce*:

If nature is so "clever" it can exploit mechanisms that amaze us with their ingenuity, is that not persuasive evidence for the existence of intelligent design behind the physical universe? If the world's finest minds can unravel only with difficulty the deeper workings of nature, how could it be supposed that those workings are merely a mindless accident, a product of blind chance?

Should we conclude that the universe is the product of design? The new physics and the new cosmology hold out a tantalizing promise: that we might be able to explain how all the physical structures in the universe have come to exist, automatically, as a result of natural processes. We should then no longer have need for a Creator in the traditional sense. Nevertheless, though science may be able to explain the world, we still have to explain science. The laws which enable the universe to come into being spontaneously seem themselves to be the product of exceedingly ingenious design. If physics is the product of design, the universe must have a purpose, and the evidence of modern physics suggests strongly to me that the purpose includes us.[24]

In reality, belief in a Creator appears to be far more widespread amongst physicists, biologists, and cosmologists than has heretofore been admitted. Such a belief is certainly understandable, given the theological background of modern science and the inherently mystical nature of physical reality itself. Speaking of his theistically minded colleagues, Paul Davies says that he is actually surprised by how many of them hold conventional religious beliefs. "In some cases," he says, "their scientific work bolsters their conventional religious positions. The majority, however, probably stand in awe of nature and aren't sure whether its subtlety and ingenuity relate to a personal God or simply an underlying order. Yet even they feel the world is more than a random accident. There has to be more to it than just fact."[25]

This gut-level feeling appears to be very firmly entrenched in American society today, where 95 percent of the population say they believe in the existence of God, 75 percent say they are certain about life after death, and 90 percent say they pray every week. Moreover, the prevalence of religious belief in this country has *not* declined in recent years; it has remained more or less the same for over half a century. According to Father Andrew Greeley, professor of sociology at the University of Arizona, fluctuations in religious belief are more a function of psychological variances in the life cycle than they are an indication of long-term societal trends: religious devotion tends to bottom out during one's late teens and early twenties, only to pick up again during one's late twenties and thirties, and it finally reaches a plateau in one's mid-forties.[26]

But if this is the case, why have so many journalists and academicians, who have ready access to the sociological data, nevertheless led us to believe that there has been a serious decline in religious devotion in this country over the last several decades? According to Father Greeley, the answer is that these writers themselves have, for one reason or another, drifted away from their religious origins and have simply projected their own lack of belief onto the remainder of society.

Notes

1. George Greenstein, *The Symbiotic Universe* (New York: William Morrow, 1988), 27.

2. I am distinguishing here between circumstantial evidence of a very convincing sort and absolute proof. For even though strong circumstantial evidence can be convincing enough to appear absolute, in actuality it doesn't even approach this lofty goal. For while the two may be functionally equivalent in a practical sense, on a strict epistemological level they may actually be separated by a vast gulf of potential information that is simply unknown to us.

3. But this isn't to say that we can't be so sure of something on a probabilistic basis that it can seem, for all practical intents and purposes, like an absolute proof. We obviously can be this certain. But when this degree of certainty is actually obtained, the practical distinction between absolute proofs and probabilistic proofs begins to blur, such that the latter can effectively begin to substitute for the former without any significant loss or compromise taking place.

4. Quoted in John Polkinghorne, *Science and Creation* (Boston: New Science Library, 1989), 28.

5. John Hick, *The Existence of God* (New York: Macmillan, 1964), 7.

6. Ibid., 7–9.

7. Paul Davies, *God and the New Physics* (New York: Simon and Schuster, 1983), 167–168.

8. Stephen W. Hawking, *A Brief History of Time* (New York: Bantam, 1988), 123.

9. Ibid., 122.

10. Ibid., 126–127.

11. Hugh Ross, *The Creator and the Cosmos* (Colorado Springs, Colo.: NavPress, 1993), 139–141

12. John D. Barrow and Frank J. Tipler, *The Anthropic Cosmological Principle* (Oxford: Oxford University Press, 1986), 133.

13. Dean L. Overman, *The Case against Accident and Self-Organization* (Lanham, Md.: Rowman & Littlefield, 1997), 59.

14. Fred Hoyle and Chandra Wickramasinghe, *Evolution from Space* (London: J. M. Dent, 1981).

15. Overman, *Case against Accident and Self-Organization*, 59.

16. Hubert Yockey, *Information Theory and Molecular Biology* (Cambridge: Cambridge University Press, 1992), 257.

17. Harold Morowitz, *Energy Flow in Biology* (Woodbridge, Conn.: Ox Bow, 1979), 68.

18. Bernd-Olaf Küppers, *Information and the Origin of Life* (Cambridge: MIT Press, 1990), 59–60.

19. Overman, *Case against Accident and Self-Organization*, 49–51.

20. Ibid., 51.

21. Francis Crick, *Life Itself: Its Origin and Nature* (New York: Simon and Schuster, 1981).

22. Ross, *Creator and the Cosmos*, 139–141.

23. Taken from A. A. Long, *Hellenistic Philosophy* (Berkeley: University of California Press, 1974), 149.

24. Paul Davies, *Superforce* (New York: Simon and Schuster, 1984), 243.

25. Quoted in A. J. S. Rayl and K. T. McKinney, "The Mind of God," *Omni*, vol. 13, no. 11 (August 1991): 46.

26. Andrew Greeley, "Keeping the Faith: Americans Hold Fast to the Rock of Ages," *Omni*, vol. 13, no. 11 (August 1991): 6.

CHAPTER THIRTEEN

~

Modern Science
and the Nature of God

For since the creation of the world God's invisible qualities—his eternal
power and divine nature—have been clearly seen, being understood from
what has been made.

—St. Paul

One of the overarching ambitions of the natural theologian during the last
several centuries has been to establish the existence and character of God beyond a reasonable doubt, purely from a careful reading of the scientific evidence. In many people's minds, the first part of this objective has already
been accomplished to an impressive degree, due to the recent deluge of scientific information about the origin and development of our Goldilocks Universe. The evidence itself—which is highly compelling in its own right—
suggests that some type of larger Designer was probably behind the genesis of
the present cosmic epoch, but most theorists have been able to infer little
more about the general character of this purported Being.

This means that the second half of the natural theologian's program—
namely, the *scientific* derivation of the various Divine attributes—has gone
essentially unfulfilled. The reason for this is not far to seek, because it is a
challenging enough task to try to establish the mere existence of a generic
Creator beyond reasonable doubt. It is a vastly more difficult one, though, to
try to infer the individual character attributes of this purported Being using
empirical data only. It is for this reason that this scientifically based goal can
be said to represent the Holy Grail for natural theologians everywhere.

Indeed, virtually everyone wants to know what the Divine character is really like in and of itself, but thus far we've only had the individual revelations of a few prophets to rely on in this critical area, along with the questionable insights of a variety of theologians and philosophers. It would therefore be nice—*very* nice—if we could gain access to a more reliable source of information about the Divine Reality. Ideally, this new source of information would be empirically based, because it would then carry with it the potential for an unsurpassed degree of accuracy (and hence reliability). Fortunately, there is indeed such an empirically based source of information in existence: the physical universe itself! This "book of nature" is *never* mistaken if it is properly read, which in turn explains why the natural theologian desperately wants to learn everything the natural world has to say about the specific attributes of the Deity.

Kevin J. Sharpe, a mathematician and theologian from New Zealand, agrees that reading the book of nature can potentially tell us a great deal about the makeup of the Divine character:

> If hair covered the universe, we could conclude that the Divine likes hair and probably is quite hirsute, long white beard and all. The universe behaves in certain ways, and since the Divine unfolds them, they say something about the Divine. The Divine acts like this, so the Divine must be like this. The pot reflects the mind and perhaps the fingers of the potter.
>
> The universe reflects the nature of the divine subuniverse, so you can examine it to learn about the Divinity. That's if you're open. . . . If the universe presents basic properties other than logic and fruitfulness, and if we accept them as divine attributes, we need to show how they emerge from our model of the Divine. If we attribute other properties to the Divine, these too should appear as basic features of the unfolding universe. That same universe founds our ideas of the Divine. Only investigation of the universe can justify a belief, though the idea may arise from any source. The empirical method, a treasure of our culture, provides a portion of the route to knowledge of the Divine. We ask the universe scientific questions about the Divine.[1]

In my own research into this area, I have been delighted to learn that many of the Divine attributes can indeed be legitimately inferred from a careful reading of the scientific evidence. Remarkably, each of these empirically derived qualities turns out to be essentially identical to most traditional monotheistic views of the Godhead. In the remainder of this chapter we shall see how.

The Value of Inferential Knowledge in Scientific Research

The elucidation of God's personal qualities from the scientific evidence alone is an inherently difficult task, because the Divine Essence is not directly amenable to the scientific method, nor is it immediately accessible to any of our five senses, since it is primarily spiritual in nature, and not physical. Nevertheless, it is possible, at least in principle, to *indirectly infer* a significant amount of descriptive information about the Creator purely from a careful reading of the scientific evidence, for if such a Being is truly responsible for creating the universe, then we should be able to apprehend at least a few of His attributes merely through a careful examination of that which He has made (as St. Paul suggests in the epigraph to this chapter).

Indeed, it can readily be seen that *all* created objects carry within themselves at least *some* of the characteristics of their respective designers.[2] If nothing else, one can thus always surmise that any given artifact will *necessarily* reveal at least some degree of intentional creative activity on the part of its particular maker, otherwise it would have never been able to come into being in the first place. While this sort of tautologous conclusion may seem unenlightening, it is just the tip of the proverbial iceberg, *because the very act of creation can be seen to imply a direct causal connection between any given creator and the created artifact itself*, and this remains true whether the particular creator in question is Michelangelo or God Himself.[3] This connection can thus be seen to contain an indirect reflection of the maker's own prior creative activity, which itself can potentially tell us a great deal about the individual characteristics that he or she actually possesses, whether the creator in question is a human being or God Himself.

In other words, there is probably no absolute difference in kind between human creativity and Divine creativity, at least as far as this particular metaphysical link is concerned, because it is clear that in both instances there *must* be an inexorable connection, or some type of initial causal contact, between the creator and the created object in question. This makes it possible, at least in principle, for us to be able to indirectly infer *from* the inherent nature of a given artifact *to* the existence of certain general qualities in its respective designer, and again, this relation would seem to hold true in a larger metaphysical sense, whether the designer in question happens to be human, Divine, or somewhere in-between.

This important point can be better illustrated by means of an example. Imagine that an abandoned flying saucer is discovered one day by an international team of experts. How would the world respond if the spacecraft were then put on public display? Among other things, people would almost certainly try to infer as much as possible about the nature of the alien race that had created the flying saucer. That is to say, they would try to infer, from a detailed analysis of the spaceship itself, as much as they possibly could about exactly *who* could have built such a mysterious contraption in the first place.

Of course, this type of inferential process isn't a fail-safe means of acquiring data, because there isn't a precise, one-to-one correspondence between the properties that are displayed by artifacts and the attributes that are possessed by their respective designers. Rather, there is almost always some degree of interpretive ambiguity involved, which in turn can lead to any number of unsubstantiated conclusions. For instance, the existence of a laser gun on board the flying saucer wouldn't necessarily mean that its alien creators are fond of war; it could also be construed as a necessary means of self-defense for a peace-loving race of extraterrestrials. Nevertheless, it is still possible to accurately infer the existence of certain traits in a given designer by vigorously pursuing this mode of inferential reasoning in both a rational and judicious manner, because the greatest limitation to be found here isn't in the indirect nature of the evidence itself, but rather in our own reasoning ability.

Interestingly, this inductive method of reasoning is not foreign to science. Rather, it is the form of logic that is most characteristic of the scientific method itself, because it moves from the particulars of individual observation to the elucidation of general physical patterns. It thus moves from effects to causes, yielding a probable (but not certain) conclusion.[4] Of course, this isn't to say that science doesn't work with propositions that are either true or false; it clearly does. It's simply to say that we can't be absolutely sure *which* propositions are true and which are false. Hence, scientists have to work through a variety of empirical channels in order to establish the most probable explanation for a given body of data, just as we are trying to do in this chapter by attempting to infer the various Divine attributes from the empirical nature of the universe itself.

This inductive method of reasoning is especially valuable to the particle physicist, because of the unobservable nature of most subatomic species. Because of this fundamental limitation, these postulated entities can only be detected in an indirect manner through a detailed examination of how they actually impinge upon their surrounding environment.

Take the ghost-like neutrino, for instance. It is a highly mysterious subatomic species that travels near the speed of light, interacts very weakly with ordinary "baryonic" matter, and may or may not have a rest mass.[5] Moreover, it cannot be directly measured in the laboratory, so a variety of *indirect* means must inevitably be resorted to if anything substantive is to be learned about its essential nature. And indeed, this is precisely what physicists have done in recent years. They have devised some of the cleverest experiments imaginable in order to be able to acquire inferential data about the nature of neutrinos.[6] In so doing, they have obtained a truly impressive understanding of the neutrino's various physical properties (although a number of question marks still remain about the nature of the neutrino, such as whether or not it actually possesses a rest mass).

Most remarkable of all, though, is the fact that *all* of this information about the neutrino has been acquired through an indirect means, by circuitously inferring its most probable qualities from its general pattern of interaction with the surrounding environment. *It is this pattern of interaction that is directly analogous to the observable impact that a designer has on his or her created artifact.* For just as we can indirectly discern many of the neutrino's unobservable properties through a careful observation of its impact on other observable entities, so too can we indirectly discern at least some of a creator's inherent properties simply through a careful examination of that which he or she has made. Once again, this is due to the fact that a designer's causal "signature" or imprint is invariably left behind whenever an artifact is designed and brought into being. It is this distinctive imprint that can subsequently be examined for indirect information about the designer's *own* idiosyncratic nature.

In the same way, then, that we can indirectly infer a great deal of information about the neutrino without ever having seen one, simply through a careful examination of how they influence the surrounding environment, so too can we infer a great deal about the nature of God without ever having seen Him or subjecting Him to rigorous experimental analysis. We can best do this by taking a careful, open-minded look at that which the Deity has supposedly made and then asking ourselves what kind of being could have originally been responsible for carrying out such a project. This is precisely the same sort of inferential activity that was advocated by the Psalmist, who confidently proclaimed that:

> The heavens declare the glory of God [and] the skies proclaim the work of his hands. Day after day they pour forth speech; night after night they display knowledge. There is no speech or language where their voice is not heard. Their voice goes out into all the earth, their words to the ends of the world. (Psalm 19:1–5, NIV)

This is a bold declaration that gives a clear stamp of approval to the natural theologian's aims, especially when it comes to the process of inferring the Divine attributes from the nature of the physical universe itself. St. Paul took this idea one step further and asserted that this inferential knowledge about God is so painfully obvious that we can't possibly claim to be ignorant about His existence and great glory:

> The wrath of God is being revealed from heaven against all the godlessness and wickedness of men who suppress the truth by their wickedness, since what may be known about God is plain to them, because God has made it plain to them. *For*

since the creation of the world God's invisible qualities—his eternal power and divine na-
ture—have been clearly seen, being understood from what has been made, so that men
are without excuse. (Rom. 1:18–20, NIV, emphasis mine)

This passage reveals St. Paul to have been the quintessential natural theologian, since he clearly believed that God's "invisible qualities" can be directly inferred from the nature of the physical universe itself. When we attempt to carry out this inferential procedure ourselves in light of our modern
scientific understanding of the cosmos, we typically find that, much to our
surprise, the results are in *direct opposition* to what we would have ordinarily
expected *a priori*, since most people in the West have been socialized to believe that modern science has long since disproven the existence of a Creator.

An increasing amount of cosmological data, however, is beginning to
show that this popular assumption is most probably *false*, as is evidenced by
the increasing number of atheistic scientists who are converting to some
form of theism.[7] For most people, however, it isn't enough to establish beyond a reasonable doubt the existence of a generic creative force in the universe. They want to know what this Cosmic Power is really *like* in and of itself. That is to say, they want to know if it is conscious, all-powerful,
benevolent, and whether or not it has any direct relevance to their own personal lives. Unfortunately, we can't directly ascertain these potential facets
of the Divine Being in an empirical manner, because His presumed nonphysical nature is not directly amenable to the scientific method. It is, however, *indirectly* available to us in a derivative sense, as we have seen, and this
is more than good enough for our purposes, because we can still discern a
great deal about God's most probable nature in this roundabout manner.

Do Any of Our Concepts Apply to God?

Of course, the validity of this sort of inferential reasoning can easily be ob-
jected to on so-called anthropomorphic grounds, insofar as it isn't necessary
(or perhaps even likely) that any of our concepts regarding the Divine will actually end up being applicable to God's true inner reality. This cynical viewpoint is buttressed by the contributions of modern sociobiology, in which it has
been argued that love, purpose, and other human-centered traits evolved not
because they have an independent, nonphysical existence, but rather because
they have biological survival value, and so were favored by natural selection.

Nevertheless, it is important to note that neither of the above statements
necessarily negates the types of inferences that we will be making in the remainder of this chapter. In fact, there is a very real sense in which both of
these statements are fundamentally *irrelevant* to the basic question that is at

issue here. For instance, whereas the cynic may be able to argue that our own values and concepts can't be transferred over to the intrinsic nature of the Godhead, the theist can just as easily counterargue that there is no necessary reason why they *cannot*. Indeed, insofar as human nature is a finite reflection of God's own Being, we would naturally *expect* there to be some correlation between our concepts and God's own intrinsic nature. Moreover, as Alvin Plantinga has aptly pointed out in his intriguing little book *Does God Have a Nature?*, the assertion that none of our concepts apply to God is itself contradictory, since it presupposes that at least one of our concepts, namely the idea that none of our concepts applies to God, *itself* applies to God.[8]

Further evidence that at least some of our concepts can validly be applied to God can be found in the enormous success of human science. For not only have we been able to crack nature's underlying quantum code, we have also been able to exploit our understanding of the natural world (including the vast potential of nuclear energy) for strategic engineering purposes. This startling fact tells us in no uncertain terms that for some mysterious reason *we do indeed have an inner cognitive connection to the way things really are in the universe*. And while this underlying connectivity to the universe doesn't necessarily translate over to the intrinsic nature of the Godhead, it would seem to make such a connection significantly more likely overall, since it tells us that on at least one level we've got intellectual access to the way things really are in the universe.[9]

A similar criticism can also be applied to modern sociobiological reasoning. For while it may be true that such things as love and purpose have their biological counterparts in the physical world, even to the point that these qualities may have evolved naturally in response to selective environmental pressures, *this doesn't necessarily mean that these same properties don't simultaneously exist in the nonphysical realm*. This would be the case if a divine Creator would have wanted to instantiate certain spiritually based traits in the physical world through natural evolutionary pathways.

We must therefore be careful not to be sidetracked by this type of cynical reasoning, even though part of it could possibly be true. For just as part of it could be true, that same part could also end up being false in the end. This being the case, we must naturally look to the scientific evidence itself in order to help us determine which alternative is probably the correct one.

A Scientific Interpretation of the Divine Character

The first quality that we can infer about the nature of the Divine Being is that He must in some sense be rational, because the entire visible universe is known to be supremely rational in terms of its basic underlying structure. Although this fact doesn't necessarily prove that God actually exists, it *does* show that *if* He exists, then He almost certainly *has* to be rational.

This rational quality is also known to extend to the creaturely realm as well, because the human thought process *itself* is also capable of being surprisingly[10] rational, especially when it comes to the mysterious process of deducing how the physical universe itself actually operates. Indeed, it is this very fact that has led many scientists to conclude that whatever else God may be, He *has* to be a supremely rational entity. Some have even christened Him as the "Divine Mathematician" because of this. The British astrophysicist Sir Fred Hoyle, as we have seen, goes so far as to call God a "Supercalculating Intellect," and he bases his conclusion on the incredible degree of technological precision that is evident throughout the physical realm.

The foundational science of quantum mechanics is another promising area from which we can glean more scientific evidence about the possible nature of God. As we have seen, the standard "Copenhagen" interpretation of quantum mechanics asserts that there is no such thing as a concrete, determined physical reality as such. Rather, the so-called physical realm actually "exists" in an indeterminate, superpositional state of all quantum possibilities until an observation is actually made upon it, because the intangible phenomenon of conscious observership is believed to somehow be the only means that is capable of "collapsing" any given combination of quantum wave functions, thereby imparting a "concrete" and determined reality to them.

This raises an obvious problem, though. For prior to the evolution of life in the universe, there were no physical observers in existence *anywhere* to be able to observe the universe into being, yet we are here nonetheless. So, given the prior validity of the Copenhagen interpretation (which most physicists readily accept), the universe *must* have somehow been observed into being from the very beginning (prior to the existence of space and time) by a transcendent "Ultimate Observer." This transcendent function, of course, can only be attributed to God, and even Barrow and Tipler have fully acknowledged this possibility, insofar as they have referred to God as the "Ultimate Observer who is in the end responsible for coordinating the separate observations of the lesser observers and is thus responsible for bringing the entire universe into existence."[11]

It is in this fashion that we can derive the Divine property of *physical transcendence* from the ostensible quantum need for an Ultimate Observer in the cosmos. But there is even more that we can surmise about God from this quantum requirement. For if God actually preceded the existence of the entire universe, then there is a very high probability that He must be an *eternally existing* being as well. This inference is supported by the realization that any being who is transcendent enough to actually precede the Big Bang must *also* be transcendent enough to be eternal.

But we can even go one step further than this. For if God is actually eternal in this manner, then there is also a substantial likelihood that He is probably *self-existent* as well. This can be seen to follow directly from the very supposition of an eternal life span for the Deity, because a Being who has always existed would *by definition* have to be uncreated, which in turn implies that He *must* have been deriving His existence from His own necessary nature for all of eternity. This is the property of *aseity*, or self-existence, in its purest form, and it can be seen to follow directly from the postulation of God's own eternal existence.

It is also possible to derive the transcendent nature of God's existence from His unique position as Creator. For if He really did bring the entire spatio-temporal realm into existence at the Big Bang, then it follows that He *must* be genuinely transcendent over the entire physical domain.

Further support for God's transcendence over the physical realm can be found in the multidimensional nature of the universe itself. Interestingly, all workable theories of particle physics that aim for a conceptual unification of nature's four fundamental forces require the existence of at least nine dimensions immediately following the Big Bang in order to be operational, yet we presently only have four observable dimensions remaining in existence (three of space and one of time).[12] Modern string theory, for instance, predicts that the universe came into being with either ten or twenty-six different dimensions, but it also predicts that soon after the creation all but four of them naturally shriveled up and disappeared.[13]

Hugh Ross, however, believes that these higher dimensions are still in existence somewhere in the cosmos, but on a level that is imperceptible to humans. He also believes that they are capable of providing a plausible avenue through which God can display much of His transcendence over the world:

> The Bible declares forthrightly that God is very close to each and every one of us. But, it just as forthrightly states that God is invisible. The Apostle Paul says that no one has ever seen God, nor can see Him. Evidently, it is impossible for us humans to make physical contact with God. How, then, can God be so close and yet be beyond physical contact?[14]

Ross finds the answer to this question in the multidimensional nature of our physical universe itself, which enables God to be both far beyond us, and yet right next to us, *simultaneously*. "It boggles the mind," Ross tells us, "to try to conceive of what can happen in seven more dimensions of space and time than we humans can experience."[15] These extra dimensions, according to Ross, enhance God's transcendence by enabling Him to carry out virtually any imaginable activity in the world that isn't logically contradictory.

While this may or may not be so, it *is* true that these higher dimensions probably exist somewhere in the universe, and it is their mere existence that most interests us here, because it illustrates quite conclusively that there are physical channels already in place for some degree of transcendence over our four-dimensional spatio-temporal realm. We can surmise from this that the concept of physical transcendence isn't implausible in and of itself, especially given the fact that these higher dimensions are directly posited by most modern particle theories. Of course, these higher dimensions are still part of the physical domain, so they aren't necessarily indicative of any absolute degree of transcendence in and of themselves. But who knows where they could lead? For all we know, they could lead directly to the transcendent spiritual realm. But even if they don't, they nevertheless appear to have set an important precedent in the universe, which revolves around the likely existence of coherent physical pathways that *lead in the direction of genuine physical transcendence.*[16]

We mustn't forget that the concept of transcendence is implicit in the very nature of the Big Bang itself, because prior to the present universal expansion there was almost certainly no such thing as space, time, or matter, which means that the state of absolute nothingness that preceded the Big Bang was itself transcended *by definition* when the Big Bang actually took place.[17] This follows necessarily from the Space-Time Theorem of General Relativity, as we have seen. So we know that something wholly other than the present spatio-temporal realm is capable of being actual, but if this is true, then it is also possible that another type of transcendent realm might be in existence *right now* in another domain of reality that totally transcends our own.[18]

This concept of transcendence is also important for our purposes because it is possible to derive the *spiritual* nature of the Divine Being directly from it. For insofar as God truly acted as the original cause of the entire spatio-temporal realm, and insofar as He is now utterly transcendent over it, it follows that He *cannot* be a physical being by definition. And if He isn't physical, then He must be something wholly other than physical, which we can call "spiritual."

We can also derive the property of *omnipresence* from the Creator's transcendent cosmic position. For insofar as God *really did* contrive the Big Bang from a position of absolute transcendence over the universe, it follows that

He must be transcendent over the *entire* spatio-temporal realm itself, which in turn means that He must be genuinely omnipresent. He is "everywhere," according to this view, because the entire Big Bang has somehow been instantiated within the ontological "umbrella" of his infinite existence. This conclusion is further supported by God's nonphysical nature, as it is much easier to see how a nonphysical being (as opposed to a physical one) can be omnipresent throughout a purely physical cosmos.

This leads us to the final Divine attribute that can be deduced directly from God's transcendent position over the universe: His proverbial *timelessness*. Prior to Einstein's theory of relativity, it was very difficult to see how God could possibly transcend the ordinary confines of time. But now we know that time isn't an absolute physical "thing" at all. It is, rather, a supremely elastic quality that can be stretched or squeezed in direct response to such relativistic items as one's velocity and one's overall proximity to a gravitational field. But if this is true for mere mortals, then how much *more* true must it be for the transcendent Creator of the cosmos, who actually created time at the Big Bang and who thus exists outside the ordinary confines of time altogether? No wonder the Psalmist could say "a thousand years in your sight are like a day that has just gone by, or like a watch in the night" (Psalm 90:4).

Indeed, God's transcendent position over time can be seen to be implicit in the biblical assertion that "God is light" (John 1:5). For if we take this statement to be a physical metaphor of God's true relationship to the temporal sphere, we find that He *must* be timeless after all, since according to Einstein, anything that travels at the speed of light is inherently timeless *by definition*. This metaphor contains the physical analogue to God's omnipresence as well, because anything that travels at the speed of light must also have infinite mass according to Einstein's relativity theory, and this is the very same thing that an infinite and omnipresent being would have if it were physical in nature! The insuperable nature of the Godhead is also cleverly concealed within this metaphor, because the speed of light, which is approximately 186,282 miles per second, is widely acknowledged to be the cosmic speed limit throughout the universe. But insofar as God *is* light, then nothing can surmount Him because absolutely nothing can move faster than Him.

However, the Bible doesn't simply tell us that God travels at the speed of light. It tells us that He *is* light. This can be understood to mean that He is the very *essence* of timelessness and insuperable omnipresence. Hence, even Einstein's theory of relativity is able to give us important scientific information about the likely nature of the Godhead.

Indeed, given the transcendent degree of intelligence that is exemplified throughout the physical universe, there is also a high probability that the Creator is *omniscient* as well (meaning He knows everything there is to know). We can say this for the simple reason that any being who is wise enough to have created our exceedingly complex universe perfectly from the start—as the most recent cosmological data[19] clearly suggests—is also likely to be all-knowing, because it is very difficult to see how such an unfathomably complex universe could possibly have been the result of anything less than a veritable *infinitude* of knowledge.[20]

This intuition can readily be supported by even a cursory glimpse into any natural science textbook, whether it is in the field of neurophysiology or quantum mechanics. For as Newton realized long ago, we have only scratched the surface of any complete knowledge of how our universe actually operates. Yet, this minuscule inkling has nevertheless turned out to be *far* more complex than any of us are capable of understanding at the present time. But if our present level of knowledge only represents the proverbial "tip of the iceberg" as far as the true degree of complexity in the universe is concerned, how much *more* complex must the whole thing *really* be? Moreover, given this complexity, how much knowledge did the Creator really need to have "on tap" in order to have been able to instantiate such an indescribably complex, fine-tuned masterpiece? It doesn't seem too much of a stretch, given these prior realizations, to assert that this degree of knowledge was most likely *infinite* in scope, especially given the corroborating fact that most theistic philosophers through the years have argued extensively for the necessity of this particular attribute.

The "groping," "jury-rigged" nature of the evolutionary process doesn't substantially weaken the power of this assertion either. For as I have shown at length elsewhere, there appears to be a morally justifiable reason as to why God would have wanted to utilize the evolutionary process to do His creating, when He presumably could have instantiated the entire biosphere instantaneously by miraculous fiat. This necessary reason appears to be related to the underlying metaphysical conditions for human existence.[21] To the extent that this speculative hypothesis turns out to be valid, the groping nature of the evolutionary process would *not* be the result of a Divine epistemological deficiency as such. It would, instead, be a paradoxical function of God's own limitless knowledge, which would have enabled Him to foresee the many extraordinary conditions that would inherently need to be satisfied before ontologically sophisticated beings such as ourselves could possibly come into being.[22]

While this may seem like a questionable leap to take, it can be justified, at least in part, on a probabilistic basis. Physicists frequently do this when they come across a physical quantity that is very steeply peaked around zero. When this happens, they tend to regard the quantity in question as being *precisely* zero, that is, until it can be shown to be otherwise. A good example of this process can be found with the cosmological constant, which turns out to be *very* steeply peaked around zero when it is measured in a low-energy world similar to our own.[23] As a consequence, most physicists tend to regard the cosmological constant as being *precisely* zero.

In the same way, we have good reason for supposing that the extreme degree of intelligence that is exemplified by our universe is actually infinite in nature, because everywhere we look, from the smallest subatomic region to the most distant nebula, we find the same unfathomable degree of intelligence and complexity staring us in the face. Moreover, there is every indication that we have obtained only a tiny glimpse of the actual amount of intelligence that pervades the cosmos. But if this is so (i.e., if the native degree of cosmic intelligence is overwhelmingly peaked toward infinity), aren't we justified in assuming that, for all practical intents and purposes, it probably *is* infinite?

Of course, this doesn't mean that an infinite degree of intelligence necessarily exists in the universe simply because we are unable to grasp it all. But what it does mean is that there appears to be an infinite amount of intelligence *in essence* remaining to be discovered in the cosmos. Indeed, we can use the Principle of Universality—which states that the same general scientific principles are probably true throughout the cosmos—to bring us to the same conclusion, by extrapolating from the known amount of intelligence in the natural sciences to the most likely degree of intelligence that is applicable throughout the cosmos.

If nothing else, we can assert with confidence that there are probably an infinite number of important mathematical relations "out there" waiting to be discovered. And since each of these relations by definition represents a small amount of cosmic intelligence that is just waiting to be understood, it follows that the universe must *necessarily* possess an infinite degree of mathematical intelligence after all. This is no trivial realization, because a significant proportion of these undiscovered relations almost certainly pertains to actual states of affairs somewhere in the cosmos. But a "significant proportion" of infinity is *itself* infinite in scope, so it would seem to follow that there must be an endless number of mathematically sophisticated states of affairs in existence after all.

This conclusion is supported by the growing realization that the physical universe itself is *infinitely* complex in terms of many of its basic underlying features (such as fractals).[24] It is hard to see how this particular feature of cosmic reality could possibly be consistent with anything *other* than an all-knowing cosmic Intelligence. For as we have already seen, it would seem to be a general metaphysical principle that any aspect of the physical universe that requires a certain amount of intelligence to understand *must* have originally required *at least* as much intelligence to initially bring about. This much only stands to reason, but this realization nevertheless has extremely far-reaching implications for us. For if the underlying complexity of the universe is truly infinite in scope, it would seem to imply that the universe *had* to have been brought about by an Intelligence that is similarly limitless in nature.[25]

While we're on the subject of infinities, now would be a good time to consider the question of the Divine power. Is there enough scientific evidence to justify the conclusion that God is infinitely powerful? If not, how much power *can* we justifiably attribute to the Deity merely through an impartial reading of the scientific evidence? Although these are clearly very difficult questions to address purely from an empirical point of view, we can nevertheless confidently assert that, given the unbelievable size and age of our universe, along with the utter grandeur of the countless celestial objects it contains, the Creator *must* be exceedingly powerful indeed.

But it is one thing to say that He is exceedingly powerful and quite another to say that He is *infinitely* powerful. But here too we can find considerable support for the traditional doctrine of omnipotence from the findings of modern science. For according to cosmologists, the present universal expansion can be traced back in time to a point when the entire universe was smashed into a point (also known as a singularity) that was *infinitely* hot and *infinitely* dense. This much alone is remarkable[26] enough, but we're also told that this infinitely dense "cosmic egg" was somehow very precisely fine-tuned so that it could detonate with just the right degree of explosive vigor to ensure the development of a life-supporting universe several billion years later.

This, in turn, leads us to ask a very pertinent question: namely, what kind of being or force could have possibly created such an infinitely hot and infinitely dense superparticle to begin with? What kind of being or force could have anticipated the many complex needs of life ahead of time and then have fine-tuned the explosion of this superparticle in such a manner as to ensure the development of these biocentric conditions several billion years later? And finally, what kind of being or force could have accomplished this stupendous feat perfectly (i.e., without error) from the very beginning? This is a spectacular achievement in and of itself, because the universe can be seen to have rapidly reached a "point of no return" within microseconds of the Big Bang, because of the so-called domino effect.

That is to say, since everything that transpired subsequent to the Big Bang built ineluctably on that which came immediately prior, there was very little possibility for these events to be significantly manipulated "downstream," particularly given the extreme explosive vigor of the Big Bang itself, along with the ostensible inviolability of the law of cause and effect. Now, insofar as this was indeed the case, it is clear that the Big Bang had to have been perfectly calibrated and fine-tuned for life from the very beginning, because there was absolutely no room for error any time thereafter. This is corroborated by the subsequent trajectory of cosmic evolution itself, which appears to have been error-free all the way to the origin of life. Even the rise of life on this planet appears to have been error-free as well, since it arose just as soon as it possibly could, which in turn suggests that it did not evolve by the time-consuming process of trial and error.

Now, what kind of being or force could have possibly been responsible for orchestrating such a perfect, error-free display of power and might, particularly in relation to the degree of foresight and balance that would have been necessary to ensure the evolution of life from the very beginning? In order for us to be able to answer this question with any degree of accuracy, we must first posit a creative force that is entirely sufficient for the task we are demanding of it. This being the case, we seem to be constrained, by the very magnificence and grandeur of the task being proposed, to posit a universal Creator who is *infinitely* powerful, because no less of a being would seem to have been capable of creating such an infinitely hot and infinitely dense particle in the first place. Indeed, this would seem to follow *necessarily* from the very infinitude of the cosmic singularity itself, because it is a metaphysical principle that *no effect can be greater than its initial cause.* Therefore, it would seem to *necessarily* follow that the creative force behind the cosmos *had* to have been *at least* as powerful as the infinitely hot and dense singularity that it brought about. And this, in turn, would seem to demand an *infinitely powerful* creative force in the universe, since an infinitely powerful cause is inherently required to generate an infinitely hot and infinitely dense effect. No wonder the astronomer John Barrow could assert that "the role of the Creator is essentially assumed by the naked big bang singularity."[27]

This situation is not unlike the time-honored conundrum concerning whether or not an omnipotent God is powerful enough to create a rock that is too big for Him to lift. While this may or may not be so (it may simply be incoherent), there is one thing about this situation that we can say with a fair degree of certainty: namely, if God is going to create an infinitely big rock, then He *has* to be infinitely powerful Himself. This much only stands to reason. But an infinitely dense singularity is in point of fact infinitely "massive" in an inverse fashion, so it *had* to have been brought about by an infinitely powerful Deity after all.

It is in this manner that the theological doctrine of omnipotence can be justified *purely from a scientific point of view*. This conclusion is corroborated by additional findings from the realm of cosmology, which indicate that the universe's many constituent parameters were perfectly fine-tuned to bring about life *from the very beginning*.[28] It was this initial perfection that, against all the odds, enabled our fledgling universe to bring about intelligent life several billion years later.

Consider, for instance, the accuracy of the so-called density parameter, which was responsible for determining the initial explosive vigor of the Big Bang in relation to the mass of the universe and the value of the gravitational constant. It had to have been fine-tuned to better than one part in 10^{60} before life would have ever been capable of evolving on this planet.[29] If the density parameter had been just a wee bit larger than it is, the universe would have collapsed back in on itself shortly after the Big Bang; if it were just a tiny bit smaller, there wouldn't have been sufficient gravitational impetus for galaxies to form. Either way, we wouldn't be here. Or what about the value of the mysterious vacuum energy or cosmological constant, which seems to have required a *stupendously* precise cancellation effect to obtain between different contributing influences to the vacuum energy before it *ever* could have been biocentric in nature? Incredibly, we now know that this cancellation effect needed to be accurate to an unbelievable *120 decimal places* before an appropriate life-supporting space could have been generated in the universe.[30] Even the noted atheistic physicist Steven Weinberg is impressed with the unprecedented nature of this fine-tuning:

> Opinions differ as to the degree to which the constants of nature must be fine-tuned to make life necessary. There are independent reasons to expect an excited state of carbon 12 near the resonant energy. But one constant does seem to require an incredible fine-tuning: it is the vacuum energy, or cosmological constant, mentioned in connection with inflationary cosmologies.
>
> Although we cannot calculate this quantity, we can calculate some contributions to it (such as the energy of quantum fluctuations in the gravitational field that have wavelengths no shorter than about 10^{-33} centimeter). These contributions come out about 120 orders of magnitude larger than the maximum value allowed by our observations of the present rate of cosmic expansion. If the various contributions to the vacuum energy did not nearly cancel, then, depending on the value of the total vacuum energy, the universe either would go through a complete cycle of expansion and contraction before life could arise or would expand so rapidly that no galaxies or stars could form.
>
> Thus, the existence of life of any kind seems to require a cancellation between different contributions to the vacuum energy, accurate to about 120 decimal places.[31]

It is hard to make sense of this profound degree of fine-tuning apart from the traditional theistic idea of an Intelligent Designer who has an unlimited amount of power at His disposal. And while it is possible to imagine alternative scenarios in which this fine-tuning might have been able to accidentally obtain (perhaps through a random varying of the constants throughout different regions of the universe), none of these question-begging alternatives is as simple or as conceptually satisfying as the traditional theistic explanation, since none purport to explain where the universe itself could have originally come from. There is also no evidence whatsoever for any varying of the physical constants throughout cosmic history. To the contrary, the evidence overwhelmingly indicates that the constants themselves have occupied their present life-supporting values from the very beginning.[32] As a consequence, natural selection is not believed to have been involved in the initial calibration of these fundamental parameters.[33]

What this means as far as we're concerned is that the universe has actually possessed its present biocentric character *from its very inception*, which again only seems to make sense in terms of an all-powerful Designer, because any force that is capable of coercing the initial conditions of the universe so perfectly from the very beginning is probably capable of doing *far more*, and this possibility only seems to be consistent with an unlimited degree of creative power.[34] When this realization is considered in light of the putative fact that only an infinite creative power is capable of bringing forth an infinitely hot and infinitely dense superparticle out of nothing, the prospect of God's all-power would seem to be a virtual certainty.

But we can take this line of argument one step further, because of the many interesting products that actually emerged from the Big Bang (namely, ourselves and the rest of the biosphere). While this doesn't necessarily prove that organic life forms were deliberately intended from the very start, this is nevertheless the most likely conclusion, all things considered, especially given the supreme amount of intelligence and power that was necessary to enable this to happen.

The basic idea here is that any creative force that is *this* intelligent and *this* powerful was, in all likelihood, more than competent enough to have actually intended the evolution of life all along, particularly given the realization that the Big Bang itself *had* to have been fine-tuned in a biocentric manner from the very outset if life was to have *ever* been capable of forming here. This implies *intelligent foresight*, which itself suggests a significant degree of *deliberate conscious intentionality* in the universe. But these are qualities that are only used in conjunction with free-willed, personal beings, because this is the only kind of being who can deliberately intend to accomplish *any* type of sophisticated, complex goal. We can infer from this that the Creator of the cosmos is most probably a forward-thinking, free-willed personal Being.

Even here, though, there is more than initially meets the eye, because any type of creative power that is conscious and powerful enough to have deliberately intended the evolution of life from the very beginning is *also* likely to have been driven by feelings of *love* and *caring* for the creation, because the entire universe seems to have been lovingly crafted, at least in part, for the sake of earthbound life forms. This is directly evidenced by the profound degree of complexity that is displayed at all levels of cosmic reality, which itself seems to indicate how far the Creator's love for us actually extends, since we clearly wouldn't be here apart from this complexity.

This is the same inference that would legitimately be drawn by an enormously loved quadriplegic child. For to the extent that this child's parents would have gone to extreme lengths to provide her with a home that catered to her every handicapped need, it would be appropriate for her to conclude that she was indeed a prized and valued person beyond measure. But this same principle can also be applied to us, because the enormous complexity of the universe is *itself* indicative of how much we are loved and valued by the Creator.

The universe is also an immensely beautiful place, where spectacular scenic vistas can be found in almost every direction one happens to look. Moreover, this natural beauty does *not* appear to be an idiosyncratic perception of our own minds, because the celestial bodies that comprise it exist independently of us and are awe-inspiring in their own right. To the extent that this is so, it follows that the Creator must possess a heightened sense of *aesthetic awareness* Himself, because any created object can only be as beautiful as the artisan who ultimately gave rise to it. This elementary principle of creativity tells us that the Divine sense of beauty must be very profound indeed. Hugh Ross agrees:

> Observe skilled sculptors, painters, or poets, artisans of any kind, and see that they always spend much more time on their masterpieces than they do on their ordinary tasks. Observe the painstaking yet joyful labor poured into each masterpiece of their design. Observe how often the artist stops to appreciate and evaluate the work in progress.
>
> Examine the creation on any scale, from a massive galaxy to the interior of an atom, from a whale to an amoeba. The splendor of each item, its beauty of form as well as of function, speaks not of instantaneous mass production but rather of patient attention to detail, of infinite care and delight. Such delight with work in progress is expressed through Genesis 1 in the oft-repeated statement, "And God saw that it was good."[35]

This brings us to the important property of *omnibenevolence*, which refers to the totality of goodness that is said to be characteristic of the Divine Being. This property can also be directly inferred from the nature of the present universal structure, because there is no question that the conditions on this planet are "good" as far as the existence of life is concerned. Everything we need for our physical sustenance is readily available in our earthly habitat, from a suitable supply of oxygen to the proper nutrients for our organismic well-being.

Indeed, the goodness of the earth becomes radically apparent when we compare the conditions here with those of *any* other celestial locale. Virtually the entire cosmos is exceedingly hostile to the needs of life, since any given area is either too hot, too cold, or otherwise too barren to be able to support the delicate needs of carbon-based life forms. But the earth is vastly different—and perhaps even unique—in its life-supporting capacity, because it lovingly caters to our needs in thousands of different ways. This fact is surely "good" for us, which in turn means that any Divine force that would have consciously intended for us to exist here must also be "good" in this instrumental sense as well, *because a good agent is almost always required to produce a good effect*, particularly when the outcome is clearly not accidental in nature.

Indeed, this goodness becomes amplified many times over when we realize how delicately balanced our world really is, *vis-à-vis* the many fine-tuned constants and other parameters that are required for our existence. Each and every aspect of this extraordinary structural precision is a direct reflection of the Divine goodness that originally produced it, as we would recognize all the more if we were somehow transported to the surface of Venus or Mars for a few seconds. These other worlds would actually be worse for us than a pre-designed hell, because we wouldn't even be capable of *surviving* anywhere else, not even for a split second. No wonder the book of Genesis repeatedly states that God saw His creation to be "very good" (Gen. 1:11, 12, 21, 25, 31).[36]

The Nature of God's Interaction with the World

Given the empirically based interpretation of the Divine Character that we have explored in this chapter, we are now in a position to ask ourselves what God's mode of interaction with the world today is likely to be. This is an important question, because a significant part of our concept of God revolves around how He chooses to interact with the world.

On the one hand, there is the theological position known as *deism*, in which God sets the universe up in the beginning and then leaves it alone to function entirely according to natural law. On the other hand, there is the much more popular theological position known as *theism*, in which God is actively involved in the affairs of the world today.

A deist therefore differs from a theist primarily in the degree to which God is believed to be directly involved in global affairs. Theists typically believe that God is intimately involved in global events, whereas deists believe He is not. Theists also differ from deists in the degree to which they believe God was involved in the creation of the biosphere. Theists believe that God was intimately involved in the world's creation at many different steps along the way, whereas deists believe that God simply created a naturalistic realm of self-organizing particles in the beginning, so that the universe could then gradually evolve by natural law into its present-day configuration. This is no small distinction, because the entire character of God hinges on the degree to which He has actually been involved in worldly affairs.

It would be a mistake, though, to assume that the terms "deism" and "theism" are mutually exclusive with respect to their description of the divine nature, for it isn't as though God had to have either been totally theistic or deistic throughout the entirety of cosmic history. To the contrary, it is quite possible for God to have acted in both a theistic *and* a deistic fashion during different stages of the creation. For instance, He could have acted in an entirely deistic fashion during the prehuman stages of cosmic history, since there may not have been any need for Him to become directly involved in the universe's evolution before the arrival of humanity. This would have been the case if God had opted to create a naturalistic realm of self-organizing particles that could subsequently evolve on its own power into our present biocentric format. With the arrival of humanity, though, we can see that there would have been a sudden need for God to become more intimately involved in worldly affairs. In response to this putative need, God could easily have changed His basic orientation to the world to be more consistent with what we call "theism."

We can see, then, that the traditional definition of deism is mistaken because it fallaciously assumes that God had to have been either totally theistic or else totally deistic throughout the entire course of cosmic history. But why should the Divine Personality be unduly constrained in this manner? We routinely alter the basic focus of our own actions in the world in direct accordance with self-perceived need, so why should it be any different for God? Why shouldn't God also be capable of altering His own fundamental orientation to the world whenever the need happens to present itself?

However, even if we assume, in sympathy with theism, that God is intimately involved in the world today, it doesn't necessarily follow from this that His actions are in violation of natural law. To the contrary, there are a variety of mechanisms that could possibly explain how God could act in the world without violating natural law. To begin with, if we work on the strong deistic assumption that God might for some reason be unable to directly intervene in the world today, it is still possible for Him to have directed the course of natural events at the Big Bang in such a way as to cause any desired effect several billion years later on this planet. Surely it is within the power of an omnipotent Being to act in this fashion. However, the laws of nature don't seem to be impervious to Divine Input in the present. To the contrary, it is possible that God is somehow directing certain events at the quantum level of reality, so as to be able to orient worldly events in a certain desired direction. It is also possible that God could be utilizing higher levels of natural law to influence worldly events without actually breaking any of the laws of nature that exist on our own level of reality.[37]

There are two additional ways in which God can be seen to be involved in worldly affairs. He can be conceptualized as the *Logos*, or the Logical Mediator, between cause and effect, much as the ancient Stoic philosophers imagined Him to be. In this case, God would be indirectly involved in all worldly events, since He would be the unseen cosmic Power that would be tying all physical causes to their own corresponding logical effects. Such a metaphysical linkage between cause and effect does indeed appear to be a necessity, because there would otherwise be no guarantee that any given cause would be followed by the "right" effect. We tend to take the fidelity engendered by the Law of Cause and Effect for granted, but each succession of cause and effect is actually comprised of a multitude of physical events that all have to be faithfully oriented in the right direction before the proper effect can result. God can be understood to be the Logical Mediator that enables this to happen without fail.[38]

This leads us to consider the final way in which God is interacting with the world today. The entire fabric of reality is inherently in need of a suitable metaphysical foundation upon which it can exist. God *is* this metaphysical pillar of reality, insofar as He functions as the underlying foundation for the whole of reality.

The Empirical Probability of Our Inferences

Earlier we saw how the inductive form of reasoning that we've used throughout this chapter yields only probable answers. This being the case, how can we be sure that our conclusions stand a good chance of actually being true in the real world?

Norman Geisler and Ronald Brooks, in their excellent book on the structure of logical thinking, describe four general ways in which we can determine the empirical probability of any inductive conclusion.[39] To begin with, they tell us that we have to take into consideration the breadth of our sample. Larger sample sizes are obviously associated with more probable conclusions. On this score, the traditional theistic conclusions that we have drawn in this chapter stand a good likelihood of actually being true in the end, because our sample size is actually the entire universe!

The second way that we can establish the empirical probability of a given conclusion is similar to the first, in that it has to do with how representative the evidence under consideration happens to be.[40] In our own case, the evidence is about as representative as it could possibly be, because once again, we're dealing with the evidence of the *entire universe*. We can, for instance, safely infer certain logical conclusions from the orderly nature of the universe itself, because a very high degree of order has empirically been discovered virtually everywhere we've looked.

The third method of establishing empirical probability, according to Geisler and Brooks, questions the degree to which the evidence itself has been examined.[41] In our own case, we can see that the evidence has been *very* carefully examined indeed, both by scientists and by our own carefully weighed interpretations of their findings.

The fourth and final method of establishing the empirical probability of our inferences questions the relationship between the data itself and the pre-existing body of knowledge in the area under consideration.[42] It is at this point that many of our theistic conclusions can be seen to have a very high degree of empirical probability overall, because all of the analogies that we have used between artisans and their artifacts are definitely known to be true in the realm of *human* creativity. In this sense our inferences are known to correspond in a direct, one-to-one fashion with virtually the entire body of knowledge on human creativity that has already been attained. Of course, this is no guarantee that our analogies will *necessarily* apply to God. However, to the extent that some type of Designer has in fact created the cosmos, the analogy with human creativity would seem to be valid, because the creative process itself is fairly straightforward in terms of its underlying fundamentals, whether the creator in question is human or Divine.

Therefore, as long as we affirm the existence of *some* type of Creator, the various inferences that we have drawn about His underlying character would seem to have a high empirical probability of being accurate in the end, because they have satisfied all four of the above criteria.

Conclusion

In this chapter, we have been able to make a number of important, empirically justifiable inferences about the nature of the Divine Being. This is significant, because it gives a substantial degree of *scientific* credibility to our view of the Godhead.

As it turns out, this scientific interpretation of the Divine nature ends up being virtually identical to the traditional monotheistic view, insofar as it indicates that God is likely to be omniscient, omnipresent, omnibenevolent, all-powerful, and supremely personal. For many modern minds, this may be more than a bit unnerving, because it stands in stark opposition to what we've been taught throughout our academic lives. Nevertheless, we shouldn't be surprised by this possibility, because a truly holistic universe is capable of giving up her secrets in numerous ways. This would seem to explain why the ancient Hebrew prophets were able to ascertain an impressive amount of theological truth in a nonempirical manner, just as we are using a more empirically based method to tap into this very same holistic reality. Actually, we should have expected this exciting theoretical convergence between science and religion all along, precisely *because* the universe is turning out to be a single, undivided whole after all.[43]

The upshot here is that our understanding of the Divine Essence needn't be contradicted, opposed, or otherwise limited by the empirical nature of the latest scientific evidence. To the contrary, our understanding of God should be greatly *bolstered* by these scientific revelations, since they are clearly capable of reflecting back to their Creator if they are viewed from the proper perspective.

Notes

1. Taken from a currently unpublished manuscript by Kevin J. Sharpe, chapter 16, 6–7.

2. My use of the word "designer" here is intended to be synonymous with the word "creator," although technically speaking, the designer of a given artifact doesn't have to be identical with its creator.

3. I am not using the male personal pronoun in relation to God in order to indicate anything specific about the nature of the Deity. I am merely using it at this point for the sake of literary convenience, although later on I will be using it to indicate that God is most likely a personal Being.

4. Norman L. Geisler and Ronald M. Brooks, *Come Let Us Reason* (Grand Rapids, Mich.: Baker, 1990), 133.

5. Paul Davies, *The Last Three Minutes* (New York: Basic, 1994), 39–41.

6. They have, for instance, studied certain supernova explosions in painstaking detail, because supernovae naturally provide one of the best sources of neutrinos for study.

7. M. A. Corey, *God and the New Cosmology* (Lanham, Md.: Rowman & Littlefield, 1993), 123–173, 202, 246, 287–291.

8. Alvin Plantinga, *Does God Have a Nature?* (Milwaukee, Wisc.: Marquette University Press, 1980), 10–28.

9. If we've got access on one level, this means that a cosmic precedent has been set, which in turn means that it's intrinsically possible for us to have access on at least one level. And if we've got access on this one level, it naturally raises the likelihood that we'll end up having access on other, higher levels as well.

10. Human rationality is surprising in three distinct ways. First, we are the only physical beings we know of who possess this trait, so we are clearly in possession of an extremely rare commodity. On a probabilistic basis alone, then, we should be surprised to find that we are in fact rational beings. (From a tautologous "weak anthropic" point of view, though, we shouldn't be surprised at all that we are rational beings because we already know that we are.) Second, we have absolutely no idea how and why our brains operate in this mysteriously rational manner. And third, it is very difficult to explain the origin of this curious property apart from the activity of a larger Creator. The fact that it ultimately facilitates survival can't be considered to be a valid explanation, because it begs the true question that is at issue here, which concerns where the original propensity for this trait ultimately came from.

11. John D. Barrow and Frank J. Tipler, *The Anthropic Cosmological Principle* (Oxford: Oxford University Press, 1986), 470.

12. Ibid., 148.

13. John D. Barrow, *The World within the World* (Oxford: Oxford University Press, 1990), 195.

14. Hugh Ross, *The Creator and the Cosmos* (Colorado Springs, Colo.: NavPress, 1993), 149.

15. Ibid., 150.

16. The very concept of physical transcendence naturally places this transcendent realm utterly beyond our present world, which in turn makes it highly unlikely that we will ever be able to detect it from a purely physical point of view. On the other hand, we don't know how far our minds can actually penetrate into the transcendent spiritual realm, so it is certainly possible that we could occasionally gain entry into this "wholly other" area from time to time by using our minds alone.

17. In speculating about what could have come "before" the Big Bang, I am not contradicting the idea that space and time actually came into existence during that primordial blast, because I am locating my question, not in the present spatio-temporal realm itself, but rather in the transcendent spiritual realm. For if God is indeed eternal in nature, then there is a very real sense in which He did exist "before" the Big Bang, even though He presumably exists outside of the ordinary constraints of time altogether.

18. I don't mean to imply here that the state of absolute nothingness that "existed" prior to the Big Bang somehow possessed existence in a positive sense. Rather, it was the utter lack of existence that was paradoxically "actual" or applicable at that point.

19. Corey, *God and the New Cosmology*, 249–257.

20. Actually, we shouldn't be unduly intimidated by the prospect of an all-knowing Deity, because the concept of infinity isn't as intangible or abstruse as we often like to believe. Many of us manipulate real infinities all the time without batting an eye, and even a young child can hold an infinite number line in her hand without much ado. Of course, these are merely symbolic representations of infinity, but they are nonetheless infinite in nature—one doesn't have to have every single number in an infinite series "on board" in order to be able to profitably manipulate infinities. But the important thing to keep in mind here is that if we, being finite, can conceptualize the idea of infinity so effectively that we can actually manipulate different infinities to our advantage, then why should it be so hard to believe that the transcendent Creator of the universe Himself has limitless knowledge? The physicist Frank J. Tipler has even gone so far as to postulate that we will one day become infinitely knowledgeable at the so-called Omega Point, even though we are clearly finite in nature. How much easier, then, should it be for us to believe that the ontologically limitless God of the universe is omniscient as well?

21. M. A. Corey, *Evolution and the Problem of Natural Evil* (Lanham, Md.: University Press of America, 2000), 93–124.

22. Ibid.

23. John D. Barrow, *Theories of Everything* (Oxford: Oxford University Press, 1991), 147–148.

24. F. David Peat, *The Philosopher's Stone* (New York: Bantam, 1991), 164–166.

25. On the other hand, there is no necessary connection between the universe's inherent degree of complexity and the amount of knowledge that is possessed by God, nor is an omniscient Creator under any sort of compulsion to create a physical universe that directly reflects His own limitless degree of understanding. To the contrary, He could very well have chosen to create a finite universe that merely displays a finite amount of knowledge. Hence, the natural theologian is not necessarily committed to the idea that the physical universe must display an infinite amount of intelligence and complexity.

26. It is ironic that we tend to be so impressed when a magician pulls a rabbit out of a hat, but when we're told that the entire universe was "pulled" out of nothing at all, we hardly sit up and take notice!

27. Barrow, *World within the World*, 315.

28. Barrow and Tipler, *Anthropic Cosmological Principle*, 288.

29. John Gribbin and Martin Rees, *Cosmic Coincidences* (New York: Bantam, 1989).

30. Steven Weinberg, "Life in the Universe," *Scientific American*, vol. 271, no. 4 (October 1994): 49.

31. Ibid.

32. Barrow and Tipler, *Anthropic Cosmological Principle*, 288.

33. Ibid.

34. Corey, *God and the New Cosmology*, 249–257.

35. Hugh Ross, *Creation and Time* (Colorado Springs, Colo.: NavPress, 1994), 142.

36. Of course, there is also a tremendous amount of evil in the world that doesn't seem to square with this presumed theological goodness, but this is only true as long as we myopically insist on viewing our existence from the smallest possible perspective. If we take

a step back, though, and try to examine the essential nature of human life from a developmental, task-oriented perspective, things begin to look much different, especially when we take the probable existence of an Afterlife into account. I say "probable" here because if a Divine Creator does in fact exist, then the odds are very good that some type of Afterlife will also exist. This would be advantageous for the theodicist, because it gives God an additional realm of existence to ensure the proper resolution of evil. For more on this fascinating issue, please refer to Corey, *Evolution and the Problem of Natural Evil*.

37. The unbroken continuity of natural law is important because it appears to be a fundamental prerequisite for human freedom. In order for free will to be legitimate, a steady, predictable environmental backdrop is required in which it can operate. But if God is capriciously interfering with this causal backdrop, by either introducing certain unpredictable events in the world or by preventing the occurrence of certain natural effects, then both the range and scope of human freedom is likely to be compromised to varying degrees.

38. This idea of God as Logos has the additional appeal of rendering certain biblical claims more understandable. For instance, we're told throughout the Bible that God was responsible for causing a large number of destructive events in the world. But how can this be? How can a totally good God be responsible for causing death and destruction in the world? This is obviously problematic, unless of course God is merely acting as the Logical Mediator between cause and effect in the world. In this case, humans would be responsible for initiating these destructive causes in the world, but God would be responsible for matching these evil causes to their own logically appropriate effects.

39. Geisler and Brooks, *Come Let Us Reason*, 137.

40. Ibid.

41. Ibid.

42. Ibid., 138.

43. Michael Talbot, *The Holographic Universe* (New York: Harperperennial Library, 1992).

CHAPTER FOURTEEN

~

Miracles

In the final analysis, God is not a magician who works cheap tricks. Rather, His magic lies in the fabric of the universe itself.

—Kenneth Miller

The word "miracle" means different things to different people. For some, it means a direct suspension of natural law by a Higher Power. For others, it simply refers to something that is inherently amazing or impressive in and of itself.

In *Back to Darwin*, I suggested that miracles are simply events that would have never taken place apart from the direct (or indirect) activity of a Supreme Being. According to this theistically based definition, everything in our world is miraculous to one degree or another, because nothing at all would be happening here apart from the primordial creativity of God Himself.

One of the chief advantages of this latter definition is that it is applicable to both natural processes and miraculous fiat, since neither one of these vehicles could have possibly existed in the absence of a larger Creator (at least not on traditional theistic premises). This widening of the scope of the miraculous to include natural cause-and-effect processes has the effect of restoring a level of sanctity to our world that has been noticeably absent since the rise of our modern age, because it asserts that *everything* on this planet is miraculous in one way or another. Even the process of evolution by natural selection turns out to be miraculous on this theistic view, since it is highly unlikely that *any* form of evolution could have possibly taken place apart from the creative activity of an Intelligent Designer. The Providential Evolutionists of the previous century, such as Robert Chambers, Richard Owen, and Asa Gray, were all keenly aware of this miraculous side of evolution, and they routinely used it in support of their position against their non-theistic opponents.

However, this isn't to say that every event in our world is equally miraculous, because this clearly isn't so. Worldly events differ from one another in their derivative distance from their original Miraculous Cause, as well as in their intrinsic goodness or badness, relative to God's higher purpose for humankind. Generally speaking, though, everything that happens on this planet is ultimately derived from the original miraculous intervention of God Himself at the Big Bang, so every single event retains a definite miraculous ancestry, whether it is openly apparent or not.

In other words, the laws of nature (along with their immediate outcomes) are the *primary miracles* that our entire universe is founded upon. They are "miraculous" because the natural course of events in a theistic universe apart from Divine Activity is absolute nothingness, as we have seen. Indeed, both modern science and traditional theism agree that a complete state of ontological nothingness actually preceded the arrival of the present cosmic order. According to traditional theism, though, God intervened in this initial nothingness by creating something with intrinsic value and substance. It was this initial act of intervention that comprised the very first miracle in the cosmos, because God interrupted this perpetual state of nonbeing to bring something of lasting value into existence. From this point onward, everything that transpired in the universe was miraculous by its very nature (to varying degrees), because all subsequent events were ultimately derived from God's original miraculous intervention. This is why we can say that the "natural" background of cause and effect that currently exists in our world is inherently miraculous, whether it superficially appears to be or not.

But even though the most mundane of natural events can be understood to be miraculous in the above-stated sense, there are nevertheless certain types of natural systems that are, by virtue of their intrinsic degree of complexity, much more ostensibly miraculous than others. These are the far-from-equilibrium systems that are formed when the primary miracles of the natural world are organized into complex functional aggregates like living cells. These complex aggregates, which we can call *first order compound miracles*, are able to manifest a deeper and more impressive type of miraculousness because they are able to tap into the underlying miraculous potential that God seems to have built into the underlying fabric of physical reality. They are "compound miracles" because they build upon the primary miraculousness of the natural world itself.

The phenomenon of life undoubtedly provides the best example of this type of advanced miraculousness, because all living organisms are more than complex enough to be seen as legitimate miracles in their own right. However, this shouldn't be taken to imply that the biological processes of life somehow contradict the natural law of cause and effect, because it is a well-known fact that all biological phenomena are mediated by concrete physiological causes. The miraculous nature of embryological development, for instance, isn't to be found in the breaking of any natural laws *per se*; it is, rather, to be found in God's remarkable ability to use unfathomably complex physiological causes to create a wondrous new echelon of reality.

Naturalistically speaking, then, a first order compound miracle is a type of *emergent* phenomenon, insofar as it is a novel property that emerges from the complex interplay of natural causes, which are themselves miraculous in their own right. This is a *eutaxiological* definition of miracles, because the miraculous influence of an Intelligent Designer is implied (in a derivative sense) by the extreme functionality that is exemplified by these very highly ordered natural states.

Arthur C. Clarke has expressed a similar view about the tremendous underlying potential of the natural world, insofar as he has stated that "any sufficiently advanced technology is indistinguishable from magic."[1] From our perspective, we can even go so far as to assert that any sufficiently advanced technology will be indistinguishable from a genuine miracle as well. This assertion, however, shouldn't be taken to denigrate the traditional doctrine of miracles; it should, instead, be taken to strongly support it, because it elevates the whole of reality to a miraculous new level of being. This "naturalistic" type of miracle, however, can only be manifested by a sufficiently advanced level of technology, because this is what is required to extract the full miraculous potential out of natural processes which are, again, inherently miraculous in their own right.

It follows from this that any miraculous suspension in the course of natural law actually constitutes a *second order compound miracle*, because the laws of nature (and their outcomes) in a theistic universe are *already* miraculous by definition, as we have seen. This may explain God's apparent reluctance to suspend the laws of nature to prove His existence—because He has, on our traditional theistic view, already given us a world that is literally overflowing with miracles!

It should be pointed out, though, that first order compound miracles (or highly ordered natural systems) tend to masquerade as miraculous suspensions of natural law (or second order compound miracles), when in fact they're nothing of the kind. This is because higher levels of emergent phenomena subjectively seem to be miraculous when they are compared with lower levels. For instance, to a person living in the seventeenth century, an instantaneous phone conversation with a person on the other side of the world would inherently seem to require a miraculous suspension of natural law, but to us it is just another unremarkable aspect of the modern telecommunications industry. In the same way, there are almost certainly higher levels of natural emergent phenomena in existence than the relatively low ones we're presently used to. To the extent that this is so, we would probably experience these higher levels as miraculous suspensions of natural law, when in fact they would "merely" be the result of a technology that is simply far more advanced than our own. For all we know, the miraculous potential of our "just right" world may be so deep that it could easily be capable of reproducing every possible miracle in this manner.

To our own subjective awareness, then, the reality of the miraculous isn't always apparent. Even if all of the natural processes in the entire cosmos are inherently miraculous, it doesn't follow from this that we will therefore be capable of directly perceiving them in this way. For to the extent that we are literally surrounded by miracles on every side, their miraculous nature will tend to become hidden from us, in the same way that the reality of water is naturally "hidden" to a fish. On this view, miracles tend to be invisible to us because we are totally inundated with them!

Nevertheless, there would seem to come a point where the complexity and functionality of a given natural system becomes so great that it cannot plausibly be attributed to chance alone. It is precisely here that the activity of an Intelligent Agent can rightfully be invoked to account for the complexity.[2]

Unfortunately, there is no clear line demarcating ostensibly miraculous natural causes from nonmiraculous ones. One person's subjectively perceived miracle is another person's mundane event. Yet, virtually everyone would agree that a Boeing 747 that could spontaneously assemble itself out of a junk pile would be unquestionably miraculous in nature. So there is a conceivable level of natural complexity that points inexorably toward the hand of an Intelligent Designer. The point I am trying to make here is simply that this critical level of complexity has already been discovered in the innate complexity of biological systems.

Recent findings by fractal theorists have only served to further substantiate this conclusion, as they have conclusively shown that most natural systems are *infinitely* complex by their very nature.[3] This conclusion applies to a whole host of natural phenomena, ranging from the physical geography of coastlines to the biochemistry of living systems. It is hard to see how such an infinite level of complexity can possibly be consistent with anything *other* than a Supreme Being.

Oxford University zoologist Richard Dawkins, author of *The Blind Watchmaker*, would disagree with this surmisal, because he is convinced that undesigned natural processes alone can account for all the observed complexity of the biosphere, especially given the fact that billions of years of evolution have already occurred. Indeed, Dawkins believes that the process of cumulative selection—wherein a complex structure is gradually built step-by-step from previous successes—constitutes powerful evidence against Intelligent Design, because it demonstrates that profound degrees of order can be achieved naturally.

Fortunately for the theist, Dawkins' argument is circular (and hence question-begging), because it assumes the prior existence of the very thing it is trying to prove, which is that natural evolutionary processes are capable of generating order without the aid of an Intelligent Designer. Given this presupposed level of functionality, it is true that extreme levels of order can be achieved "naturalistically," but it is precisely this presupposed level of functionality that we're ultimately trying to explain, so Dawkins' argument turns out to be logically fallacious after all.

Dawkins' argument is also flawed because it is founded upon a very weak premise, namely, that understanding how a natural process operates "blindly" to produce something of value automatically does away with the need for a Designer. But surely there is no logically necessary reason why this must be so. In fact, there's no good reason for believing it to be true, since no causal relationship exists between our understanding of how a natural mechanism operates, on the one hand, and the underlying likelihood that it was created by an Intelligent Designer, on the other.

Dawkins' argument also fails because it is based on yet another flawed assumption, namely, that an Intelligent Designer would have relied almost exclusively upon instantaneous fiat, and not natural evolutionary processes, to do His creating.[4] But why should we assume this to be true? Why should we assume that an omnipotent Power will always create via miraculous fiat, when even the Bible itself tells us that God created the world in six "days" (Gen. 1:31)? This passage clearly states that God created the world in time, through a temporally based series of successive developmental stages. Nowhere does it even suggest that God created the world instantaneously by miraculous fiat. Indeed, we're even told in Genesis 1:24 that God used the natural physical processes inherent in the earth to bring forth living creatures:

> And God said, "Let the earth bring forth living creatures according to their kinds: cattle and creeping things and beasts of the earth according to their kinds." And it was so.

The book of Genesis thus tells us that for six "days" (or creative stages) God delegated the actual creative work to the earth itself. But isn't this the generic process of evolution in disguise? After all, the term "evolution" itself simply means "change with respect to time." This is why we can plausibly assert that Genesis One actually describes a theistically based process of phylogenetic evolution, and not the sudden appearance of new biological forms by miraculous fiat. This conclusion significantly weakens Dawkins' assumption that an omnipotent Designer would have never utilized natural evolutionary pathways in His creation of the world.

We mustn't make the mistake, however, of assuming that this sort of naturalistic mechanism somehow counts against the existence of a providential Designer. To the contrary, the only way evolution seems to make any sense at all is in terms of larger Creator, because there doesn't appear to be a nontheistic way to plausibly account for the structural foundation of the evolutionary process (which includes the existence of our fine-tuned universe and the phenomenon of self-replication) apart from the workings of an Intelligent Designer.

So it is by no means self-evident that a divine Watchmaker would have shunned the use of natural evolutionary processes in His creation of the biosphere, especially given the fecundity of these processes at producing objects of extreme complexity, like the human brain. This being the case, how can anyone claim to know that a divine Watchmaker would have never "stooped" to such an "inefficient" means of creation as that exemplified in our own world, when we still don't even know how the first life forms originally came to exist in the first place? For no matter how low and inefficient the evolutionary process might appear, it nevertheless has been spectacularly successful at producing objects of extreme complexity, and it is very hard to argue with success.

We cannot, therefore, cogently put forth the argument that a self-driven, naturalistic process of evolution somehow eliminates the need for an Intelligent Designer, because there is no necessary connection between how a given item is made and the ultimate origin of its basic structure. It is thus distinctly possible that an omnipotent Creator could have used any number of causal mechanisms to create the world and everything that is in it. In terms of Paley's watch analogy, it doesn't ultimately matter how the watch itself is put together, since there are any number of ways that it can be physically assembled. What matters is the final product that eventually obtains.

Dawkins disagrees with this conclusion in *The Blind Watchmaker* by arguing that our world doesn't seem to have the appearance of a contrived object when it is observed with a critical eye. But isn't this precisely what we would *expect* to be the case with a supernatural Designer? It would be a very poor creator indeed whose created product openly gave the appearance of being contrived, and the same principle holds true for us as well, since we tend to judge the quality of an artist by noting the degree to which her work appears contrived; the better the artist, the less contrived the work itself appears to be.

By this same mode of reasoning, then, the work of a perfect Creator shouldn't appear to be contrived at all, and this is precisely what we find to be the case throughout our world and universe. The history of evolution, for instance, definitely has the appearance of being uncontrived (because of its naturalistic character), which explains why so many evolutionists believe that life is merely an accidental quirk of nature. But since this uncontrived appearance is precisely what we would expect *a priori* of a perfect Designer, we can profitably use it to argue *for* the existence of such a Being. On this view, our seemingly uncontrived world is not only consistent with the creative activity of an Intelligent Designer, it actually provides positive evidence for one.

Dawkins' argument fails, however, for yet another reason. For while Dawkins wants to argue that the gradual evolution of complex forms (via the process of cumulative selection) somehow eliminates the need for an Intelligent Designer, he seems to have forgotten that this is essentially the same process that human engineers routinely utilize when they design and build their own complex mechanisms. Watches, for instance, aren't built instantaneously; they are built in a gradual, stepwise fashion that is also based on the preservation of previous successes. That is, given the successful completion of the first watch-building step, the watchmaker then goes on to the next step, and then to the next one, until the watch is fully assembled. In a very real sense, then, the watchmaker also utilizes the process of cumulative selection to build his watches, since he selects each successful stage of watch assembly before advancing on to the next series of stages, until the watch itself is finally completed.

Of course, we routinely utilize the process of cumulative selection to build our machines because we have to, since we don't have the power to create them instantaneously. An omnipotent God, by contrast, presumably possesses this power.[5] But even so, it still isn't clear that He would always want to make maximum use of this ability. Indeed, the intrinsic nature of the Human Definition could very well have limited an omnipotent Creator's choice of creative mechanisms as far as our present world is concerned, without impugning His all-power one iota. For as long as we need to be psychospiritually self-creating in order to be fully human, it follows that an omnipotent God couldn't have created us ready-made by definition; and if this is true for us, it could be true in a derivative sense for the remainder of the world as well.

There are thus only three principal differences between human watch building and the natural evolution of complex biological designs: (1) the designer of the watch is plainly evident, whereas no larger Designer is immediately apparent in the natural world; (2) the same watch makes it through each successive stage of "selection" in the assembly process, whereas in the natural world, many generations of progeny are utilized to perfect a given form; and (3) in human watchmaking, a functional design is often (but not always) immediately forthcoming, whereas the evolutionary process at times seems to operate in a "blind" trial-and-error fashion, in which the final design isn't realized for many generations.[6]

None of the above differences are sufficiently great to allow us to postulate an absolute difference in kind between these two types of creative processes. A designer certainly doesn't have to be physically visible in order to exist or be ascertained. Similarly, a designer doesn't have to restrict the process of biological assembly to a single generation; he or she can just as easily spread it out over many generations. Indeed, if the production of new biological forms is dependent on natural genetic variation, then such a dissemination of the creative process over many generations seems to be logically required.

There is a sense, though, in which watches also tend to gradually evolve through a process of trial and error over many generations. For while the assembly of a single watch occurs in a single generation, a larger evolution of watch design nevertheless takes place over many generations. In this evolutionary sequence, each intermediate timepiece qualifies as an intelligent, functional design, even though each intermediate naturally leads to more advanced watch designs in the future. Similarly, the various intermediates that supposedly existed in the evolution of the living world can also be classified as intelligent, functional designs, even though they eventually led to more advanced life forms.

Our analogy breaks down, however, when these two types of designers are directly compared and contrasted with one another. The human watchmaker, for instance, builds his intermediate watches in an evolutionary sequence because he *cannot* create the final product all at once; he thus needs to go through the entire sequence in order to find out what his final product will eventually be. The assumption here is that if he could create this final product in a single generation, he almost certainly would do so. An omnipotent God, by contrast, presumably could have created the entire biosphere instantaneously by miraculous fiat, yet He deliberately chose to go through a gradual process of evolutionary development instead. One possible reason for this course of action, as we have seen, could be tied to the necessary dictates of the Human Definition, which could plausibly require a patterning of the entire biosphere after the intrinsic requirements surrounding the process of human character formation.

We can conclude from these observations that there are no major differences in kind between the human process of watch building and the divinely instituted process of biological evolution. Both processes generate intelligent functional designs using a gradual assembly process that is based upon the preservation of previous successes. But most importantly, both processes can be seen to originate in the creative mind of an intelligent designer, which in turn lends additional support to William Paley's famous watch analogy.

Paley's analogy also holds when it is applied, not to evolving life forms, but to the values of the fundamental constants themselves. This is, in fact, the best application of Paley's original argument, because we now know that the values of nature's fundamental constants have not evolved through a gradual process of natural selection.[7] They have, to the contrary, occupied their present life-supporting values from the very beginning, which means that we now have to come up with an adequate explanation for this remarkably felicitous arrangement. Since the random powers of chance are clearly not sufficient to produce this instant degree of biocentric perfection at the Big Bang, our only remaining alternative would seem to be theistic in nature.[8]

It is, therefore, not ludicrous to assert that the process of cosmic evolution is capable of generating bona fide miracles. For insofar as the instantaneous appearance of our fine-tuned universe at the Big Bang was a miracle, then those natural creative processes that were spawned "downstream" from this primordial miracle must also be considered to be miraculous in a derivative sense, including the biological process of evolution. From this point of view, the miracle of life doesn't have to appear instantaneously in order for it to qualify as being genuinely miraculous. There is, in fact, a very definite sense in which natural, evolutionary-type miracles are inherently more impressive than their instantaneous counterparts, since each of the former's principal constituent parts seems to require an individual element of design (not unlike a Rube Goldberg machine). An instantaneous miracle, by contrast, only exudes the miraculousness of its final design and sudden appearance. Indeed, the very process of trying to perform a difficult function entirely through naturalistic means would seem to be far more difficult than trying to produce the same effect instantaneously by miraculous fiat. It also seems far more impressive.

Kenneth R. Miller, a cell biologist at Brown University who believes in the fundamental compatibility between theism and evolution, would agree with this conclusion. In his book *Finding Darwin's God*, Miller shows his sympathy with this perspective by quoting the insightful words of one of his graduate school professors, who also shared this very same view:

> "If you deny evolution, then the sort of God you have in mind is a bit like a pool player who can sink fifteen balls in a row, but only by taking fifteen separate shots. My God plays the game a little differently. He walks up to the table, takes just one shot, and sinks all the balls. I ask you which pool player, which God, is more worthy of praise and worship?"[9]

There is no question that a God who can create the entire biosphere with just one direct intervention is inherently more impressive than one who has to create it piecemeal. This sort of naturalistic Creator is still transcendent in nature, and His works are still inherently miraculous. The only significant difference between this sort of Creator and His more magically based counterpart is that the miracles of the former are to be found primarily in the various outcomes of the laws of nature, and not simply in their suspension.

This eutaxiological definition of miracles also has the advantage of being consistent with all the findings and postulates of modern science, since it doesn't require a violation of the law of cause and effect in order to explain how miracles happen. To the contrary, the laws of nature are used in this particular definition to explain how miracles themselves take place. And while the traditional theist might object to this naturalistic perspective because it seems to limit the power of God to the realm of cause-and-effect processes, one could counterargue that this naturalistic perspective doesn't necessarily exclude the possibility that God *could* totally violate this causal law if He wanted to.

Notes

1. Quoted in David Deutsch, *The Fabric of Reality* (New York: Penguin, 1997), 138.

2. I am not suggesting here that a supernatural Designer must be directly responsible for generating this profound degree of complexity. I am merely suggesting that there are certain forms of natural complexity that are sufficiently profound as to require the input of a supernatural Designer at some point in our cosmological history, in order to make such a highly ordered state possible in the first place. This Divine input thus could have been limited to the creation of a highly prodigious realm of natural processes at the Big Bang—one that would have inherently been capable of generating an extreme degree of natural fecundity in the fullness of time.

3. F. David Peat, *The Philosopher's Stone* (New York: Bantam, 1991), 164–166.

4. Insofar as this premise turns out to be valid, it follows that Dawkins' conclusion must also be valid: God obviously could not have created plants and animals instantaneously by miraculous fiat and still have had them gradually construct themselves according to the principle of cumulative selection. However, Dawkins' argument fails when it is considered in light of a naturalistic Designer, who chooses to create entirely via natural cause-and-effect processes.

5. Process theists would dispute this claim because they are opposed to the idea of omnipotence in the first place. But even if one chooses to affirm the reality of an omnipotent Designer, it doesn't automatically follow from this that He can create highly complex objects instantaneously by miraculous fiat. Indeed, for all we know, such a task could be logically or metaphysically impossible by its very nature. If so, it wouldn't necessarily count against the prospect of God's all-power, because this quality has traditionally been understood to apply to coherent tasks that are inherently do-able.

6. It has also been argued that the trial-and-error character of the evolutionary process provides evidence that the biosphere couldn't have been created by an omnipotent Intelligence, but this conclusion doesn't necessarily follow. A trial-and-error process of evolutionary development doesn't have to represent a fundamental deficiency in the divine power. It can simply represent the divine intention to have evolving life forms interact in an opportunistic fashion with a constantly changing environmental milieu. On this view, the trial-and-error nature of the evolutionary process represents a critical opportunistic linkage between evolving life forms, on the one hand, and a constantly changing environment, on the other.

7. John D. Barrow and Frank J. Tipler, *The Anthropic Cosmological Principle* (Oxford: Oxford University Press, 1986), 288.

8. The only way out of this conclusion, it would seem, is by positing a form of cosmic selection before the occurrence of the Big Bang, as Lee Smolin and John Gribbin have done. However, this sort of intellectual maneuver conflicts with a significant number of scientific findings, as we have seen; it is also plagued by a number of internal inconsistencies, which explains why most astrophysicists and cosmologists have failed to come out in support of it. This leaves us, once again, with some form of theism as the best explanation for our fine-tuned universe.

9. Kenneth R. Miller, *Finding Darwin's God* (New York: HarperCollins, 1999), 283–284.

~

CHAPTER FIFTEEN

God and the
Modern Scientific Method

God is a mathematician of a very high order, and He used very advanced mathematics in constructing the universe.

—Paul Dirac

Does the concept of supernatural agency play a role in modern science? Is it even *compatible* with the scientific pursuit of knowledge? Most scientists and philosophers seem to think that the answer is no, as philosopher of science Stephen C. Meyer has pointed out:

> Biologists, and scientists generally, assume the rules of science prohibit any devia-
> tion from a strictly materialistic mode of analysis. Even most physicists sympathetic
> to design would quickly label their intuitions "religious" or "philosophical" rather
> than "scientific." Science, it is assumed, must have exclusively natural causes.
> Since the postulation of an intelligent Designer clearly violates this methodologi-
> cal norm, such a postulation cannot qualify as part of a scientific theory. Thus
> Stephen J. Gould, refers to "scientific creationism" not just as factually mistaken
> but as "self-contradictory nonsense." As Basil Willey put it, "Science must be pro-
> visionally atheistic, or cease to be itself."[1]

Scientists aren't the only ones who believe that religious matters are inherently incompatible with the scientific method. Many theists also share

this belief. Consider, for instance, the following quote from Fuller Seminary professor Nancey Murphy:

> Science *qua* science seeks naturalistic explanations for all natural processes. Christians and atheists alike must pursue scientific questions in our era without invoking a Creator. . . . Anyone who attributes the characteristics of living things to creative intelligence has by definition stepped into the arena of either metaphysics or theology.[2]

At first glance, this assertion appears to make good sense. Science does indeed seem to be centered around the exclusive pursuit of naturalistic explanations for physical phenomena. It is important to note, however, that the founding fathers of the modern scientific movement would have strongly disagreed with this conclusion. They believed that the concept of supernatural agency was *vital* to a proper understanding of the natural sciences, and indeed, it was their belief in a rational Lawgiver that initially compelled them to look for order and rationality in the cosmos.[3] With the advent of Darwin's theory of evolution by natural selection, though, scientists began to move away from theological matters in their attempt to better understand the universe in which they lived.

This "flight from religion" in the scientific community continued unabated into the twentieth century, where it eventually evolved into a philosophical doctrine known as *methodological naturalism*. Methodological naturalism is the idea that science, when properly carried out, cannot involve religious ideation, belief, or commitment.[4] This pervasive belief had two principal causes. The first of these is historical in nature. For once the Church began to oppose and persecute genuine scientific inquiry in the early days of the scientific revolution, religious matters naturally began to be separated from scientific ones. This separation was strongly reinforced by Darwin's theory of evolution, because it seemed to remove any need for an Intelligent Designer in the origin of life (since natural cause and effect processes, and not a Creator *per se*, seemed to be responsible for generating the biosphere).

This growing antagonism between science and religion was further reinforced by the so-called Principle of Objectivity, which states that the only objects or processes that can be properly studied by the scientific method are those that have an empirical, objective reality (because they are the only ones that can be accurately measured). This methodological principle in and of itself seems to exclude the idea of God from the entire realm of scientific inquiry, because God by definition is not a physical being who can be studied and measured in the laboratory.

It would be premature, however, to conclude from this methodological principle that religious matters cannot play *any* role in the modern scientific enterprise. For while there is certainly a need for objectivity in science, it doesn't follow from this that supernatural agency cannot play any role at all in scientific matters. God doesn't have to be involved in *every* aspect of the scientific method in order to be involved in *some* aspects of it. Another way of saying this is that it is possible, at least in principle, for the concept of supernatural agency to play *some* role in the proper execution of the scientific method, even if it doesn't play a role in *every* aspect of it.

It is in this fashion that we can provisionally accept the legitimacy of the Principle of Objectivity in modern science, at least in part, while simultaneously retaining the possibility of some role for supernatural agency in the overall pursuit of science. But how can this be? How can the activities of a nonempirical being who is not amenable to physical measurement nevertheless be compatible with the scientific method, whose expressed purpose is to gain a deeper understanding of the empirical world in which we live?

The answer is twofold. First, most appeals to supernatural agency are really attempts to find a sufficient explanation for the natural cause-and-effect processes that we regularly observe in the cosmos. These causal processes are the secondary causes that most theists believe were recruited by God to create the universe and everything that is in it. This employment of secondary causation in the creation of life is duly reflected in the biblical assertion that "the earth brought forth living creatures" (Gen. 1:24). This provocative statement tells us in no uncertain terms that earth-based natural processes were indeed responsible for bringing forth living creatures.

Insofar, then, as most appeals to supernatural agency are merely attempts to find a sufficient explanation for the various *secondary* causes of nature, we don't have to twist or otherwise corrupt any aspect of the scientific method in order to make an appeal to supernatural agency, since for the most part we aren't trying to credit God *directly* with the generation of any primary causes in the world *per se* (apart from His creation of the universe itself and the laws of nature that operate within it); we are merely trying to incorporate God as a sufficient metaphysical explanation for the various *secondary* causes that are at work in the world. This distinction allows the natural theologian to retain virtually the entire body of modern scientific information alongside her belief in God as Creator, since the natural theologian's expressed purpose here is simply the identification of a sufficient reason or explanation for these natural phenomena.

In other words, the natural theologian isn't trying to document the existence of an entirely new set of primary causes in the world. She is merely trying to provide a better (i.e., a more plausible and coherent) explanation for the world's *preexisting* laws and processes. This is good news indeed for the scientifically oriented theist, because it means that the notion of supernatural agency can easily be incorporated into the existing body of scientific information without any significant compromise in the latter taking place.

The second reason why the concept of supernatural agency is intrinsically compatible with the scientific pursuit of knowledge is because there is only one aspect of the scientific method—namely, the data-gathering stage—that is not directly amenable to the immediate study of supernatural agency *per se*. Again, this is because God is not an empirically observable being who can be directly studied in the laboratory. The two other stages of the scientific method—namely, the theory-building stage and the data-interpretation stage—are, by contrast, entirely compatible with the notion of supernatural agency as a potential explanatory tool. God thus only needs to be excluded from a single stage of the scientific method (the data-gathering stage), because scientific information as such is religiously neutral by its very nature.[5] But even here there is some room for movement, since the phenomenon of supernatural agency *can* be empirically investigated in an *indirect* manner without any compromise in the Principle of Objectivity taking place. One simply needs to utilize an experimental design that seeks to document, through indirect means, God's suspected influence in the world, and this can be done by attempting to observe the empirical *effects* of God's presumed influence in the world.

I am distinguishing here between two very different forms of divine action in the cosmos. In the first form, God Himself acts as an efficient cause that directly brings about certain empirically observable effects in the world. In the second form, God merely acts as an efficient cause for the various secondary causes that comprise our world and universe. From this point of view, God is the cause of the various *causes* of events in the world; He isn't the cause of the events themselves, as Charles Darwin's grandfather Erasmus once pointed out.[6]

But if God is merely the unprovable cause of these secondary causes (which themselves are responsible for bringing about the observable events in our world), what need is there to bring Him into the explanatory landscape at all? The answer has to do with the nature of scientific explanations themselves. We need to bring God into our theories so that we can arrive at a thorough and sufficient *explanation* for the various scientific phenomena that we're trying to understand.

The Nature of Scientific Explanations

The question of what actually constitutes an adequate scientific explanation is surprisingly complex. For most working scientists, an adequate scientific explanation of X is considered to be one that identifies the specific natural laws and processes that are responsible for bringing about X in the world.

Nevertheless, while such a utilitarian definition might serve its limited purpose admirably—namely, that of enabling us to better understand the workings of the natural world so that we can then manipulate it to our advantage—can we consider this sort of mechanical description to be a genuine *explanation* of the phenomenon in question? The answer, in part, depends on what one's expressed purpose happens to be. If one's intention is simply to understand the physical mechanism by which a given event transpires in the world, then this sort of explanation is indeed adequate to the task, because such an elucidation not only makes certain predictions possible about the future, it also makes it possible for the natural processes in question to be profitably manipulated to one's advantage.

However, if one's expressed goal is to understand the larger metaphysical context by which a given natural event is able to transpire in the world, then this sort of limited explanation is by no means adequate, because it leaves the implicated secondary causes *themselves* unaccounted for. It is for this reason that any thorough explanation of X must include a larger metaphysical explanation for the various secondary causes that are responsible for bringing about X in the world.

What we are really referring to here is the long-standing distinction between necessary and sufficient conditions for physical phenomena. For while the natural laws and processes that are responsible for bringing about X are surely necessary conditions for X, they still aren't *sufficient* conditions for it, because they don't include a larger explanation for their own origin. This is where the concept of supernatural agency comes into play, for by providing a sufficient explanation for the origin of these secondary causes, it can transform a partial scientific explanation, which contains only some of the necessary conditions for X, into a thorough one, which contains all of the necessary conditions which *together* are sufficient for the elicitation of X.

A useful analogy can be made here to the question of where the automobiles in a new car showroom ultimately come from. Since we are familiar with the nature of the auto-building process, we know that new cars ultimately come from huge automated factories. However, what would a totally naïve observer from another planet have to say about this issue? We can presume that such a being would probably have no idea where these new cars ultimately originate from. Nevertheless, by carefully observing the various events at the dealership that would seem to elicit the arrival of new cars, our naïve friend could surmise that the following conditions would herald the arrival of new cars on the lot: (1) a reduced inventory of new cars at the dealership, (2) the placement of a certain number of new car orders by the management, and (3) the arrival of huge double-decker trucks carrying these new automobiles.

Now, our alien friend would be entirely correct in claiming that these conditions were somehow necessary for the arrival of new cars at the dealership. Moreover, if he simply needed to identify some of the conditions that are necessary for the arrival of new cars on the lot, he wouldn't need to look any further, since he would be able to make good use of these necessary conditions to predict the approximate arrival time for each new car shipment.

Nevertheless, it is clear that this sort of practical understanding falls far short of being a thorough explanation, despite its predictive utility. For while our friend might have been able to identify some of the conditions that are necessary for the arrival of new cars on the lot, he was still a long way from identifying all of the necessary conditions for this particular outcome, and it is clear that any thorough explanation would need to account for each and every one of them.

In other words, a complete explanation needs to identify the sufficient conditions for the elicitation of any given outcome. This is why our naïve friend in the above example was nowhere near a complete explanation for the arrival of new cars at the dealership: because he didn't specify *all* of the conditions that are necessary for the elicitation of this particular event. He failed, for instance, to consider the single most important question with respect to this particular issue, namely, where did the new cars *themselves* ultimately originate from? To the contrary, he confined himself *only* to those events that can be directly observed at the dealership.[7]

Most scientific explanations today are very much like this, insofar as they tend to focus only on some of the conditions that are necessary for the elicitation of certain empirical outcomes in the physical world. This typically involves an identification of the various laws and processes that are responsible for bringing about the particular effects that are being studied. And, for the most part, scientists are delighted to have this sort of limited explanation to work with, because it gives them the powerful ability for future prediction, along with the strategic capacity to be able to elicit certain desired outcomes at will.

This sort of mechanistic understanding is clearly useful in the real world. Even so, it is still a long way off from amounting to any type of thorough explanation for the events in question. The reason for this, once again, is that limited scientific explanations typically fail to address the origin and nature of the secondary causes that were originally responsible for bringing about the effect in question. In this sense, it is like the origin of new cars in the above example, for whereas one might be able to document some of the necessary conditions for their arrival, such an explanation is still far from being complete and thoroughgoing, because it fails to address the ultimate origin of the new cars themselves. The same thing can even be said of many general laws, which are merely "descriptive and not explanatory. Many laws describe regularities but do not explain why the regular events they describe occur. A good example of this drawn from the history of science is the universal law of gravitation, which Newton himself freely admitted did not explain but instead merely described gravitational motion."[8]

So before we can hope to arrive at any thoroughgoing explanation for a particular event, we must first attempt to explain the origin and nature of the various secondary causes that are known to elicit it. This is where we can make profitable use of the notion of supernatural agency in our scientific theorizing. For by providing a sufficient explanation for the various secondary causes in our world, it can help to transform our partial scientific explanations (which contain only some of the necessary conditions for X) into complete and thorough ones (which contain all of the necessary conditions which *together* are sufficient for the elicitation of X).

This is where the notion of personal satisfaction comes into play. We all seek to have our sense of wonder and curiosity satisfied by the explanations that we regularly come into contact with in our day-to-day lives. However, some explanations are inherently more satisfying than others. It is my contention in this chapter that the partial explanations of modern science aren't nearly as satisfying for most people as comprehensive theological explanations. After all, it is hard to be satisfied by question-begging "explanations" that simply masquerade as all-encompassing ones.

For instance, trying to explain the origin of new cars in the above example by referring to certain mitigating circumstances at the dealership is question-begging by its very nature. For whereas there is a certain limited sense in which this type of explanation might be accurate, it is far from being the whole story, as we have seen, because it doesn't even attempt to address the origin of the new cars themselves. So, insofar as one's underlying question revolves around the origin of these cars, one will never be satisfied with any type of partial, question-begging answer.

In the same way, it is hardly satisfying to assert that the origin of the living world can be found in the process of evolution. For while such an assertion might be true as far as it goes, it is hardly illuminating, because it refers back to something that we already know to be true, namely, that the biosphere arose in response to various evolutionary causes. Therefore, using the theory of evolution to explain the origin of life is a partial explanation at best, because it leaves the origin of these evolutionary processes themselves unaccounted for. This is undoubtedly why so many people find the neo-Darwinian theory of evolution to be inherently unsatisfying, and this includes a growing number of evolutionary biologists and philosophers of science.

On the other hand, there are those individuals who suggest that *any* appeal to Intelligent Design is a scientific cop-out, since it seems to supplant the empirical rigors of science with nonempirical pseudo-science. Consider, for instance, the following critique of Intelligent Design:

> A scientist legitimately may suggest, as Michael Behe does, that Darwinian theory does not explain everything. But to invoke, as Behe also does, the possibility of intelligent design, is a cop-out: When something is not easily understood, a scientist should dig further to understand it. You do not understand nature by invoking the supernatural.[9]

But what if, for the sake of argument, we were to assume that an Intelligent Designer was originally responsible for creating the entire natural world itself? Would the appeal to supernatural agency still be a cop-out in this particular situation? Clearly not, because in this instance God would function as the ultimate metaphysical cause for the entire natural realm, including those laws and processes that were originally responsible for bringing about life on this planet. In this case, an appeal to supernatural agency would be a vital prerequisite for reaching an optimal *scientific* understanding of the world in which we live.

In the above citation, Alan Wolfe claims that one doesn't understand nature simply by invoking the supernatural, but this is true only insofar as one attempts to supplant a full understanding of the world's secondary causes with the empty assertion that "God did it"! The fallacy here is to assume that all appeals to supernatural agency are actually trying to do this. They are not.

There is, to the contrary, a completely different type of appeal to supernatural agency that does *not* attempt to supplant the secondary causes of the world with empty supernatural explanations. In this type of appeal, the concept of supernatural agency is used, not in place of natural cause-and-effect processes, but rather *in conjunction* with them, so that it can help to provide a sufficient explanation for their ultimate origin.

There is no doubt that "when something is not easily understood, a scientist should dig further to understand it,"[10] but it doesn't follow from this that one should never make an appeal to supernatural agency in every possible circumstance. For what if one is trying to understand the origin of the natural cause-and-effect processes that led to the origin of life long ago? In this case, it *does* make sense to dig further, but this is precisely what the natural theologian is doing when she credits God with the original creation of these natural laws and processes.

Far from being an explanatory cop-out, then, this sort of appeal to super-natural agency fits neatly within existing scientific protocol. For it is a well-known fact within the scientific community that all physical and mathematical systems require a foundational set of unquestioned axiomatic assumptions in order to be valid. One simply has to begin somewhere in order to be able to pursue a rational course of investigation; otherwise, one will spend all of one's time trying to establish a conceptual beginning point. This is particularly true in the realm of mathematics. But this is precisely what the natural theologian is doing when she credits God with the ultimate creation of the universe's natural laws and causal processes. She is simply choosing an appropriate axiomatic foundation from which to proceed with her theorizing, just like physical scientists and mathematicians are used to doing in the scientific realm. It is thus no more of a cop-out for the natural theologian to choose God as an axiomatic foundation than it is for biologists to choose the nontheistic evolutionary process as their axiomatic foundation.

If anything, the natural theologian's choice of God as an axiomatic foundation is *less* of a cop-out than most scientific axioms, because only God carries within Himself a sufficient explanation for His own existence. Everything else in the universe is contingent (and hence derivative) by its very nature. That is to say, one can trace the existence of everything in the universe back to a preceding cause, and this includes all the axioms that have ever been conceived by the human mind. However, the "metaphysical buck" has to stop somewhere; otherwise, the progression of explanatory causes would extend to infinity. This is where the concept of supernatural agency has its greatest utility in the field of natural theology. For by providing a self-sufficient metaphysical foundation for the existence of the universe and everything that is in it, the idea of God provides the *only* axiomatic foundation that is inherently adequate to the task.

The reason why this is so can be traced back to the Divine aseity—or God's self-existence and complete self-sufficiency. No other being or concept can make this unique claim, because only God *by definition* carries within Himself the reason for His own existence. Anything else that could possibly be imbued with this same attribute would thus be God in disguise.

Naturalism, Scientism, and the Principle of Objectivity

The Principle of Objectivity, which is discussed at length by the French biologist Jacques Monod[11] in his book *Chance and Necessity*, states that the only objects that can be studied scientifically are those that have an empirical, objective reality. Naturalism is, in part, a philosophical extension of the Principle of Objectivity, insofar as it states that the basic "stuff" of science (i.e., empirically measurable physical matter) is the only type of substance in existence. Its overall effect is to make it seem as though the only real substances are those that empirical science can study. The philosophical view known as scientism is also a generalization from the Principle of Objectivity, insofar as it claims that science is the only pathway to truth and rationality.

These philosophical generalizations from the Principle of Objectivity are both gratuitous and unwarranted by the existing evidence. The Principle of Objectivity is merely a methodological guideline that was originally intended to make the practice of science practical and efficient. It is therefore inappropriate for it to be extended into a far-reaching metaphysical statement about the underlying nature of reality, because it simply doesn't follow that everything in existence is material in nature, just because material objects are the only types of entities that can be properly studied by science. This is a *non sequitur* generalization that is exceptionally misleading, because there is no underlying causal connection between our epistemological limitations and the basic ontological structure of the universe itself. Science may be an extraordinarily effective means of understanding the universe in which we live, but it doesn't follow from this that the only types of substances in existence are the empirical objects that scientists can observe.

This sort of generalization from the Principle of Objectivity probably came about as various thinkers attempted to build a worldview around the throne of modern science. In so doing, however, it may have been difficult for them to separate their own personal proclivity for a single realm of existence from the overall worldview that they were constructing. They may have also been trying to fence out any religious threat to their underlying belief structure through a comprehensive attempt to undermine the metaphysical foundation of the religious worldview itself.

However, the underlying character of reality is not contingent upon the nature of our epistemological limitations, nor is it a function of what happens to be personally expedient for any given individual or group of individuals. It is, to the contrary, a reference to that which exists *entirely apart* from the affairs of human beings. This being the case, it is excessively naïve to attempt to limit the ontological structure of the universe just so it can accord well with our own epistemological limitations. For just as it would be wrong for a sentient hammer to see everything else in the universe as a nail, it is also wrong for the epistemologically limited scientist to assert that the entire universe happens to consist *only* of those objects that he is capable of observing.

Such an assertion, of course, could never be empirically demonstrated. Indeed, there is growing evidence that seems to indicate that the ontological structure of the universe is *not* limited to the material realm only. For not only does the nonmaterial character of human consciousness seem to point in the direction of an incorporeal plane of existence, the many conceptual gaps that currently exist in our scientific understanding of the universe seem to point in this direction as well. For instance, we presently have no idea where the Big Bang came from or why it exploded in just the right way to produce intelligent observers some 15 billion years later. We also have no idea where life itself came from or why it evolved just as fast as it possibly could, in total contradiction to the predictions of nontheistic evolutionary theory. We don't even have the remotest inkling about what human consciousness is in and of itself, nor do we understand why the subatomic world is fine-tuned in such an ideal biocentric manner. Last, we aren't even close to understanding how the quantum world operates, particularly with respect to the phenomenon of nonlocality (or instantaneous action at a distance). How is it possible for the actions of one particle on one side of the universe to be *instantaneously* reflected in the behavior of another particle *on the other side of the universe*? In order for this to be possible, some sort of instantaneous communication is required, and this, in turn, requires a communication speed that borders on the infinite. Such a phenomenon directly violates our modern, relativistic view of the cosmos, since it seems to require that we do away with the speed of light altogether as the cosmic speed limit.

Our universe is replete, then, with many profound mysteries that modern science is nowhere near understanding at the present time. Moreover, there is good reason to believe that we'll *never* be able to understand them from a purely naturalistic point of view, not simply because of our own epistemological limitations, but also because these mysteries inherently seem to possess a rationale that somehow transcends the boundaries of normal scientific explanation. After all, what kind of empirical explanation could the Big Bang itself possibly have? It is one thing to offer a totally naturalistic explanation in a preexisting physical context, and quite another to propose such an explanation for the universe's spontaneous appearance "out of nothing." We mustn't forget that the current consensus position in cosmology is that the universe itself began in the form of an infinitely small superparticle known as a singularity. But this is just another way of saying that it emerged out of "nothing," because an infinitely small particle is tantamount to genuine ontological nothingness. This is closer to magic than it is to genuine science, because it amounts to a genuine creation of something out of nothing. No wonder John Barrow could assert that "the role of the Creator is essentially assumed by the naked Big Bang singularity."[12]

In short, a significant chunk of the universe appears to be almost totally inexplicable from a naturalistic point of view. This being the case, why should we limit ourselves epistemologically to one-world, materialistic explanations only?

God and the Theory-Building Stage of the Scientific Method

Scientific theories are not spun in a vacuum. Rather, they are conceived in a larger cognitive environment that enables the universe to be viewed scientifically, that is, in a regular, law-like manner which is amenable to human understanding. Remarkably, the origins of this cognitive environment are theistic in nature.[13] For not only did the founding fathers of the modern scientific movement routinely utilize the concept of supernatural agency in their theorizing, they also utilized their faith in a rational Creator to justify their belief in a cosmic state of order that can be discovered and comprehended by human minds. This belief, in turn, helped to fuel the rise of modern science because it led to the general expectation of order in the universe, just as it also led to the initial motivation to look for this order in a rational and empirical manner.

John Barrow, in fact, has gone so far as to conclude that the idea of a Divine Lawgiver was essential to the development of modern science. Without this fundamental idea, according to Barrow, there would have been no pressing reason to look for comprehensible scientific laws to begin with.[14] This, in turn, explains why a productive scientific enterprise was never able to develop in cultures that lacked a formal belief in a cosmic Lawgiver.

Paul Davies has also commented on this fascinating topic:

> The mystery that now confronts us is this: How did human beings acquire their extraordinary ability to crack the cosmic code, to solve nature's cryptic crossword, to do science so effectively? I have mentioned that science emerged from a predominately Christian culture. According to the Christian tradition God is a rational being who made the universe as a free act of special creation, and has ordered it in a way that reflects his/her own rationality. Human beings are said to be "made in God's image," and might therefore be considered (on one interpretation of "image") to share, albeit in grossly diminished form, some aspect of God's own rationality. If one subscribes to this point of view it is then no surprise that we can do science, because in so doing we are exercising a form of rationality that finds a common basis in the Architect of the very natural world that we are exploring.
>
> Early scientists such as Newton believed this. They thought that in doing science they were uncovering part of God's rational plan for the cosmos. The laws of nature were regarded as "thoughts in the mind of God," so that by using our God-given rationality in the form of the scientific method, we are able to glimpse the mind of God. Thus they inherited a view of the world—one which actually

stretches back at least to Plato—that places mind at the basis of physical reality. Given the (unexplained) existence of rational mind, the existence of a rationally ordered universe containing rational conscious beings is then no surprise.[15]

Indeed, many of science's greatest discoveries can be traced back to some form of theistic belief. Take, for instance, the discovery of Nicholas Copernicus (1473–1543) that the earth revolves around the sun, and not vice versa. Although this landmark achievement is routinely cited as supporting evidence for atheism (since it shows that the earth is not at the center of the universe), Copernicus himself[16] was a thoroughgoing teleologist who used his theistic belief in the necessary harmony and order of the cosmos to construct a purely mechanistic view of the solar system.[17] Johannes Kepler (1571–1630) also used his belief in a Divine Creator to great advantage, insofar as it helped him to discern the nature of the planetary orbits. For by believing that God had created the universe in accordance with some perfect numerological principle, Kepler was subsequently able to decipher the mathematical nature of the various planetary motions.[18] William Harvey (1578–1657) also made brilliant use of his belief in God, since he deliberately used it to unravel the nature of the human circulatory system. Harvey tried to imagine how a purposeful Creator would have constructed a system of motion in the human body, and it was precisely this sort of design-based thinking that ultimately led him to make his epic discovery.[19]

Harvey's way of thinking is related to what has been called "anthropic reasoning," because one begins with the fact of human existence and then reasons backward to the conditions that must have been necessary to bring about this existence. This typically leads to a very highly constrained set of initial conditions in the universe, which itself is most consistent with the deliberate workings of an Intelligent Designer.[20]

Now, when one begins theorizing in this anthropic manner, the natural tendency is to begin anticipating the creative strategies of a possible Designer for the above-stated reason. Moreover, history has shown that this type of strategy can lead to pioneering discoveries that probably would have never been made otherwise.

This anthropic style of reasoning has been so fertile over the years because it tends to lead the scientific theorist down the same "creative road" that a possible Designer might have utilized in His creation of the universe. When one begins to think in this manner, one implicitly begins to theorize in accordance with the basic principles of Intelligent Design, and it is this designer-based reasoning that tends to lead to exciting discoveries in virtually all of the natural sciences.[21]

Abduction

According to the founder of American pragmatism, C. S. Peirce (1839–1914), there are three types of reasoning that can be used in science: inductive, deductive, and *abductive*. Abductive reasoning is better known as reasoning to the best explanation, and Peirce believed that it plays an essential role in the progression of science.[22]

Abduction is the only type of reasoning that is *ampliative* in nature, since it is able to give us more information than is contained in the premises. As a consequence, it is the only form of reasoning "which can introduce novel ideas differing in kind from those found in the premises or explanandum. This sort of reasoning takes place at the very beginning of scientific inquiry."[23] In fact, Peirce went so far as to claim that "all the ideas of science come to it by way of abduction."[24]

Peirce describes the actual process of abductive reasoning in the following manner:

> Upon finding himself confronted with a phenomenon unlike what he would have expected under the circumstances, he looks over its features and notices some remarkable character or relation among them, which he at once recognizes as being characteristic of some conception with which his mind is already stored, so that a theory is suggested which would explain that which is surprising in the phenomena.[25]

Terry G. Pence, a philosopher from Northern Kentucky University, describes the logical format of abductive reasoning thusly:

> The surprising fact C is observed. But if A were true, C would be a matter of course. Hence, there is reason to suspect that A is true.[26]

From this description, it is clear that abductive reasoning has a strong intuitive aspect to it, insofar as it represents an "appeal to instinct"[27] that often strikes one like a flash of light. This is the "aha!" experience that is so typical of major scientific advances. The history of science is, of course, replete with this kind of intuitive breakthrough, but we must also keep in mind that this type of reasoning can also be quite fallible in nature. However, this fallibility is an inescapable part of the abductive process itself, since intuitively reasoning to the best explanation naturally produces a multiplicity of possible explanations, only one of which usually turns out to be true.

What is significant for our purposes is that Peirce did *not* believe that the process of abductive reasoning in science necessarily precludes the supernatural from the explanans. As far as Peirce was concerned, then, "there is no essential hostility between the most essential aspect of scientific reasoning and broadly theistic conclusions."[28]

Terry G. Pence argues this very point in an article entitled "Charles S. Peirce, Scientific Method, and God."[29] In fact, Pence goes so far as to claim that for Peirce, abductive inferences that appeal to God as an explanation are inherently just as legitimate as any scientific explanation.[30] But how can this be, given God's invisible, nonempirical nature? The answer, of course, is that many of the objects that are studied by science *are* in fact invisible, which in turn means that they are not directly measurable after all. In Peirce's own words:

> Nor is it in the least true that physicists confine themselves to such a "strictly positivistic point of view." Students of heat are not deterred by the impossibility of directly observing molecules from considering and accepting the kinetic theory; students of light do not brand speculation on the luminiferous ether as metaphysical; and the substantiality of matter itself is called in question in the vortex theory, which is nevertheless considered as perfectly germane to physics. All these are "attempts to explain phenomenally given elements as products of deeper-lying entities." In fact this phrase describes, as well as loose language can, the general character of scientific hypotheses.[31]

Indeed, what does it really mean for an object to be "empirically measurable"? It means that the object in question must be empirically detectable by our scientific measuring instruments. But if this is so, then the essential limitation with respect to "empirical measurability" can be seen to lie, *not* in the nature of objects themselves, but rather in the essential limitations surrounding our measuring instruments. This would be readily apparent if a machine were to be invented that could empirically detect the existence of objects in the spiritual realm. In this case, these nonphysical objects would suddenly become "empirical" in nature, because they would then be capable of being measured by our instrumentation.

From this point of view, there are no nonempirical objects *per se*; there are only objects that cannot yet be measured by human scientists. However, if and when such advanced instruments are ever invented, these "nonempirical" realms will suddenly become "empirical" in nature, because they will then become amenable to empirical measurement. It follows from this assertion that everything in existence is ultimately "empirical" in nature, insofar as everything has some type of reality that can, at least in principle, eventually become amenable to human measurement.

But if this is so, then why should we exclude entire realms of possible existence from scientific consideration, simply because we're not yet able to directly measure them? Of course, I am not referring here to the data-gathering stage of the scientific method, because we obviously cannot accumulate data on objects that aren't empirically measurable. I am referring, instead, to stage one of the scientific method, in which scientific theories are first conceived, and also to stage three, in which the data that is accumulated in stage two is then interpreted in terms of the initial presenting theory. One can easily appeal to the existence of these other nonempirical realms when one is initially forging a scientific theory, or later, when one is interpreting the data that has previously been empirically acquired.

It therefore makes no sense to exclude, simply on the basis of our own measuring limitations, an entire realm of possible existence from our scientific analyses. For it is becoming increasingly clear that we live in a unified universe, in which everything that exists somehow interacts with everything else to form a single, interconnected whole. But if this is so, then everything that exists (and not simply everything that can be empirically measured) should be a fundamental part of our scientific pursuit for truth, because in the end, the behavior of everything we can observe is probably being influenced by the *whole* of reality, and not just the limited part that we can presently measure. To thus restrict our scientific explorations to only those objects that can be measured today is to severely limit our potential understanding of the universe in which we live.

We can readily see the effect of this epistemological limitation in many different areas of scientific inquiry. Take Bell's Theorem for instance. It postulates the existence of a mysterious quantum phenomenon known as "nonlocality," in which it is possible for two particles to somehow be connected to one another in a direct causal manner, such that a change in the momentum of one particle will *instantaneously* be reflected in the behavior of the other particle, even though the two particles might exist at opposite ends of the universe.

This nonlocal phenomenon has repeatedly been verified in the laboratory, yet there is currently no way for modern science to account for this "spooky" action at a distance (as Einstein once called it). To the contrary, quantum nonlocality breaks one of the most fundamental "laws" in the entire repertoire of science, namely, that nothing can travel faster than the speed of light.[32] But if nothing can travel faster than light, how is it possible for two particles at opposite ends of the universe to be in direct causal contact with one another? Obviously, it must be possible for *something* in the universe to travel faster than light, because the phenomenon of quantum nonlocality requires there to be an *instantaneous* connection between particles that have been in causal contact with one another.

It is at this point that we can begin to detect the existence (and subsequent influence) of another plane of reality in the universe that transcends the present one in which we live. And while it might simply represent an unseen dimension in the physical realm, it could just as easily represent another plane of reality altogether, which is somehow able to interact with the physical realm to produce the "paradoxical" nonlocal effects that we presently observe. But such effects are only paradoxical as long as we restrict the scope of our scientific inquiry to the realm of the physically measurable. But once we broaden our scope to include the *whole* of reality, the paradoxes that we presently observe could very well turn out to be indicative of another plane of reality that is somehow causally interacting with our own. This is why it is imperative that we broaden the scope of our scientific inquiry to include the whole of reality, because the holistic nature of the universe directly implies that there is a significant causal interaction between *everything* that is in existence. Insofar as this is indeed the case, we will never be able to understand such paradoxes as quantum nonlocality as long as we continue to exclude the possible existence of these nonempirical realms from our scientific theorizing.

We mustn't make the mistake, however, of assuming that the possible existence of these other realms is totally beyond the reach of scientific investigation. They aren't. To the contrary, it is possible to compensate for this lack of direct measurability by devising experiments that are cleverly designed to detect the *effects* of these potential unseen realms. For while unseen objects and processes may not be directly measurable in the laboratory, they nevertheless can have important *effects* on that segment of reality that we *can* observe and measure. So, by carefully designing our experiments to take advantage of such empirically observable effects, we can *indirectly* document the potential existence of unseen objects and processes. And this, in turn, makes it possible for us, at least in principle, to examine the potential effects of supernatural agency from a scientific point of view.

That is to say, there are two possible ways in which an object or process can be empirical in nature (and hence open to scientific investigation). On the one hand, it can be directly empirical, which means that it can be directly detected and measured in the laboratory. However, it is also possible for an object or process to be *indirectly* empirical in nature. This would be the case if the object or process *itself* was invisible, but yet somehow was able to impinge upon our empirical world in a directly measurable way.

The ghostlike subatomic particle known as the neutrino provides a good case in point. For years, particle physicists questioned the possible existence of the neutrino, on the basis of their preexisting theory of subatomic particles. However, due to the postulated nature of the neutrino[33] itself, it was impossible to directly detect the existence of these hypothetical particles in the empirical world.[34] In response to this challenge, several very clever experiments were proposed to compensate for this complete lack of direct empirical information. Researchers simply devised a situation in which they were able to indirectly document the existence of the neutrino by directly measuring its projected effects on known physical processes. They were able to do this using what they had already hypothesized to be true about the neutrino from existing quantum theory.

Although they had to wait for a rare supernova explosion[35] before they could have potential access to these mysterious particles, they got precisely what they were looking for in the great supernova event of 1987. Remarkably, they were able to *indirectly* document the existence and nature of neutrinos from this one event, even though the neutrino itself is invisible and is thus not directly amenable to empirical scientific study. They were able to do this by circuitously inferring the neutrino's most probable qualities from its general pattern of interaction with the surrounding environment.

Now, if scientists can document the existence of invisible particles in this indirect fashion, they can in principle study *other* types of invisible objects in this same indirect manner, including potentially spiritual ones. Peirce would have agreed with this surmisal, particularly since he believed that supernatural agency can and should play an important role in the modern scientific method. In fact, Peirce actually went so far as to conclude that reasoning to the best explanation often requires a direct appeal to supernatural agency, as his article on abduction, entitled "A Neglected Argument for the Reality of God," well illustrates.[36]

Peirce also believed that the notion of supernatural agency is inherently able to meet the demands of Ockham's Razor as well. For whereas the inclusion of God into the physical realm might initially appear to multiply causes needlessly (by bringing an entirely different realm of potential causation into account), Peirce had a different idea. He didn't believe that the "simplicity criterion" could be reduced to numbers alone. That is, he didn't believe that the "fewest is always the truest."[37] Rather, Peirce preferred to believe in what Pence has called "natural simplicity," which can be used to describe hypotheses that are more natural, facile, and in accordance with human instinct.[38] According to Peirce, then, it isn't merely the number of ingredients in a scientific hypothesis that determines its overall degree of simplicity; it is also the degree to which the hypothesis itself is natural, facile, and in accordance with human instinct that helps to make this determination.

It is with this revised definition of the simplicity criterion in hand that Peirce was able to claim that, in many instances, supernatural agency *is* in fact the simplest of all possible explanations. The reason for this, once again, is that when one abductively reasons to the best possible explanation, the God Hypothesis often turns out to be the simplest possible alternative after all, particularly for events such as the Big Bang, which exist at the metaphysical horizon of natural causation. It is the best explanation in these instances because it is the one that is most natural, facile, and in accordance with human instinct.

The Data-Gathering Stage

It is the data-gathering stage of the scientific method where one is ultimately obliged to respect the Principle of Objectivity. This means that a researcher *qua* scientist can only study those objects and processes that are able to produce measurable empirical effects in the world. There are two ways this can happen. On the one hand, the object or process itself can be objectively observable, in which case it will naturally be directly amenable to empirical measurement. On the other hand, the object of study can actually be invisible, in which case it will only be amenable to scientific study in an *indirect* fashion, through a notation of the effects that it has on our empirically measurable world, particularly in response to deliberate scientific manipulation.

Many scientists, however, routinely overlook the fact that science *can* profitably study, in the above-stated manner, invisible objects and processes that are not directly observable in any type of empirical fashion. Moreover, there is no necessary requirement that these invisible objects or processes must be physical in nature. They could conceivably be made up of any type of fundamental "substance," but most nontheistic interpretations of the scientific method typically don't allow for this. Instead, there is the implicit expectation throughout most of the scientific world that *all* potential objects for scientific study will fundamentally be physical in nature, whether they are visible or not. This expectation appears to be partly the result of an inappropriate philosophical generalization from the Principle of Objectivity, which recognizes the need for empirical measurability in one part of the scientific method, but then concludes from this that all objects for scientific study must ultimately be comprised of the same material "stuff" that our larger world consists of. However, it doesn't at all follow that the objects for scientific study must *themselves* be constructed of material building blocks, just because there is an underlying epistemological need for *something* in the scientific method to be empirically measurable.[39]

That is to say, there is no necessary reason why the objects of scientific study must *themselves* be constructed of the same type of physical material that happens to comprise the remainder of the empirically observable world. To draw such a conclusion, based on the underlying need for objectivity in science, is to commit a serious category mistake, because it confuses one category of explanation (namely, a methodological one that is based on the partial need for empirical measurability in science) for a completely different category (namely, an ontological one that is based on the need for the objects themselves to have the same sort of material constitution as our measuring instruments). But methodology isn't ontology by any stretch of the imagination, so it makes no sense to try to extend the methodological need for objectivity in science all the way out to the ontological status of the objects *themselves* that are being studied.

It is this particular methodological limitation, in fact, that is routinely used to justify the exclusion of all nonmaterial causes and explanations from science. This argument can be stated as follows:

1. Science is, by definition, the study of natural objects and processes that can be empirically measured, either directly (through direct observation and subsequent measurement) or indirectly (by observing and measuring, in an indirect fashion, the *effect* that some invisible object or process has in the world).
2. Supernatural agency is, by definition, a nonmaterial cause and explanation.
3. Therefore, supernatural agency cannot be a part of any legitimate science.

This conclusion is *non sequitur* for two reasons. First, it doesn't follow that the underlying composition of an object for scientific study must *itself* be material in nature, just because the process of empirical measurement happens to be materially based. Second, it doesn't follow that the *interpretation* of empirical data must itself be empirical in nature. We are distinguishing here between: (a) the nature of the data in question and (b) the subsequent *interpretation* of that data. Surely there is no necessary connection between the need for objective data in science and the subsequent need for a similarly objective *interpretation* of that data.

We are talking here about two distinct aspects of the modern scientific method, the first pertaining to the process of data-acquisition, and the second pertaining to the subsequent interpretation of that data. Moreover, because these two aspects are fundamentally and methodologically distinct from one another, we cannot apply the same epistemological limitations indiscriminately to both. But this is precisely what the antitheistic proponents of methodological naturalism have done: they have conflated two distinct aspects of the scientific method into a single all-encompassing process that reflects the same set of epistemological restrictions. But an empirical measurement is not the same type of activity as the subsequent interpretation of empirical data. Objective measurement is inherently precise, and it is naturally restricted to the empirical world only. The process of data interpretation, by contrast, extends throughout the unlimited range of the human imagination, so it isn't nearly as epistemologically limited. However, by attempting to restrict all aspects of "true science" to the empirical realm, methodological naturalists are mistakenly conflating two epistemologically and methodologically distinct parts of the scientific method, with unnecessarily restrictive consequences.

Certainly there is no necessary reason why an objective phenomenon has to have a similarly objective interpretation or explanation. Indeed, not only is it possible for an objective phenomenon to have a legitimate nonobjective interpretation, it is also quite likely overall, given the current paucity of *genuine* empirical explanations in the scientific world. For while there is a towering overabundance of empirical data in all of the natural sciences, there is simultaneously almost a complete *lack* of any authentic empirical explanations for that data.

Indeed, we would be hard-pressed to come up with a *single* empirical explanation of an objective phenomenon in our world. The startling fact of the matter is that there are virtually *no* satisfying explanations of empirical phenomena in the scientific world, even though we have elucidated thousands of mechanisms by which the natural world operates. It is one thing to understand how a given process functions in terms of its underlying mechanism, and quite another to have a larger explanation in hand that explains what the object or process really is in itself and why it exists in the world the way it does. This is one of the chief reasons why Aristotle devised his four-part analysis of causation to begin with—because he realized that understanding what a thing is made of and how it operates *still* doesn't provide a truly satisfying explanation for it. For this we also need to know the *final cause* for the object in question, which is the larger purpose or function for which it exists. However, modern science has virtually banished the study of final causes in nature, so most theorists don't even bother to consider the question of why things exist in the natural world. They focus instead on empirical descriptions of objective phenomena, and while these descriptions might be eminently useful, they are still a far cry from being fully explanatory.

But even if we agree to restrict the subject matter of science to the empirical world, we can still make credible references to the agency of an Intelligent Designer, because this empirical requirement, as we have seen, only applies to the process of observation itself; it doesn't necessarily apply to the object or process that is actually being measured. Accordingly, scientists can profitably study particles and forces which are themselves invisible without any compromise in the Principle of Objectivity taking place, and they routinely do so by studying the *effects* that these invisible things have on the observable world. Moreover, it doesn't necessarily follow that an invisible force, such as gravity, that somehow emanates from physical matter and also acts on physical matter, must *itself* be material in nature. For all we know, the force of gravity could be emanating entirely from the spiritual realm, even though its principal effect is on the material world. In the same way, it is possible, at least in principle, to *indirectly* measure the *effects* of certain potential religious forces in the empirical realm. For just as the invisible neutrino was discovered by *indirectly* documenting its existence through its effect on the empirical world, so too can we potentially document the existence of an invisible God indirectly through the various *effects* that His putative existence might have on the physical world.

Take the healing properties of prayer for instance. While we may not be able to directly document the spiritual source of this healing, we can nevertheless devise controlled experiments that can indirectly document prayer's healing power, and we can do so in a scientific manner. For while the spiritual source of this healing might itself be invisible, the resulting effect is empirically measurable. We can therefore test the legitimacy of this religious belief in a totally "scientific" manner by devising experiments in which certain measurable changes in the world are predicted in response to the act of praying. For instance, we can divide a test population into two groups. One group is prayed for and the other (control) group is not. The results can then be rigorously evaluated for their statistical significance.

The physician-turned-philosopher Larry Dossey has done precisely this. In an intriguing series of books and articles, Dossey has assembled an impressive list of scientific experiments that conclusively demonstrate the healing power of prayer.[40]

These experiments are no less scientific because they postulate the existence of an unseen spiritual realm through which prayer can conceivably act. For while these experiments might be predicated on the possible existence of an unseen spiritual realm, they can nevertheless make testable predictions because the effects of prayer *can* be empirically measured in the real world. The nonempirical nature of God is thus a Red Herring when it comes to the possible inclusion of supernatural agency in the modern pursuit of science, because experiments can be designed to manipulate this ostensible unseen power in such a way that objectively measurable changes *can* potentially result.

The Data-Interpretation Stage

The idea of supernatural agency is very much at home in the third stage of the scientific method, as we saw in the previous section, since one can profitably utilize nonempirical explanans in the subsequent interpretation of empirical data without any violation to the Principle of Objectivity taking place. For while the quest for objectivity rightfully resides in the nature of the observed data, there is no need to hold one's underlying explanation for the data to a similar epistemological standard.

Take the origin of the universe, for example. According to the most widely accepted cosmological model, absolutely nothing—not even space or time—preceded the Big Bang.[41] Moreover, a large amount of empirical evidence indicates that the Big Bang itself was a genuine event, yet we don't have a clue about what actually caused it or why it occurred the way it did.

Here, then, we have an empirically documented event that has no larger empirical explanation. But it isn't as if this lack of an explanation is simply the result of our scientific ignorance. To the contrary, an empirical explanation for the Big Bang doesn't seem to be possible *in principle*, because of the epistemological dead end known as Planck's Wall. All of our theories and measuring abilities break down completely at this point, when the universe was but a mere 10^{-43} seconds old. It doesn't appear that human science will *ever* be able to transcend this fundamental limitation because of the inability of material particles to carry information beyond it. But even if we do eventually get beyond it, we still will *never* be able to document an empirical explanation for the Big Bang, because any such explanation would inherently presuppose the prior existence of space and time, neither of which existed before the Big Bang itself.

The same epistemological limitation exists in quantum mechanics. For whereas we might be able to empirically document the behavior of a quantum system, we do not appear to be capable of putting forth an empirical explanation for this quantum behavior. Once again, this inability does not appear to be a function of our own limited measuring capacity. Rather, it appears to be built into the underlying nature of the quantum system itself. The best that we can do is to assert that any given quantum event is due to "chance," and nothing more, but this is a far cry from being a true empirical explanation.

However, this paucity of genuine explanations for empirical data shouldn't deter scientists and philosophers from proposing tentative nonempirical explanations for the events in question. This is good science, because the lack of an empirical explanation should not, in itself, preclude us from trying to find a good, rational explanation for the phenomena we are trying to understand.

The upshot here is that good, empirically based science *can* allow for the proffering of nonempirical explanations for empirical data. And it is precisely here that the concept of supernatural agency can properly be included in the modern scientific method.

Indeed, there is a very real sense in which theological explanations can be more "scientific" than bona fide scientific ones. This can be seen from the very nature of explanations themselves:

> Explanations are answers to why-questions. If one is asked to explain an action that she has performed, she will tell *why* she performed it, listing as explanans her reasons, her intentions, or the external forces that constrained her. Or, in order to explain the fact or explanandum that two magnets move together in a certain manner, one will give an account of why they did so, referring to the laws of magnetic attraction and the way that these particular magnets were aligned.[42]

But if an explanation is an answer to a why-question, then it follows that much of science is only partially explanatory at best, since scientists typically only try to answer how-questions about the natural world. And insofar as they *do* attempt to answer a why-question, it is usually only in terms of explaining *how* something took place. True explanations, or why things exist the way they do, are thus beyond the ken of modern empirical science, as the following quote from Paul Davies well illustrates:

> I should like to . . . [address] the question of whether, in my scheme, science can explain the emergence of life, consciousness, and intelligent beings who can come to know the laws that have produced them. I have argued that, given the laws of nature, evolutionary processes can do the rest, without the need to invoke a God who intervenes either sporadically or continually to guide evolutionary progress. As I understand the discipline of science, its job is to explain the world on the basis of laws. The question of the nature of the laws themselves lies outside the scope of the scientific enterprise as it is customarily defined. This does not mean that it is worthless to inquire into the nature of the laws. However, that inquiry, while it might be pursued in a scientific spirit, properly belongs to the subject of metaphysics and not science. So a scientist might claim, quite correctly, that the remarkableness of the above mentioned emergence occurs entirely in accordance with the laws of nature. But is it thereby explained? In the narrow scientific sense it is explained, but this limited notion of explanation is unlikely to satisfy many people. We want to know why the laws of nature are what they are, and in particular why they are so ingenious and felicitous that they enable matter and energy to self-organize in the unexpectedly remarkable way I have described, a way sugges-

tive of design or purpose (in some suitably modified sense). To me, it points to a deeper level of explanation than just accepting the laws as a brute fact. Whether this deeper level can legitimately be called God is for others to decide.[43]

In his examination of the so-called anthropic question, G. F. R. Ellis addresses this same issue:

> The essential possibilities that arise in the anthropic issue are, (a) it can be interpreted in terms of a selection principle, but then there must be an ensemble of universe states in which it can act; one needs to account for the existence of this ensemble of universes, and give some hint of how the proposal could be confirmed; and no ultimate explanation is considered. Alternatively, (b) it can plausibly be interpreted in fundamental terms as either due to pure chance, or else as purposeful design. In the former case we a complete but unsatisfying explanation; in the latter case there is nothing more for science *per se* to say (from the scientific viewpoint, it will have occurred just by chance, for science itself does not have room for a designer).
>
> If we look at the situation from a purely scientific basis, we end up without any solid resolution, basically because science attains reasonable certainty by limiting its considerations to restricted aspects of reality; even if it occasionally strays into the area, it is not designed to deal with ultimate causation. Thus something like a religious viewpoint is required to make progress, because religion is indeed concerned with ultimate issues. . . . [The] anthropic question can be viewed in this [religious] way without there being an incompatibility with science, and . . . indeed, a far more satisfactory overall view is attained [in this manner] than if we restrict our considerations to the purely scientific.[44]

In short, science itself is only capable of proffering limited explanations of the natural world, because it focuses primarily on answering how-questions, and not the deeper why-questions that characterize ultimate explanations. It is for this reason that theology indeed qualifies as the "queen of the sciences" after all, because it is the only human discipline that is capable of generating satisfying, ultimate explanations of the natural world. In this sense, theology is truly "super" to all of the other natural sciences, as Nancey Murphy points out:

> The best approach is to argue that theology is a science (or very science-like), but that it deals with reality at a higher level of complexity than do the other sciences—it takes its place at the top of the hierarchy of sciences. A somewhat similar view is that of Wolfhart Pannenberg, who argues that theology is the science that provides the most all-encompassing context for the other sciences.[45]

To some readers, it may come as a shock to see theology described as a science, but there is a very real sense in which this is so. For insofar as science seeks to understand the nature of the universe and everything that is in it, and insofar as theology concerns itself with ultimate explanations, then theology really is a science after all, because it seeks to understand the *whole* of reality from the largest possible vantage point. This is the manner in which theology can rightfully be said to be the "queen of the sciences"—because theology does indeed provide an all-encompassing context for the other sciences, through its emphasis on answering the why-questions of human existence.

The natural sciences, by contrast, are only able to address the empirically observable portion of reality, because of the aforementioned objectivity stipulation. For while the various sciences might endeavor in principle to understand the whole of reality, they are not able to follow through with the desire, because of our limited ability to measure and manipulate the physical world. Scientific explanations also tend to be only partial at best, since they focus primarily on how natural processes operate in the universe. But discerning how something functions is a far cry from understanding *why* it exists in the first place.

It is thus no accident that the human mind tends to migrate from how-explanations toward why-explanations. For as Philip Clayton has pointed out, the most complete explanations tend to describe *why* things are the way they are in the universe, and not just how things operate.[46] This is why the empirical explanations of modern science tend to point *away* from themselves, and toward the deeper question of *why* the natural world is the way it is—because the human mind naturally tends to seek out full and comprehensive why-explanations to natural phenomena. This is why we can say that the empirical observations of modern science regularly tend to give way to a scientifically oriented metaphysics—because only metaphysical explanations are able to address the why-questions that are regularly brought up by our scientific inquiries.[47]

In effect, then, there are two principal aspects to the modern scientific method: an empirically based aspect, which is centered around the gathering of objectively measurable data, and a more philosophical aspect, which is centered around the *interpretation* of this data. Earlier in the history of science these two aspects were not distinct from one another. Instead, they both formed a larger discipline known as "natural philosophy." Today, however, with our emphasis on epistemological reductionism, we have endeavored to separate the empirical aspects of science from its more philosophical aspects, and it is precisely here in this separation that the issue of God's role in the natural world has been lost.

Supernatural Agency and the Definition of Science

Although there is widespread disagreement amongst scientists and philosophers of science as to what constitutes "true science," several key criteria have been cited in recent years as being basic to the scientific pursuit for understanding. Significantly, the idea of supernatural agency is *not* at odds with most of these criteria.

For one thing, the fundamental purpose of science is to discern the truth about our world and universe. At this basic level, science is entirely open to the possibility of Intelligent Design, because insofar as God actually exists, then the deepest scientific truth of them all would be that the universe has actually been created by an intelligent and purposive Being.

This being so, how should we judge the merits of theological explanations that purport to explain physical phenomena? According to electrical engineer and computer scientist Paul Penfield Jr., theological explanations should be judged according to several of the same criteria that apply to scientific explanations:

> The concept of God is often invoked to explain phenomena. If the phenomenon is one that has a scientific explanation, then it is possible to compare the scientific merits of the two explanations, one based on science and the other or God or, more generally, on faith.
>
> The nature of what constitutes a good scientific theory is not universally understood. As a result, sometimes reasoning based on faith is seriously promoted as scientific. Scientists tend to judge scientific theories on their accuracy, simplicity, and suggestiveness. Any faith-based theory that is represented as scientific should be subjected to those three criteria. Not all phenomena can be successfully explained by science. In some cases a scientific explanation is possible but not yet available. In others, such explanations will never exist. In still others, people will have different opinions as to whether and when such explanations will be developed.
>
> In cases where science does not (yet) have a needed answer, what are we to do? We scientists use scientific theories as long as they seem to do the job. In the same spirit, we can use arguments based on faith so long as they seem to work, and as long as we keep in mind the assumptions made.
>
> Without this kind of approach we would be severely limited in what we could do. Much of the work of many professions, including engineering, deals with human nature, for which we have no scientific theories. In addition, science itself rests on assumptions about nature and the rational thought process that are not, in the final analysis, provable. Finally, we scientists are ourselves humans, and so our activities "off the job" require dealing with matters for which no scientific theory will work.[48]

In other words, the notion of supernatural agency isn't inherently precluded by the presumed nature of scientific inquiry. Indeed, when we examine the four principal criteria that are routinely used to help define true science, we see that the basic idea of supernatural agency isn't precluded by any of them.

For instance, a theory that purports to be scientific must be capable of explaining certain aspects of the natural world according to a self-consistent logical structure.[49] The concept of supernatural agency is entirely consistent with this criterion, because it does indeed explain the existence and nature of the empirical world according to a self-consistent logical structure.

The philosopher Michael Ruse has expanded on this particular criterion by arguing that a theory must also explain *by reference to natural law* before it can be considered to be true science.[50] However, many appeals to supernatural agency also make reference to natural law. This is especially true for theists who believe that God acts in the world through the various laws of nature that He ostensibly designed and created. Even Darwin himself believed that God acts in the world through these "secondary causes," but insofar as this is true, then there must be some degree of explanatory equivalence between appeals to supernatural agency and appeals to natural law. This is just another way of saying that as long as God acts in the world through secondary causes, then any concomitant appeal to supernatural agency as an explanatory mechanism is essentially an appeal to natural law as well, since the latter can coherently be construed as being one of God's chief creative tools.

Indeed, there is a very real sense in which God's every action provides an instantiation of the natural[51] law of cause and effect, because every effect that God chooses to bring about in the universe is always elicited by the preceding cause of His own will to act. It follows from this that all of God's actions in the world are mediated by this form of the law of cause and effect. This is significant for our purposes, because it means that God's actions in the world are compatible, at least in principle, with one of the chief hallmarks of the scientific method, namely, the desire to study and understand natural causal processes.

Going one step further, the natural theologian sees God as being the metaphysical origin of *all* natural laws. This is an important point, because modern science hasn't even approached an understanding of where the various laws of nature themselves ultimately originated from. Instead, scientists simply assume the prior existence of these laws in an axiomatic fashion and then work from there. However, such a maneuver only begs the real question that is at issue here, which is this: where did the laws *themselves* ultimately come from and why do they have the specific character that they do? It isn't enough to simply take the existence of these laws for granted, because it is the origin and nature of these laws that we're really trying to understand here. Therefore, to attempt to explain any given event in terms of the workings of natural law is almost tautological by its very nature, because we already *know* that virtually all natural phenomena are mediated by natural law.

Of course, it always helps to identify the specific laws and mechanisms by which certain events take place in the universe, but this is still a long way from being a genuine explanation, because it fails to address the origin of the laws themselves.

Genuine scientific theories are also said to be predictive, testable, and hence falsifiable. But here too we find that appeals to supernatural agency are indeed compatible with true science, because they are also capable of generating coherent predictions about the natural world. For instance, if we are going to utilize the concept of Intelligent Design to help explain the origin of genetic information in the DNA molecule, we can predict the existence of a single all-encompassing evolutionary program inside that genome that somehow directed the evolution of all life on earth.[52] We can make this prediction because only an Intelligent Designer could have been responsible for infusing this sort of evolutionary program into the genome long ago.

This prediction also has the advantage of being both empirically testable and falsifiable. We simply need to study the informational content of the genome in painstaking detail in order to discern whether such an evolutionary program actually exists or not.[53] By the same token, though, if such a program is never found, despite years of rigorous searching, then this particular prediction will have been empirically falsified after all.

Real science is also said to be tentative in nature, since it can never achieve absolute certainty about anything (except for the certainty that we will never have absolute certainty). Supernatural agency fits in nicely here as well, because the very openness of the modern scientific perspective lends itself beautifully to the possibility that an unseen Being is somehow responsible for the characteristics and behavior of the physical world. And lastly, the idea of supernatural agency fits in well with two of the three principal stages of the modern scientific method. The idea of God can be used very effectively, as we have seen, in both the theory-building and data-interpretation stages of modern science. Again, the reason for this is that the Principle of Objectivity only applies to the data-gathering stage of the scientific method. The other two stages are open to all self-consistent explanatory principles that can be supported by the strength of the empirical data, and this clearly *includes* the possibility of an Intelligent Designer.

Philip Kitcher has come up with three additional criteria that seem to underlie all forms of successful science, and interestingly enough, the notion of supernatural agency is easily compatible with all three of these as well.[54] Kitcher's first requirement is *independent testability*, which is "achieved when it is possible to test auxiliary hypotheses independent of the particular cases for which they are introduced"[55] This requirement poses no problem for supernatural agency, since any experiment that involves God will nevertheless be independently testable, since it will necessarily revolve around empirical measurements that can usually be duplicated.

That is to say, experimental designs that revolve around the concept of supernatural agency are really no different from other types of experimental designs because they are all empirically based, and are hence repeatable. But how can this be, when any potential Divine activity is nonempirical by its very nature? The answer is simply that most appeals to supernatural agency in modern science have nothing directly to do with the data itself; rather, they have to do with the general orientation of scientific theories, as well as with the *ex post facto* interpretation of the observed data. In short, we aren't trying to attribute any given set of observations *directly* to the activity of an Intelligent Designer. We are simply trying to find a sufficient explanation for the empirical data that we have already amassed.

The implicit assumption here is that God works primarily through secondary causes, as we have seen. But insofar as this is so, then most scientific appeals to supernatural agency can be reduced to the following complaint, namely, that the physical process being studied is *itself* causally insufficient to account for the noted observation. It is at this point that the role of supernatural agency can plausibly be resorted to, not as a primary cause, but rather as a conceptually adequate cause for the various secondary causes that are being studied.

Take the fine-tuned Big Bang "coincidences" for example. Modern science has produced a vast body of empirical data that carefully describes how the universe evolved in such a finely tuned, anthropic direction. It is at this point that a major problem develops, though, since these anthropic coincidences don't seem to be capable of carrying within themselves the reason for their own fine-tuned existence. Something more seems to be required, which in this case would amount to a sufficient reason for the initial appearance of these anthropic events.

Much of science revolves around this search for "adequate" reasons and explanations. However, there are many instances in which a sufficient reason for a given phenomenon is *not* to be found solely with the natural cause and effect processes that gave rise to it. It is at this point that the concept of supernatural agency can properly be invoked, not as a primary cause for the observed phenomenon, but as a sufficient explanation for the various secondary causes that originally produced it. It is in this fashion that we can transcend the accusation that we are resorting to a God-of-the-gaps pseudo-explanation, since we aren't using God as a primary or direct cause for any observed phenomena. Rather, we're simply using Him as a sufficient explanation for the various secondary causes that are at work in the universe.

This is a critical distinction that goes a long way toward legitimizing the inclusion of supernatural agency in the modern scientific method. The question thus becomes one of explanatory satisfaction, namely, are we satisfied with the empirically based explanations that we have been offered in the various natural sciences, or is something more inherently required to produce a satisfactory explanation? In terms of the anthropic coincidences mentioned above, it is clear that the various cause-and-effect processes that led up to these coincidences were themselves incapable of accounting for the observed fine-tuning. So while these secondary causes may have been necessary for the production of these coincidences, it doesn't follow from this that they were also *sufficient* for their development. To the contrary, these secondary causes by themselves do *not* appear to be a sufficient explanation for the various anthropic coincidences. This is why we feel compelled to look elsewhere for a sufficient explanation to begin with, because mindless cause-and-effect processes do *not* seem to be capable of fine-tuning themselves in a biocentric manner.

This is where the invocation of supernatural agency in the modern scientific method becomes methodologically appropriate. It is appropriate, not because we are using God as a direct explanation for these coincidences, but rather because we are using Him as an *indirect* explanation for them, *via* the various *secondary causes* that helped to produce them.

Indeed, by focusing our attention on secondary causes, and not primary ones, we are going a long way toward legitimizing the inclusion of supernatural agency in modern science. For in so doing, we aren't trying to credit a nonmaterial cause (e.g., God) with the production of certain empirical effects; we are merely trying to find a sufficient explanation for the various secondary causes that modern science has documented. The advantage of this methodological maneuver is that it does *not* require an abandonment of the Principle of Objectivity. To the contrary, it keeps the content of our scientific pursuit for knowledge anchored squarely in the material realm, such that it is no longer necessary for scientists and philosophers to fear that they will be abandoning science if they try to make a sensible appeal to supernatural agency.

This same rationale also explains why the concept of supernatural agency turns out to be compatible in principle with Kitcher's other two criteria for a successful science. They are: (1) *theoretical unification* (or "the result of applying a small family of problem-solving strategies to a broad class of cases") and (2) *fecundity* (when new lines of investigation eventually grow out of a theory's incompleteness).[56] Both of these criteria are routinely utilized by the natural theologian in her study of God's possible relationship to the natural order, but this shouldn't be surprising in the least. For as long as experimental designs that make an appeal to supernatural agency are methodologically similar to those that do not make such an appeal, then the same qualities that characterize a successful science will also characterize useful appeals to supernatural agency. Accordingly, a good, theistically oriented science will be characterized by the same type of theoretical unity and fecundity as a good nontheistically oriented science is.

The founding fathers of the modern scientific movement wouldn't have been surprised by this conclusion. In fact, they would have actually *expected* it, because they regarded the Creator as the chief unifying feature of the entire natural realm.

The Methodological Equivalence of Design and Neo-Darwinian Evolution

With all this talk about the compatibility between supernatural agency and the modern scientific method, the reader might be surprised to learn that, contrary to popular belief, there are no good criteria that can reliably be utilized to help demarcate science from nonscience.[57] Indeed, there is now a consensus amongst philosophers of science in this area that such an attempt to demarcate science from nonscience is both "intractable and ill-conceived."[58] This means that any attempt to eliminate supernatural agency from the realm of science on the basis of its "unscientific nature" is likely to be problematic.

Stephen C. Meyer agrees that any attempt to demarcate science from nonscience will ultimately fail. He has examined all of the criteria that have traditionally been used to demarcate science from nonscience (such as Popper's falsifiability criterion and the positivistic emphasis on empirical verifiability) and he has found them all wanting.[59] For not only do these alleged criteria fail to effectively demarcate real science from pseudo-science, we sometimes find good scientific theories that also exhibit pseudo-scientific properties:

> Many theories that have been repudiated on evidential grounds express the very epistemic and methodological virtues (testability, falsifiability, observability, etc.) that have been alleged to characterize true science. Many theories that are held in high esteem lack some of the allegedly necessary and sufficient features of proper science. As a result, with few exceptions most contemporary philosophers of science regard the question "What methods distinguish science from non-science?" as both intractable and uninteresting. What, after all, is in a name? Certainly not automatic epistemic warrant or authority. Thus philosophers of science have increas-

ingly realized that the real issue is not whether a theory is scientific but whether it is true or warranted by the evidence. . . .

The question of whether a theory is scientific is really a red herring. What we want to know is not whether a theory is scientific but whether a theory is true or false, well confirmed or not, worthy of our belief or not. One cannot decide the truth of a theory or the warrant for believing a theory to be true by applying a set of abstract criteria that purport to tell in advance how all good scientific theories are constructed or what they will in general look like.[60]

The philosopher of science Larry Laudan agrees that demarcationist arguments have failed completely. "If we could stand up on the side of reason," Laudan argues, "we ought to drop terms like 'pseudo-science.' They do only emotive work for us."[61] The upshot of this realization, according to Meyer, is that "one cannot define in such a way as to confer automatic epistemic authority on favored theories simply because they happen to manifest features alleged to characterize all 'true science.' When evaluating the warrant or truth claims of theories, we cannot substitute abstractions about the nature of science for empirical evaluation."[62] Meyer concludes from this that:

A stalemate exists in our analysis of [theistic] design and [neo-Darwinian] descent. Neither can automatically qualify as science; neither can be necessarily disqualified either. The a priori methodological merit of design and descent are indistinguishable if no agreed criteria exist by which to judge their merits.[63]

This is a radical conclusion indeed, which Meyer proceeds to document with several powerful arguments. For instance, it is often claimed that the neo-Darwinian account of life's origin is scientific in nature because it makes an explicit reference to natural law, whereas the theistic account is supposed to be unscientific because it makes no such reference to natural law.

This is a flawed conclusion for several reasons. First, natural laws are not explanations.[64] They merely describe the regularities of nature, so they do not explain *why* these regularities happen.[65] Second, not all scientific explanations make reference to natural law:

While scientists may often use laws to assess or enhance the plausibility of explanations of particular events, analysis of the logical requirements of explanation has made clear that the citation of laws is not necessary to many such explanations. Instead, many such explanations of particular events or facts, especially in the historical sciences, depend primarily, even exclusively, upon the specification of past causal conditions and events rather than laws to do what might be called the "explanatory work." That is, citing past causal events often explains a particular event better than, and sometimes without reference to, a law or regularity in nature.[66]

Meyer is distinguishing here between empirical science and historical science. With empirical science, of course, there is an emphasis on observability, repeatability, and testability. With historical science, on the other hand, these criteria are difficult or impossible to attain, because the causal event that one is trying to explain is buried deep in the past. Therefore, one must rely on a different set of criteria to evaluate historical science, such as the specification of past causal conditions, along with the events that they are supposed to have elicited. This is why laws aren't used in many historical explanations, because "many particular events come into existence via a series of events that will not regularly occur. In such cases laws are not relevant to explaining the contrast between the event that has occurred and what could have or might have ordinarily been expected to occur."[67]

The crucial point here is that the science of origins is historical by its very nature. Therefore, appeals to natural law won't generally be as useful here as the elucidation of the specific causes and events that led up to the origin of life. This not only puts design and nontheistic descent in the same overall branch of science, it also helps to level the "playing field" between these two disciplines, since the various historical sciences *are* by their very nature amenable to one-time, theistic-type causes.

At this point, the demarcationist might object to a theistic science of origins because a supernatural cause seems to imply a miraculous contradiction or violation of natural law, which in turn would seem to make any type of science impossible. However, it doesn't follow that a supernatural cause will necessarily violate or contradict natural law. For while a given law might be *transcended* by the actions of a supernatural Being, this transcendence doesn't have to be the result of a broken law as such. It could just as easily result from the use of a more sophisticated form of natural law. To a technologically naïve person from the first century, using a telephone to talk to someone on the other side of the world would seem to involve a miraculous violation of natural law, but this isn't so at all. With the advent of modern technology, we can now transcend the "lower" laws of nature with higher, more sophisticated laws, and it is easy to see how this could seem to be a miraculous violation of natural law to a technologically naïve individual. But clearly no such violation has occurred in this instance. It only *seems* like a miracle has occurred because the higher laws of nature are able to make it look *as though* certain lower laws have been violated, when in fact they have not.

By the same token, the postulation of supernatural agency in the origin of life needn't involve a miraculous "violation" of natural law as such—only the transcending of a lower law with a higher one.[68] Meyer agrees that "the action of agency (whether divine or human) need not violate the laws of nature; in most cases it merely changes the initial and boundary conditions on which the laws of nature operate."[69]

It is also regularly claimed that the unobservable nature of the Designer automatically renders Him inaccessible to empirical study. But we have already seen how observability as such is *not* an essential prerequisite of true science after all. Meyer agrees:

> Claims about unobservables are routinely tested in science indirectly against observable phenomena. That is, the existence of unobservable entities is established by testing the explanatory power that would result if a given hypothetical entity (i.e., an unobservable) were accepted as actual. This process usually involves some assessment of the established or theoretically plausible causal powers of a given unobservable entity. In any case, many scientific theories must be evaluated indirectly by comparing their explanatory power against competing hypotheses.[70]

Meyer concludes his exhaustive coverage of this area by noting that "an unexpected equivalence emerges when design and descent are evaluated against their ability to meet specific demarcation criteria."

> The demand that the theoretical entities necessary to origins theories must be directly observable if they are to be considered testable and scientific would, in applied universally and disinterestedly, require the exclusion not only of design but also of descent. Those who insist on the joint criteria of observability and testability, conceived in a positivistic sense, promulgate a definition of correct science that evolutionary theory manifestly cannot meet. If, however, a less severe standard of testability is allowed, the original reason for excluding design evaporates. Here an analysis of specific attempts to apply demarcation criteria against design actually demonstrates a methodological equivalence between design and descent.[71]

This methodological equivalence has two ramifications that are relevant for our purposes. First, since no good reason has yet been proposed that would exclude design from science, design should be afforded the same scientific status that is possessed by the neo-Darwinian theory of evolution. Second, this methodological equivalence means that the science of origins should be just as open to the possibility of design as it is to the various neo-Darwinian postulates:

> A rational historical biology must not only address the question "Which materialistic or naturalistic evolutionary scenario provides the most adequate explanation of biological complexity?" but also the question "Does a strictly materialistic evolutionary scenario or one involving intelligent agency or some other theory best explain the origin of biological complexity, given all relevant evidence?" To insist

otherwise is to insist that materialism holds a metaphysically privileged position. Since there seems no reason to concede that assumption, I see no reason to concede that origins theories must be strictly naturalistic.[72]

Supernatural Agency and the God of the Gaps

The chief criticism that has been levied against the inclusion of supernatural agency in modern science has to do with the ignorance factor. Both scientists and philosophers alike are afraid that we will be giving in to ignorance if we begin making scientific appeals to supernatural agency.

> The received view within scientific and academic circles generally is that science is on safest ground when it remains committed to naturalistic explanation. To invoke a Designer is seen as a serious compromise not only of scientific endeavor generally but also of scientific integrity. The worry is always that by invoking the supernatural, we give in to ignorance and superstition. A well-known Sidney Harris cartoon makes the point well. Two scientists are standing at a blackboard. A course of calculations is interrupted by the phrase "Then a miracle occurs." In the caption, one of the scientists asks the other whether he might not be more explicit on this last point.[73]

There is no question that inappropriate appeals to supernatural agency *are* scientifically stultifying. Recent history has confirmed the truth of this assertion, because modern science has indeed discovered natural causes for many phenomena that were believed to be beyond scientific explanation just a few short years ago. But does it follow from this that *all* appeals to supernatural agency are inappropriate, just because many of them are presently known to be? Of course not. It is quite possible for there to be appropriate appeals to supernatural agency in modern science, even if we can name a thousand instances where such an appeal is flagrantly inappropriate.

This being the case, how are we to differentiate appropriate appeals to supernatural agency from inappropriate ones? As William A. Dembski[74] has pointed out, we can take the lead from a statement made by the great astronomer Edwin Hubble:

> Not until the empirical resources are exhausted need we pass on to the dreamy realms of speculation.

This is a mission-critical statement as far as my message in this chapter is concerned, because it lays the essential groundwork for distinguishing between appropriate appeals to supernatural agency and inappropriate ones.

We can make this distinction based on the criterion of whether or not we have exhausted the full range of naturalistic explanations for any given phenomenon, as Dembski explains:

> Methodological naturalism confuses appeals to God that mask our ignorance of natural causes with appeals to God that arise because we have exhausted the full range of possible natural causes. . . . When Hubble wrote . . . [the above-quoted] line in the 1930s, he clearly believed that our empirical resources would not be exhausted and that our entrance into the dreamy realms of speculation could be postponed indefinitely. . . . Nevertheless, Hubble's statement is a concession. What's more, it is a non-vacuous concession, because empirical resources come in limited supplies and do get exhausted. Moreover, as soon as empirical resources are exhausted, naturalistic explanation loses its monopoly as the only legitimate explanatory strategy for science.[75]

Of course, it is impossible to know for a certainty that we have exhausted the full range of naturalistic explanations, for unless we could somehow be omniscient, there is always the chance that we will end up finding a naturalistic explanation for any given phenomenon. This is why we should never block the road of (nondestructive) scientific inquiry, because it is important that we continue searching for empirical causes since we'll never know for sure whether or not we've exhausted the full range of naturalistic explanations.

By the same token, though, it is also quite possible that we *have* exceeded the full range of naturalistic explanations in certain areas of science, for as Dembski reminds us, "empirical resources come in limited supplies and do get exhausted."[76] And while we may not be able to tell for a certainty whether or not this finite supply has been exceeded, what we can say is that if this finite supply is ever exceeded with respect to any particular phenomenon, modern science will be incapable of arriving at an adequate explanation without first making an appeal to supernatural agency.

It may be the case that no such appeal to supernatural agency will turn out to be appropriate following the Big Bang. In this case, the deist's central premise—namely, that God created a self-organizing universe in the beginning and then left it alone to evolve according to natural law—will be correct. Or, it could be the case that the theist's central premise of a God who regularly intervenes in the world will turn out to be correct. Of course, we'll never know the answer to this question for a certainty until we gain access to a much greater storehouse of knowledge.

In the meantime, we can feel safe in invoking supernatural agency to account for what is perhaps the most perplexing part of modern science: the origin of the laws of nature. Naturalistic science seems utterly incapable of finding the answer to this question, not just in fact but also in principle. For as Gödel's theorem reminds us, no self-contained human discipline can achieve a coherent self-explanation without venturing outside of itself. What this means for us is that the laws of nature cannot be manipulated scientifically so as to be able to derive a sufficient accounting of their own origin. It cannot be done for the same reason that undecidable propositions will always be able to be generated in arithmetic or in any larger branch of self-contained mathematics—because no self-contained human discipline can provide a coherent self-explanation without venturing outside of itself. Gödel, of course, was fully aware of the implications of this stunning realization, so much so, in fact, that he was able to devise an elaborate proof for the existence of God based on it.

On the other hand, we may feel a little less inclined to invoke supernatural agency to account for the Big Bang. For while cosmologists presently believe that everything in the universe, including space and time, had its ultimate origin[77] in the Big Bang, there is always the chance that we will eventually discover a naturalistic explanation for the birth of the universe itself.[78]

In all likelihood, an appeal to supernatural agency *will* turn out to be appropriate at the Big Bang, not simply to account for the universe's sudden appearance out of nothing, but also to explain its perfect orchestration for life some 15 billion years later. Again, the present cosmological consensus is that absolutely *nothing* of a material nature preceded the Big Bang. If this consensus turns out to be valid, it would mean that there were no natural processes in existence at all prior to the Big Bang to bring the universe into being. To the extent that this turns out to be so, we will have been successful in locating an instance in which natural processes were in fact totally exhausted, which, in turn, leaves room for the *appropriate* invocation of supernatural agency to account for the birth of the universe.

This same principle can also be applied to the mysterious origin of the laws of nature. Since we'll never be able to come up with a self-consistent accounting for the origin of these laws by using the laws themselves as an empirical guide, it would seem as though we've totally exhausted the full range of naturalistic explanations when it comes to the origin of these laws. This again leaves room for the *appropriate* invocation of supernatural agency in modern science.

The founding fathers of the modern scientific movement wouldn't have been surprised by this conclusion. They recognized that empirical science is inherently incapable of coming up with a sufficient explanation for its own existence, and it is partly for this reason that they blended philosophy, theology, and empirical science into a single, all-encompassing intellectual discipline known as "natural philosophy."

We needn't fear that this type of conceptual integration will end up compromising the objectivity of modern science. To the contrary, it will go a long way toward ensuring the openness and accuracy that scientists crave, because it will reinstate the proper context to the current practice of science, just as it will also restore what is arguably the single most important part of our modern understanding of the universe: the role of a possible Creator. It doesn't really matter whether such a Deity *actually* exists or not, because the best way to approach this issue is to assume from the very outset that He *might* exist. For in so doing, one automatically orients oneself to the various possibilities that naturally surround these two possibilities. One cannot simply assume that it is impossible for such a Being to exist, because in this case one will have closed oneself off to the single most important scientific possibility of them all, namely, the Author and Creator of the various natural sciences. And this, in turn, would naturally end up jeopardizing the accuracy of one's scientific conclusions. After all, how can one possibly gain an accurate scientific understanding of an intelligently designed universe if one has already fully committed oneself to the opposite metaphysical situation?

Since we'll never know for a certainty in this world whether or not God truly exists, the prudent strategy, it would seem, is to adopt the scientific equivalent of Pascal's Wager. Pascal's Wager, you may recall, asserts that the safest thing to do, given God's possible existence, is to believe in Him no matter what, for if He turns out to be real, then one will be appropriately rewarded in the end, but if He turns out to be a fiction, one will have at least given God's possible existence the benefit of the doubt, while living a good and productive life in the meantime.

This manner of reasoning is somewhat analogous to receiving a package in the mail that *could* turn out to be a bomb, based on the package's superficial appearance. In this case, the prudent thing to do would be to *assume* that there is a bomb in the package and to then act accordingly. The very possibility of a potentially deadly consequence logically demands that one give the situation the benefit of the doubt by assuming that it is a bomb until proven otherwise.

In the same way, it is a distinct possibility that God exists after all. This being the case, there is a much greater advantage to be gained by assuming His existence and then acting accordingly, instead of simply doing the opposite. For if God does in fact exist, one will then benefit for the rest of eternity by having assumed this existence no matter what, but if He doesn't exist, one won't be any worse off for having given this possibility the benefit of the doubt. On the other hand, if one flagrantly rejects the possibility of God's existence, one is taking a very large risk indeed if one turns out to be wrong. Clearly, the wise thing to do is to believe in God no matter what.

This same rationale can also be used to justify the inclusion of supernatural agency in the modern scientific enterprise, if only as a potential, provisional explanation. For if God turns out to exist after all, then this inclusion will have given us the greatest possible degree of accuracy in our scientific theorizing, since the most accurate types of theories in an intelligent designed universe will naturally acknowledge the existence of a Designer. If, however, God doesn't exist after all, then His provisional inclusion in the modern scientific method will turn out to have had no significant negative consequences associated with it. If, on the other hand, the inclusion of supernatural agency is not allowed in modern science, then scientists run the risk of being flagrantly wrong in their understanding of the natural realm.

The only way, then, that the "provisional atheism" of the methodological naturalist can ultimately pay off is if God turns out not to exist after all. However, since we will never be able to know this for a certainty in this lifetime, and since the potential risk of being wrong is so great, it makes sense to provisionally *assume* the possible existence of God in one's scientific theorizing. The potential reward from doing this far outweighs any concomitant risk, as we have seen.

We mustn't forget that one of the defining parameters of the modern scientific enterprise is its openness to new explanations. A closed-minded science therefore isn't a real science at all. Accordingly, conceptual prejudice, and not theistic science *per se*, is the real enemy of modern science. We shouldn't close the door to *any* potential explanation in the natural world.

This dictum is all the more appropriate when we consider the fact that modern science doesn't even have a rudimentary understanding of *what* the various components of the natural sciences really *are* in themselves. We have no idea, for instance, what the gravitational force really *is* in itself or how it ultimately goes about accomplishing its effect in the cosmos. All we really understand is the value of the acceleration that it induces on earth (9.8 meters per second).

For all we know, the gravitational force could actually be generated by the direct activity of the Divine Spirit on the physical universe. We just don't know at this point. But what we *do* know is that, given our tremendous ignorance about the true nature of things, it would be foolhardy in the extreme for us to begin ruling out possible explanations for natural phenomena based on our own metaphysical prejudices, and this is all the more true when we consider the overwhelming evidence for design that cosmologists have recently generated.[79]

The Nature of Theistic Science

The essence of "theistic science," as Alvin Plantinga, J. P. Moreland, and others have pointed out, is that theists should make use of all the conceptual tools at their disposal when they go about constructing hypotheses and research proposals. In the words of J. P. Moreland:

> Theistic science is rooted in the idea that . . . [theists] ought to consult all they know or have reason to believe in forming and testing hypotheses, explaining things in science and evaluating the plausibility of various scientific hypotheses, and among the things they should consult are propositions of theology (and philosophy). Theistic science can be considered a research program . . . that, among other things, is based on two propositions: 1) God, conceived of as a personal, transcendent agent of great power and intelligence, has through direct, primary agent causation and indirect, secondary causation, created and designed the world for a purpose and has intervened in the course of its development at various times, and 2) The commitment expressed in proposition 1 can appropriately enter into the very fabric of the practice of science and the utilization of scientific methodology.[80]

We have already seen how the concept of supernatural agency can legitimately be included in the scientific method without any compromise in the integrity of the latter taking place. For not only can the idea of God be coherently proposed as a possible indirect explanation for various empirical phenomena, the existence of this possible entity can also be empirically tested in an indirect manner as well by noting how such a being might conceivably affect the visible world.

According to Moreland, theistic science possesses the following additional characteristics:

> Theology can provide metaphysical pictures of what was and was not going on in the formation of some entity (the universe, first life, the basic kinds of life, humankind or, for some, the geological column. These pictures can serve as guides for new research (e.g., by postulating that a purpose will be found for vestigial organs), they can yield predictions that certain theories (e.g., theories of naturalistic mechanisms like natural selection working at the level of macroevolution, theories entailing a beginningless universe) will be falsified, and they can yield predictions that certain discoveries will be made (e.g., the Cambrian explosion, gaps in the fossil record, fixity of created "kinds." In this way theology can serve as a resource for a negative heuristic (paths of research to avoid . . .) and a positive heuristic (paths of research to pursue). . . .
>
> Further, theology can provide and help to solve external and internal conceptual problems. Scientific laws and theories typically involve observational concepts and their associated observational terms (e.g., "is red," "sinks"), as well as theoretical concepts and their associated terms (e.g., "is an electron," "has zero rest mass"). Often scientists try to solve both empirical and conceptual problems. Roughly, an empirical problem is one of the observational aspects of some range of scientific data that strikes us as odd and in need of an explanation. For example, what is the precise movement of the tides, and why do they move as they do?

Frequently scientists will try to solve conceptual problems, which come in two types: internal and external. Internal conceptual problems arise when the theoretical concepts within a theory are defective in some way—perhaps they are vague, unclear, contradictory, or circularly defined. External conceptual problems arise for some theory, T, when T conflicts with some doctrine of another theory, T', and that doctrine of T' is rationally well founded, regardless of the discipline with which T' is associated. Natural science has always interacted with other fields of study in complicated, multifaceted ways that defy a simple characterization.[81]

Moreland goes on to describe how both philosophy and theology can interface with science precisely at the point where external conceptual problems arise for the latter:

An external conceptual problem can arise in philosophy or theology, but enters into the very fabric of science because it interfaces with and tends to count against a given scientific theory. Part of the practice of science is to make sure that a scientific theory solves its problems, external conceptual problems included. Thus external conceptual problems provide counterexamples to the complementarian model of science-theology integration, because they are cases where science and another discipline like philosophy of theology interact at the same level in an epistemically positive or negative way.[82]

The Role of Supernatural Agency in Modern Science

I believe that the concept of supernatural agency should be returned to the modern scientific enterprise for several reasons. First, the concept of God appears to be a fundamental (and therefore necessary) ingredient in the underlying theoretical matrix out of which scientific assertions obtain their coherence. In this sense, the role of a Creator appears to be presupposed by the fundamental axioms of modern science. Insofar as this is so, it follows that most scientific claims will ultimately turn out to be incomplete until the foundational role of a Creator is first acknowledged.

I am not suggesting here that the concept of God should be included in the actual content of most scientific claims, nor do I believe that the idea of God should be invoked in the vast majority of scientific explanations. The notion of supernatural agency as such does not appear to be a mode of causation that is appropriate for empirical scientific analysis, nor does it seem to be a direct explanation for most types of discrete physical phenomena. It appears instead to be a vast theoretical matrix out of which modern science is able to obtain its own internal coherence. This is no small point, because the various presuppositions that are relied upon in modern science must first be internally coherent before they can be capable of constituting valid scientific explanations.

The advantage of this conceptual rearrangement is that it enables science and religion to comfortably coexist beside one another as mutual partners in our ongoing quest for knowledge and understanding. For by confining the role of God in modern science to the underlying theoretical matrix out of which scientific claims obtain their coherence, God is kept *out of* most scientific claims themselves. This enables scientists to do their work without fearing that their work will be trumped or invalidated by inappropriate religious pseudo-explanations.

Moreover, I do not believe that the concept of supernatural agency should be excluded from the realm of modern science simply because many scientists are prejudiced against it. Conceptual prejudice as such should not be part of the modern scientific enterprise. Potential explanations should not be excluded from the available pool of explanatory resources simply because they fail to meet someone's preconceived idea of what constitutes true science. If the goal is simply to pare down the list of possible explanations, it would be better—and more in line with the underlying character of modern science itself—to employ a Darwinian-style process of selection with these possible explanations, so that only the "fittest" among them can continue to survive in the available pool of explanatory resources. Fitness in this case would refer to the overall notion of explanatory adequacy, for example, how well does the idea or concept account for the data in question? If the "fit" between the data and the proposed explanation is good, the explanation itself can be retained for future testing and analysis, whereas if the fit is poor, it can either be retired to a list of inactive explanations or else eliminated altogether (depending on how poor the fit happens to be).

This leads us to the third reason why I believe that the concept of supernatural agency should be included in the modern scientific enterprise: because it provides a far more plausible—and hence more believable—account of the cosmological evidence than atheistic science does. After all, how are we to account for the incredible fine-tuning that cosmologists have discovered in our nascent cosmos, especially given the fact that this calibration was obviously directed toward the goal of making the universe life-supporting? Modern science hasn't even approached an adequate explanation for this uncanny phenomenon, yet demarcationists like Michael Ruse want to eliminate the possibility of a supernatural explanation altogether because it isn't "real science."

Why should we go against our better judgment here? For if we reason abductively to the best possible explanation, we find that the concept of Intelligent

Design is in fact the best explanation after all, as the following quote from physicist George Greenstein makes clear:

> As we survey all the evidence, the thought insistently arises that some supernatural agency—or, rather, Agency—must be involved. Is it possible that suddenly, without intending to, we have stumbled upon scientific proof of the existence of a Supreme Being? Was it God who stepped in and so providentially crafted the cosmos for our benefit?[83]

Although Paul Davies began his famous writing career being skeptical about the plausibility of the design hypothesis, he has since revised his position on the weight of the evidence alone:

> The essential feature of our universe is that something of value emerges as the result of processing according to some ingenious pre-existing set of rules. It looks *as if* they are the product of intelligent design. I do not see how this can be denied. Whether you wish to believe that they really *have* been so designed, and if so by what sort of being, must remain a matter of personal taste. My own inclination is to suppose that qualities such as ingenuity, economy, beauty, and so on have a genuine transcendent reality—they are not merely the product of human experience—and that these qualities are reflected in the structure of the natural world.[84]

And again:

> We have cracked part of the cosmic code. Why this should be, just why *Homo sapiens* should carry the spark of rationality that provides the key to the universe, is a deep enigma. We, who are children of the universe—animated stardust—can nevertheless reflect on the nature of the same universe, even to the extent of glimpsing the rules on which it runs. How we have become linked into this cosmic dimension is a mystery. Yet the linkage cannot be denied.
>
> What does it mean? What is Man that we might be party to such privilege? I cannot believe that our existence in this universe is a mere quirk of fate, an accident of history, an incidental blip in the great cosmic drama. Our involvement is too intimate. The physical species *Homo* may count for nothing, but the existence of mind in some organism on some planet in the universe is surely a fact of fundamental significance. This can be no trivial detail, no minor byproduct of mindless, purposeless forces. We are truly meant to be here.[85]

Sir Fred Hoyle—the pioneering astrophysicist who discovered the fascinating connection between stellar nuclear resonances and the process of carbon formation—has even gone so far as to conclude that *any* scientist who examined the evidence of intrastellar carbon formation would likely "draw the inference that the laws of nuclear physics have been deliberately designed with regard to the consequences they produce inside the stars."[86]

If Hoyle's assertion is correct, then the concept of supernatural agency should indeed be a part of our modern scientific enterprise after all, precisely *because* it provides the best explanation for the current data at hand. This is why the idea of a theistic science is particularly tantalizing to an increasing number of scientists and philosophers, because a theistically oriented science is inherently better equipped—given the inherent persuasiveness of the evidence itself—to decipher the underlying truth of our own origins than any type of atheistic science could ever be.

The final reason why I believe that the concept of supernatural agency should be returned to the modern scientific enterprise has to do with the holistic nature of the universe itself. With the advent of quantum mechanics in the previous century, we've learned that our entire universe is like a hologram, insofar as it is a complete, undivided whole. This cosmic holism is one of the chief unifying principles of modern science, as David Bohm and many others have pointed out.[87] This means, amongst other things, that each of the universe's constituent parts is somehow causally connected to all of its other parts, so that there are no truly isolated segments of the cosmos.

But if this is so (and a large body of experimental evidence suggests that it is), then this means that the universe doesn't reflect the same disconnectedness and compartmentalization that is so characteristic of our scientific understanding of the natural world. It is, instead, a pulsating, interconnected gestalt of mutually interdependent particles and energy fields, all working together to produce a single, coherent universe that is fit for life.

What this means is that there is no one-to-one correspondence between the underlying nature of the universe itself and our own epistemological divisions and distinctions. That is to say, there *is* no such thing as biology, chemistry, or physics *per se* in the real world. There is, instead, a single universal reality that happens to manifest itself to our distinction-seeking minds as separate intellectual disciplines. We are thus only deceiving ourselves if we believe that the physical universe can somehow be divided into neat little categories for our own explanatory convenience. The real world simply does not operate this way. To the contrary, every segment of cosmic reality is holistically interconnected with all the other parts, such that there are truly no isolated causes to be found anywhere in the natural realm. Instead, there is a single, interconnected plenum of causes throughout the cosmos, which in turn means that any attempt to isolate a particular cause from the rest of cosmic reality is bound to be only part of the story when it comes to understanding how and why things happen the way they do in the universe.

This is the principal reason why I believe we should include the possibility of supernatural agency in our scientific theorizing, because in the end there are no truly isolated causes to be found anywhere in the entire universe. Instead, there are material causes that are somehow interconnected with everything else that exists in and around the cosmos, including God Himself.[88] This is why the concept of supernatural agency should be returned to the modern scientific enterprise—because the principle of cosmic holism tells us that His existence is almost certainly impinging upon the physical universe in a wide variety of different ways.

Notes

1. Stephen C. Meyer, "The Methodological Equivalence of Design and Descent," in *The Creation Hypothesis*, ed. J. P. Moreland (Downers Grove, Ill.: Intervarsity Press, 1994), 69.

2. Nancey Murphy, "Phillip Johnson on Trial: A Critique of His Critique of Darwin," *Perspectives on Science and Christian Faith* vol. 45, no. 1 (1993): 33.

3. David C. Lindberg, "Science and the Early Church," in *God and Nature*, ed. David C. Lindberg and Ronald Numbers (Berkeley: University of California Press, 1986), 19–48.

4. Alvin Plantinga, "Methodological Naturalism?" *Perspectives on Science and Christian Faith*, vol. 49, no. 3, 144.

5. While scientific information per se may be religiously neutral, the concept of supernatural agency can nevertheless be profitably utilized in both the building of scientific theories and in the final interpretation of empirical data.

6. Interestingly enough, Erasmus Darwin, who was a physician by training, wrote extensively about the evolutionary process long before his grandson Charles arrived on the scene. His ideas are contained in a work of poetry entitled *Zoonomia*.

7. It is important to note, however, that our alien friend didn't really need to know where the new cars themselves were ultimately coming from. He simply needed to know how to elicit their arrival at the dealership, and for this limited purpose he was quite successful, since he had no practical need to understand the ultimate origin of the new cars themselves.

8. Meyer, "Methodological Equivalence of Design and Descent," 78.

9. Alan Wolfe, "A Welcome Revival of Religion in the Academy," *Chronicle of Higher Education*, 19 September 1997, B4–B5.

10. Ibid.

11. Jacques Monod, *Chance and Necessity* (New York: Knopf, 1971).

12. John D. Barrow, *The World within the World* (Oxford: Oxford University Press, 1990), 315.

13. Lindberg, "Science and the Early Church," 19–48.

14. Barrow, *World within the World*, 31–38.

15. Paul Davies, "The Intelligibility of Nature," in *Quantum Cosmology and the Laws of Nature*, ed. Robert John Russell, Nancey Murphy, and C. J. Isham (Vatican City State: Vatican Observatory Publications, 1996), 155.

16. John D. Barrow and Frank J. Tipler, *The Anthropic Cosmological Principle* (Oxford: Oxford University Press, 1986), 49–50.

17. Copernicus was such a devoted anthropocentrist, in fact, that he felt uneasy giving up humanity's physical centrality in the cosmos. He was, however, able to reconcile his anthropocentrism with his heliocentric discovery by pointing out that humanity's displacement from the center of the cosmos is infinitesimally slight when compared to the immense size of the universe itself.

18. Barrow and Tipler, *Anthropic Cosmological Principle*, 50.

19. Ibid., 52–53.

20. M. A. Corey, *God and the New Cosmology* (Lanham, Md.: Rowman & Littlefield, 1993), 232.

21. This, of course, is to be expected in a universe that has been intelligently designed. However, it might also be expected in a universe that only seems as though it has been designed. For if the various laws of nature can truly counterfeit the workings of an Intelligent Designer, then it is possible that this counterfeiting might also extend to the basic underlying principles of the physical world itself, such that by anticipating the activities of this counterfeit designer, one might then be better able to unmask the actual principles that are at work in the natural world.

22. Terry G. Pence, "Charles S. Peirce, Scientific Method, and God," *Perspectives on Science and Christian Faith*, vol. 49, no. 3 (September 1997): 156.

23. Ibid.

24. C. S. Peirce, Harvard Lecture 5, "On Three Kinds of Goodness," vol. 5 (1903): 145.

25. C. S. Peirce, "Syllabus," vol. 2 (1903): 776.

26. Pence, "Charles S. Peirce," 157.

27. C. S. Peirce, Cambridge Lectures, Lecture 1, "Philosophy and the Conduct of Life," vol. 1 (1898): 630.

28. Pence, "Charles S. Peirce," 156.

29. Ibid.

30. Ibid., 160.

31. Review of William James, "The Principles of Psychology," vol. 7 (1891): 60.

32. The curious behavior of objects traveling near the speed of light explicitly forbids anything from traveling at precisely the speed of light, because the mass of even the "tiniest" object is thought to suddenly become infinite at this point.

33. The neutrino may or may not have a rest mass, and it is believed to travel near the speed of light. It is also thought to interact very weakly with ordinary "baryonic" matter.

34. Paul Davies, *The Last Three Minutes* (New York: Basic, 1994), 39–41.

35. Supernova explosions are believed to be accompanied by an incredibly massive release of neutrinos.

36. C. S. Peirce, "A Neglected Argument for the Reality of God," vol. 6 (1908).

37. Pence, "Charles S. Peirce," 159.

38. Ibid.

39. One wonders how the proponents of the Principle of Objectivity would respond if a device were invented one day that could detect and measure the existence of unseen objects in the spiritual realm. Would religious issues suddenly become the focus of legitimate

science? Indeed, something similar has already transpired with the work of Larry Dossey, a physician who has written a series of books on the empirically proven efficaciousness of prayer.

40. Larry Dossey, *Prayer Is Good Medicine* (San Francisco: HarperSanFrancisco, 1997).

41. Barrow, *World within the World*, 228.

42. Philip Clayton, *Explanation from Physics to Theology* (New Haven, Conn.: Yale University Press, 1991), 2.

43. Davies, "Intelligibility of Nature," 164.

44. G. F. R. Ellis, "The Theology of the Anthropic Principle," in *Quantum Cosmology and the Laws of Nature*, ed. Robert John Russell, Nancey Murphy, and C. J. Isham (Vatican City State: Vatican Observatory Publications, 1996), p. 376.

45. Nancey Murphy, "Evidence of Design in the Fine-Tuning of the Universe," in *Quantum Cosmology and the Laws of Nature*, ed. Robert John Russell, Nancey Murphy, and C. J. Isham (Vatican City State: Vatican Observatory Publications, 1996), p. 418.

46. Clayton, *Explanation from Physics to Theology*, 2.

47. We see, then, that the same factor that is responsible for the tremendous success of modern science (the demand for objectivity) is also responsible for its explanatory shortcomings. For while this empirical limitation might be able to facilitate our understanding of how things operate in the natural world, it doesn't go very far in helping us to understand why things are the way they are. For this more all-encompassing type of explanation, we need to move beyond the world of empirical observation only into the realm of philosophical interpretation.

48. Paul Penfield Jr., in a lecture at MIT entitled "God the Scientist."

49. Walter James ReMine, *The Biotic Message: Evolution versus Message Theory* (St. Paul, Minn.: St. Paul Science, 1993), 32.

50. Michael Ruse, "A Philosopher's Day in Court," in *But Is It Science?*, ed. Michael Ruse (Buffalo, N.Y.: Prometheus, 1988), 21–26.

51. We are defining the word "natural" here to be "that which exists naturally apart from the works of human beings." From this point of view, who or what could possibly be more "natural" than the self-existent Creator of the universe who has existed for all eternity? After all, we are talking here about a being whose very essence is to exist, so from this viewpoint God is indeed the most "natural" entity imaginable.

52. M. A. Corey, *Back to Darwin* (Lanham, Md.: University Press of America, 1994), 293–298.

53. If such a program is ever discovered, it will go a long way toward confirming the theory of origins that initially gave rise to this prediction.

54. Philip Kitcher, *Abusing Science* (Cambridge: MIT Press, 1982), 45.

55. Quoted in Keith Abney, "Naturalism and Nonteleological Science: A Way to Resolve the Demarcation Problem between Science and Nonscience," *Perspectives on Science and Christian Faith*, vol. 49, no. 3 (September 1997): 166.

56. Ibid.

57. Meyer, "Methodological Equivalence of Design and Descent," 67–102.

58. Ibid., 76.

59. Ibid., 72–88.

60. Ibid., 75, 99.

61. Larry Laudan, "The Demise of the Demarcation Problem," in *But Is It Science?*, ed. Michael Ruse (Buffalo, N.Y.: Prometheus, 1988), 349.

62. Meyer, "Methodological Equivalence of Design and Descent," 76.

63. Ibid., 75.

64. Ibid., 78.

65. Ibid.

66. Ibid., 78–79.

67. Ibid., 79.

68. In *The Natural History of Creation*, I defined a miracle as "any action that is performed by God." See M. A. Corey, *The Natural History of Creation* (Lanham, Md.: University Press of America, 1995), 309–311. With this broad definition, it follows that everything that happens in the universe in literally miraculous, but only in a derivative sense, since every causal event that transpires in the universe is ultimately derived from the creatorship of God.

69. Meyer, "Methodological Equivalence of Design and Descent," 81.

70. Ibid., 83.

71. Ibid., 85.

72. Ibid., 102.

73. William A. Dembski, "On the Very Possibility of Intelligent Design," in *The Design Hypothesis*, ed. J. P. Moreland (Downers Grove, Ill.: Intervarsity Press, 1994), 131.

74. Quoted in Dembski, "On the Very Possibility of Intelligent Design," 132.

75. Ibid.

76. Ibid.

77. In this case, an appeal to God would be appropriate to account for the Big Bang since there would be no natural processes prior to the Big Bang to bring the universe into existence.

78. An appeal to supernatural agency here would in fact be an appeal to a God of the gaps.

79. Corey, *God and the New Cosmology*, 42–116.

80. J. P. Moreland, ed., *The Design Hypothesis* (Downers Grove, Ill.: Intervarsity Press, 1994), 12–13.

81. Ibid., 51–52.

82. Ibid., 52–53.

83. George Greenstein, *The Symbiotic Universe* (New York: William Morrow, 1988), 27.

84. Paul Davies, *The Mind of God* (New York: Simon and Schuster, 1992), 214.

85. Ibid., 232.

86. Fred Hoyle, *Religion and the Scientists* (London: SCM, 1959).

87. Kevin J. Sharpe, *David Bohm's World* (Lewisburg, Pa.: Bucknell University Press, 1993), 51–55.

88. Many people find it difficult to imagine how God could possibly be related to the natural world of empirical science. One of the biggest problems in this area has been the widespread tendency for people to believe that a valid scientific explanation for a physical

event somehow obviates the need for a Divine Creator. This attitude can be traced all the way back to Laplace, who believed that the "God hypothesis" is no longer necessary, since scientists can now explain physical events in terms of purely natural causes. The hidden assumption behind Laplace's way of thinking is that God does not or cannot work through purely physical causes. People who think in this fashion expect any physical evidence of God to be blatantly apparent and even magical in nature. While it is difficult to pinpoint the historical origin of this way of thinking, there is one thing we can say for sure: it has nothing at all to do with biblical teaching on this subject. To the contrary, the Bible repeatedly emphasizes the many naturalistic aspects of God's universe. For instance, we are told in the first chapter of Genesis that the earth brought forth living creatures, in response to God's Command (Gen. 1:24). This directly speaks of a series of naturalistic processes in the origin of life, which God, through His Supernatural Creativity, somehow made possible.

~

CHAPTER SIXTEEN

Hope for the Future

Whether or not it is clear to you, no doubt the universe is unfolding as it should.

—Max Ehrmann

Is there a cause for hope in today's overly violent, pollution-ridden world? There are many who would argue that the answer to this question is a self-evident "No." And from a certain point of view they would seem to be correct: the human population is rapidly outgrowing the earth's underlying capacity to support it, while at the same time we are aggressively destroying our precious ecosystem with reckless abandon. Species are going extinct at a truly alarming rate, and the ecological damage that we're doing to our planet will almost certainly persist for thousands of years. It will take centuries for the earth's rapidly diminishing ozone layer to be adequately replenished, and the many nuclear poisons that we have concocted during the last few decades will remain unbelievably toxic for millions of years to come.

We are also using our rapidly increasing technological prowess to devise weapons of mass destruction that were inconceivable just a few short years ago. Unfortunately, the human race has never invented a weapon that it didn't eventually use, so our immediate future looks very grim indeed, especially given the many areas of political unrest that can be found throughout the globe. And when we pause to consider what would happen if a terrorist organization ever got their hands on a functional nuclear device, fear rapidly gives way to outright panic, especially since it's likely to be just a matter of time until this eventually happens.

Most frightening of all, though, is the realization that no matter what tragic event threatens the future of humanity, God will almost certainly *not* intervene to prevent it. He didn't intervene to prevent World Wars I or II, and it seems unlikely in the extreme that He will ever openly intervene in human affairs until the very end.[1]

With this in mind, is it possible to find a glimmer of hope in today's increasingly hopeless world? I believe that the answer to this question is an unequivocal "Yes"! Moreover, I believe that this cause for hope is objectively rational because it is based upon the conclusions of modern empirical science.

This cause for hope, in a nutshell, is founded upon the extreme structural complexity of our entire Goldilocks Universe. We didn't create this complexity, nor do we know where it ultimately came from or how it came to possess its present biocentric configuration. All we know for sure is that this complexity does indeed exist and that our lives are possible because of it.

This being the case, we can now go one step further and utilize this profound complexity as a logical springboard to bring us to a dramatic, far-reaching conclusion. For if the universe has indeed been designed by a Supreme Intelligence for a particular purpose (as we previously concluded), then this divinely instituted purpose isn't going to be thwarted by anything that the human race can possibly do on this planet. In fact, insofar as this cosmic Power actually foresaw the destiny of the human race when He created the cosmos at the beginning of time, it follows that He had to have known from the very outset how we were going to turn out, yet He chose to instantiate us anyway! This suggests that humanity's future trajectory somehow fits into God's cosmic Plan, despite its extremely ominous appearance from an earthbound point of view.

Insofar as this is so, it means that nothing that ever transpires on this planet is capable of taking our Creator by surprise. This realization is eminently reassuring in itself, because it means that events are unfolding here largely according to plan, no matter what nightmarish cataclysms may end up transpiring in our society. This belief, of course, involves a significant element of faith, *but it isn't a form of faith that we are unfamiliar with*. To the contrary, it is a type of faith that we implicitly rely on every single day.

Whether we are aware of it or not, we all routinely express a tremendous amount of faith in the natural cosmic order, because it is the natural order itself that has given us our very lives on this planet. After all, we don't really know how our bodies work or how our minds are able to consciously experience the world, but we don't let these questions stop us from trying to live our lives to the fullest anyway.

In short, we tend to take all of the fundamental ingredients of life for granted, but this is just another way of saying that we actually have a great deal of unspoken faith in the entire natural order, whether we are consciously aware of it or not. David Ray Griffin calls this sort of tacit belief a "hardcore commonsense notion," because it is something that we regularly affirm in practice, even if we happen to verbally deny it. This is significant, because it reveals a pervasive level of unconscious trust in the cosmic *status quo*.

But if this is so, then it is just another step to express a similar degree of trust in the future trajectory of the entire universe itself. This isn't as preposterous as it may initially seem, for if we can trust "Mother Nature" to give us a world that caters to our minds and bodies in thousands of different ways, why can't we also trust her to provide us with a future trajectory for our lives that is both positive and hopeful?

Think about this for a moment. We weren't responsible for designing the universe at the beginning of time, nor were we responsible for creating our bodies, the atmosphere, or the food we have to regularly eat in order to remain alive. All of these vital ingredients, and hundreds more like them, have mysteriously been provided *for* us, and to a large extent they tend to function very effectively in our day to day lives. We therefore feel compelled to accept the trustworthiness of these items on faith, even though we don't really know how they operate or where they ultimately came from.

Each time we eat something, then, we are expressing an unspoken degree of faith in the way things naturally are, because it is the natural order itself that originally gave us the ability to transform food into life-giving energy. This same principle is also applicable when we try to get a suntan at the beach.[2] In this case, we are expressing faith in the sun's natural ability to tan us without exploding and annihilating us all. This is no small thing, because the sun is an unimaginably huge hydrogen bomb that is continuously detonating in precisely the right manner to provide us with a safe amount of heat and energy.

This fact is all the more amazing because of the many intricate forces inside the sun that are perfectly counterbalanced with one another to encourage its structural stability over the long term. If even a single one of these fine-tuned parameters ever lost its perfect degree of balance, we'd all be incinerated in a moment's notice, yet no one gives serious thought to this issue because of their unspoken faith in the natural order. This faith in Mother Nature is essentially ubiquitous amongst human beings, yet for some reason we tend to forget it when we look out into the future. For instead of trusting the natural world to provide us with a safe and secure destination as we grow older, we tend to become afraid whenever we contemplate the future.[3]

There is, however, no logical reason to abandon our underlying faith in the natural order simply because we're looking out into the future. The "future," after all, transforms itself into the "present" with each passing second, so it necessarily follows from this that the "future" must be fundamentally comprised of the same metaphysical stuff as the "present." Accordingly, if we find it expedient to have faith in the natural cosmic order in our present-day lives, then we should also find it equally expedient to express a similar type of faith when it comes to the future, since the future relentlessly becomes the present with each passing moment. This is why we can assert that the "future" must be comprised of the same fundamental building blocks as the "present."

This perspective makes a good deal of sense, for if we can express faith in Mother Nature when it comes to the present-day functioning of our world and universe, then we should also be able to express a similar degree of faith when it comes to these very same things in the future. The basic idea here is that if Mother Nature is going to go to *such* incredible lengths to provide us with a trustworthy world to live in today, then she is almost certainly *not* going to abandon us in the future, no matter how much we might feel to the contrary.

Human beings, however, have always experienced a certain amount of foreboding when it comes to the future because of their instinctive fear of the unknown, particularly when it comes to the reality of death.[4] Moreover, fear also naturally tends to negate our sense of faith, so it isn't surprising that our faith in the natural world should rapidly dissipate whenever we look out into the future. However, we mustn't allow this fear to deteriorate into irrationality, because it makes little sense to abandon our instinctive faith in Mother Nature simply because it involves the future instead of the present. *For insofar as it is rational to have a certain amount of faith in the natural order in today's world, then it is also rational to express a similar type of faith in the future as well, because the future will most assuredly become the present in due time.*

This argument can be reduced to the following:

1. Most individuals implicitly express a substantial degree of faith in the natural order, because it is the natural order itself that has given us the ability to live and thrive in a remarkably complex world and universe. Without this implicit faith in the cosmic *status quo*, we would be unable to act with equanimity in the present, since we would be unable to trust the various aspects of our existence to the point of being able to act on them.

2. This implicit faith in Mother Nature is essentially limited to the present.

3. The future, however, is not fundamentally distinct from the present, since the future seamlessly *becomes* the present with each passing moment.

4. Therefore, the present and the future are essentially comprised of the same overall character and nature.

5. Hence, anyone who expresses faith in Mother Nature in the present should logically express a similar degree of faith toward the future as well, since both are comprised of the same fundamental character and nature.

6. This is proven by the realization that any justifiable lack of faith in the future should simultaneously be applicable to the present, for if the future natural order cannot be trusted, then the present natural order should not be trusted either.

7. Nevertheless, we instinctively tend to express trust in the present natural order, since this trust is a necessary precondition for *any* type of constructive action in the world.

8. Therefore, we should put an equal amount of trust in the future natural order as well, since it is fundamentally comprised of the same general character as the present natural order.

9. It is therefore rational to express hope in the future, because it is similarly rational to express hope in the present-day *status quo*.

10. The extreme complexity that permeates the entire cosmos supports us in this contention, because if Mother Nature is going to go to such radical lengths to give us a comfortable world to live in today, then she probably *won't* be abandoning us in the future.

Insofar as the above argument is valid, we can see that our instinctive sense of foreboding regarding the future is primarily a function of our own existential fears, and *not* a lack of faith in the future natural order *per se*. It is very easy, however, to confuse and conflate these two issues because they *feel* so similar. We must, therefore, do our best to protect our ongoing faith in the cosmic *status quo* so that it isn't quietly supplanted by our many existential fears regarding the future. For only then will we feel secure enough to be able to fully experience the happiness and joy that Mother Nature is patiently waiting to bestow upon us.

Notes

1. According to Matthew 24:22, God will intervene in global affairs near the end of this earthly age to prevent the total destruction of the human race (presumably from the effects of a worldwide nuclear holocaust).

2. Of course, we all know about the sun's ability to cause skin cancer, but the severity of this threat is a comparatively recent phenomenon that can be directly traced to the on-going destruction of the earth's protective ozone layer. It is this ozone depletion that has made sunlight so much more carcinogenic in recent years than it used to be. But this fact only serves to highlight the central point that I am trying to make here, since "Mother Nature" herself initially provided the earth's ozone layer for our protection. It is only when the human race thoughtlessly began dumping millions of tons of ozone-depleting pollu-tants into the atmosphere that the carcinogenic power of sunlight started to become a se-rious issue. The "take home" point here is that Mother Nature is clearly far more trust-worthy than most human beings ever thought her to be, so if we continue to assault her with our mindless polluting we will almost certainly be forced to pay a proportionally higher price in the future.

3. Part of this fear may exist because we instinctively realize how hard we are making it for ourselves when we deliberately institute immoral principles that are designed to rape and exploit both people and the environment for monetary advantage.

4. Ernest Becker, *The Denial of Death* (New York: Free Press, 1973), 26–27.

Glossary

ACCIDENT: The unintended consequence of an action that was consciously intended to produce a very different result. Because genuine accidents presuppose a preexisting realm of volition where some things happen in a desirable and predictable manner, and others do not, it is inappropriate to use this word to refer to an uncreated cosmos.

ANTHROPIC PRINCIPLE: The scientific view which seeks to demonstrate that conscious biological organisms can only arise in a universe in which the laws of nature have a certain special form.

ASEITY: A theological term that applies exclusively to God; it signifies complete and total independence from all other possible things.

BIG BANG: The cosmological theory which states that the entire universe exploded into being several billion years ago from an infinitely small point of matter-energy.

COMPOUND MIRACLE: Sophisticated instances of natural order that build upon the primary miraculousness of the natural world itself.

COPENHAGEN INTERPRETATION OF QUANTUM MECHANICS: The belief that there isn't any one specific reality in the physical world. There is, instead, a variety of possibilities, from which a single one is ultimately chosen by the act of observation. It is here with the "collapse of the quantum wave function" that all of the other possibilities are believed to instantly vanish.

COPERNICAN PRINCIPLE: A cosmological perspective which states that life is probably plentiful in the universe because there is nothing special or unique about human existence as such.

COSMOLOGICAL ARGUMENT: A time-honored attempt to prove the existence of God by tracing the cosmic chain of cause and effect back to an original Uncaused Cause.

CREATION EX NIHILO: The belief that God created the universe out of absolute nothingness.

DESIGN-CENTERED ANTHROPIC PRINCIPLE: The universe possesses a life-supporting configuration because it was deliberately infused with these properties by a Higher Power.

EPISTEMIC DISTANCE STIPULATION: A theological teaching which states that the world must superficially appear as if there is no God if human freedom is to remain intact.

FINAL ANTHROPIC PRINCIPLE: Intelligent life must come into existence in the universe, and once it comes into existence, it will never die out.

FIRST-ORDER COMPOUND MIRACLE: The organization of primary miracles (e.g., miraculous natural processes) into highly ordered states, which themselves are able to generate even more miraculous outcomes.

FREE WILL: Our natural feeling that we can always do otherwise than we actually do.

FUNDAMENTAL CONTANTS OF NATURE: A collection of numbers that enter into the mathematical equations that characterize the laws of physics.

GENERAL RELATIVITY THEORY: Einstein's conceptualization of gravity as a function of the geometry of four-dimensional space-time.

LOGOS: A view of God that can be traced back to the Stoic philosophers of ancient Greece, which regards the Deity as the Logical Mediator between cause and effect in the world.

METAPHYSICAL NATURALISM: The philosophical perspective which asserts that the realm of material particles is the only type of being and existence in the entire universe.

METHODOLOGICAL NATURALISM: The idea that science, when properly carried out, cannot involve religious ideation, belief, or commitment.

MIRACLE: Anything that emanates, either directly or indirectly, from the Hand of God. Since everything in our world is ultimately derived from God's primordial activity at the Big Bang, everything in our world is ultimately miraculous in a derivative sense (to varying degrees).

MODERATE ANTHROPOCENTRISM: A philosophical view that regards *Homo sapiens* as one of the most important species in the entire universe. This leaves room for the possible existence of other intelligent beings elsewhere in the cosmos.

MULTIVERSE: The whole of physical reality, which may or may not contain a vast realm of parallel universes.

NATURAL THEOLOGY: A theology that is based on the belief that God can be known through the rational study of the natural realm without the aid of special revelation.

OCKHAM'S RAZOR: The Principle of Economy which states that one should not "multiply causes beyond necessity" in the construction of valid scientific hypotheses (also known as the Principle of Theoretical Economy).

PARALLEL UNIVERSE: A hypothetical, quantum-based copy of our own tangible universe.

PARTICIPATORY ANTHROPIC PRINCIPLE: Observers are necessary to bring the universe into being.

PAULI EXCLUSION PRINCIPLE: A subatomic ordering principle which guarantees that no more than one kind of particle and spin can occupy a single quantum state at the same time.

PHOTON: A particle of light.

POINCARÈ RECURRENCE THEOREM: Almost any bounded mechanical system with finite potential energy and finite kinetic energy will necessarily return to any previous initial state.

PRIMARY MIRACLE: The miraculousness exemplified by the laws of nature.

PRINCIPLE OF DECEPTIVE APPEARANCES: Things are rarely, if ever, the way they superficially seem to the naked eye.

PRINCIPLE OF THE EMPEROR'S NEW CLOTHES: The pressure to conform to a widely held, though mistaken, belief out of the fear of appearing ignorant.

PRINCIPLE OF QUANTIZATION: The phenomenon wherein electrons are only able to exist at discrete levels about the nucleus, which amount to multiples of Planck's universal quantum of energy.

PRINCIPLE OF SUFFICIENT REASON: Nothing can be so without a reason, causal or otherwise, why it is so.

PRINCIPLE OF THEORETICAL ECONOMY: A philosophical guideline which states that the simplest hypothesis is usually the correct one (also known as "Ockham's Razor").

PRINCIPLE OF UNIVERSALITY: The applicability of the same general laws and principles throughout the cosmos.

QUANTIZATION: The property of having a discrete (and not continuous) set of possible values.

QUANTUM MECHANICS: Currently the most fundamental theory of matter and motion, which is based in part on the uncertain nature of the subatomic realm.

SECOND-ORDER COMPOUND MIRACLE: A Divinely inspired suspension of natural law.

SELF-ORGANIZATION: The process by which an extensive degree of structure and organization arises in a system because of ordering processes that are internal to the system itself.

SINGULARITY: A region of space-time where a fundamental physical quantity, such as the strength of gravity, becomes infinite.

SPACE-TIME THEOREM OF GENERAL RELATIVITY: A corollary of Einstein's General Theory of Relativity, which asserts that space, time, and matter *all* came into existence at the Big Bang.

STRONG ANTHROPIC PRINCIPLE: The universe must have those properties that allow life to develop within it at some stage in its history.

SUPERNATURAL NATURALISM: The philosophical position espoused by my developmentally based theology, which asserts that a supernatural Being designed and instituted the realm of natural law for a higher, instrumental purpose, which centers on the psychospiritual development of human beings.

TELEOLOGICAL ARGUMENT: An argument for the existence of God that interprets the purposiveness, or goal-directedness, of the natural world as evidence for design.

THEISM: Belief in one God who is actively involved in His creation.

WEAK ANTHROPIC PRINCIPLE: Given the reality of human life, the physical universe must contain areas that are compatible with our own existence as observers.

Bibliography

Abbott, Larry. "The Mystery of the Cosmological Constant." *Scientific American*, vol. 3, no. 1 (1991).

Abney, Keith. "Naturalism and Nonteleological Science: A Way to Resolve the Demarcation Problem between Science and Nonscience." *Perspectives on Science and Christian Faith*, vol. 49, no. 3 (September 1997).

Angrist, Stanley W., and Loren G. Hepler. *Order and Chaos*. New York: Basic, 1967.

Aquinas, Thomas. "The Summa Theologica." In *Great Books of the Western World*. Vol. 19. Ed. R. M. Hutchins. Chicago: Encyclopaedia Britannica, 1952.

Argyll, Duke of. *The Reign of Law*. New York: Lovell, n.d.

Ayer, Alfred Jules. *Language Truth and Logic*. Oxford: Oxford University Press, 1936.

Barbour, Ian. *Religion in an Age of Science*. San Francisco: Harper and Row, 1990.

Barrow, John D. *Pi in the Sky*. Boston: Little, Brown, 1992.

———. *Theories of Everything*. Oxford: Oxford University Press, 1991.

———. *The World within the World*. Oxford: Oxford University Press, 1990.

Barrow, John D., and Frank J. Tipler. *The Anthropic Cosmological Principle*. Oxford: Oxford University Press, 1986.

Basinger, David. *The Case for Freewill Theism*. Downers Grove, Ill.: Intervarsity Press, 1996.

Becker, Ernest. *The Denial of Death*. New York: Free Press, 1973.

Behe, Michael J. *Darwin's Black Box*. New York: Simon and Schuster, 1996.

Bohm, David. "Postmodern Science and a Postmodern World." In *The Reenchantment of Science*, ed. David Ray Griffin. Albany: SUNY Press, 1988.

———. *Wholeness and the Implicate Order*. London: Routledge and Kegan Paul, 1980.

Bondi, Herman. *Cosmology*. Cambridge: Cambridge University Press, 1960.

Boslough, John. *Stephen Hawking's Universe*. New York: William Morrow, 1985.

Bowler, Peter J. *The Eclipse of Darwinism*. Baltimore, Md.: Johns Hopkins University Press, 1983.

———. *Evolution: The History of an Idea*. Los Angeles: University of California Press, 1989.

Brooks, Daniel R., and E. O. Wiley. *Evolution As Entropy*. Chicago: University of Chicago Press, 1986.

Brown, Michael H. *The Search for Eve*. San Francisco: Harper and Row, 1990.

Burnet, Thomas. *Sacred Theory of the Earth*. Reprint, London: Centaur, 1965 [1691].

Campbell, John H. "An Organizational Interpretation of Evolution." In *Evolution at a Crossroads*, ed. David J. Depew and Bruce H. Weber. Cambridge: MIT Press, 1985.

Carter, Brandon. "Large Number Coincidences and the Anthropic Principle in Cosmology." In *Confrontation of Cosmological Theories with Observation*. Dordrecht: Reidel, 1974.

Casti, John L. *Paradox Lost*. New York: William Morrow, 1989.

Caullery, Maurice. *Genetics and Heredity*. New York: Walker, 1964.

Chambers, Robert. *Vestiges of the Natural History of the Creation*. London: Churchill, 1844.

Cicero. *The Nature of the Gods*. Trans. H. C. P. McGregor. London: Penguin, 1972.

Clayton, Philip. *Explanation from Physics to Theology*. New Haven, Conn.: Yale University Press, 1991.

Collins, C. B., and S. W. Hawking. *Astrophys. J*. vol. 317 (1973).

Copernicus, Nicholas. *On the Revolution of the Heavenly Spheres*. Bk. 1. Ch. 6. Trans. C. G. Wallis. Ed. R. M. Hutchins. Encyclopedia Britannica, 1952.

Corey, M. A. *Back to Darwin*. Lanham, Md.: University Press of America, 1994.

———. *Evolution and the Problem of Natural Evil*. Lanham, Md.: University Press of America, 2000.

———. *God and the New Cosmology*. Lanham, Md.: Rowman & Littlefield, 1993.

———. *Job, Jonah, and the Unconscious*. Lanham, Md.: University Press of America, 1995.

———. *The Natural History of Creation*. Lanham, Md.: University Press of America, 1995.

Crick, Francis. *Life Itself: Its Origin and Nature*. New York: Simon and Schuster, 1981.

Darwin, Charles. *The Origin of Species*. New York: Collier, 1909.

Darwin, Erasmus. *Zoonomia*. 2 vols. London: 1974.

Darwin, F. *The Life and Letters of Charles Darwin*. London: John Murray, 1888.

Davies, Paul. *The Accidental Universe*. New York: Cambridge University Press, 1982.

———. *Are We Alone?* New York: Basic, 1995.

———. *The Cosmic Blueprint*. New York: Simon and Schuster, 1989.

———. *The Fifth Miracle*. New York: Simon and Schuster, 1999.

———. *God and the New Physics*. New York: Simon and Schuster, 1983.

———. "The Intelligibility of Nature." In *Quantum Cosmology and the Laws of Nature*, ed. Robert Russell, Nancey Murphy, and C. J. Isham. Vatican City State: Vatican Observatory Publications, 1996.

———. *The Last Three Minutes*. New York: Basic, 1994.

———. *The Mind of God*. New York: Simon and Schuster, 1992.

———. *Other Worlds*. New York: Simon and Schuster, 1980.

———. *Superforce*. New York: Simon and Schuster, 1984.

Dawkins, Richard. *The Blind Watchmaker*. New York: Norton, 1986.

Dembski, William A. *Intelligent Design*. Downers Grove, Ill.: Intervarsity Press, 1999.

———. "On the Very Possibility of Intelligent Design." In *The Design Hypothesis*, ed. J. P. Moreland. Downers Grove, Ill.: Intervarsity Press, 1994.

Denton, Michael. *Evolution: A Theory in Crisis*. Bethesda, Md.: Adler and Adler, 1986.

———. *Nature's Destiny*. New York: Free Press, 1998.

Deutsch, David. *The Fabric of Reality*. New York: Penguin, 1997.

Dossey, Larry. *Prayer Is Good Medicine*. San Francisco: HarperSanFrancisco, 1997.

du Nouy, Lecomte. *Human Destiny*. New York: Longmans, Green, 1947.

Dyson, Freeman. *Disturbing the Universe*. New York: Harper and Row, 1979.

———. "Honoring Dirac." *Science*, vol. 185 (September 27, 1974).

Eccles, Sir John. "Modern Biology and the Turn to Belief in God." In *The Intellectuals Speak Out about God*, ed. Roy Abraham Varghese. Chicago: Regnery Gateway, 1984.

Eccles, John, and Daniel N. Robinson. *The Wonder of Being Human*. Boston: Shambhala, 1985.

Eden, Murray. "Inadequacies of Neo-Darwinian Evolution as a Scientific Theory." In *Mathematical Challenges to the Neo-Darwinian Interpretation of Evolution*, ed. P. Moorhead and M. Kaplan. Philadelphia: Wistar Institute Press, 1967.

Einstein, Albert. *Essays in Science*. New York: Philosophical Library, 1934.

Ellis, G. F. R. "The Theology of the Anthropic Principle." In *Quantum Cosmology and the Laws of Nature*, ed. Robert John Russell, Nancey Murphy, and C. J. Isham. Vatican City State: Vatican Observatory Publications, 1996.

Flamsteed, Sam. "Probing the Edge of the Universe." *Discover*, vol. 12, no. 7 (July 1991).

Flew, Antony, R. M. Hare, and Basil Mitchell. "Theology and Falsification." In *New Essays in Philosophical Theology*, ed. Antony Flew and Alasdair MacIntyre. London: SCM, 1955.

Freedman, Wendy L. "The Expansion Rate and Size of the Universe." *Scientific American*, vol. 267, no. 5 (November 1992).

Gaylin, Willard. *The Male Ego*. New York: Viking, 1992.

Geisler, Norman L., and Ronald M. Brooks. *Come Let Us Reason*. Grand Rapids, Mich.: Baker, 1990.

Gillespie, Neal C. *Charles Darwin and the Problem of Creation*. Chicago: University of Chicago Press, 1979.

Gingerich, Owen. "Let There Be Light: Modern Cosmogony and Biblical Creation." In *Is God a Creationist?*, ed. Roland Mushat Frye. New York: Scribner's, 1983.

———. "Modern Cosmogony and Biblical Creation." In *Is God a Creationist?*, ed. Roland Mushat Frye. New York: Scribner's, 1983.

Godfrey, Laurie R, ed. *Scientists Confront Creationism*. New York: Norton, 1983.

Goldschmidt, Richard. *The Material Basis of Evolution*. New Haven, Conn.: Yale University Press, 1940.

Gould, Stephen Jay. *Bully for Brontosaurus*. New York: Norton, 1992.

———. *The Flamingo's Smile*. New York: Norton, 1985.

———. *Hen's Teeth and Horse's Toes*. New York: Norton, 1980.

———. *The Panda's Thumb*. Norton, 1980.

Gray, Asa. *Darwiniana*. New York: Appleton, 1876.

Greeley, Andrew. "Keeping the Faith: Americans Hold Fast to the Rock of Ages." *Omni*, vol. 13, no. 11 (August 1991).

Greenstein, George. *The Symbiotic Universe*. New York: William Morrow, 1988.

Gribbin, John. *In the Beginning*. Boston: Little, Brown, 1993.

———. *In Search of the Double Helix*. New York: Bantam, 1987.

———. *The Omega Point*. New York: Bantam, 1988.

Gribbin, John, and Martin Rees. *Cosmic Coincidences*. New York: Bantam, 1989.

Griffin, David Ray. *God and Religion in the Postmodern World*. Albany: SUNY Press, 1989.

———. *God, Power, and Evil*. Philadelphia: Westminster, 1976.

———, ed. *The Reenchantment of Science*. Albany: SUNY Press, 1988.

Hadd, John R. *Evolution: Reconciling the Controversy*. Glassboro, N.J.: Kronos, 1979.

Hardy, Alister. *Darwin and the Spirit of Man*. London: Collins, 1984.

Harris, Errol E. *Cosmos and Anthropos*. Atlantic Highlands, N.J.: Humanities Press International, 1991.

Hartshorne, Charles. *Omnipotence and Other Theological Mistakes*. Albany: SUNY Press, 1984.

Haught, John. *God after Darwin*. Boulder, Colo.: Westview, 2000.

Hawking, Stephen W. *Black Holes and Baby Universes*. New York: Bantam, 1993.

———. *A Brief History of Time*. New York: Bantam, 1988.

Helitzer, Florence. "The Princeton Galaxy." *Intellectual Digest*, no. 10 (June 1973).

Henderson, Charles P. *God and Science*. Atlanta: John Knox, 1973.

Henderson, Lawrence J. *The Fitness of the Environment*. Glouster: Peter Smith, 1970.

———. *The Order of Nature*. Cambridge, Mass.: Harvard University Press, 1917.

Hick, John. *Death and Eternal Life*. Louisville: Westminster/John Knox, 1994.

———. *Evil and the God of Love*. New York: Harper and Row, 1977.

———. *The Existence of God*. New York: Macmillan, 1964.

———. *An Interpretation of Religion*. New York: Macmillan, 1989.

———. "Rational Theistic Belief without Proof." In *Arguments for the Existence of God*. New York: Macmillan, 1971.

Hiebert, Erwin N. "Modern Physics and Christian Faith." In *God and Nature*, ed. David C. Lindberg and Ronald L. Numbers. Berkeley: University of California Press, 1986.

Himmelfarb, Gertrude. *Darwin and the Darwinian Revolution*. New York: Norton, 1959.

Hogben, L. T. *The Nature of Living Matter*. London: Routledge and Kegan Paul, 1931.

Hoyle, Fred. "The Big Bang in Astronomy." *New Scientist*, vol. 92, no. 1280 (November 19, 1981).

———. *Religion and the Scientists*. London: SCM, 1959.

———. "The Universe: Past and Present Reflections." *Engineering and Science* (November 1981).

Hoyle, Fred, and Chandra Wickramasinghe. *Evolution from Space*. London: J. M. Dent, 1981.

Hume, David. *Dialogues Concerning Natural Religion*. London: Penguin, 1990.

Jaki, Stanley L. *Cosmos and Creator*. Edinburgh: Scottish Academic Press, 1980.

———. *The Paradox of Olbers' Paradox*. New York: Herder and Herder, 1969.

James, William. "The Principles of Psychology." Vol. 7 (1891).

———. *The Varieties of Religious Experience*. New York: Longman, 1902.

Jantsch, Erich. *The Self-Organizing Universe*. Oxford: Pergamon, 1980.

Jastrow, Robert. *God and the Astronomers*. New York: Warner, 1978.

———. *Until the Sun Dies*. New York: Warner, 1977.

Johnson, Philip E. *Darwin on Trial*. Washington, D.C.: Regnery Gateway, 1991.

Kaku, Michio, and Jennifer Trainer. *Beyond Einstein: The Cosmic Quest for the Theory of the Universe*. New York: Bantam, 1987.

Kauffman, Stuart A. "Antichaos and Adaptation." *Scientific American*, vol. 265, no. 2 (August 1991).

———. *At Home in the Universe*. New York: Oxford University Press, 1995.

———. "Self-Organization, Selective Adaptation, and Its Limits." In *Evolution at a Crossroads*, ed. David J. Depew and Bruce H. Weber. Cambridge: MIT Press, 1985.

Kitcher, Philip. *Abusing Science*. Cambridge: MIT Press, 1982.

Knoll, Andrew H. "End of the Proterozoic Eon." *Scientific American*, vol. 265, no. 4 (October 1991).

Kuhn, Thomas S. *The Structure of Scientific Revolutions*. Chicago: University of Chicago Press, 1962.

Küppers, Bernd-Olaf. *Information and the Origin of Life*. Cambridge: MIT Press, 1990.

Laszlo, Ervin. *Evolution: The Grand Synthesis*. Boston: Shambhala, 1987.

Laudan, Larry. "The Demise of the Demarcation Problem." In *But Is It Science?*, ed. Michael Ruse. Buffalo, N.Y.: Prometheus, 1988.

Leakey, Richard. *The Making of Mankind*. New York: Dutton, 1981.

Leakey, Richard, and Roger Lewin. *Origins Reconsidered*. New York: Doubleday, 1992.

Leibniz, G. W. *Theodicy*. La Salle, Ill.: Open Court, 1985.

Leslie, John. "Anthropic Principle, World Ensemble, Design." *American Philosophical Quarterly*, no. 19 (1982).

Lewin, Roger. *Complexity*. New York: Macmillan, 1992.

Lindberg, David C. "Science and the Early Church." In *God and Nature*, ed. David C. Lindberg and Ronald L. Numbers. Berkeley: University of California Press, 1986.

Long, A. A. *Hellenistic Philosophy*. Berkeley: University of California Press, 1974.

Lovejoy, C. O. *Life in the Universe*. Ed. J. Billingham. Cambridge: MIT Press, 1981.

Mayr, Ernst. *Animal Species and Evolution*. Cambridge, Mass.: Belknap, 1963.

McDonough, Thomas R., and David Brin. "The Bubbling Universe." *Omni*, vol. 15, no. 1 (1992).

Mendillo, M., and R. Hart. "Resonances." *Physics Today*, vol. 27, no. 2 (February 1974).

Meyer, Stephen C. "The Methodological Equivalence of Design and Descent." In *The Creation Hypothesis*, ed. J. P. Moreland. Downers Grove, Ill.: Intervarsity Press, 1994.

Miller, Kenneth R. *Finding Darwin's God*. New York: HarperCollins, 1999.

Mivart, St. George Jackson. *On the Genesis of Species*. London: Macmillan, 1871.

Monod, Jacques. *Chance and Necessity*. New York: Knopf, 1971.

Moore, John N. *Should Evolution Be Taught?* San Diego, Calif.: Institute for Creation Research, 1971.

Moorehead, P. S., and M. M. Kaplan, eds. *Mathematical Challenges to the Neo-Darwinian Interpretation of Evolution*. Philadelphia: Wistar Institute Press, 1967.

Moreland, J. P., ed. *The Design Hypothesis*. Downers Grove, Ill.: Intervarsity Press, 1994.

Morgan, T. H. *The Scientific Basis of Evolution*. London: Faber and Faber, 1932.

Morowitz, Harold. *Energy Flow in Biology*. Woodbridge, Conn.: Ox Bow, 1979.

Murchie, Guy. *The Seven Mysteries of Life*. Boston: Houghton Mifflin, 1978.

Murphy, Nancey. "Evidence of Design in the Fine-Tuning of the Universe." In *Quantum Cosmology and the Laws of Nature*, ed. Robert John Russell, Nancey Murphy, and C. J. Isham. Vatican City State: Vatican Observatory Publications, 1996.

———. "Phillip Johnson on Trial: A Critique of His Critique of Darwin." *Perspectives on Science and Christian Faith*, vol. 45, no. 1 (1993).

Naeye, Robert. "Moon of Our Delight." *Discover*, vol. 15, no. 1 (January 1994).

Novikov, Igor D., and Yakob Zel'dovich. "Physical Processes Near Cosmological Singularities." *Annual Review of Astronomy and Astrophysics*, no. 11 (1973).

Ohno, Susumu. *Evolution by Gene Duplication*. New York: Springer-Verlag, 1970.

Oldroyd, D. R. *Darwinian Impacts*. Atlantic Highlands, N.J.: Humanities Press, 1980.

Overman, Dean L. *The Case against Accident and Self-Organization*. Lanham, Md.: Rowman & Littlefield, 1997.

Paley, William. *Natural Theology*. Reprint, London: Baldwyn, 1819 [1802].

Peat, F. David. *The Philosopher's Stone*. New York: Bantam, 1991.

———. *Superstrings and the Search for the Theory of Everything*. Chicago: Contemporary Books, 1988.

Peirce, C. S. Cambridge Lectures, Lecture 1. "Philosophy and the Conduct of Life." Vol. 1 (1898).

———. Harvard Lecture 5. "On Three Kinds of Goodness." Vol. 5 (1903).

———. "A Neglected Argument for the Reality of God." Vol. 6 (1908).

———. "Syllabus." Vol. 2 (1903).

Pence, Terry G. "Charles S. Peirce, Scientific Method, and God." *Perspectives on Science and Christian Faith*, vol. 49, no. 3 (September 1997).

Penrose, Roger. *Shadows of the Mind*. Oxford: Oxford University Press, 1994.

Plantinga, Alvin. *Does God Have a Nature?* Milwaukee, Wisc.: Marquette University Press, 1980.

———. *God, Freedom, and Evil*. Grand Rapids, Mich.: Eerdmans, 1974.

———. "Methodological Naturalism?" *Perspectives on Science and Christian Faith*, vol. 49, no. 3.

———. *The Nature of Necessity*. Oxford: Oxford University Press, 1974.

———. "Religious Belief without Evidence." In *Rationality and Religious Belief*, ed. C. F. Delaney. Notre Dame, Ind.: University of Notre Dame Press, 1979.

Pojman, Louis P. *Philosophy of Religion*. Belmont, Calif.: Wadsworth, 1987.

Polkinghorne, John. *Science and Creation*. Boston: New Science Library, 1989.

Popper, Karl. *Unended Quest*. Glasgow: Fontana Books of Collins, 1976.

Powell, Corey S. "The Golden Age of Cosmology." *Scientific American*, vol. 267, no. 1 (July 1992).

———. "Greenhouse Gusher." *Scientific American*, vol. 265, no. 4 (October 1991).

Radetsky, Peter. "How Did Life Start?" *Discover*, vol. 13, no. 11 (November 1992).

Ratzsch, Del. *Nature, Design, and Science*. Albany: SUNY Press, 2001.

Raup, David M. "Conflicts between Darwinism and Paleontology." *Field Museum of Natural History Bulletin*, vol. 50, no. 1 (January 1979).

———. *Extinction: Bad Genes or Bad Luck?* New York: Norton, 1991.

Rayl, A. J. S., and K. T. McKinney. "The Mind of God." *Omni*, vol. 13, no. 11 (August 1991).

Reichenbach, Bruce. *Evil and a Good God*. New York: Fordham University Press, 1982.

ReMine, Walter James. *The Biotic Message: Evolution versus Message Theory*. St. Paul, Minn.: St. Paul Science, 1993.

Rifkin, Jeremy. *Algeny*. New York: Viking, 1983.

Rolston, Holmes. *Science and Religion*. Philadelphia: Temple University Press, 1987.

Ross, Hugh. *Creation and Time*. Colorado Springs, Colo.: NavPress, 1994.

———. *The Creator and the Cosmos*. Colorado Springs, Colo.: NavPress, 1993.

———."Einstein Exonerated in Breakthrough Discovery." *Facts and Faith*, vol. 1, no. 3 (1999).

———. *The Fingerprint of God*. Orange, Calif.: Promise Publishing, 1991.

———. *Genesis One: A Scientific Perspective*. Sierra Madre, Calif.: Wisemen Productions, 1983.

Ruse, Michael. "A Philosopher's Day in Court." In *But Is It Science?*, ed. Michael Ruse. Buffalo, N.Y.: Prometheus, 1988.

Russell, Bertrand. *Religion and Science*. New York: Oxford University Press, 1968.

Sagan, Carl. *Cosmos*. New York: Random House, 1980.

Sanford, John A. *Evil: The Shadow Side of Reality*. New York: Crossroad, 1981.

———. *The Kingdom Within*. San Francisco: Harper and Row, 1987.

Schrödinger, Erwin. *What Is Life?* Cambridge: Cambridge University Press, 1967.

Schroeder, Gerald L. *Genesis and the Big Bang*. New York: Bantam, 1990.

———. *The Science of God*. New York: Free Press, 1997.

Scriven, Michael. "The Presumption of Atheism." In *Philosophy of Religion*, by Louis P. Pojman. Belmont, Calif.: Wadsworth, 1987.

Shapiro, Robert. "Prebiotic Ribose Synthesis: A Critical Analysis." *Origin of Life and Evolution of the Biosphere*, no. 18 (1988).

Sharpe, Kevin J. *David Bohm's World*. Lewisburg, Pa.: Bucknell University Press, 1993.

Sheldrake, Rupert. *A New Science of Life*. Los Angeles: Tarcher, 1981.

Shermer, Michael. *How We Believe*. New York: Freeman, 2000.

Simpson, George Gaylord. *The Meaning of Evolution*. New Haven, Conn.: Yale University Press, 1967.

Smart, Ninian. "Omnipotence, Evil, and Supermen." *Philosophy*, vol. 36, no. 137 (1961).

Smith, John Maynard. *Did Darwin Get It Right?* New York: Chapman and Hall, 1989.

Smolin, Lee. *The Life of the Cosmos*. Oxford: Oxford University Press, 1997.

Spergel, David N., and Neil G. Turok. "Textures and Cosmic Structure." *Scientific American*, vol. 266, no. 3 (March 1992).

Spetner, Lee. *Not by Chance*. Brooklyn, N.Y.: Judaica Press, 1998.

Stahler, Steven W. "The Early Life of Stars." *Scientific American*, vol. 265, no. 1 (July 1991).

Stansfield, William D. *The Science of Evolution*. New York: Macmillan, 1977.

Steele, Edward J., Robyn A. Lindley, and Robert V. Blanden. *Lamarck's Signature*. Reading, Mass.: Perseus, 1998.

Stoner, Peter W., and Robert C. Newman. *Science Speaks*. Chicago: Moody, 1968.

Swimme, Brian. "The Cosmic Creation Story." In *The Reenchantment of Science*, ed. David Ray Griffin. Albany: SUNY Press, 1988.

Swinburne, Richard. "Argument from the Fine-Tuning of the Universe." In *Physical Cosmology and Philosophy*, ed. J. Leslie. London: Macmillan, 1990.

———. *The Existence of God*. Oxford: Clarendon, 1979.

———. *Providence and the Problem of Evil*. Oxford: Clarendon, 1998.

Talbot, Michael. *The Holographic Universe*. New York: Harperperennial Library, 1992.

Tennant, F. R. "Cosmic Teleology." In *Philosophical Theology*. Vol. 2. Ch. 4. New York: Cambridge University Press, 1930.

Thompson, D'Arcy Wentworth. *On Growth and Form*. New York: Macmillan, 1942.

Trefil, James. *The Dark Side of the Universe*. New York: Doubleday, 1988.

———. *Reading the Mind of God*. New York: Scribner's, 1989.

Trumpler, Robert J. "Absorption of Light in the Galactic System." *Publications of the Astronomical Society of the Pacific*, no. 42 (1930).

Van Till, Howard J. *The Fourth Day*. Grand Rapids, Mich.: Eerdmans, 1986.

Wallace, Alfred Russell. *Natural Selection and Tropical Nature*. London: Macmillan, 1895.

Ward, Keith. *God, Chance, and Necessity*. Oxford: Oxford University Press, 1996.

Ward, Peter D., and Donald Brownlee. *Rare Earth*. New York: Copernicus, 2000.

Weinberg, Steven. *The First Three Minutes*. New York: Basic Books, 1977.

———. "Life in the Universe." *Scientific American*, vol. 271, no. 4 (October 1994).

Weisskopf, Victor. "The Frontiers and Limits of Science." *American Scientist*, vol. 65 (August 1977).

Wheeler, John A. "The Princeton Galaxy." *Intellectual Digest* 3, no. 10 (June 1973).

Yockey, Hubert. *Information Theory and Molecular Biology*. Cambridge: Cambridge University Press, 1992.

Zehavi, Idit, and Avishai Dekel. "Evidence for a Positive Cosmological Constant from Flows of Galaxies and Distant Supernovae." *Nature*, vol. 401, no. 6750 (September 16, 1999).

Index

About the Author

Michael A. Corey is a graduate of Claremont Graduate University and the Union Institute. He has spent the last decade traveling the world and lecturing on the various issues pertaining to science and religion and is the author of several books on the subject, including *God and the New Cosmology* and *Evolution and the Problem of Natural Evil*. He lives in Charleston, West Virginia.